Mikoyan MiG-29

Fulcrum

MULTI-ROLE FIGHTER

Yefim Gordon

Airlife
England

First published in the UK in 1999
by Airlife Publishing Ltd

British Library Cataloguing-in-Publication Data
A catalogue record for this book
is available from the British Library

ISBN 1 84037 028 9

Typeset by Servis Filmsetting Ltd, Manchester
Printed in Hong Kong

Airlife Publishing Ltd
101 Longden Road, Shrewsbury, SY3 9EB, England
E-mail: airlife@airlifebooks.com
Website: www.airlifebooks.com

Acknowledgements

The author wishes to express his deepest thanks to:

Mikhail R. Val'denberg,
former MiG-29 chief project engineer;

Valeriy V. Novikov,
current MiG-29 chief project engineer;

Vano A. Mikoyan,
deputy MiG-29 chief project engineer;

Anatoliy P. Kikhtenko,
ANPK MiG flight test facility chief;

Sergey P. Belyasnik,
a leading engineer at ANPK MiG;

Valentin S. Vetlitskiy, artist;

Andrey Yurgenson, draftsman;

Andrey V. Fomin, an aviation writer;

Anatoliy A. Komarov, VPK-MAPO;

Viktor Drooshlyakov, aviation writer and photographer;

Vladimir Petrov at LII;

Mikhail Ye. Yevdokimov, my son, for his computer
skills and support;

and Dmitriy S. Komissarov – the book could not have
been accomplished without his excellent translation.

Contents

Mikoyan MiG-29 Fulcrum
MULTI-ROLE FIGHTER

Author's Introduction

By the end of the '60s the air forces of most countries of the world having a well-developed aircraft industry were equipped with second-generation jet fighters – the Mikoyan MiG-21 'Fishbed', the McDonnell (later McDonnell Douglas) F-4 Phantom II, the Northrop F-5 Tiger/Freedom Fighter and the Dassault Mirage III. The principal requirements which these fighters were designed to meet were high performance (a top speed of Mach 2.0 or better and a 19,000–20,000-m/62,335–65,616-ft service ceiling), guided air-to-air missile (AAM) armament and the provision of a fire control radar enabling the aircraft to operate day and night in all weather conditions.

At the same time third-generation fighters were about to emerge, such as the MiG-23 'Flogger' in the Soviet Union, the Dassault Mirage F.1 in France and the SAAB JA/AJ-37 Viggen in Sweden. No quantum leap in speed and altitude performance was needed at this stage. The main requirements were longer range, better manoeuvrability, the ability to operate from semi-prepared tactical airstrips and versatility.

Third-generation fighters were to enter service in the early '70s, along with upgraded versions of the MiG-21 and the F-4. However, by then the fighter makers both sides of the Iron Curtain had started working on fourth-generation aircraft which would form the backbone of NATO and Warsaw Pact air forces in the next decade. The USA made the first move by announcing the FX (Fighter Experimental) programme in March 1966. Boeing, Lockheed and North American entered the competition, followed later on by Republic (a division of Fairchild-Hiller Corporation).

Originally the single-seat twin-engined FX was to have a 27-ton (59,523-lb) gross weight and a Mach 3 top speed. However, operational experience gained in Vietnam forced the USAF to redefine totally the advanced fighter concept. The powerful radar and heavy missile armament of the F-4 gave it an advantage over the MiG-21 at long and medium range only; in a dogfight the lighter and nimbler MiGs came out on top. Hence the new general operational requirement (GOR) for the FX called for a lightweight fighter, armed with only an internal gun and short-range AAMs. Later, however, the USAF thought better of it and revised the GOR to include a fire control radar and medium-range AAMs. Gross weight was set in the 20-ton (44,091-lb) class and top speed at Mach 2.5.

US aircraft manufacturers began designing fighters to meet the new requirements in 1969; McDonnell Douglas won the FX contest with the F-15 Eagle, securing a contract by the end of the year. The prototype YF-15A took off on 27 July 1972 and deliveries of production F-15As commenced in November 1974.

Still, the lightweight tactical fighter idea was not altogether dead and buried. In the early '70s the USAF General Staff decided it was advisable to complement the costly heavy fighters with much lighter and cheaper aircraft grossing at 9–10 tons (19,841–22,045 lb). Such a fighter would have simpler avionics and a limited weapons range (internal gun and short-range AAMs only) but high manoeuvrability. The LWF (LightWeight Fighter) programme was announced in January 1972, with the MiG-21 as a reference point for the designers; the USAF was well aware that in a dogfight the 'Fishbed' was more than a match for the more sophisticated and better armed but less agile Phantom.

In February 1972 General Dynamics (ex-Convair), Northrop, Boeing, LTV-Aerospace and Lockheed submitted their proposals for the LWF contest. GD's Model 401 and Northrop's P.600 were selected for full-scale development. The former project was based on studies made by Convair for the FX programme, while the latter was an evolution of the P.530 project developed in 1966 as an F-5 replacement. In April GD and Northrop were awarded contracts for the completion and testing of prototypes of the two fighters as the YF-16 and YF-17 respectively.

Both aircraft entered flight test in 1974; the YF-16 won the flyoff in January 1975. The USAF requested that the aircraft be given strike capability under the ACF (Air Combat Fighter) programme. The definitive F-16A Fighting Falcon made its first flight on 8 December 1976 and entered production in August 1978.

However, Northrop's efforts were not lost. McDonnell Douglas decided that the YF-17 could be modified at minimum cost to fit the US Navy's NACF (Naval Air Combat Fighter) requirement. The aircraft then entered full-scale development in January 1976 as the McDD F/A-18 Hornet shipboard air superiority fighter/attack aircraft; the prototype made its first flight on 18 November 1978 and production commenced in 1979.

1

Taking Shape

Early studies and the PFI/PLMI programmes

In the late '60s the Soviet Union was also working on the fourth-generation fighter concept. Analysing operational experience with fighters in regional conflicts, the engineers began considering ways and means of enhancing combat capabilities. The latest know-how and technologies and the entire potential of the Soviet aerospace industry were brought into play. Fourth-generation fighters were to be armed with new air-to-air missiles and feature a sophisticated weapons control system.

All three of the Soviet Union's leading fighter makers joined the research and development effort. These were the design bureau led by Artyom Ivanovich Mikoyan (aka OKB-155[1] or MMZ[2] 'Zenit'), the OKB led by Pavel Osipovich Sukhoi, aka MZ 'Koolon' (Coulomb)[3], and the bureau led by Aleksandr Sergeyevich Yakovlev, aka OKB-115 or MMZ 'Skorost' (Speed).

In 1971 TsNII-30,[4] a division of the Soviet Ministry of Defence, issued the first GOR for a fourth-generation fighter tentatively designated PFI (*perspektivnyy frontovoy istrebeetel'* – advanced tactical fighter). The primary rôles of the PFI comprised destroying enemy fighters in close-in combat with short-range AAMs and an internal gun, intercepting aerial targets at long range (either by means of its own radar or with guidance from ground control

and intelligence (GCI) centres) and destroying them with medium-range AAMs, providing top cover for friendly troops and point defence of important targets, destroying enemy reconnaissance vehicles, escorting heavy aircraft, performing tactical recce and destroying small ground targets in daytime conditions with bombs, unguided rockets and gunfire.

The aircraft had to possess a look-down/shoot-down capability (i.e., destroy aerial targets both above and below its own flight level) and operate in any weather conditions, day and night, in an active and passive electronic countermeasures (ECM) environment. The F-15 and Northrop P.530 and YF-17 were regarded as the PFI's principal adversaries in air-to-air combat (though the Northrop fighters were replaced by the General Dynamics (now Lockheed Martin) F-16 when the results of the LWF contest became known). Typical aerial targets in the interceptor or hunter-killer rôle included the F-4E, GD F-111A, Panavia MRCA (Tornado) and SEPECAT Jaguar fighter-bombers.

The PFI differed from third-generation fighters mainly in having higher manoeuvrability, a completely new avionics suite and highly effective new weapons. The higher manoeuvrability would be attained by employing new aerodynamic layouts improving the lift/drag ratio and installing lightweight, powerful and fuel-efficient engines to achieve a thrust-to-weight ratio in excess of 1. The integrated weapons control system (WCS) would feature digital computers, an infra-red search and track (IRST) unit complementing the customary radar and be based on semiconductors rather than vacuum tubes for greater reliability. The armament would comprise a fast-firing gun and

[1] *Opytno-konstrooktorskoye byuro* – experimental design bureau; there were no 'companies' as such in the USSR. The number is a code allocated for security reasons.

[2] *Moskovskiy mashinostroitel'nyy zavod* – Moscow Machinery Plant. MMZ Zenit or MMZ No. 155 was the name of Mikoyan's experimental shop.

[3] The name of a physical unit. The Sukhoi OKB's experimental shop was prefixed MZ, *not* MMZ.

[4] *Tsentrahl'nyy naoochno-issledovatel'skiy institoot* – Central R&D Institute No. 30

Artyom I. Mikoyan, the founder of the renowned design bureau. (Yefim Gordon archive)

new short- and medium-range AAMs.

The Mikoyan OKB started working on a fourth-generation fighter in 1970; at a very early stage the aircraft was designated MiG-29. Initially the MiG-29 programme as a whole was the responsibility of Gleb Ye. Lozino-Lozinskiy who was also the chief project engineer of the MiG-25MP heavy interceptor (the future MiG-31 'Foxhound'). The actual work on the fighter's general arrangement, however, was directed by preliminary design (PD) section chief A. A. Choomachenko, Doctor of Technical Sciences,[5] a prominent aerodynamicist.

Two major research bodies were actively involved in the MiG-29 programme. The Central Aerodynamics & Hydrodynamics Institute named after Nikolay V. Zhukovskiy (TsAGI – *Tsentrahl'nyy aero- i gidrodinameecheskiy institoot*) aided with the general arrangement while the State Research Institute of Aircraft Systems (GosNIIAS – *Gosoodahrstvennyy naoochno-issledovatel'skiy institoot aviatseeonnykh sistem*)[6] worked on the fighter's advanced avionics. (Both are located in the town of Zhukovskiy south of Moscow.)

Selecting the proper general arrangement and aerodynamic layout was the key issue at the PD stage. The engineers considered both conventional arrangements and the so-called integral layout when the wings and fuselage blend into a single lifting body.

Much thought was given to the powerplant. Placing the air intake in the nose *à la* MiG-21 was ruled out immediately since the inlet ducts would occupy a disproportionately large portion of the internal volume; it had to be two intakes mounted laterally. Choosing the number of engines was easy. A version powered by a single large turbojet proposed at first was quickly rejected. Building on operational experience with the best single-engined third-generation fighters (MiG-21, MiG-23, Mirage III etc.), Mikoyan opted for a twin-engined aircraft. This improved survivability in combat and reduced accident attrition risk in peacetime.

An early configuration of the MiG-29 had shoulder-mounted trapezoidal wings, a low-mounted horizontal tail and a single fin and rudder. The wings featured leading-edge root extensions (LERXes) and full-span leading-edge slats. The sharply raked two-dimensional air intakes with horizontal airflow control ramps were strongly reminiscent of the MiG-25 'Foxbat' interceptor or the F-15. There

were six underwing hardpoints: four for medium-range AAMs and two for short-range dogfight missiles.

Another early configuration was a sort of cross-breed between the MiG-29 and the MiG-31 (as each came to look eventually). Likewise it had boxy 'Foxbat'-style air intakes; the nose gear unit had twin wheels while the main units featured twin-wheel bogies but with the wheels located in tandem *à la* SAAB Viggen; not in the MiG-31's staggered-tandem arrangement. The aircraft was to be armed with four medium-range K-25 AAMs based on the Raytheon AIM-7E Sparrow (a handful of these had been captured in Vietnam and shipped to the USSR for examination), but eventually work on this missile was discontinued.

A third study utilised the integral layout with the fuselage, wings and engine nacelles all blended together. Unlike the two previous projects, this was a light fighter with a normal gross weight of some 13.5 tons (29,761 lb). Thus it was not only lighter than other Mikoyan projects but also lighter than Sukhoi's entry for the PFI competition, the T-10 (the future Su-27 'Flanker') with a normal TOW of 21 tons (46,296 lb) and the production single-engined MiG-23M 'Flogger-B' which grossed at 15.7 tons (34,611 lb) fully armed. Another advantage of the integral layout was that the prominent LERXes provided a convenient location for the internal gun; finding a good place for it turned into a major problem in the 'conventional' projects. The aircraft was shorter than the actual MiG-29 and had a wing area of only 25 m² (268.8 sq. ft).

The integral layout had its opponents. Some of the engineers claimed the conventional fighter was easier to build; moreover, they were armed with calculations showing that the conventional layout offered a smaller maximum cross-section. PD section engineer Yakov I. Seletskiy had to reduce the height of No. 3 fuel tank by 50 mm (2 in.) and came up with a cross-section identical to that of the conventional version.

In 1971 research institutes within the framework of the Ministry of Aircraft Industry (MAP – *Ministerstvo aviatseeonnoy promyshlennosti*) and the Soviet Air Force (VVS – *Voyenno-vozdooshnyye seely*) began developing fighter force re-equipment concepts for the '80s. Analysis of trends in hardware and tactics development showed that fighters were facing a broader range of missions in contemporary warfare.

Ideally the air force should have several kinds of fighters with different weapons systems optimised for the various mission types. E.g., to intercept an enemy strike

---

[5] The Soviet equivalent of the Dr. Rer. Techn. degree (USA)

[6] Originally called NIIAS (without the 'state' prefix)

group over territory held by friendly troops a fighter had to be tied to GCI centres guiding it to the target. Conversely, maximum independence from ground control was required when hunting over enemy territory. An interceptor needed good acceleration and rate of climb, heavy armament and capable avionics giving it look-down/shoot-down capability. An escort fighter should have sufficient range to operate 250–300 km (138–166 nm) beyond the frontlines. High manoeuvrability, a high thrust-to-weight ratio, a wide speed range and special short-range missiles were a must for close-in combat.

Designing a single aircraft to meet all these contradictory requirements didn't seem possible. Yet the Soviet Union could not afford to have a multitude of specialized fighters in its inventory. A possible compromise solution was to build up the future fighter force with two basic types complementing each other: an advanced tactical fighter (PFI), i.e., a heavy fighter capable of operating singly or in groups 250–300 km (138–166 nm) beyond the frontlines, and an advanced mass-produced light fighter (PLMI – *perspektivnyy lyohkiy massovyy istrebeetel'*)[7] optimised for operations above friendly territory and the tactical battle area – i.e.,

100–150 km (55–83 nm) beyond the frontlines.

The PFI would have a sizeable internal fuel and ordnance load (at least four medium-range air-to-air missiles in addition to short-range or dogfight AAMs and a built-in gun) and a comprehensive navigation, communications and electronic support measures (ESM) suite. With a specially configured avionics and weapons fit it could be operated by the PVO (*protivovozdooshnaya oborona* – Air Defence Force). Conversely, the PLMI was to be as easy to build and maintain as possible, use semi-prepared airstrips and be operated by average-skill pilots and ground personnel. Its armament would be limited to two medium-range AAMs and short-range weapons. The PFI and PLMI would account for 30–35% and 65–70% of the fighter force respectively, being the Soviet answer to the F-16 and the F-15 respectively.

This concept was developed jointly by the fighter design bureaux, the air force's R&D establishments and the aircraft industry. It was at this stage that specific

---

7 Later changed to Lightweight Tactical Fighter (LFI – *lyohkiy frontovoy istrebeetel'*)

A model depicting the MiG-29 at an early development stage. The aircraft is something of a cross-breed between the MiG-25 and the future MiG-29. (Yefim Gordon)

Another early version of the MiG-29 project with a single fin and rudder and lateral air intakes. (Yefim Gordon archive)

operational requirements (SORs) for fourth-generation fighters were developed. The key demand was the ability to win in close-in combat by virtue of agility, a high thrust-to-weight ratio and an effective WCS. Col. Sookhankin, director of TsNII-30, and P. V. Fedosov, director of NIIAS, played a key role in defining the two-types concept and getting it accepted. This was no easy task; air force C-in-C Marshal P. S. Kootakhov took a lot of convincing. It got worse when Marshal Dmitriy F. Ustinov was appointed Defence Minister, and worse still when Mikhail S. Gorbachov became head of the Soviet state and defence spending cuts ensued.

In 1972, having revised the SORs, the VVS issued a request for proposals concerning fourth-generation fighters. The Mikoyan OKB[8] submitted two versions of the MiG-29 project; Yakovlev entered the Yak-45M light fighter and the Yak-47 heavy fighter (neither of which materialized in the end), while Sukhoi's entries were the T10-1 and T10-2 (integral-layout and conventional

versions respectively). After evaluating the projects the air force tasked the Sukhoi and Mikoyan bureaux with building the heavy PFI and LFI respectively; Yakovlev had to walk away empty-handed. The MiG-29 project was then swiftly reassigned to the LFI rôle to fit the new policy – all the more so because Mikoyan hoped to get (and eventually did get) an order for the MiG-31 heavy interceptor.

MiG-29 (*izdeliye* 9.11) and MiG-29A (*izdeliye* 9.11A) light tactical fighter (advanced development projects)

In 1973 the fighter force re-equipment research was largely complete, with the T-10 and MiG-29 selected as the primary types after the PFI/PLMI contest. In the same year TsNII-30 issued SORs for the two types with revisions based on the research results. The most stringent demands applied to the avionics, primarily the WCS. The fire control radar was to work in multiple wavebands and be capable of detecting and tracking multiple targets. The avionics were to be based on semiconductors instead of the vacuum tubes used hitherto, be lighter, more compact and more reliable. The

---

[8] Artyom I. Mikoyan died on 9 December 1970. His deputy Rostislav Appollosovich Belyakov succeeded him as General Designer (the official title of the head of an OKB and the design bureau was named after its founder – a common practice in the Soviet Union.

aircraft were to be equipped with an optoelectronic targeting system comprising an infra-red search and track (IRST) unit and a laser rangefinder. The cockpit was to feature a head-up display (HUD) and a cathode-ray tube (CRT) indicator.

Originally both the PFI and the LFI were to be armed with a 23-mm (.90-in calibre) Gryazev/Shipoonov GSh-23 or a 30-mm (1.18-in calibre) GSh-30 twin-barrel fast-firing automatic gun, K-27[9] advanced medium-range AAMs and K-14 or K-73 short-range AAMs. However, this had to be changed very soon. Development of the S-29 fire control radar originally planned for the MiG-29 was taking longer than anticipated, and Mikoyan had to undertake a crash redesign programme to speed up development and ensure that the air force's requirements were met. The S-29 was substituted by the production Sapfeer-23ML (Sapphire) radar fitted to the MiG-23ML 'Flogger-G', and the K-14 and K-73 AAMs were replaced by the K-23M (K-24) missile (NATO code name AA-7 'Apex') intended for the same fighter and production R-60/R-60M (AA-8 'Aphid') dogfight missiles.

The original version equipped with the S-29 radar bore the manufacturer's designation *izdeliye* 9.11, while the stopgap version with MiG-23 avionics and armament was designated *izdeliye* 9.11A.[10] Quite simply, 9 stood for (MiG-2)9 while 11 was probably an allusion for some obscure reason to the manufacturer's designation of the 'true' 'Flogger' prototypes (*izdeliye* 23-11).[11] Production costs of the MiG-29 in low cost configuration would be little more than half those of the T-10; with the two types making up 70% and 30% of the fighter force respectively, this would ensure maximum cost-effectiveness.

Work on the MiG-29A project proceeded throughout 1973-74, and the proponents of the conventional layout were not about to give up the fight yet. In early 1973 design team chief A. Nazarov approached PD section chief A. A. Choomachenko, saying that an integral-layout aircraft had a bigger surface area and hence created more drag than a conventional aircraft. He was backed by Deputy General Designer Z. Ye. Bersoodskiy, fuselage design team head I. V. Lipets and some other OKB

employees who claimed the integral layout could not give adequate structural strength and in general it was a dead duck.

Yakov I. Seletskiy, the main 'author' of the integral layout, and Anatoliy Pavlov stood up against the traditionalists. Choomachenko himself favoured the new design; however, being a cautious person, he decided to let the two projects proceed in parallel and let the 'innovators' and 'conservatives' fight out the issue. Eventually the innovators won. The conventional version with lateral intakes proved to have poor performance in tight turns during a dogfight when the leeward intake operated in extremely unfavourable conditions; moreover, it could not attain angles of attack (AOAs) in excess of 20°. This was not the case with the integral layout where the intakes were mounted under the fuselage/wing centre section, continuing into the engine nacelles.

TsAGI participated actively in the development of the fourth-generation fighters from the start, evaluating the competing aerodynamic layouts of the MiG-29 and T-10. Mikoyan engineers recalled that N. K. Lebed', a female TsAGI employee in charge of the fourth-generation fighter research programme, showed them plan views of the integral versions of both aircraft; the similarity was striking.

However, like the OKB, the institute had its share of traditionalists who insisted that both the MiG-29 and T-10 should be designed along conventional lines, period. G. S. Büschgens, the then director of TsAGI, kept urging Rostislav A. Belyakov to abandon the integral layout. V. Mikeladze, Irodov, Koorochkin and other influential TsAGI engineers also swore to the conventional layout; N. K. Lebed' maintained neutrality. Belyakov, for his part, was unwilling to speak openly on this all-important issue because, unlike Büschgens, he was not yet a fully-fledged member of the USSR Academy of Sciences and thus was not authoritative enough. (The General Designer did not participate directly in developing the MiG-29's general arrangement.)

Choomachenko, who had been appointed project chief and Deputy General Designer on 29 December 1972, was instrumental in the choice of the integral layout over the conventional one. Vano Artyomovich Mikoyan, the nephew of the OKB's founder, was appointed Choomachenko's deputy the same day. Zinaida Zhevyrkina, an OKB employee who helped Choomachenko stand for his doctor's degree, did a lot of work, analysing the strengths and weaknesses of the competing layouts. This analysis was later sent to TsAGI

---

[9] K stands for *kompleks (vo'orouzheniya)* – armament system

[10] Pronounced *izdayliye* – product, a term often used for coding Soviet military hardware items

[11] There was also the MiG-23-01 'Faithless', an experimental delta-wing STOL fighter with Kolesov RD36-35 lift-jets which had little in common with the 'Flogger', and the MiG-23-31 (*izdeliye* 92) STOL technology demonstrator – actually a much-modified MiG-21PFM 'Fishbed-F' obstinately misidentified in the West as the MiG-21PD (*podyomnyye dveegateli* – lift engines).

and was one of the reasons that made the institute's leaders change their attitude. Later G. S. Büschgens led a major aerodynamics research and wind tunnel test programme (the first wooden models of the 'integral' MiG-29 were tested in TsAGI's wind tunnels in 1973). A lot of structural strength research was made by academician A. I. Makarevskiy and his successor A. F. Selikhov, both notable TsAGI engineers.

On 15 July 1974 the General Designer formally approved 1/20th scale drawings of the MiG-29A. Anatoliy Pavlov working under project engineer[12] Yakov I. Seletskiy had executed the drawings which illustrated not only the fighter's general arrangement but all main structural elements, even indicating calculated structural loads. The smoothly blended wings and fuselage minimised drag and maximised lift throughout the speed range while providing ample internal space for fuel and avionics. The wings featured prominent LERXes for better lift at high alpha and powerful high-lift devices (automatic leading-edge flaps, trailing-edge flaps and flaperons). The stabilators were deflected differentially for roll control, augmenting the ailerons and enabling the aircraft to manoeuvre vigorously throughout its flight envelope (speed, altitude and AOA).

The SOR issued by the air force for the T-10 did not specify leading-edge flaps; however, the SOR for the MiG-29 did, and this decision was promptly proved correct when wind tunnel tests began. The very first wind tunnel model of the 'integral' MiG-29 *sans* LE flaps immediately showed poor directional stability at AOAs in excess of 20° (the flaps had been omitted for purely technological reasons). This was remedied by making saw-cuts at certain angles in the wooden wings to imitate the LE flaps and the maximum AOA immediately increased to 25°. (Actually a wind tunnel model incorporating LE flaps was not built until the real aircraft was flying!)

The axes of the stabilator hinges were slightly inclined downwards to increase stabilator momentum. To maintain a 90° angle between the vertical and horizontal tails the fins were canted slightly outwards. This made the aircraft statically stable (unlike the T-10 which was statically unstable).

The T-10 as originally flown (the aircraft known in the West as 'Flanker-A') had no LE flaps. However, a complete redesign proved necessary before the aircraft entered production as the Su-27 (T10-S or 'Flanker-B'), and *this* aircraft did have LE flaps. Being competitors, Mikoyan and Sukhoi are not exactly the best of friends and some Mikoyan employees have accused Sukhoi of filching the idea, as well as the idea of outward-canted vertical tails. (The latter claim does not hold water. The first two 'Flanker-A' prototypes had the fins placed vertically; outward-canted fins were indeed introduced on the next seven development aircraft (T10-3 to T10-6 and T10-9 to T10-11) but the production T10-S reverted to vertical fins! To paraphrase a popular saying, what is a sauce for a MiG is not always a sauce for the Su.)

As noted earlier, all Soviet fourth-generation fighter projects were strictly twin-engined aircraft. This improved survivability in combat, reduced accident attrition risk in peacetime and gave the aircraft a thrust-to-weight ratio in excess of 1. However, the advantages of the twin-engined layout could be used to the full on a modern light fighter only by fitting advanced jet engines with a low specific fuel consumption (SFC) and a high specific thrust.

Several Soviet engine design bureaux started working on such engines in the late '60s. These were the State machinery plant named after Vladimir Yakovlevich Klimov (OKB-117 led by Klimov's successor, Sergey Petrovich Izotov), the Soyuz (Union) machinery plant in Moscow (OKB-300 led by Sergey Konstantinovich Tumanskiy), the engine design bureau led by Arkhip Mikhaylovich Lyul'ka and the Perm' engine design bureau led by Pavel Aleksandrovich Solovyov. They received scientific support from the Central Institute of Aero Engines (TsIAM – *Tsentrahl'nyy institootaviat seeonnovo motorostroyeniya*).

Lyul'ka and Solovyov came up with the AL-31F and D-30F6 afterburning turbofans (all previous Soviet fighter engines had been strictly turbojets). However, these were rather too large for a light fighter like the MiG-29, being rated at 12,500 kgp (27,557 lb st) and 15,500 kgp (34,171 lb st) respectively in full afterburner. The MiG-29 required an afterburning turbofan in the 7,500–8,500 kgp (16,534–18,738 lb st) thrust class. The Izotov OKB (better known for its turboshaft engines used in Mil' and Kamov helicopters) offered such an engine – the RD-33 rated at 8,300 kgp (18,298 lb st). Before long, however, competition showed up in the form of the Tumanskiy OKB with the R67-300 afterburning turbofan rated at 7,500 kgp, and an unofficial contest began.

Tumanskiy listed his engine's lower dry weight as a strong point; however, Mikoyan engineers were sceptical

---

[12] The next in command after the chief project engineer. He is a workhorse doing actual design work while the chief project engineer mostly superintends and coordinates the whole programme, reporting to the General Designer.

about this. The point was that the R67-300 was a three-shaft turbofan while the RD-33 was a two-shaft turbofan. Why was the R67-300 lighter when the extra turbine and compressor should have weighed some 50 kg (110 lb)? A complicated design issue was the engine's accessory gearbox driving generators, fuel and oil pumps. Izotov proposed a mechanical drive for the gearbox while Tumanskiy suggested a compressed-air turbine instead; this necessitated air supply lines which again resulted in a weight penalty.

After studying the two projects carefully the Mikoyan OKB selected the RD-33 in 1973. TsIAM also spoke in favour of the Izotov turbofan, proving that the R67-300 would be heavier than Tumanskiy claimed because of design shortcomings. Using Izotov's accessory gearbox drive gave an overall weight saving of about 250 kg (551 lb).

By 1974 the MiG-29 powerplant had been finalised. The RD-33 (aka *izdeliye* 88) had a specified thrust of 5,040 kgp (11,111 lb st) dry/8,300 kgp (18,298 lb st) reheat and a bypass ratio of 0.475. By comparison, the turbojets powering production tactical fighters of the time – the Tumanskiy R25-300 of the MiG-21*bis* 'Fishbed-L/N' and the Tumanskiy R29-300 of the MiG-23M – had afterburner ratings of 7,100 kgp (15,652 lb st) and 12,500 kgp (27,557 lb st) respectively.

The turbofan's turbine temperature was 1,650°K versus 1,313°K for the R25-300 and 1,443°K for the R29-300. Overall engine pressure ratio (EPR) was 21.5 versus 9.5 for the R25-300 and 13.1 for the R29-300. The RD-33 had a 20% lower SFC at full military power than both Tumanskiy turbojets and a weight/thrust ratio 26% and 11% better respectively; with a 1,055-kg (2,325-lb) dry weight, the RD-33 was even 15% lighter than the less powerful R25-300.

Actually the Izotov OKB had been working on the RD-33 since 1968 at its own risk. Bench testing of engine components began in 1972 and the prototype engine ran in late 1974. The advanced development project of the RD-33 was completed the same year, along with several pre-production 'batch zero' engines; the design task, however, was not officially issued by MAP until 15 July 1975 when the RD-33 project had been duly approved and Mikoyan had agreed to use the engine in the MiG-29. In 1976 a flight-cleared RD-33 took to the air for the first time, suspended under one of the ten Tupolev Tu-16LL engine testbeds[13] (converted 'Badger-A' medium bombers) operated by LII.[14]

The engines were located in spaced nacelles and the low-slung intakes attached to the fuselage underside made them extremely vulnerable to foreign object damage (FOD). Mikoyan engineers found a very unconventional and singularly effective solution to the problem not used by any fighter maker before. On the ground the main air intakes were blanked off completely by perforated panels (FOD protection doors) hinged at the top and the engines breathed through a series of spring-loaded blow-in doors on the upper sides of the LERXes. During rotation the FOD protection doors swung up into a horizontal position, triggered by weight coming off the nose gear, allowing the engines to operate normally, and the dorsal blow-in doors closed automatically.

The integrated weapons control system (WCS) developed by NIIAS was one of the fighter's most important systems. The MiG-29 was the world's first fighter to have three targeting systems: a pulse-Doppler fire control radar with look-down/shoot-down capability, an IRST and a helmet-mounted sight (HMS). They were to work in concert, exchanging data via computers; this gave a high degree of automation, higher reliability and ECM resistance and the ability to attack covertly. Apart from its stealth feature (the ability to attack without switching on the radar), the IRST could establish the target's position with high accuracy, allowing the pilot to score a hit with the first burst of gunfire – a useful feature since the gun is regarded as a secondary weapon on a modern fighter and hence the ammunition capacity is rather limited. The IRST was located in a characteristic transparent 'ball' offset to starboard ahead of the windscreen.

Development of the IRST was subcontracted out to NPO Elektroavtomatika in Leningrad while the Radio Research Institute (NIIR) in Moscow, a division of NPO Phazotron, was tasked with designing the radar.[15] NIIAS itself developed mathematical models and software for the unique weapons control system and was responsible for systems integration.

A major issue was the fighter's control system. After considering fly-by-wire (FBW) controls the engineers decided to play safe and opted for a conventional control system with mechanical linkages. Sure enough, FBW controls offered higher manoeuvrability but conventional

---

[13] LL = *letayuschchaya laboratoriya* – lit. flying laboratory, i.e., either testbed or research aircraft, depending on the aircraft's actual role

[14] LII – *Lyotno-ispytahtel'nyy institoot* – Flight Test Institute named after test pilot Mikhail M. Gromov and located in Zhukovskiy

[15] NPO = *naoochno-proizvodstvennoye obyedineniye* – research and production association

controls were considered more reliable. The control system featured irreversible hydraulic actuators in all three control circuits and an artificial-feel unit to facilitate flying and reduce pilot fatigue during prolonged high-G manoeuvring.

On 26 June 1974 the Central Committee of the Communist Party and the Council of Ministers issued a directive ordering the development of the MiG-29 light tactical fighter. The same year TsNII-30 issued a SOR for the type with still more updates reflecting the results of research made in 1971-74. An interdepartmental plan for advanced development project completion was drawn up. Such a document was necessary because the MiG-29 programme was a major effort involving numerous organizations within the aerospace, electronics and defence industries and their efforts needed a lot of coordinating. Besides, time was running short; the F-15A had already achieved initial operational capability (IOC) with the USAF, the YF-16 had entered flight test, and Avions Marcel Dassault were working on the Mirage 2000 fighter.

As noted earlier, the MiG-29 programme was unusual in that development proceeded in two parallel lines – the 'pure' MiG-29 with advanced mission avionics and weapons and the downgraded MiG-29A with simplified radar and weapons based on current production models. The MiG-29A was regarded as an 'entry-level' version designed to save time; it could achieve IOC in the late '70s and do the job until the more sophisticated equipment and weapons came along. Besides, the idea of a cheap light tactical fighter was actively supported by the MoD while the MiG-29 with a new radar and new missiles still had to be accepted.

Both versions had identical airframes, powerplants and systems, including the flight instrumentation system, navigation and communications equipment; flight performance was also nearly identical. The MiG-29A featured the SUV-23ML-2 (SUV-29A) WCS (*sistema oopravleniya vo'orouzheniyem* – weapons control system). It included the Phazotron Yantar' (Amber) fire control radar (a derivative of the Sapfeer-23ML and Sapfeer-23D-III fitted to the MiG-23ML and MiG-23M respectively) with associated analogue computer and target illumination channel for missiles with semi-active radar homing (SARH), the OEPrNK-29A optoelectronic targeting/nav suite, data transfer equipment for feeding target data to the missiles' guidance units etc. The OEPrNK-29A (*optiko-elektronnyy preetsel'no-navigatseeonnyy kompleks*) comprised the OEPS-29A

optoelectronic targeting system, an HUD, a direct-vision CRT display, an Orbita-20 digital computer and an SN-29A navigation system.

The Yantar' radar (aka Sapfeer-23ML-2) developed by NPO Phazotron under General Designer Yuriy N. Figoorovskiy was to be capable of detecting small aerial targets such as fighters at 55 km (30 nm) in open airspace and 20 km (11 nm) in look-down/shoot-down mode. For large targets such as bombers the required detection range was 80 km (44 nm) and 25 km (13.8 nm) respectively.

The OEPS-29A optoelectronic targeting system was designed by the Gheofizika (Geophysics) Central Design Bureau in Moscow. It comprised an IRST unit and a laser rangefinder. Its functions included target search, acquisition and tracking, distance measuring to targets and ground, and establishing the targets' angle coordinates and angle speed. The system could operate throughout the aircraft's altitude envelope in visual meteorological conditions (VMC), day or night, and was immune to ECM. In pursuit mode a fighter-type target could be detected at more than 15 km (8.3 nm); target lock-on range was 8–10 km (4.4–5.5 nm).

Besides the WCS, the avionics would include an identification friend-or-foe (IFF) transponder, the Biryuza command link system (Turquoise; pronounced biryoozah), the SAU-29 automatic control system (*sistema avtomateecheskovo oopravleniya*),[16] the SO-69 air traffic control (ATC) transponder, the Beryoza-L radar homing and warning system (Birch; pronounced beryoza), the Reper-M ('Benchmark') radio altimeter, the Olenyok automatic direction finder (ADF), the MRP-56P marker beacon receiver, the Zhooravl'-30 ('Crane') radio set etc.

The MiG-29A was armed with an AO-17A twin-barrel 30-mm gun with 150 rounds. Missile armament comprised two K-24 (K-23M) medium-range AAMs then under development (alternatively, two production R-23R SARH missiles also code-named AA-7 'Apex') and four K-60/K-60M IR-homing dogfight AAMs. The latter could be substituted by two to four R-13M (AA-2 'Atoll') short-range AAMs or the projected growth version, K-13M1, eventually produced as the R-13M1 (AA-2-2 'Advanced Atoll'). In the strike/close air support (CAS) rôle the aircraft could carry 100-kg (220-lb), 250-kg (551-lb) and 500-kg (1,102-lb) free-fall bombs; the total bomb load was 2,000 kg (4,409 lb). Other compatible air-to-ground

---

[16] I.e., advanced autopilot/ILS

A MiG-29 display model on General Designer Rostislav A. Belyakov's desk (stills from a Mikoyan video).

weapons included UB-32 rocket pods with thirty-two 57-mm (2.24-in.) S-5 folding-fin aircraft rockets (FFARs) each, B-8M rocket pods with twenty 80-mm (3.15-in.) S-8 FFARs each, S-24 and S-25 heavy unguided rockets, and two UPK-23-250 gun pods (each housing a GSh-23 twin-barrel 23-mm gun with 250 rounds).[17] The armament was carried on six underwing hardpoints.

The K-24 AAM was a product of the Vympel (Pennant) OKB led by A. L. Lyapin; V. A. Poostovoytov, his deputy, was the missile's project chief. Developed for the MiG-23ML tactical fighter, the K-24 was a major upgrade of the production R-23 medium-range AAM introduced in 1973. It was broadly comparable in performance to the newly-introduced AIM-7F (the latest version of the

Sparrow) and had a range increased to 50 km (27 nm) and a more powerful warhead. The missile came in two versions – the K-24R with a monopulse radar guidance unit (with enhanced ECM resistance, incidentally) and the IR-homing K-24T; a passive radar-homing version (anti-radiation missile) and a version with combined IR/radar guidance were to follow later.

The K-13M1 emanating from the same bureau was an improved version of the R-13M missile used by most Soviet tactical aircraft since 1973. It had extended G limits (allowing it to be fired during tighter turns), a shorter minimum safe launch range and an upgraded Iney-M ('Hoar frost') IR tracker head.

The R-60M was developed by the rival Molniya (Lightning) OKB under Marat R. Bisnovat (his deputy V. N. Yelagin was project chief). Like the K-13M1, the R-60M was an upgrade of an existing missile (the R-60). However, in this case the engineers concentrated on

[17] B = *blok* – unit or module. This term is used in many contexts – e.g., when speaking of avionics etc.; in this case it means FFAR pod. UB = *oonifitseerovannyy blok* – standardized FFAR pod. UPK = *oonifitseerovannyy pushechnyy konteyner* – standardized gun pod.

increasing the field of view and IRCM resistance of the Komar-M ('Mosquito') tracker head and improving warhead effectiveness. The K-13M1 project was completed in 1974, the other two missiles following next year.

The AO-17A twin-barrel gun, also designated 9A623, was a product of A. G. Shipoonov's bureau of instrument engineering – a division of NPO Tochnost' (Accuracy) – in Toola south of Moscow, a town renowned for its gun-makers. It used the AO-18 30-mm round and utilised the same operating principle as the lighter GSh-23 (AO-9), one barrel being loaded by the recoil action of the other and vice versa. The AO-17A had a rate of fire of 3,000 rounds per minute, a muzzle velocity of 850 m/sec (2,788 ft/sec) and weighed about 100 kg (220 lb).

Originally, as mentioned earlier, Mikoyan had intended to equip the MiG-29 with a version of the GSh-23L – the gun fitted to third-generation versions of the MiG-21 and the MiG-23. However, the survivability of fighters (including the MiG-29's potential adversaries) had improved considerably since GSh-23 days and a 23-mm gun just did not pack a punch that was big enough; 30 mm was the calibre required to really put some holes in the enemy. The AO-17A successfully passed its State acceptance trials in 1976 and was fitted to production Su-25 'Frogfoot' strike aircraft and Mi-24P 'Hind-F' assault helicopters as the GSh-30.

The 'proper' MiG-29 differed from the entry-level MiG-29A mainly in having an SUV-29 (S-29) WCS comprising the RLPK-29 (*rahdiolokatseeonnyy preetsel'nyy kompleks*) and the OEPrNK-29 (S-31) optoelectronic targeting/nav suite. The latter was almost identical to that of the MiG-29A but featured a helmet-mounted sight enabling the pilot to point the missile tracker heads towards the target and feed target data to the radar and IRST simply by turning his head towards it – a major asset in a dogfight.

The RLPK-29 radar targeting system was built around the Phazotron N-019 Rubin radar[18] (Ruby, pronounced roobin) developed under project chief Yuriy P. Kirpichov (Deputy General Designer at NPO Phazotron). It was a new-generation pulse-Doppler radar which was both lighter and more capable than current models, tracking up to ten targets at a time. A fighter-type target could be detected at 60–70 km (33–38 nm) in open airspace and

40 km (22 nm) in look-down/shoot-down mode. The NATO code name was 'Slot Back'. The MiG-29 also featured an improved digital computer and changes to the weapons selection system and the SN-29 navigation system.

The gun and air-to-ground weapons were identical in both versions but the missile armament was totally new. In standard configuration the MiG-29 was to carry two new K-27 medium-range AAMs and four K-14 or K-73 short-range AAMs. Alternatively, six K-14, K-13M1, K-60M or K-73 missiles could be carried. The GOR for air-to-air missiles intended for fourth-generation fighters drawn up in 1973, and a government directive ordering the development of such weapons was issued next year. Specialists from GosNIIAS (notably R. D. Kooz'minskiy and A. N. Davydov) had a hand in making the GOR and closely monitored the missile development work.

At the same time there was a contest going on between the missile makers. The Vympel and Molniya bureaux were vying for the K-27 medium-range AAM. The missile was required to have better performance than the AIM-7F introduced in 1975 and a modular construction allowing it to be configured with different guidance systems and powerplants. The basic K-27A with a range of 70–80 km (38–44 nm) and a launch weight of 250 kg (551 lb) was intended chiefly for the MiG-29, while a version with a longer-burn rocket motor designated K-27B had a range of 120–130 km (66–72 nm) and a 350-kg (771 lb) launch weight was destined for the T-10. The A and B versions were intended mainly for the MiG-29 and T-10 respectively. Vympel's entry developed by chief project engineer A. L. Lyapin came out as the winner. Vympel proposed two configurations of the K-27. One had normal tail surfaces while the other had large forward-swept canards; the latter configuration was selected at the advice of TsAGI. The missile came in four versions: the K-27R with SARH, the IR-homing K-27T (both with regular rocket motors) and the extended-range K-27ER and K-27ET.[19]

Unlike all AAMs existing in the Soviet Union or elsewhere, the K-27 had an inertial guidance mode. The target was initially illuminated by the fighter's radar and the missile switched to active radar homing at the terminal guidance phase. This considerably increased effective kill range, allowing the pilot to fire his missiles before the 'bad guy' did so, and was expected to give

---

18 Curiously, the same name was also used for a very different radar – the RBP-4 ground mapping/bombing radar fitted to the Tu-16 'Badger', Tu-22A/R 'Blinder-A/C' and Tu-95 'Bear-A' bombers (RBP = *rahdiolokatseeonnyy bombardeerovochnyy preetsel* – lit. radar bomb sight).

19 R = *rahdiolokatseeonnaya golovka samonavedeniya* – radar homing unit; T = *teplovaya golovka samonavedeniya* – IR homing unit. E means 'high energy', i.e., long-burn rocket motor.

Soviet fighters a considerable advantage over the F-15 and McDD F/A-18 Hornet armed with Sparrows. The modular construction with interchangeable guidance units made the missile easily adaptable to the changing tactical situation and posed countermeasures problems for the enemy. The basic K-27R/T was broadly similar to the AIM-7F while the 'heavy' K-27ER/ET had much better speed and range. (After entering production in 1984-87 the missile was redesignated R-27 for *raketa* and received the NATO code name AA-10 'Alamo'.)

The same two bureaux were working on short-range (12–20 km/6–11 nm) AAMs, or dogfight missiles. Vympel developed the K-14; a thorough update of the K-13M and K-13M1 with an omnidirectional IR tracker head and higher G limits. Molniya designed the all-new K-73 high-manoeuvrability wingless missile with a jet control system and an IR tracker head with a limited field of view. It was designed along the same lines as the K-60 (R-60 in production form/AA-8 'Aphid') which weighed a mere 45 kg (99 lb). However, aerial combat tactics and experience with foreign missiles showed that an omnidirectional tracker head was a must for a dogfight missile. The VVS urged the company to alter the K-73 project and incorporate the Mayak (Beacon) wide-angle tracker head developed by the Arsenal factory in Kiev under project chief A. V. Molodyk. The new tracker head was rather large and heavy, resulting in an increase in the missile's dimensions; still, the basic concept remained unchanged.

In 1976 the K-73 had to be redesigned once again, as the original layout had some serious shortcomings, including poor manoeuvrability and limited flight time. The engineers opted for a mixed jet/aerodynamic control system and added cruciform wings. This decision was influenced by reports of the US Navy's Agile AAM, a wingless missile with a jet control system which had been terminated for much the same reasons. In its definitive form the K-73 weighed 110 kg (242.5 lb).

The K-73 development programme was originally led by Marat R. Bisnovat until his death in 1977. Later, G. I. Khokhlov was assigned responsibility for guided missiles in the newly-formed NPO Molniya with Gleb Yevgen'yevich Lozino-Lozinskiy as General Director. In 1983 NPO Molniya switched to ballistic missiles; the aircraft armament group was transferred to the ex-rival Vympel OKB – which thus got all the credit when the missile entered production two years later as the R-73 (AA-11 'Archer'). As for Vympel, their competing K-14 project was completed in 1976 and it was immediately apparent that the two missiles were virtually identical in

class, performance, weight and dimensions. The K-14 had the advantage of a simpler design, employing a purely aerodynamic control system, and a good deal of commonality with the proven R-3S (AA-3 'Anab') and R-13M/R-13M1 which meant it could be readily launched from the MiG-21, MiG-23, MiG-27 'Flogger-D', Yak-28P 'Firebar', Su-17 'Fitter-B', 'Fitter-K' and other fighters and fighter-bombers in service with the VVS.

To expand the G limits at which the missile could be fired the K-14 incorporated an unusual device called a feathering rudder. For a long time work on the two missiles progressed in parallel and the reason why the K-14 was eventually rejected was that its 'so-called' non-autopilot control system (which dated all the way back to the 1960-vintage R-3S) was hopelessly antiquated. GosNII AS engineers urged the OKB to redesign the control system completely but Vympel was not in a position to do so, having a lot of other air-to-air missile programmes on its hands (the K-24, K-27, K-33 etc.)

Combat efficiency analysis in 1974-76 showed that the entry-level MiG-29A was quite capable of filling the rôle which the more sophisticated MiG-29 had been designed to fill. It could successfully destroy advanced Western fighters at medium and close range, intercept low-flying multi-rôle tactical aircraft and take out stationary or slow-moving ground targets in VMC conditions. In the air defence rôle it was capable of intercepting aircraft flying at up to 23,000–24,000 m (75,459–78,740 ft) and 2,500–2,600 km/h (1,388–1,444 kts). In the strike/CAS rôle the MiG-29A's combat efficiency was two to four times that of the MiG-21PFM 'Fishbed-F'.

On 19 January 1976 the Central Committee of the Communist Party and the Council of Ministers issued a new directive ordering the development of two fourth-generation fighters; the MiG-29 light fighter and the Su-27 heavy fighter. Both types were to pass their State acceptance trials in 1977. This, at long last, was the official go-ahead. The two aircraft were to feature an advanced weapons control system and highly effective new-generation weapons matching or even surpassing those of the F-15 and F-16. That took care of the two versions issue; the low cost MiG-29A was cancelled and the OKB concentrated wholly on the MiG-29 as originally proposed.

The new-generation WCS proved to be one of the greatest challenges. Data available on the F-15 and F-16 showed that Western fighters were way ahead of Soviet ones in avionics, especially radar and processors. Therefore, the Su-27 and MiG-29 programmes involved a massive and high-priority R&D effort concerning primarily radar, digital aircraft processor, data exchange and data presentation technologies, as well as avionics integration.

An R&D programme code-named Soyuz aided a lot in the development of radars for the new-generation fighters. The programme was initiated by NIIR's chief G. M. Koonyavskiy. He was responsible for the RP-21 Sapfeer (Sapphire/NATO 'Jay Bird') radar of the MiG-21, the Oryol (Eagle/NATO 'Skip Spin') radar of the initial production Su-15 'Flagon-A' and the Tayfoon (Typhoon/NATO 'Twin Scan') radar of the Su-15T 'Flagon-D'. In the late '70s Koonyavskiy left NPO Phazotron and went on to work at GosNII AS.

The main contractor under the Soyuz programme was NPO Istok (Source) under General Designer S. I. Rebrov which designed and built three prototypes of a fire control radar also known as Soyuz. One was retained by the manufacturer for debugging, another was turned over to GosNII AS for trials in simulated service conditions and the third was tested by LII on an avionics testbed. The Soyuz was a pulse-Doppler radar broadly similar in design and performance to the Hughes Electronics AN/APG-65 fitted to the F/A-18. It featured semiconductor technology and a high-speed digital processor permitting ultra-accurate ground mapping. Ground and flight tests went well and, though the Soyuz was strictly a technology demonstrator, some of its features went into the N-001 and N-019 radars fitted to the Su-27 and MiG-29 respectively.

MiG-29E experimental fighter (project)

Development of digital computers for tactical aircraft and software for these computers progressed in the Soviet Union since the late '60s. Aerospace, electronics and defence industry enterprises involved included GosNIIAS, LII, NPO Elektroavtomatika, NPO Fazotron, NPO Leninets (Lenin's Follower) in Leningrad, NIITsEVT[20] and MNIIP[21] (aka NPO Vega-M). It was not long before this massive effort bore fruit: starting in the early '70s, digital computers were fitted to Soviet tactical aircraft, including fourth-generation fighters.

In the Su-27 and MiG-29, the first Soviet fighters with digital avionics, the extremely stringent operational requirements (high processing speed and multiple functions) meant the engineers faced a cartload of problems. The Mikoyan OKB had to undertake a special R&D programme named Feniks (Phoenix) to tackle them. Under this programme supervised by Yuriy A. Yanyshev, the BTsK-29 digital avionics suite[22] would be developed and tested on the purpose-built MiG-29E experimental fighter. Numerous research and engineering organizations, including NPO Elektroavtomatika, NIIAS, NPO Phazotron, NIITsEVT etc., participated in the Feniks programme. The BTsK-29 avionics suite and the MiG-29E never got beyond the PD stage. However, the results of the research effort were put to good use later. The programme made it possible to formulate the main principles of the avionics hardware structure, cockpit data presentation and controls placement. Eventually NIITsEVT led by A. A. Solovyov developed the Ts100 series main computer's WCS while NPO Elektroavtomatika produced a similar TsVM-80 computer for the Su-27.[23]

NIIAS led by Academician Yevgeniy A. Fedosov contributed much to designing and refining the MiG-29's avionics suite; P. V. Poznyakov supervised all of the institute's research programmes for the MiG-29. A laboratory managed by Z. A. Kaploon was specially organized at NIIAS for developing and debugging avionics software for fourth-generation fighters. Jointly with the Mikoyan OKB the institute built a special S-2900 simulation complex for testing the fire control radar, optoelectronic targeting system and weapons control system. Data obtained on the KPM-2300 combat simulator enabled the engineers to estimate how the MiG-29 would fare against the F-15 and F-16 in a dogfight. Later, NIIAS engineers participated in the State acceptance trials of the actual aircraft at NII VVS (the Air Force Research Institute).

MiG-29 (*izdeliye* 9.12) and MiG-29A (*izdeliye* 9.12A) light tactical fighter (definitive projects)

The MiG-29 project was finally frozen in 1977. However, preparation of drawings and project documents had gone on steadily for the previous four years. When approving the 1/20th scale drawings of the MiG-29A on 15 July 1974, General Designer Rostislav A. Belyakov had deemed it necessary to increase wing area from 34 m^2

---

20 *Naoochno-issledovatel'skiy institoot tsifrovykh elektronno-vychisleetel'nykh tekhnologiy* – Digital Computing Technologies Research Institute

21 *Moskovskiy naoochno-issledovatel'skiy institoot priborostroyeniya* – Moscow Research Institute of Instrument Engineering

22 BTsK = *bortovoy tsifrovoy kompleks* – lit. on-board digital complex

23 TsVM = *tsentrahl'naya vychisleetel'naya masheena* – main computer

(365.6 sq. ft) to 38m² (408.6 sq. ft). The rewinged fighter received a new manufacturer's designation, *izdeliye* 9.12; the 'entry-level' version with MiG-23 avionics and armament became *izdeliye* 9.12A. The general arrangement, however, remained unaltered; *izdeliye* 9.12 was an integral-layout mid-wing monoplane with prominent LERXes and powerful high-lift devices, twin tails and differentially-movable low-set stabilators, RD-33 afterburning turbofans in underslung spaced nacelles with inlet FOD protection doors and auxiliary dorsal intakes, and a heavy-duty tricycle landing gear.

The integral layout provided a good lift/drag ratio and ample structural strength reserves, enabling the aircraft to pull high G loads and manoeuvre at high AOAs. Wing lift was increased by means of camber, programmable automatic leading-edge flaps, trailing-edge flaps and flaperons. The LERXes increased wing lift at high alpha, reducing the risk of stalling and/or spinning. The multi-mode air intakes were highly efficient at high alpha, rendering the aircraft safe and easy to fly. The MiG-29 made large-scale use of composites and aluminium-lithium alloys to cut airframe weight. The elevated position of the cockpit and the bubble canopy with one-piece windscreen offered the pilot excellent all-round visibility; this was helped by the triple rear-view mirrors on the windscreen frame. The pilot sat on a K-36DM zero-zero ejection seat developed by the Zvezda (Star) design bureau under Guy Il'yich Severin; it enabled safe ejection throughout the aircraft's flight envelope.

In definitive form the MiG-29 had a length of 15.0 m (49 ft 2.55 in.) less pitot boom, a wingspan of 10.8 m (35 ft 5.19 in.), a wing area of 38.0 m² (408.6 sq. ft) and a height on ground of 4.56 m (14 ft 11.52 in.). Empty weight was 9,670 kg (21,318 lb) and normal takeoff weight with a 3,650-kg (8,046-lb) internal fuel load was 13,570 kg (29,916 lb).[24] Takeoff thrust-to-weight ratio was 1.23 and specific wing loading was 350 kg/m² (1,706 lb/sq. ft).

Unlike the Su-27 which was designed to operate up to 400 km (222 nm) beyond the frontline, the MiG-29 was to operate mostly over friendly territory, venturing only some 100 km (55 nm) beyond the frontline. It had higher performance and more capable avionics and armament than the MiG-23 then forming the backbone of the Soviet Air Force's tactical fighter element. The higher performance was due to the integral layout increasing speed and manoeuvrability and to the twin engines giving a significantly better thrust-to-weight ratio (compared with

the 'Flogger's single engine). The highly effective K-27, K-73 and K-14 new-generation AAMs and twin-barrel 30-mm gun enabled the MiG-29 to destroy highly manoeuvrable targets within a broad speed and altitude range.

The SOR stated the MiG-29's rôles first of all as counter-air and top cover for ground troops. The CAS/strike rôle was viewed as very secondary, which, as Mikoyan conceded, was a big mistake. The aircraft was required to have a top speed of 2,500 km/h (1,388 kts) at high altitude, 1,500 km/h (833 kts) at sea level and go from 600 to 1,100 km/h (333 to 611 kts) in 13 seconds and from 1,100 to 1,300 km/h (722 kts) in 7 seconds. Service ceiling with 50% fuel was 19,500 m (63,976 ft); maximum rate of climb at 1,000 m (3,280 ft) was 325 m/sec (1,066 ft/sec). Range was 800 km (444 nm) at S/L and 2,750 km (1,527 nm) at high altitude with a single 1,500-lit. (33 Imp. gal.) drop tank on the fuselage centreline. The aircraft was stressed for 9 Gs. This and the high alpha limit, broad speed and altitude range, high thrust-to-weight ratio and carefully designed aerodynamics enhanced flight safety, allowing prolonged violent manoeuvring in combat.

Combat efficiency estimates showed that the MiG-29 could destroy an F-4E, an F-111A, a Tornado or a Jaguar flying at 30–23,000 m (98–75,459 ft) and up to 2,500 km/h (1,388 kts) with K-27 missiles in both head-on and pursuit mode. In a dogfight with an F-15 or an F-16 armed with AIM-9L Sidewinder missiles the chances of a kill were 1.4 and 1.5 times better than the respective enemy's. In a long-range missile duel with an incoming F-15 the MiG-29 (aided by GCI centres) was superior to the enemy throughout its flight envelope thanks to the higher agility of the K-27 AAM as compared with the AIM-7F. It was also decidedly superior to the F-16A because the N-019 radar had much longer detection range than the US fighter's Westinghouse AN/APG-66. The probability of scoring a hit on an F-4E pulling 4 Gs with a 0.5-second burst of gunfire at 200–800 m (656–2,624 ft) range was 40–80%; it was estimated that four or six rounds would do the job. Efficiency against ground targets was also deemed to be adequate.

The gun armament was changed before long. Mikoyan soon decided that the AO-17A (GSh-30) was rather too heavy for a light fighter like the MiG-29. A joint effort of the OKB (notably PD section chief Tyapkin) and NPO Tochnost resulted in the development of an acceptable weapon brought out in 1976. The new gun, designated TKB-687 or 9A4071, used the same AO-18 round; it was

---

[24] The specific operational requirement stated a 12,800-kg (28,218-lb) TOW

based on a single barrel borrowed from a naval twin-barrel 30-mm automatic gun and shortened by 500 mm (1 ft 7.68 in.). This decreased muzzle velocity to 850–900 m/sec (2,788–2,952 ft/sec) as compared with that of the naval weapon but even so it was actually higher than that of the AO-17A! At 50 kg (110 lb), the TKB-687 was twice as light as the AO-17A and had a rate of fire of 1,500–1,800 rpm. A prototype was built in 1977; six years later the

production gun (redesignated GSh-301) was fitted to the MiG-29 and Su-27. With this weapon, the probability of scoring a hit on an F-4E pulling 4 Gs with a 0.5-second burst at 200–800 m range was 20–70% (one barrel is less than two, after all).

The definitive version of the MiG-29 advanced development project was examined and approved when the first prototype was actually flying.

MiG-29 full-scale mockup in the Mikoyan experimental factory's assembly shop. (Mikoyan OKB archive)

The first prototype MiG-29 (Aircraft 901) shows the twin gun muzzles to advantage. (Mikoyan OKB archive)

2

Learning to Fly

MiG-29 prototypes and pre-production aircraft (901 to 904, 908 and 917 to 925)

Originally the Mikoyan OKB had planned to build no less than 25 flying prototypes and a number of static test airframes. The unusually large number of development aircraft was due to the extreme complexity of the flight test programme. Performance and handling trials, avionics trials, armament trials etc. would have to be assigned to different aircraft. And so they were; each of the flight test aircraft was allocated a code number (901 to 925)[1]. For the first time in Soviet aircraft design history the three-digit prototype numbers were included in government decrees, so changing them or reallocating them to a different airframe was out of the question.

Each of the prototypes would have mission equipment and flight test equipment (sensors and data recorders) to match the specific part of the trials programme for which the aircraft was built. For the first time in Mikoyan's design practice a full-scale aircraft was to be tested in the TsAGI wind tunnel and special airframes built for test avionics trials and avionics compatibility testing.

[1] I.e., 901 = (MiG-29) flight test article No. 1

In keeping with the original two-stage development concept part of the development aircraft was earmarked for completion to MiG-29A standard with the SUV-23ML-2 weapons control system. However, it soon turned out that the radar set of the Yantar (Sapfeer-23ML-2) radar did not fit the MiG-29 airframe. In the MiG-23 the bulky cubic radar set fitted nicely into a bay aft of the cockpit but, try as they would, Mikoyan engineers could not squeeze it into the MiG-29A. NPO Phazotron offered to develop a horseshoe-shaped unit that would fit under the cockpit. However, when the engineers tried fitting the restyled radar set to the full-scale mockup the result was pure frustration: the unit was too large again. The problem was cured by making the LERXes slightly thicker to provide more room in the avionics bay.

However, as was mentioned earlier, the MiG-29A was cancelled in 1976, leaving only the full-blooded MiG-29. Besides, after Lt. Viktor I. Belenko's notorious defection to Japan with the MiG-25P 'Foxbat-A' interceptor on 6 September the same year NPO Phazotron had to concentrate wholly on developing the S-25 (Sapfeer-25)

Aircraft 901 had the nose gear unit located well forward. However, early test flights made it imperative to move the nose gear aft for FOD prevention reasons. (Mikoyan OKB archive)

Freshly-completed MiG-29s in the final assembly shop of the Lookhovitsy Mechanical Plant. (Yefim Gordon)

fire control radar for the upgraded MiG-25PD 'Foxbat-E', which meant the Yantar radar had to be shelved. As a result the MiG-29A airframes (aircraft 905 to 907 and 909 to 916) were never built. The code number 908 originally allocated to a MiG-29A was later reused for a powerplant development aircraft built to replace the third prototype which had crashed during trials. Thus a total of 14 flight test aircraft was actually built.

The first four prototypes were built at Mikoyan's experimental shop (MMZ No. 155) with assistance from MMZ No. 30 Znamya Truda (pronounced *znahmya troodah* – Banner of Labour).[2] This factory located at Moscow's Central airfield named after Mikhail V. Frunze (better known as the Khodynka airfield) was gearing up to manufacture production MiG-29s and supplied major structural components such as main integral fuel tanks for all prototypes. The aircraft sported a two-digit tactical code[3] in blue on the air intakes and the full prototype

code number in white on the dielectric fin caps. E.g., the first prototype was 01 Blue (901 White), the second was 02 Blue (902 White) etc.

All manufacturing drawings released by the OKB had to be duly approved by the factory, the All-Union Institute of Aviation Structural Materials (VIAM – *Vsesoyouznyy institoot aviatseeonnykh materialov*) and the Research Institute of Aviation Technologies (NIAT – *Naoochno-issledovatel'skiy institoot aviatseeonnykh tekhnologiy*). To make sure the prototypes were completed on schedule V. Bykov, a Mikoyan employee, drew up an interdepartmental plan roughly equivalent to a bar chart. Representatives of organizations involved in the MiG-29 programme would come to Moscow from all over the land to report on progress and sign the plan, showing what had actually been done. Both MMZ No. 30 and the Mikoyan experimental shop had to buy state-of-the-art manufacturing equipment. The experimental shop participated in assembling all prototypes and fitting them out with test instrumentation.

The first prototype was rolled out in 1977 and commenced ground systems tests same year. Having as yet no practical knowledge of the structural strength reserves of an integral-layout aircraft, Mikoyan engineers had incorporated excessive structural strength in the MiG-29, just to be on the safe side, making the aircraft

---

[2] Now called MAPO, *Moskovskoye aviatseeonnoye proizvodstvennoye obyedineniye* – the Moscow Aviation Production Association named after Pyotr V. Demen'tyev (ex-Minister of Aircraft Industry)

[3] Unlike Western military aircraft which have serial numbers allowing positive identification, Soviet military aircraft have two-digit tactical codes which are usually simply the aircraft's number in the unit which operates it. Three-digit codes are rare and are usually allocated to development aircraft only, often tying in with the aircraft's construction number (manufacturer's serial number).

rather overweight. For the first time in Soviet fighter design practice a service life limit had been set, so measures had to be taken to reduce stress build up in the fighter's structural elements. Both VIAM and TsAGI had expressly recommended the use of composites, and Mikoyan had high hopes, expecting to save some 400 kg (881 lb) of airframe weight by using them. The real weight saving, however, was only about 200 kg (440 lb). As a result, the first prototype's TOW was 700 kg (1,543 lb) above the specified limit. Since 01 Blue was intended primarily for handling and performance trials, no gun was fitted, although the aircraft had provisions for a GSh-30

(AO-17A) gun and featured twin muzzle openings in the port LERX. A gun mockup was originally installed but later removed and the gun ports were faired over.

On 6 October 1977 the MiG-29 became airborne for the first time with Mikoyan chief test pilot Aleksandr V. Fedotov at the controls. Valeriy Ye. Menitskiy also flew the first prototype. Later, as more prototypes became available and the scope of the trials programme widened, other test pilots joined in.

Manufacturer's flight tests with three prototypes made up the greater part of the trials programme until the spring of 1981. The first prototype was used to evaluate performance

Briefing before a mission. (Aviatsiya i Kosmonavtika)

and handling and measure airframe loads (stress in the main structural elements); engineer A. B. Slobodskiy was in charge of the test programme. As early as 1978 Fedotov began low-speed handling and stalling/spinning trials. Ventral fins were added in the course of these trials at the insistence of TsAGI to improve directional stability at high alpha and facilitate spin recovery (TsAGI engineers claimed that pitch control in a spin would otherwise be inadequate). All of the 14 prototypes and pre-production aircraft had these ventral fins.

Early test flights revealed that the designers had unfortunately picked the only possible location for the nose gear unit where all debris flung up by the nosewheels (despite the mud/snow/slush guard) was projected squarely into the air intakes. Since the MiG-29 had the patented FOD protection doors, this didn't seem to matter much and the nose gear unit was left as it was. Nevertheless a MiG-23B 'Flogger-D' prototype was converted into a Test Dirt aircraft to investigate debris distribution patterns on takeoff and landing, with wire mesh screens protecting the air intakes. The first prototype was retired in Zhukovskiy after making 230 flights. Several years later it was donated to the VVS Museum in Monino southeast of Moscow where it resides in the open-air display.

Construction of the second and third prototypes (aircraft 902 and 903) started almost simultaneously, but the latter aircraft was actually completed first. Initially aircraft 902 was identical to the first prototype but even before it was completed the nose gear unit was moved aft 1.5 m (4 ft 11 in.) to reduce further the risk of foreign object ingestion: a decision inspired by early flight tests. The nose gear was also shortened slightly.

Coded 02 Blue (902), the second prototype, which was actually the *third* flight test article, entered flight tests in November 1979, making seven flights before the year was out; three more flights were made by 15 March 1980. 02 Blue had no radar and was therefore used to verify the optoelectronic targeting/navigation system. This was the first MiG-29 to have the intended GSh-301 single-barrel gun; it was also the first aircraft to participate in the State acceptance trials programme at NII VVS in Akhtoobinsk in southern Russia (near Saratov on the river Volga). Anatoliy A. Belosvet was in charge of the flight test programme on the OKB's part and I. G. Kristinov headed the VVS test team.

Aircraft 902 was first in many respects. The FOD problem was eventually found to be serious enough to cause a relocation of the nose gear unit, intake doors

notwithstanding. Therefore, from 02 Blue onwards the nose gear was moved 1.5 m (4 ft 11 in.) aft. This aircraft was also the first to have integral wing fuel tanks.

It soon turned out that the aircraft's AOA limit was 5° lower than specified in the project, as violent vibration was encountered at high alpha. The cause of the trouble was traced to sections of the leading-edge flaps which had been eliminated at Belyakov's orders; this gave a weight saving of 15 kg (33 lb) but created turbulence. Since the wings had been redesigned, the original flap configuration could not be restored and the engineers found a different solution, modifying the wingtips to smooth the airflow. After making 229 test flights the aircraft was relegated to the aircraft systems test facility in Faustovo near Moscow (GosNIPAS)[4]. There it was used at first to test the fire suppression system and later shot up to check if the fuel tanks would explode after taking a hit.

The third prototype, 03 Blue (903), was rolled out ahead of the second one and made its first flight in June 1978; this aircraft was virtually identical to the first one

---

[4] *Gosoodahrstvennyy naoochno-ispytahtel'nyy poligon aviatseeonnykh sistem* – State Research and Test Range for Aircraft Systems

The experienced pilots at Kubinka had no trouble mastering the advanced fourth-generation fighter. (Aviatsiya i Kosmonavtika)

TOP: *The only known photograph of the second prototype, 'Aircraft 902'. (Yefim Gordon archive)*
ABOVE: *The fourth prototype, 'Aircraft 904'. (Yefim Gordon)*

and served for powerplant testing. Unfortunately, its career proved to be extremely short. On 15 June the aircraft crashed on its ninth flight when one of the engines suffered an uncontained compressor failure and fragments severed the control runs. The fighter became uncontrollable and test pilot Valeriy Menitskiy ejected safely. Flight data recorder readouts showed that the good engine had continued running steadily right to the point of impact, thus proving that the powerplant operated well during a spin with no tendency to flame out.

Interestingly, on the first two flight test aircraft (901 and 903) the No. 1 integral fuselage fuel tank was larger than on subsequent aircraft, having two sections projecting forward. In plan view these resembled the legs of a sitting man seen from above and thus were promptly dubbed legs by Mikoyan engineers. When the nose gear unit was moved aft on aircraft 902 this necessitated a relocation of the equipment bay, which in turn led to a

change in the No. 1 tank's shape. As Mikoyan engineers put it, 'the legs were cut off'! Also, the first two flight test aircraft lacked integral wing tanks but did have provisions for them – 'in case range proved to be inadequate'.

The fourth prototype, 04 Blue (904), was intended mainly for dynamic load measurement and equipped with numerous stress sensors. It took to the air on 15 May 1979. After making 40 flights within the manufacturer's flight test programme the aircraft was handed over to LII in July 1981; the institute operated it until the type had successfully passed its state acceptance trials. LII representatives, however, tell a different story, claiming that 04 Blue made only 11 flights with Mikoyan before being transferred to LII and making a further 148 flights there. The fourth prototype was used in a comprehensive dynamic load measurement programme at LII; lead engineer A. V. Pochando was responsible for the flight tests. After retiring in July 1991 the aircraft was briefly displayed near Frunzenskaya underground station in

Bombs on a 'Fulcrum'?? The fourth prototype was used to look into the possibility of using the MiG-29 as a fighter-bomber and is shown here in bombed-up condition. (Yefim Gordon archive)

downtown Moscow; later it was transferred to the open-air museum at Khodynka airfield. Powerplant testing continued with the fifth prototype (aircraft 908) which made its first flight on 5 April 1979. However, this aircraft fared little better than its predecessor. It was lost on its 48th flight on 31 October 1980 when a combustion chamber failed; the resulting fire burned through control runs and the aircraft dived into the ground. A. V. Fedotov ejected, receiving a spinal injury that kept him in hospital for several months.

Aircraft 901, 903 and 908 took part only in manufacturer's trials; the other prototypes were used in the state acceptance trials as well. In the course of tests the fighter was modified to incorporate the GSh-301 single-barrel 30-mm gun (also designated TKB-687 and 9A4071K). This gun developed by V. P. Gryazev and A. G. Shipoonov at NPO Tochnost was designed for fixed and movable installations; it used the AO-18 round and had a rate of fire of 1,600 rpm. The new gun necessitated changes to the fittings and ammo box.

The sixth prototype or aircraft 917 (17 Blue) was the standard-setter for the production MiG-29 and incorporated various improvements made in the course of the test programme. All subassemblies were manufactured at MMZ No. 30 but final assembly took place in Mikoyan's experimental shop. This aircraft later became the first MiG-29 to feature the extended-chord rudders protruding beyond the fin trailing edge that were characteristic of late-production aircraft. 17 Blue made its first flight in December 1979. It was used in the aerodynamics research part of the trials programme and for performance and handling testing, making a total of 369 test flights before it was retired. It is now an instructional airframe at the Air Force Engineering Academy named after Nikolay Yegorovich Zhukovskiy in Moscow.

The seventh development aircraft, 18 Blue (918), was the reverse of aircraft 902 as regards mission avionics. It was the first MiG-29 prototype to have a fire control radar but had no optoelectronic targeting system. It took to the air on 22 May 1980 and made 265 flights (including 163 flights within the weapons control system test programme), gaining the distinction of the type's first air-to-air kill with a K-27R IR-homing missile. In 1982 aircraft 918 was modified under the MiG-29K shipboard fighter programme with an arrester hook under the aft fuselage and unofficially designated MiG-29KVP; this will be described in more detail later.

Between them the prototypes made 331 test flights under the state acceptance trials programme by the end of 1980. The intensity of the trials increased greatly when four more single-seaters (aircraft 919, 920, 921 and 923) the prototype of the MiG-29UB trainer (aircraft 951) joined the programme in 1981. By the end of the year the total number of test flights had increased to 700 (647 for the single-seaters and 53 for the two-seater).

Aircraft 919 (19 Blue), which first flew on 30 July 1981, was another radar test vehicle. Unlike 18 Blue, however, it featured the new Ts100 digital computer replacing the Orbita-20 analogue computer. This aircraft was the first to score a kill with a K-73 short-range AAM, destroying an M-21 target drone (remote-controlled MiG-21 conversion; M = mishen' – target). In July 1985 after making 266 flights with Mikoyan the eighth prototype was transferred to LII which used it to investigate the effect of vibration and high temperatures on the aircraft's systems at the request of the VVS, as equipment failures were a constant source of annoyance on initial production 'Fulcrums'. It was also used to examine the effect of G loads on gun and missile firing.

On 16 August 1988, the eighth prototype was displayed

'Aircraft 919' on display in the city park in Zhukovskiy on Aviation Day (16 August 1988). (Yefim Gordon)

ЦЕНТР АВИАЦИОННОЙ НАУКИ

'Aircraft 924' on display in front of TsAGI's administrative building in Zhukovskiy on Aviation Day (18 August 1991), one day before the military coup which brought an end to the Soviet Union's existence. (Yefim Gordon)

in the city park in Zhukovskiy on Aviation Day.[5] Finally, retiring in 1991 with 364 flights to its credit, it became an instructional airframe at a technical training unit in the town of Elektrougli near Moscow where it is used to demonstrate in-service repair techniques. The ninth aircraft, 20 Blue (920), was the first to feature a complete set of mission avionics and was used for avionics compatibility testing. It entered flight test on 6 March 1981. After making 373 flights it went to the nuclear test range on the Novaya Zemlya archipelago in the Barents Sea (probably to test its tactical nuclear weapons delivery capability).

Powerplant testing was finally completed on the tenth aircraft (21 Blue/921) which first flew on 21 August 1981; this included investigating the effect of gun firing and missile launches on engine operation. After making 376 flights under the MiG-29's flight test programme 21 Blue

found further use as a testbed for the uprated RD-33K engine developed for the vastly upgraded MiG-29M version. The aircraft still survives at Mikoyan's test facility at LII, Zhukovskiy. Aircraft 922 joined the test programme on 20 May 1982 but was withdrawn from use after only four flights, including three for WCS testing. It was then handed over to TsAGI for full-scale wind tunnel tests.

The next development aircraft, 23 Blue (923), made its first flight at Zhukovskiy on 4 November 1981 and was soon ferried to NII VVS in Akhtoobinsk for testing the optoelectronic targeting/nav system and internal gun. This aircraft proved the gun's effectiveness by destroying a Lavochkin La-17 jet-propelled target drone. 23 Blue introduced redesigned fittings for the landing/taxi lights which had been a problem on earlier prototypes, turning downwards on their own accord every now and again. Nevertheless, red reference lines were painted on the main gear doors to which the lights were attached; these

---

[5] Celebrated on the third Sunday in August.

'901' Prototype

'901' Prototype

'901' Upgraded Prototype

'904' Prototype

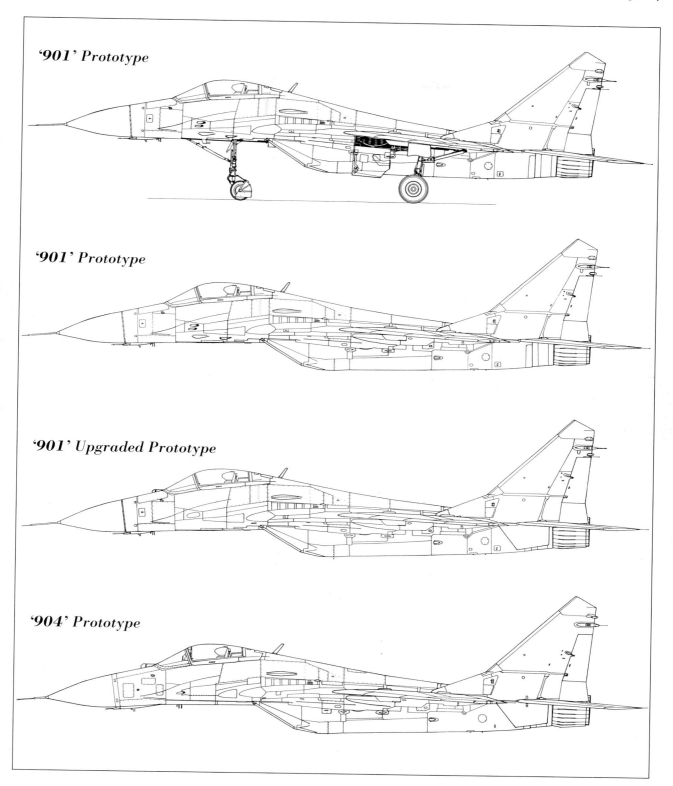

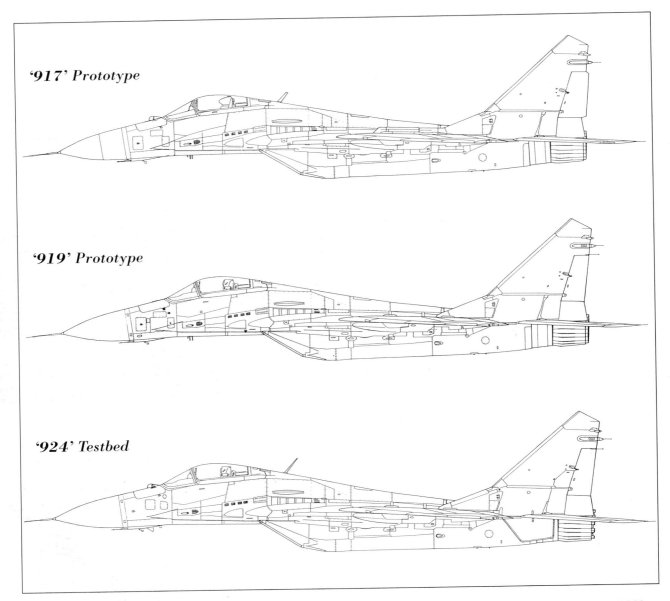

'917' Prototype

'919' Prototype

'924' Testbed

are present on all production MiG-29s. This aircraft ended its days at GosNIPAS in Faustovo after 281 flights as another fire suppression system test rig.

24 Blue (924, construction number 0390501625)[6] was rolled out by the Znamya Truda factory on 30 September 1981 but did not make its first flight until 9 September 1983 at the hands of OKB test pilot Boris A. Orlov. It was transferred to LII after 22 flights; on 29 December 1983, Rimas A. A. Stankiavicius made the first acceptance flight.[7] The institute used 24 Blue for dynamic load measurement and later for evaluating modified engine

nozzles and modified air intakes. On 18 August 1991, a day before the military *coup d'état* which brought an end to the existence of the Soviet Union, the aircraft was in the Aviation Day static display in front of TsAGI's administrative building in Zhukovskiy. By 1997 the

---

6 The construction number (c/n) or manufacturer's serial number is non-standard because this was a pre-production aircraft (see footnote in 'Fulcrum-C' section in next chapter).

7 According to LII sources, Mikoyan test pilots A. V. Fedotov and A. N. Kvochur made only 11 flights in 24 Blue before the aircraft went to LII.

A standard production MiG-29 (izdeliye 9.12). (Yefim Gordon)

aircraft had made 360 flights, logging 233 hours. The fourteenth and final development aircraft, 25 Blue (925) was the definitive standard-setter for full-scale production incorporating all the changes made in the course of the trials. It took off for the first time on 30 December 1982, making 235 test flights before it was withdrawn from use at LII. 25 Blue was used, among other things, to check the interaction between the fire control radar and the IRST. Next year the MiG-29 entered production at MMZ No. 30 under the in-house designation *izdeliye 9.12*.

Improvements started coming as soon as the first fighters rolled off the production line at Khodynka. Operational experience in Afghanistan where the Mujahideen guerrillas were often using portable IR-homing surface-to-air missiles such as Stinger and Redeye. This forced the engineers to devise countermeasures. Thus the MiG-29 received infra-red countermeasures (IRCM) flare dispensers; these were initially located on the wings ahead of the fin fillets. The arrangement was tested on the sixth prototype (17 Blue). Dorsal strakes (boundary layer fences) of varying length incorporating the chaff/flare dispensers were tested during

the aerodynamics refining programme which was to continue for a long time yet. Eventually, however, they were found to be unnecessary and on the MiG-29K and MiG-29M the dispensers were fitted flush with the rear fuselage skin. The final pre-production aircraft also participated in IRCM testing.

Aleksandr V. Fedotov investigated the MiG-29's spinning characteristics. It transpired that if you really wanted the MiG-29 to spin you had to force it. The aircraft simply would not spin of its own accord! When the pilot let go of the controls after initiating a spin the fighter recovered automatically. On the minus side, high-alpha handling did pose problems. The MiG-29 was found to have reverse roll reaction to rudder input at high AOAs; i.e., if the pilot applied right rudder the aircraft rolled to the left instead of to the right. Conversely, the fighter behaved normally if bank was countered by rudder input. This quirk initially caused the AOA to be limited to 20°; this was later increased to 22°, then 24° etc. as flight tests progressed and the aircraft's behaviour was studied.

However, both Mikoyan and the VVS were unhappy about having to correct bank at high AOAs by rudder

'Aircraft 925', the final aircraft of the experimental batch, during flight tests. (Mikoyan OKB archive)

input. The reason was that the MiG-29 was supposed to be the backbone of the Soviet Union's fighter force, superseding not only the MiG-23 but the MiG-21 as well. Now 'Fishbed' pilots did not have to work the rudder pedals all that much, and getting them into the habit of vigorous footwork in the MiG-29 would call for a lot of effort. Therefore, Mikoyan introduced an automatic bank corrector into the control system. When the AOA passed certain limits the autopilot automatically deflected the rudders as necessary to eliminate excessive bank. Calculations showed the required rudder deflection was 8°; for safety's sake the bank corrector was adjusted in increments of 2°.

Stage B of the state acceptance trials held by Mikoyan and the VVS was completed successfully on 27 October 1983 with the twelfth prototype (23 Blue). All in all the prototypes had made some 2,500 test flights, with the loss of two aircraft due to uncontained engine failure. The aircraft was officially included in the VVS inventory in 1984; full-scale production and initial operational capability (IOC), however, had been achieved two years earlier.

The West got news of the MiG-29's existence in the spring of 1979 when a US surveillance satellite photographed one of the prototypes on LII's airfield in Zhukovskiy. The manufacturer was unknown at the time, so the aircraft received the provisional reporting name 'Ram-L' because Zhukovskiy was then erroneously referred

to as Ramenskoye.[8] By 1982, when the true designation became known, the MiG-29 was allocated the ASCC reporting name 'Fulcrum'. However, it was a long time before the West had any idea what the fighter really looked like. Provisional three-view drawings published in 1982 were wildly inaccurate, showing almost a copy of the Northrop YF-17, though in fact the resemblance is purely superficial.

Later, when the MiG-29 was fully operational, the people that created it received high government awards. Mikhail R. Val'denberg, who succeeded Choomachenko as chief project engineer around 1982, was awarded the honorary Hero of Socialist Labour title, many other engineers received decorations. Anatoliy A. Belosvet (Deputy General Designer at Mikoyan), P. V. Pozdnyakov (Deputy Director of GosNIIAS), Gen. L. I. Agoorin (head of NII VVS), Mikoyan test pilot Valeriy Menitskiy, Yuriy P. Kirpichov (head of NIIR) and V. G. Stepanov (head of the Klimov engine design bureau) were awarded the prestigious Lenin Prize – a neat sum of money. Twelve Mikoyan employees, including Rostislav A. Belyakov, Vano A. Mikoyan, Anatoliy Pavlov, V. Godoonov, A. B. Slobodskiy, M. Yakubovich, Stepanov, Bezlyud'ko and four others, received the State Prize.

---

8 Ramenskoye is actually a separate town located right next to Zhukovskiy

TOP: *10 Blue during a training sortie. (Mikoyan OKB)*

ABOVE: *10 Blue was retained by Mikoyan for demonstration and training purposes. (Yefim Gordon archive)*

BELOW: *An experimental MiG-29 ('Aircraft 970') used as a weapons testbed for the R-27 and R-77 (RVV-AE) medium-range AAMs. (Yefim Gordon archive)*

The Family Starts Growing

MiG-29 tactical fighter (*izdeliye 9.12* or *izdeliye 5*), 'Fulcrum-A'

The first major production version of the MiG-29 known around Mikoyan as *izdeliye 9.12* was referred to in Air Force documents as *izdeliye 5*. (Multiple codes for the same equipment item were common practice intended to make it harder for Western spies.) As mentioned earlier, the fighter entered production at MMZ No. 30 Znamya truda in 1982. This version, featuring the RLPK-29 targeting system (built around the N-019 Rubin radar) and the OEPrNK-29 (S-31) optoelectronic targeting/nav system, stayed in production until 1990. Mikhail R. Val'denberg became MiG-29 project chief when production started; he was superseded by V. V. Novikov in 1993.

Despite being designed in Leningrad the RD-33 turbofan was built in Moscow. The Krasnyy Oktyabr' (Red October) plant[1] in Tushino, Moscow, assembled the first pre-production engines in 1977; production began in 1980, initially on a small scale, and really got under way

two years later. The Soyuz engine design bureau (TMKB Soyuz) at the same location had a hand in debugging and improving the RD-33. The result was better performance and a greatly increased engine life. RD-33s manufactured in the early '90s had a 1,400-hr service life and a 700-hr TBO; by comparison, for early-production engines built in the mid-80s these were a mere 350 and 800 hrs respectively. Current production engines are even better, with a 2,000-hr service life.

A lot of enterprises in the aerospace, electronics, defence and other industries supplied components for the MiG-29. E.g., the Krasnyy Oktyabr' factory in Leningrad – there were a lot of Red Octobers! – manufactured the Izotov GTDE-117 auxiliary power unit (APU). The N-019 radar was built by the state instrument factory in Ryazan' while the IRST came from the Ural Optical Equipment Factory (UOMZ) in Sverdlovsk (now Yekaterinburg). The production run was split into batches of fifteen aircraft (though some batches contained more). Like the prototypes, the first 70 aircraft had ventral fins outboard of the engine nacelles to improve spinning characteristics

---

[1] Currently known as the Machinery plant named after V. V. Chernyshov (public limited company)

A production MiG-29 (izdeliye 9.13). (Yefim Gordon)

TOP: *The izdeliye 9.13 can be distingushed from the initial production version by its characteristic bulged spine. (Yefim Gordon)*

ABOVE: *A production MiG-29 (11 Blue, 'Aircraft 211') used by Mikoyan for research. Note the additional pitot heads on the forward fuselage. (Viktor Drooshlyakov)*

and directional stability at high alpha. By 1984, however, the automatic bank corrector in the rudder control circuit had passed its trials and was introduced on production aircraft, rendering the ventral fins unnecessary; besides, they complicated access to the engine cowlings. Most early production aircraft had them removed in service.

The increased-chord rudders tested on the sixth prototype and introduced on late-production aircraft were also associated with high-alpha handling. Large rudder deflection in order to counter bank at high AOAs proved inadvisable, as the pilot had difficulty in bringing the rudders manually to neutral position in the event of an autopilot or actuator failure. The solution was to reduce rudder deflection in this mode and compensate for this by increasing rudder area. Another change made on late MiG-29s was the ailerons set at 5° upward deflection in the neutral position to further improve spinning characteristics. The production MiG-29's AOA limit set by the manufacturer was 26°. However, in service the VVS imposed a 24° limit, just to be on the safe side.

Another characteristic feature of initial production aircraft (besides the ventral fins) was a nose gear door section attached to the oleo ahead of the nosewheels and doubling as a gravel deflector! The reason for this was that stones would sometimes stick to the nosewheels and then, coming loose, be projected forward by the centrifugal force, whereupon the aircraft caught up with them. This was dangerous because the FOD protection doors retracted on rotation, leaving the intakes wide open to such 'stray bullets'. (Some research on the MiG-29's mudguards *had* been done but generally experience accumulated with the MiG-23 was considered to be sufficient.)

Because of its characteristic shape the deflector was promptly dubbed *bahbochka* (butterfly). However, it sometimes made contact with the ground during taxiing and was soon deleted; the few aircraft fitted with this deflector had it removed. The original solid mudguard enclosing the entire rear half of the nosewheels was soon replaced by a small grid-type mudguard.

Soon after production entry the MiG-29 was equipped with BVP-30-26M chaff/flare dispensers[2] ahead of the fins, with 30 26-mm (1.02-in.) infrared countermeasures (IRCM) flares each. A vortex generator was added to the pitot boom in a similar fashion to the final version of the 'Flogger' – the MiG-23MLD 'Flogger-K'.

Originally the MiG-29 was to incorporate a good deal of composites. Indeed, on the first thirty production aircraft the inlet ducts, engine cowlings, leading-edge flaps, control surfaces, wingtips, fuselage spine, fins and numerous access panels were made of composites, not to mention the radome and dielectric fin caps concealing communications aerials. The ailerons, rudders and aft portions of the stabilators had honeycomb construction. However, the composite panels failed on several occasions during trials and in service, even causing two serious accidents in late 1984. The trouble was traced to microscopic cracks which appeared during riveting. The riveting technology was changed, with prior drilling of holes to preclude crack formation. Still the problem persisted; it turned out that aircraft built by MAPO's division in Lookhovitsy outside Moscow suffered from defective riveting. On one occasion test pilot Abramovich had a hair-raising near-accident when an engine inlet duct failed in flight; the aircraft landed with a gaping hole in the engine nacelle – half the duct was gone. This was the last straw. Minister of Aircraft Industry Pyotr V. Demen'tyev demanded that composites be excluded from structurally important areas of the aircraft. From the 31st production aircraft (fuselage number 0301)[3] onwards the inlet ducts, leading-edge flaps and some other components were made of D19 aluminium alloy which resulted in a 20-kg (44-lb) weight penalty.

Mikoyan stuck to composite cowlings for quite some time. These were expendable items and were replaced by new ones during overhauls, hence the demand was fairly high. However, the aerospace industry was unable to produce enough and started lobbying for a replacement that would last longer. Demen'tyev intervened again, demanding that the cowlings be made of metal too; and so they were, adding another 40 kg (88 lb) of airframe weight. In the end only the composite fins, radome and access panels remained (the fins were found to be strong enough).

The MiG-29 (*izdeliye* 9.12) had an internal fuel capacity of 4,300 lit. (946 Imp. gal.); the fuel was carried in four fuselage integral tanks and two wing tanks. For long-range operations and ferry flights a 1,520-lit. (334.4 Imp. gal.) drop tank could be carried on the fuselage centreline. Unlike most Soviet fighters which used standardised drop tanks, the 'Fulcrum's' tank was tailored to the aircraft. It was semi-conformal to cut drag. The rather bulky drop tank obstructed the APU exhaust

---

2 BVP = *blok vybrosa pomekh* – lit. interference ejector

3 The fuselage numbers (f/n) appear only in Mikoyan documents and are not to be found anywhere on the aircraft and even in the factory's papers.

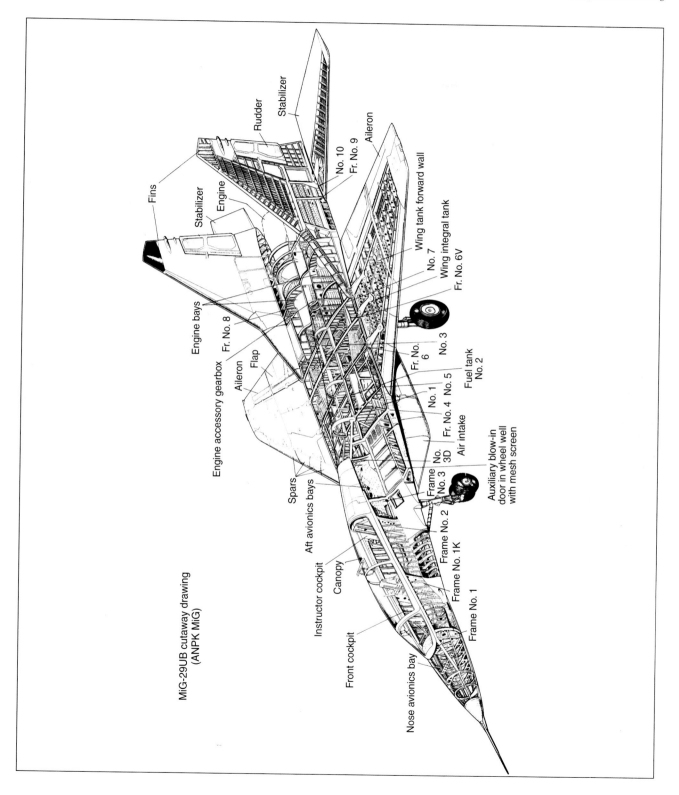

MiG-29UB cutaway drawing
(ANPK MiG)

Rudder

Stabilizer

No. 10

Fr. No. 9

Aileron

Wing tank forward wall

Wing integral tank

No. 7

Fr. No. 6V

Fr. No. 3

Fins

Stabilizer

Engine

No. 3

Fuel tank
No. 2

Engine bays

Fr. No. 8

Fr. No.
6

No. 5

Engine accessory gearbox

Aileron

Flap

No. 1

Fr. No. 4

Air intake

Auxiliary blow-in
door in wheel well
with mesh screen

Spars

Frame No.
3D

Aft avionics bays

Frame No. 3

Instructor cockpit

Canopy

Frame No. 2

Frame No. 1K

Front cockpit

Frame No. 1

Nose avionics bay

Instrument equipment

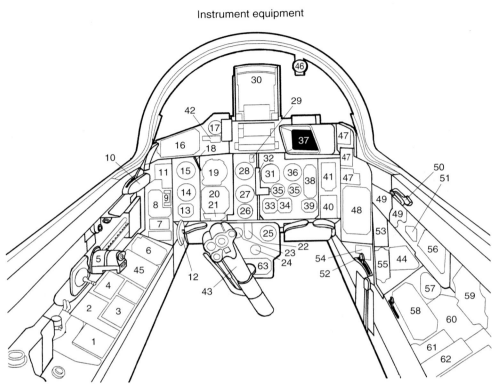

1. Oxygen control panel
2. Automatic flight control system control panel
3. Communication control panel
4. Flaps control panel
5. Throttle control lever
6. Aiming complex control panel
7. Automatic flight control system controller
8. Radar complex control panel
9. Landing gear control valve
10. Canopy manual operating handle
11. Landing-lamp control panel
12. Landing gear emergency extension handle
13. Pilot approach display
14. Altitude indicator
15. Speed indicator
16. Optical and electronic aiming and navigation complex control panel
17. Angle-of-attack and acceleration indicator
18. Emergency braking valve handle
19. Flight director indicator
20. Navigation instrument
21. Heading setting panel for attitude and heading reference system

22. Pitot static tube selector switch
23. Voltmeter
24. Cabin air temperature selector
25. Braking system pressure gauge
26. Clock
27. Machmeter
28. Vertical speed, turn-and-slip indicator
29. Nose wheel braking handle
30. Head-up display and its control panel
31. Radio altimeter altitude indicator
32. Jamming release system control panel
33. Pilot oxygen supply indicator
34. Hydraulic and pneumatic system pressure indicator
35. Gas temperature indicator
36. Tachometer indicator
37. Direct visibility indicator
38. Fuel quantity and flow meter system indicator
39. Ramp position indicator
40. Illumination warning station indicator
41. Display of system EKRAN
42. Jamming station control panel (MiG-29SE only)
43. Aircraft control stick

44. IFF system panel
45. Power plant emergency modes control board
46. Magnetic compass KI
47. Annunciators
48. Short-range navigation and landing system control panel
49. Cabin, glass, probe heating control panel
50. Canopy emergency jettison handle
51. Internal and external lighting panel
52. Ventilation selector switch CANOPY-PILOT
53. Radio equipment control panel
54. Illumination warning station control panel
55. Radio compass control panel
56. Intercabin lighting panel
57. IFF system panel
58. Guidance system control panel
59. Aircraft power generating system switching board
60. Engines starting control panel
61. Aircraft systems switching board
62. Aircraft systems control panel
63. Combined armament-control system control panel

Rostislav Belyakov (second from the right) discusses the MiG-29's trials programme with Air Force top brass at NII VVS in Akhtoobinsk. First from left is MiG-29 programme chief Anatoliy Belosvet who did a lot to help the aircraft enter service. Both men, along with other Mikoyan officers involved with the MiG-29, later received government awards for the fighter's development. (Mikhail Val'denberg archive)

located between the engine nacelles, so Mikoyan incorporated a unique feature: the tank had a straight-through vertical duct or pipe at the rear enabling the APU to exhaust right through it! Flying with the centreline drop tank had its limitations: the airbrake could not be used. It formed the aft extremity of the fuselage and consisted of upper and lower halves, with the brake parachute container in between. If the airbrake were deployed the lower half would strike the drop tank.

The SUV-29 (S-29) weapons control system of the initial production version (*izdeliye* 9.12) included the RPLK-29 radar targeting system (N-019 Rubin radar plus Ts100 digital processor) and the OEPrNK-29 targeting/navigation complex. The latter comprised the OEPS-29 optoelectronic targeting system (IRST/laser ranger plus Schchel'-3UM helmet-mounted sight), another Ts100 processor and the SN-29 navigation system. The 'Fulcrum's' standard weapons included two R-27R

medium-range IR-homing AAMs (*izdeliye* 470), two R-73 IR-homing dogfight AAMs (*izdeliye* 72) and the GSh-301 internal gun with 150 rounds.

Izdeliye 9.12 could attack ground targets in a dive (dropping bombs, firing unguided rockets, and strafing), during recovery from a dive (dropping bombs) and in level flight (dropping bombs and submunitions). Alternative ordnance loads in the strike/CAS rôle included four 500-kg (1,102-lb) FAB-500M54 or FAB-500M62 iron bombs, four 500-kg ZB-500 napalm bombs or six 250-kg (551-lb) FAB-250 bombs on BD3-UMK single bomb racks (i.e., one per pylon), up to sixteen 100-kg (220-lb) OFAB-100 or 120-kg (264-lb) OFAB-120 bombs totalling up to 2,000 kg (4,409 lb) on MBD2-67U multiple ejector racks (MERs), two to four 240-mm (9.44-in.) S-24 heavy unguided rockets, up to four UB-32A-73 rocket pods with a total of 128 S-5K/S-5M 57-mm (2.24-in) folding-fin aircraft rockets or B-8M1 pods with a total of 80 S-8 80-

mm (3.14-in.) FFARs. Of course, a mix of these weapons could be carried.[4]

The weapons control system switched to the appropriate channel automatically to suit the type of target the fighter was attacking. In strike mode the high-precision laser rangefinder continuously measured target range; if for some reason the laser ranger could not be used the WCS automatically computed target range, using altitude and attitude (pitch angle) as reference data. This was then used to calculate the weapon impact point and issue signals to the pilot to adjust course, commence and finish the attack. Adjustments for target speed and drift were made semi-automatically by memorizing the initial and terminal target sighting lines. A fixed grid in the HUD is used as a backup for 'manual' sighting.

Testing continued both at LII and NII VVS even after the fighter entered production (a test pilot's work is never done!). Not all flights ended well. One aircraft was lost at LII when a missile parted company with the aircraft, striking the stabilator and damaging it. The aircraft became uncontrollable and the pilot had to eject.

Like most Soviet fighters, early production MiG-29s had a dark green/dark earth camouflage scheme. At Le Bourget, however, General Designer Rostislav A. Belyakov noticed that USAF fighters displayed at the airshow sported a two-tone grey colour scheme (the so-called Egypt One camouflage). At his orders the OKB hastily developed a range of new camouflage patterns (including grey ones) and showed them to VVS officials. The Air Force requested that Mikoyan lend them two MiG-29s for grey camouflage evaluation purposes; the ninth prototype, 20 Blue (920), was the first of these. The results proved encouraging and the Soviet Air Force adopted the two-tone grey colour scheme as standard for the type; the early dark green/dark earth aircraft were soon repainted.

Hungarian, Polish and Yugoslav MiG-29s, along with a few others, wore the same grey camouflage. Some foreign operators of the 'Fulcrum', however, thought differently. East German and Czech aircraft had a dark green/dark earth colour scheme; Syrian and Iraqi MiG-29s sported a desert camouflage, while North Korean aircraft had green

upper surfaces and light blue undersurfaces. The two-tone grey camouflage was fairly effective, as witnessed by RAF Tornado F.2 pilots which escorted a pair of company-owned MiG-29 demonstrators on the way to the Farnborough International '88 airshow.

MiG-29UB conversion trainer (*izdeliye* 9.51 or *izdeliye* 30), 'Fulcrum-B'

To facilitate conversion training of Air Force pilots the Mikoyan OKB developed a combat-capable trainer version of the fighter designated MiG-29UB (*oochebno-boyevoy* [*samolyot*] – combat-capable trainer). The *sparka*,[5] as the aircraft was informally known, bore the manufacturer's designation *izdeliye* 9.51, eventually entering production under the same product code.

The trainee and instructor sat in tandem cockpits enclosed by a common aft-hinged canopy giving shorter ejection time in an emergency. To avoid a major redesign and ensure maximum commonality with the single-seater the fire control radar was deleted, leaving only the IRST and HMS; hence the R-27R medium-range AAM with semi-active radar homing was excluded from the MiG-29UB's weapons range. The OEPrNK-29UB optoelectronic targeting/nav system was modified to include a second set of indicators and controls. The R-73 and R-60 (R-60M) IR-homing AAMs, air-to-ground armament and internal gun were retained.

Despite the lack of radar, the MiG-29UB retained dogfighting and strike capability, as the IRST could engage targets at 25–30 km (13–16 nm) range. Special emulators were fitted to allow pilots to train in intercept techniques, using the radar, firing SARH missiles and dealing with systems failures. The aircraft featured flight and mission data recorders allowing sorties to be analysed quickly and possible pilot errors detected. It was designed to operate in visual and instrumental meteorological conditions, day and night, enabling transition to the single-seat MiG-29 within a very short time frame. The two cockpits featured identical controls and K-36DM ejection seats. To give the instructor better forward visibility the rear cockpit was equipped with a retractable periscope which was raised during landing and taxying. By eliminating the radar the engineers managed to avoid a reduction in internal fuel capacity as compared to the

---

[4] FAB = *foogahsnaya aviabomba* – high-explosive bomb; OFAB = *oskolochno-foogahsnaya aviabomba* – HE/fragmentation bomb. ZB = *zazhigahtel'nyy bahk* – lit. incendiary tank. MBD = *mnogozamkovyy bahlochnyy derzhahtel'* – multi-lock beam-type (weapons) rack (as distinct from cassette-type racks). B = *blok* – unit or module (used in many contexts – e.g., when speaking of avionics etc.), in this case, FFAR pod; UB = *oonifitseerovannyy blok* – standardised (FFAR) pod. S = *snaryad* – cannon shell *or* unguided missile (guided ones are designated R for *raketa*).

[5] This is a common Soviet (Russian) Air Force slang term for conversion trainer derivatives of fighters and translates loosely as Two-Sticks, being derived from *spahrennoye oopravleniye* – dual controls. (Double Trouble would be more fitting, perhaps?)

TOP: *The still unpainted first prototype MiG-29UB combat trainer in Mikoyan's experimental shop. (Yefim Gordon archive)*

ABOVE: *A production MiG-29UB. The* sparka *has a common aft-hinged canopy over the tandem cockpits. (Yefim Gordon archive)*

BELOW: *Blue 51, the first prototype MiG-29UB, during flight tests. (Yefim Gordon archive)*

single-seater (*izdeliye* 9.12) – 3,200 kg (7,054 lb) less reserves. At 17.42 m (57 ft 1.82 in.) the trainer was only 100 mm (3.93 in.) longer than the basic MiG-29.

Performance, too was almost identical: with a normal takeoff weight of 14,600 kg (32,187 lb) in clean condition (i.e., with no external stores) the MiG-29UB had a 1,400-km/h (777-kt) top speed at sea level and a rate of climb of 330 m/sec (1,082 ft/sec). Like the single-seater, the *sparka* was stressed for 9 Gs. Top speed at high altitude was slightly lower (2,230 km/h or 1,238 kts); so was the service ceiling (17,500 m/57,414 ft). Range also decreased slightly to 680 km (377 nm) at S/L and 1,410 km (783 nm) at high altitude.

Coded 51 Blue (951), the MiG-29UB prototype (referred to as aircraft 951 in OKB documents) took off for the first time on 29 April 1981 with Aviard G. Fastovets at the controls. By the end of the year the aircraft had made 53 flights. The second prototype (aircraft 952, coded 52 Blue) was usd in the State acceptance trials programme. The third prototype or preproduction aircraft (53 Blue) had a non-standard c/n, 4029692486;[6] this aircraft was retained by Mikoyan and much used for demonstration purposes. After successfully passing the manufacturer's flight tests and State acceptance trials the MiG-29UB entered production at the Gor'kiy aircraft factory No. 21 named after Sergo Ordzhonikidze.[7] 'Assembly' would be more accurate, since the main airframe components were manufactured in Moscow by MMZ No. 30 and shipped to Gor'kiy (now Nizhniy Novgorod) for final assembly and equipment installation. In VVS documents the MiG-29UB was referred to as *izdeliye* 30. The trainer's NATO code name was 'Fulcrum-B', the single-seater (*izdeliye* 9.12) becoming the 'Fulcrum-A'.

MiG-29, export version A (*izdeliye* 9.12A), 'Fulcrum-A'

Soon after the initial production version became operational with the VVS the factory at Moscow-Khodynka began manufacturing a slightly downgraded export version intended for the Soviet Union's Central European allies (the Warsaw Pact countries). Known as *izdeliye* 9.12A, the aircraft featured an RLPK-29E (*eksportnyy*) radar targeting system based on the N-019EA Rubin radar, a modified OEPrNK-29E (S-31E) optoelectronic targeting/nav system and different

identification friend-or-foe (IFF) transponders. Performance was identical to Soviet Air Force 'Fulcrums'. Export version A stayed in production from 1988 to 1991 and was supplied to Bulgaria, Czechoslovakia, East Germany, Poland and Romania.

MiG-29, export version B (*izdeliye* 9.12B), 'Fulcrum-A'

An even more downgraded export version designated *izdeliye* 9.12B was developed for 'friendly' states outside the Warsaw Pact. This aircraft featured the simplified N-019EB radar and OEPrNK-29E2 targeting/nav system. Version B entered production at MMZ No. 30 in 1986 and was supplied to Hungary, India, Iraq, Syria, Yugoslavia and some other states. (The practice of supplying downgraded equipment to foreign customers was probably a sort of insurance policy in case today's allies would turn into enemies tomorrow and use weapons purchased in the Soviet Union against it. In that case having slightly better weapons would give the Soviet Union an advantage.)

Initially the aircraft was armed with R-60 and R-27R missiles, later supplanted by R-27R1 and R-73 AAMs. In the strike rôle it could carry up to four FAB-250 or FAB-500 HE bombs, ZB-500 napalm bombs or KMGU submunitions pods,[8] four S-24 unguided rockets or four B-8M1 pods with 80 S-8 FFARs.

MiG-29 tactical fighter (*izdeliye* 9.13 or *izdeliye* 7), 'Fulcrum-C'

One of the biggest problems facing the designers of Soviet fourth-generation fighters was meeting the specified range requirements. When the T10-1 (first prototype of the first-generation Su-27, alias 'Flanker-A') and the first prototype MiG-29 (aircraft 901) entered flight test in 1977, both were found to have insufficient range. Sukhoi went the hard way, scrapping the original design altogether and coming up eventually with a new aircraft, the T10-S which entered production as the second-generation Su-27 or 'Flanker-B'.

Mikoyan did not have to resort to such drastic measures since the requirements for the light tactical fighter were less stringent. Still, the problem was there and had to be dealt with. The advanced development project specified a range of 800 km (444 nm) at S/L and 2,750 km (1,527 nm) at high altitude with one centreline drop tank; in

---

6 See note on c/ns in 'Fulcrum-C' section.

7 This long-standing Mikoyan partner is now called the Nizhniy Novgorod aircraft factory Sokol (Falcon)

8 KMGU = *konteyner dlya malogabaritnykh groozov ooniversahl'nyy* – 'all-purpose small items container'

The fat spine of the izdeliye *9.13 is well illustrated by this view from above. (Yefim Gordon archive)*

reality it was 700 km (388 nm) and 2,100 km (1,166 nm) respectively for the production MiG-29 (*izdeliye* 9.12). Increasing the internal fuel volume on the MiG-29 was something of a problem since the patented dorsal auxiliary air intakes ate up a lot of space in the LERXes which could otherwise be used for fuel. Only the No. 1 fuselage tank in the spine could be readily enlarged; its capacity was increased by 240 lit. (52.8 Imp. gal.), giving an internal fuel volume of 4,540 lit. (998.8 Imp. gal.). As the next-best solution the engineers introduced wet wing pylons permitting the carriage of two 1,150-lit. (253 Imp. gal.) drop tanks. Fitting three drop tanks increased the total fuel volume to 8,340 lit. (1,834.8 Imp. gal.) which gave a ferry range of 3,000 km (1,666 nm). With the drop tanks speed was limited to 850 km/h (472 kts or Mach 0.8).

Another requirement not met on the initial production model was the provision of a comprehensive electronic countermeasures (ECM) suite. This took longer to develop than anticipated, which is why the initial MiG-29 featured only an L006LM (Beryoza) radar homing and warning system (RHAWS) and BVP-30-26M chaff/flare dispensers. In contrast, Sukhoi engineers designing the Su-27 opted for podded ECM gear from the outset, which meant it could be fitted to all versions of the 'Flanker' without requiring modifications. Late MiG-29s were to feature an L-203B (Gardeniya-1FU) jammer in the avionics bay aft of the cockpit. This and the enlarged No. 1 fuel tank necessitated a change in the shape of the fuselage spine. The upper fuselage contour became convex instead of concave, giving the fighter a distinctive humpbacked appearance and earning it the nickname *gorbahtyy* – hunchback (though fatback would be more appropriate perhaps). The ECM aerials were located

A MiG-29 (izdeliye 9.13) on test at NII VVS, operating from Akhtoobinsk. (Yefim Gordon)

under four prominent dielectric panels at the wingtips to give 360° coverage.

In 1983 the Mikoyan OKB converted three standard Batch 4 aircraft – 04 Blue/404 White (c/n 2960525975, f/n 0404), 05 Blue/405 White (c/n 2960705533?, f/n 0405) and 06 Blue/406 White (f/n 0406) – into prototypes of the new version. The c/n of 05 Blue was possibly changed following conversion to 'Fulcrum-C' (*IF* it is correct, that is!), as it does not tie in with that of the preceding aircraft. Trials began in April 1984, the three prototypes making more than 400 flights between them. All three had the recontoured fuselage spine but the first two may have been used for aerodynamics research only; 06 Blue *did* have the enlarged No. 1 fuel tank and Gardeniya-1FU jammer.

The first prototype was retained by the State Flight Test Centre in Akhtoobinsk (GLITs)[9] after completing its State acceptance trials and used in various research programmes. E.g., the radar was tested for ECM

resistance on this aircraft. The aircraft entered production at MAPO (Moscow-Khodynka) in 1986 as *izdeliye* 9.13; the Air Force's code was *izdeliye* 7. Production ended in 1991 when the VVS completed its acquisition programme. Even so, 'Fulcrum-A' production continued in parallel on a small scale, mainly for export. The first production *izdeliye* 9.13 (26 Blue, c/n 2960705560, f/n 1616) was the standard-setter for the production 'Fulcrum-C', incorporating all the refinements made in the course of flight tests.[10] This aircraft made more than 500 test flights

---

[9] *Gosoodahrstvennyy lyotno-ispytahtel'nyy tsentr*, formerly NII VVS.

[10] On single-seaters the construction number usually contains ten digits, e.g., 2960507682. 29 is almost certainly the type; 60 could be a code denoting the factory while the fifth digit could denote the version (5 = *izdeliye* 5, *aka izdeliye* 9.12). The remaining five digits do not signify anything and are selected at random to confuse would-be spies; the first two and last three of these accrue independently. (It's much the same story with these last five digits on other Soviet types, civil as well as military.)

Only the 'famous last five' are usually quoted and are sometimes stencilled on the fins, chaff/flare dispenser fairings and inboard pylons. The number embossed on the nose gear is *NOT* the aircraft's c/n but the nose gear oleo's c/n.

The MiG-29UB has a separate c/n system – e.g., N50903016577. The first four digits appear to relate to the factory, 30 almost certainly means *izdeliye* 30 (MiG-29UB), plus the 'famous last five'.

A pair of fatback 'Fulcrums' taking off. (Yefim Gordon)

at GLITs; when the programme was completed in November 1988 it was donated to the Great Patriotic War Museum on Poklonnaya Gora in Moscow. (Curiously, the first 15 aircraft of Batch 16 were 'Fulcrum-As'; for some obscure reason the first 'Fulcrum-C' batch began with f/n 1616 instead of 1701, continuing to f/n 1630!)

The first production fatbacks were deployed in East Germany and operated by the 4th VA (*vozdooshnaya armiya* – air army, = air force). The new version promptly attracted the attention of Western military intelligence and received the reporting name 'Fulcrum-C'.

Apart from the fuel system and ECM suite, the MiG-29 (*izdeliye* 9.13) had an ordnance load increased to 3,200 kg (7,054 lb) and could carry a wider range of air-to-ground weapons. These included KMGU-2 submunitions containers with BKF cassettes containing anti-personnel and anti-tank bomblets and mines weighing 0.5–2.5 kg (1.1–5.5 lb). Six FAB-500M54 bombs could be carried instead of four by fitting MBD3-U2T-1 MERs to the inboard pylons, each with two bombs in tandem. A typical

load for a strike mission was four FAB-500s plus two R-73 or R-60M AAMs for self-defence. The 'Fulcrum-C's' maximum takeoff weight was 18,480 kg (40,740 lb).

More than 400 fatbacks were built in all. Of them 233 remained in Russia after the collapse of the Soviet Union; 155 were retained by the Ukraine, seven more by Moldavia and a handful by the Central Asian republics. 30 aircraft unclaimed by the VVS and not yet fitted with the Gardeniya jammer sat at the factory airfield in Lookhovitsy.

MiG-29 experimental fighter (*izdeliye* 9.14), 'Fulcrum-C'

In 1984 the Mikoyan OKB developed a version of the MiG-29 (*izdeliye* 9.13) with enhanced strike capability known in-house as *izdeliye* 9.14. The aircraft featured a new weapons control system including a Ryabina (Rowan, pronounced ryabina) low light level TV/laser designator pod. This had been developed for the upgraded MiG-27M 'Flogger-J' attack aircraft and projected light strike/counter-insurgency (COIN) versions of the MiG-101 twin-turboprop

Mikoyan CTP Roman Taskayev demonstrates the MiG-29UB's STOL capabilities. (Yefim Gordon)

utility aircraft (still a 'paper airplane' in 1997) and the Yak-58 five-seat piston-engined light aircraft.

The weapons range was expanded to include Zvezda[11] Kh-25M (AS-10 'Karen') and Spetstekhnika Kh-29 (AS-14 'Kedge') TV-guided or laser-guided air-to-ground missiles and KAB-500 smart bombs.[12] The maximum bomb load was 4,500 kg (9,920 lb) with eight bombs on MERs under the wings and one on the fuselage centreline.

The prototype *izdeliye* 9.14, 407 Blue (c/n 2960507682), was a converted 'Fulcrum-A' (the tactical code was derived from the aircraft's f/n, 0407). Defying superstition, it flew for the first time on 13 February 1985 with Toktar O. Aubakirov at the controls. The Ryabina LLLTV/laser designator system was still under development at the time, so the aircraft served to test the augmented bomb armament and examine the possibility of operations from dirt strips. It was also used for performance testing within the 'Fulcrum-C's State

acceptance trials. Later 407 Blue was used in the MiG-29S upgrade programme. In 1991-92 it participated in several international airshows. However, *izdeliye* 9.14 did not enter production because in the mid-80s the Mikoyan OKB began working on a major upgrade of the 'Fulcrum' – the MiG-29M which also had pinpoint strike capability. The prototype remained a one-off and is still operational at GLITs in Akhtoobinsk, with more than 800 flights to its credit.

Testbeds and research aircraft

a) Aircraft 970 and aircraft 971 weapons testbeds

Two production 'Fulcrum-A's known in-house as aircraft 970 and aircraft 971 had a modified WCS, serving as weapons with the Vympel weapons design bureau. They were used to test the R-27T/TE, R-27RE and K-77 (RVV-AE/AA-12 'Adder')[13] medium-range air-to-air missiles. The first aircraft took off in May 1985, followed by the second in January 1986.

---

11 Not to be confused with G. I. Severin's bureau responsible for the K-36DM ejection seat.

12 KAB = *korrekteerooyemaya aviabomba* – guided bomb.

13 Designated R-77 in production form.

The programme which was completed in August 1989 included missile separation safety trials in all flight modes, verification of changes to the N-019 radar introduced on the later N-019M Topaz and live firing trials against La-17M, M-21 and Tu-16M 'Badger' target drones. Both aircraft lacked tactical codes, sporting only the prototype code (970 and 971) in white on the dielectric fin caps.

b) MiG-29 stealth technology testbed

To investigate ways of reducing the aircraft's radar signature a standard production MiG-29 was coated experimentally with a radar-absorbent material (RAM). Similar experiments were conducted with the Su-25 'Frogfoot' attack aircraft. Trials showed that the RAM significantly reduced the fighter's RCS, thus reducing radar detection range, the accuracy of missiles' target lock-on and proximity fuse detonation.

c) Uprated RD-33 (izdeliye 21) engine testbed

After completing its State acceptance trials programme the tenth MiG-29 prototype, 21 Blue (921), was converted into a testbed for a version of the RD-33K engine (*izdeliye* 21) uprated to 8,800 kgp (19,400 lb st) in full afterburner; this had been developed for the upgraded MiG-29M (*izdeliye* 9.15). The prototype engine was installed in the fighter's port nacelle (the starboard engine remained standard). The air intakes were converted to MiG-29M standard with downward-hinging FOD protection grilles some way downstream instead of solid doors at the mouth and no auxiliary dorsal intakes.

d) MiG-29KVP

In 1982, when the N-019 radar had passed its trials, the eighth prototype (18 Blue/918) was converted under the MiG-29K programme. The objective was to test the type's compatibility with a conventional takeoff and landing

A pair of fatback MiG-29s from Kubinka performing aerobatics. The lead aircraft is piloted by Col. Aleksandr Gornov, one of the Display Centre's best pilots. (Yefim Gordon)

(CTOL) aircraft carrier and perfect carrier operations techniques. Unnecessary equipment was removed, resulting in a gross weight of only 12 metric tons (26448), and an arrester hook fitted under the aft fuselage which meant the airframe had to be reinforced. In this guise the aircraft was unofficially designated MiG-29KVP (*korotkiy vzlyot i posahdka* – STOL).

Carrier operations trials proceeded at the Novofyodorovka airbase near the city of Saki on the Crimea Peninsula, home to the AV-MF[14] Flight Test Centre. A special 'unsinkable carrier' had been built there, featuring a ski jump and an arrester wire system. On 21 August 1982 Aviard G. Fastovets made the first takeoff from the provisional T-1 ski jump (T = *tramplin*). The aircraft became airborne at 240 km/h (133 kts) after a 250-m (820-ft) takeoff run. Between 1 October and 25 October 1984 the MiG-29KVP made a number of takeoffs from the restyled T-2 ski jump. Two other Mikoyan test

pilots, Toktar O. Aubakirov and A. Krootov, also participated in the ski-jump takeoff and automatic carrier approach trials. Air Force pilots had to wait their turn, using breaks in the OKB's flight test programme while the results were analysed. E.g., NII VVS test pilot V. M. Kandaoorov made 200 flights at Novofyodorovka, including 65 wire engagements; part of these were on the MiG-29KVP.

Initially the aircraft was repainted in a greenish-blue naval colour scheme. However, this was a bad idea, as the naval camouflage turned out to be an anti-camouflage; as Toktar Aubakirov put it, the aircraft was 'eye-catching as a butterfly'. Therefore, the MiG-29KVP soon reverted to its original grey colour scheme.

18 Blue was in the static park at MosAeroShow-92 in Zhukovskiy (11-16 August 1992), Russia's first major airshow. Later the aircraft was briefly used as an instructional airframe by the Moscow Energy Institute before being donated to the VVS Museum in Monino. For some obscure reason the MiG-29KVP had Mikron written

---

14 *Aviatsiya voyenno-morskovo flota* – Naval Aviation.

The appearance of a single-seat MiG-29 and a two-seat MiG-29UB at the 1988 Farnborough International airshow really made the headlines. (Yefim Gordon archive)

10 Blue about to start on another demo flight at FI'88 with Anatoliy Kvochur in the driver's seat. (Yefim Gordon archive)

All aviation magazines published detail photos of the MiG-29 after its Farnborough appearance. This particular photo comes from the cover of the Czech mag Létectvi a Kosmonautika (Flying and Spaceflight).

on both stabilators after being transferred to the museum.

e) Aircraft 211 (izdeliye 9.21)

In the late '70s and early '80s GosNIIAS began examining the possibilities of integrating digital avionics into the MiG-29. The BTsK-29 digital avionics suite enabled multiplex data exchange between the aircraft's systems, significantly enhancing combat potential. To this end an early production MiG-29, 11 Blue (211 White, f/n 1601), was converted into an avionics testbed in late 1987. Since the aircraft was known in-house as *izdeliye* 9.21, the code 211 was applied to the dielectric

fin caps in small white digits. Outwardly the aircraft could be identified by numerous additional pitots on the standard nose pitot boom and immediately aft of the radome. Flight tests began in April 1988 but were suspended shortly afterwards.

f) Equipment reliability research aircraft

After completing an equipment reliability test programme on aircraft 919, LII began further research in order to deal with the MiG-29's teething troubles. The research aircraft this time was a standard production 'Fulcrum-A' (10 Blue, c/n 2960516767) borrowed from the Air Force'combat training centre in Lipetsk. This aircraft later became Mikoyan's demonstrator workhorse (apparently because the OKB had no aircraft of its own free for this purpose), eventually crashing spectacularly at the 1989 Paris airshow (see Chapter 6).

g) N-010 radar testbed (izdeliye 9.16)

A production fatback MiG-29 (16 Blue) was converted into an avionics testbed for the Phazotron N-010 Zhuk radar developed for the MiG-29M (see next chapter). Quite simply, the nose was severed and replaced by a new one incorporating the experimental radar. 16 Blue made the first post-conversion flight on 12 January 1987 but the trials had to be suspended for an extended period because the radar failed and finding out and eliminating the cause took a lot of time. When the radar was repaired the aircraft went to Akhtoobinsk where it remained operational until 1990. However, the MiG-29M had

entered flight tests by then and further trials of the new radar proceeded on the the the real thing.

MiG-29S tactical fighter (izdeliye 9.13S), 'Fulcrum-C'

In the late '80s Mikoyan conducted additional research in order to adapt the new R-77 (RVV-AE) active radar homing missile to the 'Fulcrum'. The result was an upgraded version of the 'Fulcrum-C' designated MiG-29S or *izdeliye 9.13S*. Unlike *izdeliye 9.14*, this upgrade centred on enhancing the aircraft's counter-air capability. The main new feature of the MiG-29S was the improved RLPK-29M targeting system; this was based on the N-019M Topaz fire control radar having better ECM resistance.[15] It could guide missiles to two targets at a time

---

[15]This was probably tested on a Tupolev Tu-134UBL 'Crusty' bomber crew trainer (uncoded, ex 21 Red, c/n 64740) converted by NPO Phazotron into an avionics testbed

Anatoliy Kvochur, one of the world's best test pilots, is about to show the spectators what the 'Fulcrum' can do, after a remarkably short takeoff. (Yefim Gordon archive)

and operated in concert with R-27RE and R-77 AAMs.

Modifications to the control system increased the fighter's maximum AOA to 28°. The airframe was reinforced, permitting an increase in MTOW to 20,000 kg (44,091 lb). The ordnance load in the strike rôle was increased to 4,000 kg (8,818 lb) of bombs on four MERs under the wings (two 500-kg/1,102-lb bombs per station). Like the standard 'Fulcrum-C', the MiG-29S had provisions for three drop tanks. By Mikoyan estimates, the new missiles, especially the R-77 which was more capable than the AIM-120 AMRAAM, increased the fighter's combat efficiency 2.5 to 3 times. The R-77 featured a unique combined guidance system with inertial guidance initially and active radar homing at the terminal guidance phase. In a long-range missile duel the MiG-29S had a 10% better chance than the Lockheed Martin F-16C and Dassault Rafale and a 25% better chance than the SAAB JAS39 Gripen and Dassault Mirage 2000-5.

Two 'Fulcrum-C' prototypes, 05 Blue (f/n 0405) and 04 Blue (f/n 0404), were modified in 1988 and 1989 respectively to integrate the R-77 AAM with the new radar. 05 Blue entered flight test in January 1989, with 04 Blue following in June the same year. Another development aircraft, the sole *izdeliye* 9.14 (407 Blue), also participated in the MiG-29S programme. The first 'real' prototype entered flight test on 23 December 1990. When the trials programme was completed, VVS aircraft overhaul plant No. 121 at Kubinka AB began upgrading early-production 'Fulcrum-A/Cs' to MiG-29S standard. The new version attained IOC with the fighter regiment at Shaykovka AB. When testing of the R-77 missile was completed aircraft No. 0405 continued as a testbed for new high-accuracy air-to-ground weapons intended to further boost the capabilities of the MiG-29S.

MiG-29S tactical fighter (*izdeliye* 9.12S), 'Fulcrum-A'

A similar upgrade of the original production version, 'Fulcrum-A', bore the same service designation, MiG-29S; quite logically, however, the manufacturer's designation was different – *izdeliye* 9.12S. Outwardly the aircraft differed from the version described above in having the original concave fuselage spine; thus, it had less internal fuel and lacked the L203B (Gardeniya-1FU) jammer. Four MiG-29S (*izdeliye* 9.12S) fighters were retained by MAPO-MiG for demonstration purposes and painted in a rather bizarre metallic green/blue/silver camouflage. The aircraft were coded 333 White (c/n 2960536093), 555 White (c/n 2960540157), 777 White and 999 White (c/n

2960536591) and participated in international airshows on a regular basis.

MiG-29SD export version (*izdeliye* 9.12SD), 'Fulcrum-A'

Predictably, an export version of the 'skinny' MiG-29S (*izdeliye* 9.12S) appeared before long under the designation MiG-29SD or *izdeliye* 9.12SD; the D means *dozaprahvka* – refuelling. It featured an RLPK-29ME (export) radar targeting system (N-019ME radar) and an OEPrNK-29-1E optoelectronic targeting/nav system offering a major improvement in combat capabilities over the standard export 'Fulcrum'. The aircraft had provision for three drop tanks increasing total fuel volume to 8,100 lit. (1,782 Imp. gal.). Western avionics could be integrated as an option.

Malaysia was the launch customer and the aircraft entered production in 1995. Aircraft delivered to the Malaysian Air Force (TUDM), and sometimes identified as MiG-29N, though this designation is nowhere to be found in Mikoyan documents, have Western tactical

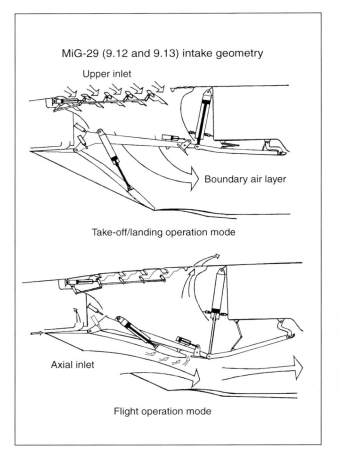

MiG-29 (9.12 and 9.13) intake geometry

Upper inlet

Boundary air layer

Take-off/landing operation mode

Axial inlet

Flight operation mode

navigation equipment (TACAN), VOR/ILS, IFF and ATC transponders, additional HF and UHF radios and other avionics. The flight instruments are marked in feet and knots according to Western standards.

The upgraded weapons control system enabled the MiG-29SD to engage two aerial targets at a time, firing two missiles consecutively or simultaneously. This was possible if target azimuths differed by more than 8° or if the targets were on a common azimuth but more than 10 km (5.5 nm) apart. The radar consecutively engaged the two targets as they approached the authorised launch zone (i.e., when target range was adequate); target lock-on occurred manually or automatically. As both targets entered the authorised launch zone, the common indication display showed 'fire when ready' symbols. The portside missile was then fired at the left-hand target and the starboard-side missile at the right-hand target. If only one target entered the authorised launch zone, the system fired on it first and waited for the other target to come within range.

A hose-and-drogue aerial refuelling system with a strap-on refuelling probe was developed for the MiG-29SD to be fitted at customer request; this was tested on 'Fulcrum-A' 357 Blue (see below).

MiG-29SE export version *(izdeliye 9.13SE)*, 'Fulcrum-C'

A similar export version of the 'fatback' MiG-29S *(izdeliye 9.13S)* was designated MiG-29SE or *izdeliye 9.13SE* (E for export). It differed from the MiG-29SD only in having a bigger internal fuel capacity; the WCS and the bomb load were identical.

MiG-29SM multi-rôle fighter

To enhance the 'Fulcrum's' strike capability the MiG-29S was developed into the MiG-29SM (*modernizeer ovannyy* – upgraded). It could carry Kh-29T TV-guided AGMs and KAB-500KR TV-guided bombs. The weapon projected a bomb's eye view to a display in the cockpit, enabling the pilot to hit targets with pinpoint accuracy. The ordnance load was 4,000 kg (8,818 lb). In production form the MiG-29SM was to have flight refuelling capability with a fully-retractable L-shaped probe. Mikoyan estimated the modification to have tripled the aircraft's combat potential as compared to *izdeliye 9.12*. The MiG-29SM was presented at Le Bourget in 1995. In reality, however, the aircraft in the static park was a perfectly standard 'Fulcrum-A' with an impressive array of weapons in front of it – which it could not carry.

MiG-29 refuelling system testbed

The Malaysian contract signed on 7 June 1994 stated that 14 out of 16 'Fulcrums' ordered by TUDM (i.e., all of the single-seat MiG-29SDs) were to be retrofitted with refuelling probes upon completion of deliveries. To this end a standard production MiG-29 (*izdeliye 9.12*) was converted into a testbed for the optional flight refuelling probe developed for the MiG-29SD/SE/SM.

Unlike the MiG-29K and MiG-29M which had a completely retractable L-shaped probe offset to port ahead of the windscreen, this probe was semi-retractable and removable. The largish elongated fairing, rather like that of the Tornado GR.1, was located on the port side of the forward fuselage (starboard-side installation was impossible because the No. 2 pitot was located there). The probe itself weighed 65 kg (143 lb); the additional fuel lines, valves and other fuel system components increased the aircraft's weight by another 30 kg (66 lb). The system made it possible to fill both internal tanks and drop tanks.

In developing the system Mikoyan built on experience with the probe tested on the MiG-25PDZ 'Foxbat-E', MiG-25RBVDZ and MiG-25RBShDZ 'Foxbat-B' refuelling system testbeds and later fitted to production MiG-31B 'Foxhound' interceptors. The MiG-29's probe was adapted for working both with the Russian Ilyushin Il-78 (Il-78M) 'Midas' three-point tanker and with Western hose-and-drogue tankers such as the Lockheed C-130K Hercules and McDonnell Douglas KC-10A Extender (the latter with an adapter on the flying boom). The only problem was how to squeeze the new components into the very limited space available. Originally the engineers wanted to place the probe immediately below the cockpit canopy but later moved it downward a little. The fuel line could not be stowed completely in the fuselage and part of it adjacent to the probe had to be covered by a fairing. The probe, complete with attachment frame and the protruding part of the fuel line could be removed or reinstalled within an hour if need arose. The system could be retrofitted to any version of the 'Fulcrum' with minimum modifications and at minimum cost. Aerial refuelling is a complex procedure demanding great concentration and skill, so changes were made to the semi-automatic control system to facilitate approach to and contact with the tanker. A short-range radio navigation (SHORAN) system ensured rendezvous with the tanker. After extending the refuelling probe the pilot switched the control system to the refuelling stabilization mode.

MiG-29 Type 9.12 (Blue 10)

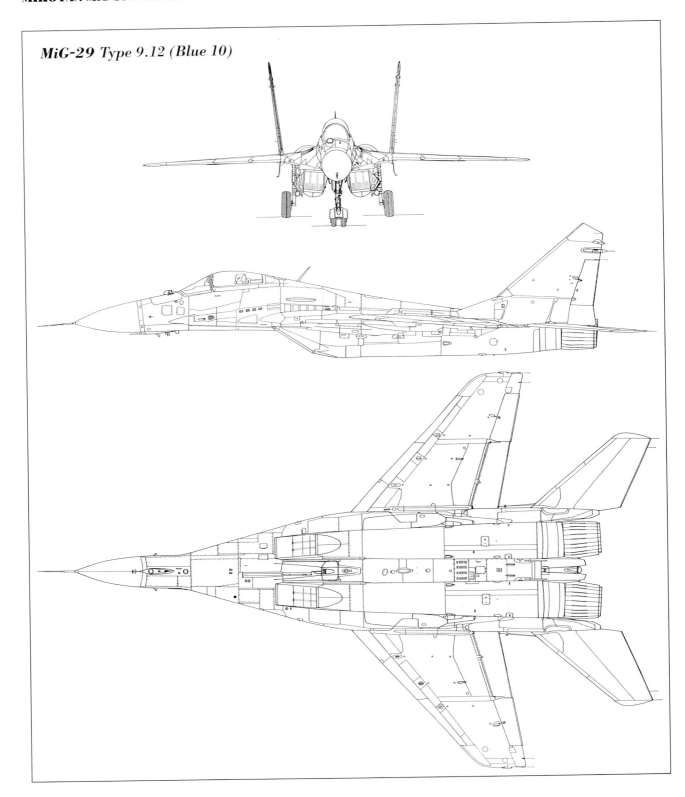

MiG-29SMT 'Increasing fuel capacity' early project

MiG-29SMT 'Increasing fuel capacity' latest project

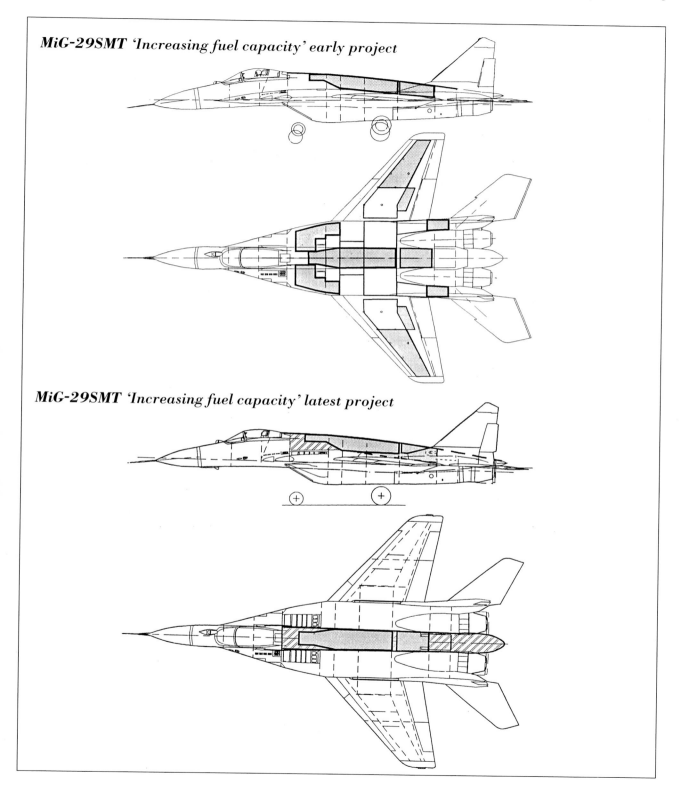

The experimental aircraft (c/n 2960536034, f/n 4808) originally flew in primer and *sans* tactical code; in this guise it was used for refuelling trials. On 16 November 1995 MAPO-MiG CTP Roman P. Taskayev made the first successful refuelling from an Il-78 registered SSSR-78782 (c/n 0083489673, f/n 6709).[16] Mikoyan test pilot Marat A. Alykov and Air Force test pilots V. D. Shooshoonov and A. A. Goncharov also flew the aircraft. Mikoyan engineers and test pilots claimed that the improved flight control and stabilization system was better than all others used by Russian combat aircraft with flight refuelling capability. Refilling one fuselage tank and three drop tanks extended the MiG-29's ferry range to 6,000 km (3,333 nm). The refuelling probe fairing had no adverse effect on the fighter's performance and handling. Contact with the Il-78 was made at altitudes up to 8,000 m (26,246 ft) and speeds between 400 and 600 km/h

16 Many Soviet Air Force transport aircraft ostensibly wore civil registrations and the colours of the national airline, Aeroflot, and a few retained the old SSSR-prefix (i.e., CCCP- in Cyrillic characters) and the Soviet flag even in 1997.

(222–333 kts). Refuelling was also performed at 350–500 km/h (194–277 kts) to simulate working with the slower KC-130 turboprop tanker. This was because the Malaysian Air Force had six C-130 transports which could be readily converted into tankers.

The trials programme was completed in January 1996. The fighter was then painted in the standard two-tone grey camouflage and coded 357 Blue. It was displayed the same year at two major airshows – ILA'96 at Berlin-Schönefeld and Farnborough International '96. In June 1997 the aircraft participated in the Le Bourget airshow under the exhibit code 353, appearing later in the static park at the MAKS-97 airshow in Zhukovskiy (19-24 August).

From ILA'96 onwards 357 Blue was called MiG-29SM by aviation specialists (though the data plate at MAKS-97 read MiG-29SD!) but both designations are hardly applicable to this particular aircraft since it was merely a refuelling systems testbed. Curiously, a stencil on the nose immediately aft of the radome read N-019EM – which was probably a 'misprint' as the radar was designated

When the MAPO industrial association was formed, company demonstrators were adorned with the MAPO logo on the nose. (MAPO)

MAPO demonstrator 'Fulcrum-A' 777 White with a full ordnance load. (MAPO)

N-019ME. Indeed, there is no positive confirmation that 357 Blue is really equipped with this radar!

MiG-29SMT multi-rôle fighter (*izdeliye* 9.17)

Operational experience with the MiG-29 proved that it was indeed a high-performance combat aircraft with better manoeuvrability, speed, rate of climb and service ceiling than the best Western fighters in its class – the F-16, F/A-18 and Mirage 2000. Range, on the other hand, was inadequate. Besides, the 'Fulcrum's' armament developed in the early '80s no longer met the more stringent modern requirements in full. Given Russia's economic situation of the early '90s, the VVS could not afford to buy new hardware in the near future; a mid-life update (MLU) for existing aircraft was the only alternative. This led MAPO-MiG to begin a radical upgrade of the production fighter in 1997.

Designated *izdeliye* 9.17, the new version was based on the 'fatback' MiG-29S (*izdeliye* 9.13S). It incorporated some features of the MiG-29M (*izdeliye* 9.15) and some projects that never materialised or were still in the making. In its original form the air intakes were borrowed straight from the MiG-29M, with FOD protection grilles replacing the earlier solid doors; the upper auxiliary intakes were thus deleted, making room for 930 lit. (204.6 Imp. gal.) of extra fuel in the LERXes. The forward fuselage was identical to the MiG-29M's, featuring a raised cockpit and options for a refuelling probe. The spine was even fatter than on the 'Fulcrum-C', increasing avionics bay volume by 500 lit. (110 Imp. gal.). It incorporated two strap-on fuel tanks totalling 1,650 lit. (363 Imp. gal.), a MiG-29M-style dorsal airbrake (the ventral airbrake was retained, albeit in modified form) and a MiG-29M-style boat-tail fairing between the engine nozzles. The wings were modified to incorporate four hardpoints each instead of three and hold 390 lit. (85.8 Imp. gal.) of extra fuel. The fighter had increased-area stabilators with dogtooth and broader-chord fin root sections, again borrowed straight from the MiG-29M.

The main gear units were beefed up. Fuselage integral tank No. 3 was also reinforced and enlarged by 200 lit. (44 Imp. gal.); additionally, the aircraft could carry enlarged 1,800-lit. (396 Imp. gal.) drop tanks under the wings and had provisions for a fully-retractable MiG-29K-style refuelling probe. As originally designed the aircraft had an increase in internal fuel capacity of 3,170 lit. (697.4 Imp. gal.) or 2,490 kg (5,489 lb).

The multi-function N-019MP 'Topaz' radar could engage both aerial and ground targets (the P stands for *poverkhnost*'). The latter was possible thanks to a synthetic aperture radar (SAR) mode allowing ground mapping with a 15-m (49-ft) resolution. Mikoyan opted for upgrading the radar, as this was cheaper than fitting a new radar. The N-019MP is a centimetre-waveband radar which is unaffected by fog, rain or snow, giving the aircraft true all-weather capability. By comparison, millimetre-waveband radars do not work well in these conditions because the waves are absorbed and dissipated by rain etc.

In ground mapping mode the radar enabled the aircraft to be used as a reconnaissance platform, scanning an area of land measuring 15×15 km (9.3×9.3 mi.), 24×24 km (14.9×14.9 mi.), 50×50 km (31×31 mi.) or 77×77 km (47.8×47.8 mi.) depending on resolution. Radar imagery could be transmitted to GCI centres in real time via satellite, A-50 'Mainstay' AWACS aircraft or directly by data link.

Speaking of reconnaissance, the weapons control system incorporated a 'two-stage' function. While the radar could detect such objects as bridges, vehicles etc., a more detailed view was often necessary for tactical reconnaissance. In that case a marker on the radar screen would be placed over an area of particular interest as commanded by ground control (or by the pilot, using a small joystick). The tracker heads of optically-guided weapons which have a higher resolution than the radar are then aimed at the target and a 'bomb's eye view' is transmitted. Depending on the situation, the pilot or ground controller can identify a high-priority target and take it out immediately with a high-precision weapon.

The weapons range included R-27R and R-27R1 SARH medium-range AAMs, R-27T and R-27T1 IR-homing medium-range AAMs, R-27ER and R-27ET extended-range missiles, R-77 (RVV-AE) active radar-homing medium-range AAMs, R-73E IR-homing short-range AAMs, Zvezda Kh-31A (AS-17 'Krypton') anti-shipping missiles, Kh-31P anti-radiation missiles, Kh-29T (Kh-29TE) TV-guided AGMs and KAB-500KR TV-guided 'smart bombs'. Gun pods with movable guns were also planned.

The air-to-surface weapons could be aimed and fired automatically at known targets, using target data supplied

ABOVE and OPPOSITE ABOVE: *Close-ups of the MiG-29SM's refuelling probe. The probe is to be retrofitted to Malaysian Air Force (TUDM) 'Fulcrums' (unofficially called MiG-29N). (Yefim Gordon)*

BELOW: *The experimental probe-equipped MiG-29 during trials with an Il-78 'Midas' tanker (SSSR-78782). (MAPO – Artur Sarkisyan)*

The long since retired Aircraft 925 converted to a mockup of the MiG-29SMT as originally projected, seen here at LII in December 1997. (Yefim Gordon)

to GCI centres by reconnaissance aircraft and then uploaded to the fighter by data link. This feature increased combat efficiency and survivability in low-level strike. Typically in low cloudbase conditions aircraft equipped with millimetre-waveband radars have to fly a low-level high-speed attack profile to use the radar and TV/laser-guided weapons. This leaves the pilot very little time for taking aim and complicates weapon targeting. Reducing speed inevitably increases the danger of being shot down; also, many aircraft are unstable in fully-loaded condition at low speed, as proved by Chechen war experience. The new WCS allowed this situation to be avoided.

An advanced control system utilising the HOTAS (hands on throttle and stick) concept was incorporated, allowing the pilot to select and fire weapons without letting go of the throttles and stick. The cockpit featured an electronic flight instrumentation system (EFIS) with four rectangular displays: two 130×180 mm (5.1×8.1 in.) colour liquid crystal displays (LCDs) on the instrument panel and two 75×75 mm (2.95×2.95 in.) monochrome LCDs on the side consoles. These had better backlight compensation than cathode-ray tubes. For safety's sake backup electromechanical instruments were retained in the centre of the panel. The avionics and weapons used a

MIL-STD-1553B digital databus, enabling Western avionics and weapons to be integrated at customer request. Finally, a combined FBW/mechanical control system similar to that of the MiG-29M was incorporated.

Izdeliye 9.17 received the official designation MiG-29SMT, the T denoting *toplivo* (fuel) and referring to the increased fuel load. The designation is clearly patterned on the MiG-21SMT 'Fishbed-K', another 'fatback fighter'. In the original project normal takeoff weight (by manufacturer's estimates) was 16,000 kg (35,273 lb) and MTOW in overload condition 21,000 kg (46,296 lb). Range was increased to 3,500 km (1,944 nm) on internal fuel only or 6,700 km (3,722 nm) with a single refill if a refuelling probe was fitted. Thrust-to-weight ratio was 1.04 on takeoff and 1.5 in combat mode. Like other 'Fulcrums', the MiG-29SMT was stressed for 9 Gs.

However, in late 1997 the engineers changed the project considerably – not least because MAPO objected to such drastic structural changes. The main problem was that the complicated redesign of the air intakes was not worth the effort, giving only a slight increase in fuel capacity. Therefore, Mikoyan engineers retained the anti-FOD doors and dorsal auxiliary intakes of the 'Fulcrum-A/B/C', adding only strap-on fuselage tanks to increase range. The wings and tail unit were likewise left

TOP: *The first prototype MiG-29SMT, 405 Blue (ex-331 Blue), at its rollout in Zhukovskiy on 22 April 1998. This view illustrates clearly the extraordinarily bulged spine of the new version. (Yefim Gordon)*

ABOVE: *MiG-29SMT 917 Blue with its impressive array of external stores. (Yefim Gordon)*

unchanged. Thus, the enhanced combat potential was due solely to improved avionics and weapons; Mikoyan decided the aerodynamic potential of the MiG-29's airframe had been used to the full.

The technical outlook of the MiG-29/*izdeliye* 9.17 (a document of that name was authorised by chief project engineer Valeriy V. Novikov on 2 December 1997) stated that current internal fuel capacity was only increased by 1,880 lit. (413.6 Imp. gal.) or 1,475 kg (3,251 lb). The forward strap-on tank holding 1,400 lit. (308 Imp. gal.) or 1,100 kg (2,425 lb) of fuel would be located between frames No. 3-B and 7 and shaped in such a way so as not to obstruct existing access hatches. The aft strap-on tank holding 480 lit. (105.6 Imp. gal.) or 375 kg (826 lb) of fuel would be located between frames No. 7 and 8. The two tanks would be removable to facilitate access to control system components and other equipment during maintenance.

These would give the MiG-29SMT a 2,100-km (1,166-nm) range on internal fuel with a normal weapons load, which is equal to the 'Fulcrum-A's' range with centreline drop tank. This increased to 2,700 km (1,500 nm) with one drop tank and 3,300 km (1,833 nm) with three drop tanks. If a refuelling probe was fitted, range became effectively unlimited. Changes would be made to the fuel delivery, drainage, neutral gas pressurisation, single-point refuelling and fuel metering subsystems, and a fuel jettison subsystem would be introduced. A MiG-29M-style dorsal airbrake would be fitted after all and the ventral airbrake would be modified. The aircraft would feature twin brake parachutes and KT-209 mainwheels borrowed from the MiG-29M.

Izdeliye 9.17 would retain the basic 'Fulcrum-C's' six underwing hardpoints and standard underwing drop tanks. The weapons range would include two R-27R1/RE1 medium-range AAMs, two R-27T1/TE1 medium-range AAMs, up to six R-77 medium-range AAMs or R-73E short-range AAMs, two Kh-29T/TD AGMs, two Kh-31A anti-shipping missiles or Kh-31P anti-radiation missiles, up to four KAB-500KR or KAB-500-OD guided bombs (the latter is a fuel/air bomb), B-8M1 rocket pods with S-8 FFARs and S-24 heavy unguided rockets. The maximum ordnance load in current project form is 4,000 kg (8,818 lb). The design is not finalised yet and a lot depends on customer demands. Mikoyan believes the upgraded MiG-29SMT will be able to take on such advanced fighters as the Dassault Rafale, Eurofighter EF2000 and McDD F/A-18E Super Hornet which are scheduled to enter service in the beginning of the 21st century.

Production aircraft would probably be powered by upgraded RD-33 engines with a service life of 2,000 hrs. Such a figure had been unheard-of for Russian fighter engines until now. This upgrade placed the RD-33 among the world's best fighter engines, vastly improving its export potential; low engine life had been the chief source of criticism levelled at this engine by Western specialists.

A mockup of the EFIS-equipped MiG-29 cockpit was displayed at Le Bourget in June 1997. The complete aircraft was unveiled at the MAKS-97 airshow on 19 August creating a minor sensation in itself. However, this was in reality a mockup of the original project configuration hastily converted from the long-since retired last pre-production *izdeliye* 9.12, as evidenced by the tactical code '25 Blue' and original narrow-chord rudders. Surprisingly, the aircraft sported the construction number 25975 – probably applied as an afterthought, obviously bogus and intended to pass it off as a new-build aircraft, since this c/n belongs to the first prototype 'Fulcrum-C' (04 Blue)!!!

The mockup was demonstrated to the Russian President Boris N. Yeltsin who visited the airshow on opening day amid stepped-up security measures (which, incidentally, created a traffic jam beyond description and general confusion). Yeltsin climbed into the cockpit, inspecting it thoroughly, and, after listening to the explanations and arguments of Mikoyan representatives, agreed that the MLU idea was a good one.

In the autumn of 1997 one of the 'Fulcrum-Cs' previously operated by GLITs in Akhtoobinsk as a weapons testbed (c/n 2960705533, f/n 0405 – i.e., the original second prototype 'Fulcrum-C') was modified by Mikoyan for trials under the MiG-29SMT programme. The conversion concerned only the cockpit which was equipped with an EFIS to MiG-29SMT standard to improve flight and target data presentation.

Coded 331 Blue (ex 05 Blue) and sporting ten red star 'kill markings' on the port side of the nose to mark successful missile launches, the aircraft was to make its first post-conversion flight at LII on 27 November. However, the flight actually took place two days later because of poor weather. The IA PVO C-in-C, the Deputy Minister of Defence and numerous TV and aviation journalists were there to witness the 8-minute first flight performed by test pilot (1st class) Marat Alykov, one of the company's youngest test pilots.

On 22 April 1998 the MiG-29SMT was unveiled to aviation dignitaries and the aviation press at Mikoyan's flight test facility in Zhukovskiy – *again*. This time,

A view of the wind tunnel model showing the nose gear unit relocated aft. (Yefim Gordon archive)

The instrument panel of a standard MiG-29. (Yefim Gordon)

The left control console of a standard MiG-29. (Yefim Gordon)

The right control console of a standard MiG-29. (Yefim Gordon)

This view of the mockup clearly shows the twin orifices for the double-barrelled gun originally intended for the MiG-29. (Mikoyan OKB archive)

TOP & ABOVE: *The first prototype. (Yefim Gordon)*

'Aircraft 917', the 17th flight test aircraft, seen here after modification with extended-chord rudders to improve the MiG-29's directional control, these were a late addition during flight tests. (Mikoyan OKB archive)

Pre-production MiG-29 during tests. (Mikoyan OKB archive)

Old and new 'Fulcrums'. . . .and they're both dead. The original wooden mockup of the MiG-29 is seen here sitting in the open at Mikoyan's flight test facility next to the MiG-29M static test airframe. Zhukovskiy, April 1998. (Yefim Gordon)

The first prototype MiG-29UB (Aircraft 951) retired at Mikoyan's flight test facility in Zhukovskiy. As this photo shows, the 'Fulcrum-B' had increased-chord rudders from the start. (Yefim Gordon)

This 'Fulcrum-A' (01 White) was flown by the CO of the 120th IAP based at Domna AB. Note how the tactical code is repeated on the inner faces of the fins. (Aleksandr Vasil'yev)

75 White, a sharkmouthed MiG-29UB operated by the 120th IAP at Domna AB. (Aleksandr Vasil'yev)

As 'Fulcrum-C' 407 Blue prepares to get away on a post-repair checkout flight, MiG-29UB 304 Blue waits, ready to fly as chase plane. Mikoyan flight test facility, Zhukovskiy, April 1998. (Yefim Gordon)

04 Blue (c/n 2960525975), the first prototype 'fatback' converted from a 'Fulcrum-A'. (Yefim Gordon)

The 'Fulcrum' was a tough competitor both for the GD F-16 and the Dassault Mirage 2000 on the world weapons market. Even though the avionics were considered rather primitive, the MiG-29 did exceptionally well in mock combat with Western fighters, both in Western and Eastern Europe. (MAPO)

As on the Su-27, a typical ordnance load comprises two medium-range R-27 AAMs and four R-73 'dogfight missiles'. (MAPO)

Even with a full weapons load the MiG-29 has an excellent rate of climb. (MAPO/Artur Sarkisyan)

A MiG-29 (izdeliye 9.13) on test at NII VVS, operating from Akhtoobinsk. (Yefim Gordon)

One of the best factory test pilots at the Lookhovitsy plant was killed in an accident while practising for the MAKS-95 airshow. This picture was taken a month before his death. (Yefim Gordon)

The unit at Kubinka AB was one of the first to convert to the izdeliye 9.13. (Yefim Gordon)

One of the trainers resident at Kubinka. (Yefim Gordon)

ABOVE: *A trio of 'fatback' MiG-29s takes off on an aerobatics training sortie. (Yefim Gordon)*
OPPOSITE: *The instructor's instrument panel in a MiG-29UB. (Yefim Gordon)*

A MiG-29UB belonging to the Strizhi (Swifts) display team. (Yefim Gordon)

The experimental probe-equipped MiG-29 during trials with an Il-78 'Midas' tanker (SSSR-78782). (MAPO/Artur Sarkisyan)

TOP & ABOVE: *The cockpit of the so-called MiG-29N differs slightly from that of the standard fighter. (Yefim Gordon)*

'. . . into position and hold'. Toktar Aubakirov aligns 311 Blue for takeoff. (Yefim Gordon archive)

ABOVE: OKB staff and RNS Admiral Kuznetsov's crew congratulating Toktar Aubakirov after yet another deck landing. (Yefim Gordon archive)

BELOW: 312 Blue was present again at MAKS-93 in Zhukovskiy, armed with two Kh-25 ASMs, two R-77s and four short-range AAMs (two R-60Ms and two R-73s). (Yefim Gordon)

however, it was the real thing, and it was very different to the mockup presented in November 1997. Coded 405 Blue to reflect the fuselage number (0405), the prototype was in fact none other than the aircraft previously used as a testbed for the MiG-29SMT's glass cockpit described previously (ex 331 Blue).

Since then the aircraft had been extensively modified to bring it, externally at least, to MiG-29SMT standard with a much more convex upper fuselage, extended MiG-29SM-style 'beaver tail' and one-piece dorsal airbrake. Still, this was little more than an avionics and aerodynamics testbed for the *izdeliye* 9.17, as the two additional strap-on fuel tanks in the recontoured spine were non-functional! 405 Blue was intended for stability and handling trials and testing the upgraded avionics suite.

The MiG-29SMT made its first flight the same day at the hands of Vladimir M. Gorboonov, Hero of Russia, who succeeded Roman P. Taskayev as Mikoyan's CTP in the autumn of 1997. Speaking to the journalists after the flight, Gorboonov said that the MiG-29SMT had much enhanced combat capabilities while retaining the unique handling characteristics of the 'Fulcrum'.

MiG-29SMT 405 Blue was displayed statically at the ILA'98 airshow at Berlin-Schönefeld airport carrying a Thomson-CSF CLDP laser designator pod under the fuselage. A non-functional semi-retractable refuelling probe similar to that of Royal Malaysian Air Force MiG-29SDs was fitted to the port side of the nose to demonstrate the type's unlimited upgrade capabilities.

The second prototype, a converted late-production 'Fulcrum-C' (c/n 2960735400, f/n 4710), was set aside by Mikoyan for conversion in late 1997. Originally the aircraft carried only a single 500-lit. (100 Imp. gal.) strap-on tank for fuel system and aerodynamics testing, giving a range increase of only 180 km (100 nm); in this guise it entered flight test on 28 November 1997. In March 1998 the aircraft was turned over to Mikoyan's experimental shop for complete conversion to MiG-29SMT standard, becoming the first 'true' MiG-29SMT, meeting project specifications completely.

Aptly coded 917 Blue to match the manufacturer's designation (Product 9.17), the aircraft took to the air on 14 July 1998 at the hands of Vladimir Gorboonov. The first flight lasted more than an hour, giving some indication of the fighter's capabilities.

Throughout August 1998 test pilot Marat Alykov practised his flying display for the FI'98 airshow. Then, on 2 September, 917 Blue took off for Tver' with three drop tanks. Next day the fighter arrived at Farnborough after a non-stop flight; the stopover at Tver' was necessary because headwinds are less probable on the Tver'-Farnborough route, helping to save fuel. The MiG-29SMT's flying display at Farnborough showed that the fatter spine had virtually no adverse effect on the fighter's manoeuvrability. In late November the MiG-29SMT was displayed at the Zhuhai'98 airshow, since China had expressed an interest in the aircraft.

On 29 December 1998 the first 'production' MiG-29SMT (01 Blue, c/n 2960720165, f/n 26...) was completed at Mikoyan's experimental shop and crated for delivery to Zhukovskiy. The aircraft had previously been in service with the 4th TsBPiPLS (Combat and Conversion Training Centre) in Lipetsk and wore the Guards badge on the nose. On 12 January 1999 the aircraft was demonstrated to top-ranking Russian officials, foreign military attachés and the press along with other new Mikoyan products, including the MFI fifth-generation fighter demonstrator (*izdeliye* 1.14). Guests at the ceremony included Army General Igor' Sergeyev (Defence Minister), Col.-Gen. Anatoliy Kornookov (Air Force/Air Defence Force C-in-C), Lt.-Gen. Yuriy Klishin (deputy C-in-C) and Yevgeniy Shaposhnikov (Presidential adviser on aviation matters).

As mentioned earlier, the MiG-29SMT can fill the strike, interceptor, tactical reconnaissance and tactical airborne command post rôles. Experts claim the fighter's combat potential is eight times that of the baseline MiG-29 'Fulcrum-A' while direct operating costs are 35–40% lower.

New avionics will enable the MiG-29SMT Stage 1 to carry all kinds of aircraft weapons, including Western missiles. Each of the fighter's seven computers will equal ten of the computers fitted to 1982–standard production MiG-29s. Using modern electronic components has produced a weight saving of some 600 kg (1,322 lb). Speaking at the MiG-29SMT's first flight ceremony, Russian MoD weaponry department chief Col.-Gen. Anatoliy Sitnov stated that the aircraft's avionics represent the fifth generation of fighters and will be the baseline avionics fit of all present-day Russian combat aircraft.

The upgrade programme is a joint effort of the MoD, the Mikoyan OKB and the primary Russian arms exporter, the Rosvo'orouzheniye State Company which has agreed to supply most of the finance. Rosvo'orouzheniye's General Director Yevgeniy Anan'yev believes the new MiG has excellent export potential, as the basic type is in service with more than twenty nations which could be looking for an upgrade.

MiG-29UBT combat trainer (*izdeliye* 9.52)

In the summer of 1998 Mikoyan's experimental shop began converting a MiG-29UB combat trainer into the prototype MiG-29UBT. The aircraft in question was Mikoyan's well-known demonstrator, 304 Blue, which was a regular participant of numerous international airshows. The MiG-29UBT features increased fuel tankage in a bulged fuselage spine *à la* MiG-29SMT (once again, T stands for *toplivo* – [extra] fuel) and updated avionics, including glass cockpits. The front cockpit is virtually identical to the MiG-29SMT's and the rear cockpit features three large LCDs.

The upgraded WCS enable the MiG-29UBT to fire R-27T AAMs in addition to the familiar R-73s. The trainer also has strike and air defence suppression capability; the air-to-air surface weapons range includes Kh-31P anti-radiation missiles, Kh-29T TV-guided AGMs, Kh-25ML laser-guided AGMs and KAB-500L laser-guided bombs.

The fatback trainer entered flight on 25 August 1998 at the hands of Oleg Antonovich (front seat) and Vladimir Gorboonov. On 3 September the aircraft arrived at Farnborough in company with the second prototype MiG-29SMT to participate in the FI'98 airshow.

In late May 1999 the second prototype MiG-29UBT converted from a standard 'Fulcrum-B' – 52 Blue (also marked 952 White on the fin caps), f/n 2410 – and was delivered to LII from Mikoyan's experimental shop; the tactical code was derived from the manufacturer's designation, *izdeliye* 9.52. This was the first-ever two-seat MiG-29 to feature flight refuelling capability; the semi-retractable refuelling probe was identical to that of the MiG-29SD and MiG-29SMT. 52 Blue made its first post-conversion flight on 26 May.

MiG-29MF multi-rôle fighter (proposal)

In 1997 Russia began negotiations with the Philippines, offering the MiG-29 to the Philippine Air Force (PAF, *Hukbong Himpapawid ng Pilipinas*). The Philippine version is referred to by Mikoyan as MiG-29MF, i.e., *modifikahtsiya dlya Filippeen* – version for the Philippines. It seems Russian manufacturers are adopting the Western practice of incorporating the customer's name into the aircraft's designation – e.g., McDD CF-18A (C for Canadian), McDD EAV-8C Matador (E for *Español*) etc.! (Incidentally, in the Russian press the aircraft has been referred to as MiG-29FM.) No technical details of the MiG-29MF have been published so far, since the negotiators were mainly concerned with range, avionics fit and armament. However, the aircraft is quite probably based on the MiG-29SD or SM. What is certain is that the MiG-29MF is to be equipped with a semi-retractable refuelling probe and that usable fuel weight is 3,300 kg (7,275 lb).

A still from a video showing a MiG-29 dropping a 500-kg (1,102-lb) KAB-500KR TV-guided bomb. (ANPK MiG video)

4

A New Generation

MiG-29M Multi-rôle fighter (*izdeliye* 9.15, *izdeliye* 9)

A s far back as the late '70s Mikoyan started looking for ways of enhancing the MiG-29's combat potential. The obvious way was to incorporate the latest technologies, new hard-hitting weapons and more capable avionics. Another area open for improvement was the RD-33 engine which needed uprating. Thus began a new development stage which resulted in what could be called the second-generation 'Fulcrum' – the MiG-29M (*modernizeerovannyy* – upgraded) known around the OKB as *izdeliye* 9.15 and in the VVS as *izdeliye* 9.

The main objectives of the upgrade programme were higher versatility, longer range, better working conditions for the pilot and lower losses in action. This could be accomplished by installing a new-generation weapons control system and an ESM suite, integrating new high-accuracy air-to-air and air-to-ground weapons, increasing internal fuel capacity (and possibly providing flight refuelling capability), uprating the engines and fitting

advanced flight instrumentation and cockpit indication systems. Whilst being basically similar in layout and structure to the production 'Fulcrum', the MiG-29M would feature aerodynamic refinements, changes improving stability and handling, and technological changes making the aircraft easier to build. The result was, in effect, a new aircraft so different from the basic MiG-29 as to be placed in a new category – the so-called Generation 4+ multi-rôle fighters.

To power the MiG-29M the Klimov OKB developed a landlubber version of the RD-33K engine (*izdeliye* 21) designed for the MiG-29K shipboard fighter (see next chapter). Modifications to the engine core, including improved turbine first stage cooling, increased thrust to 5,500 kgp (12,125 lb st) at full military power and 8,800 kgp (19,400 lb st) in full afterburner. The RD-33K had a 6–7% lower SFC in full afterburner and a higher weight/thrust ratio. Unlike the naval engine, the version

The top view illustrates the changes to the rear fuselage and the dog-tooth on the stabilator leading edges characteristic of the MiG-29M. Note the false dorsal intake louvres à la production 'Fulcrums' added to confuse Westerners studying satellite imagery. (Yefim Gordon archive)

As the tactical code 151 Blue reveals, this was izdeliye 9.15 No. 1. Note the black and white phototheodolite targets on the fins. (Viktor Drooshlyakov)

fitted to the MiG-29M lacked the 9,400-kgp (20,723 lb st) contingency rating used for ski-jump takeoffs from the aircraft carrier because field performance requirements for land-based fighters were not so stringent. The new engine had a duplex full authority digital engine control (FADEC) system replacing the traditional analog engine controls of the basic RD-33, a duplex automatic fuel flow management system and a new accessory gearbox. Besides having greater reliability, the FADEC enabled the engine to accelerate quicker.

The MiG-29M featured redesigned air intakes which, like the engines, had been tested on the tenth MiG-29 prototype (21 Blue). The solid FOD protection doors and dorsal auxiliary intakes of the 'Fulcrum-A/B/C' were deleted and replaced by downward-hinging grids further downstream. The walls of the mainwheel wells were

perforated to admit additional air when the grids were down. Unlike the basic MiG-29, the intakes had a lower lip that could be deflected 20° down to improve engine operation at high alpha; the FADEC controlled these and the intake ramps.

Major changes were made to the airframe. Most of it, especially the forward fuselage, was made of 01420 aluminium-lithium (Al-Li) alloy. Unlike production 'Fulcrums', the structure was welded, not riveted. This saved structural weight because there was no need to seal rivet joints or leave margins for riveting and the new alloy had a lower specific gravity. Besides, more internal volume could be used for fuel (on the basic MiG-29 fuel tank capacity was limited by the impossibility to seal all rivet joints. The share of composites was increased; besides the fins and various dielectric and access panels, composites were used for the airbrake, engine cowlings and inlet ducts. The use of radar-absorbent materials (RAM) reduced the aircraft's radar cross-section (RCS) ten times!

The pilot's seat was raised to improve visibility (the pilot's downward field of view was 15°); this necessitated a change in the shape of the canopy which was more convex than the 'Fulcrum-A/C's'. The LERXes received a sharper leading edge to generate more powerful vortices at high alpha; this and the increased-span ailerons substantially improved the aircraft's low-speed handling. Stabilator area was increased for the same reason by

extending the leading edge, resulting in a characteristic dogtooth which also energised the airflow over the stabilators at maximum deflection. Fin chord was increased below the rudders.

The upper fuselage was reshaped; its contour was a straight line; something in between the slightly concave spine of the 'Fulcrum-A' and the strongly convex back of the 'Fulcrum-C'. The APU air intake was relocated to starboard. The split airbrake of the standard MiG-29 was replaced by a Su-27 style one-piece dorsal airbrake located further forward (between the fins); this, however, was rather smaller than the 'Flanker's', having an area of

A group of Mikoyan test pilots with Mikoyan engineers, including the then MiG-29 project chief Novikov (centre of far row). (Yefim Gordon archive)

approximately 1 m^2 (10.75 sq. ft). The control system automatically compensated for pitch-up force generated by the airbrake when deployed.

The engineers had met insistent requests from Air Force pilots to increase the MiG-29's combat radius. Deletion of the dorsal auxiliary air intakes and other airframe changes made room for more than 1,000 lit. (220 Imp. gal.) of additional fuel, increasing the internal fuel capacity to 5,720 lit. (1,258.4 Imp. gal.) or 4,460 kg (9,832 lb) of usable fuel and extending range by 30–40%. With three drop tanks the fuel load increased to 9,200 lit. (2,024 Imp. gal.). The landing gear was beefed up to absorb the higher gross weight. The single cruciform brake parachute intakes of the 'Fulcrum-A/B/C' with an area of 17 m^2 (182.79 sq. ft) gave way to twin chutes with an area of 13 m^2 (139.78 sq. ft) each and more powerful wheel brakes were fitted for more effective deceleration on landing.

The MiG-29M had an unusual combined control system featuring a quadruplex analog fly-by-wire (FBW) pitch control channel with no mechanical backup and triplex FBW roll and yaw control channels with mechanical backup enabling 50% control surface deflection. Making the fighter statically unstable in the pitch control channel reduced drag caused by pitch trim in cruise mode and hence improved fuel economy, contributing to the increase in range.

The S-29M weapons control system was completely new, comprising an RLPK-29M radar targeting system and an OEPrNK-29M targeting/navigation complex. The former was built around the brand-new Phazotron N-010 Zhuk (Beetle) fire control radar. The WCS incorporated more effective Ts101 series digital processors and also old Ts100 series processors with new software. The N-010 pulse-Doppler radar developed under Phazotron's General Designer A. I. Kanaschchenkov could track ten aerial targets while guiding AAMs to four priority threats. Detection range for a fighter-type target[1] in the forward hemisphere was 80 km (44 nm) versus 70 km (38 nm) for the N-019. The radar had a flat-plate slotted array with mechanical scanning in azimuth (90° versus 70° in the N-019) and electronic scanning in elevation. It could work in ground mapping mode with low, medium or high resolution (in standard beam, Doppler beam compression and synthetic aperture radar modes respectively), determining target coordinates, freezing or enlarging the picture if necessary, measuring the aircraft's ground speed (for navigation or making corrections during missile firing) and enabling automatic terrain following.

At 220 kg (485 lb), the N-010 was 60% lighter than the N-019 (350 kg/771 lb). Outwardly it could be recognized by a reprofiled radome with simple curvature instead of the N-019's double curvature. This was due to the fact that the N-010 had a much smaller and neater scanner replacing the N-019's bulky twist-cassegrain 'bin', allowing the radome to be made cleaner aerodynamically. The radar was probably tested on a modified Tu-134AK 'Crusty' airliner (SSSR-65907, c/n 63996, f/n 6333), one of Phazotron's avionics testbeds.[2]

The updated OEPrNK-29M optoelectronic targeting/navigation complex comprised an OLS-M (*optiko-lokatseeonnaya stahntsiya, modernizeer ovannaya*) combined IR/TV search and track/laser ranger unit and an HMS. Besides having increased range, it not only detected aerial targets and measured their coordinates but designated ground targets for laser-guided and TV-guided weapons and tracked them in real time. Unlike first-generation MiG-29s, the characteristic IRST ball was opaque, looking like an eyeball with the TV lens in the middle as the pupil, and was mounted atop an elongated fairing.

The new high-sensitivity IRST unit had a deep-cooling system increasing detection range several times. The TV camera could identify aerial and ground targets at long range, thus having the same function as the Northrop AN/ASX-1 electro-optical target identification system (TISEO) fitted to the McDD F-4E+. The higher-power laser ranger/designator improved the chances of target acquisition in the forward hemisphere and accurate guidance of missiles. The helmet-mounted sight supplied target data to other targeting systems and IR-homing missiles. For more efficient aiming at ground targets (especially at night) the aircraft could be fitted with a podded laser designator combined with a low light level TV or thermal imaging system.

The MiG-29M had a completely new 'glass cockpit' (EFIS) with an improved HUD and two multi-function monochrome cathode-ray tube (CRT) displays for flight and target/weapons data; colour CRTs could be integrated later on. Small backup electromechanical instruments were retained in the centre of the instrument panel. The cockpit utilised the HOTAS concept. The aircraft also

---

[1] A target with an RCS of 3 m^2 (32.25 sq. ft)

[2] This ex-VIP aircraft was spotted at LII in August 1992 with the experimental radar supplanting the navigator's glazing. By August 1995 it was reconverted to standard configuration and sold to Alrosa-Avia, a Russian airline, as RA-65907.

The MiG-29M shows off its characteristic ordnance load: two Kh-29 AGMs, two Kh-31 AGMs, two R-73 AAMs and two R-77 AAMs. (Yefim Gordon)

featured a new inertial navigation system (INS), secure data link for interaction with automated GCI centres, a new communications suite and IFF transponders.

The maximum ordnance load on eight underwing hardpoints and one centreline station was 4,500 kg (9,920 lb). The weapons range included the latest product of the Vympel design bureau, the R-77 (RVV-AE) AAM developed since 1982 with the bureau's leader G. A. Sokolovskiy as project chief. It was conceived as the Soviet answer to the GM-Hughes AIM-120A advanced medium-range air-to-air missile (AMRAAM) and therefore promptly nicknamed AMRAAMski in the West. The R-77 was the first Soviet AAM with active radar homing. At the initial guidance phase it had inertial

guidance with mid-course correction using signals from the fighter's radar, switching to active radar homing at the terminal guidance phase; this made it an effective weapon at up to 90 km (50 nm) range, and several targets could be attacked at once. The R-77 was a fire-and-forget weapon – a feature previously found only on IR-homing AAMs. Novel design features, such as the lattice-like rudders (a world's first), gave the missile unparalleled manoeuvrability, enabling it to score a kill against a target taking violent evasive action with up to 12 Gs.

The R-77 had been tested on two MiG-29s converted by Mikoyan into weapons testbeds (aircraft 970 and 971) even before construction of the first prototype MiG-29M began. So were various systems and equipment; e.g., the powerplant had been put through its paces on the tenth prototype 'Fulcrum-A' (21 Blue), as mentioned previously. The MiG-29M could carry up to eight R-77s or R-73 IR-homing short-range AAMs, up to four R-27R1/R-27T1 IR-homing/SARH medium-range AAMs, two R-27RE1/R-27TE1 extended-range AAMs, up to six Kh-29T TV-guided air-to-ground missiles, Kh-29L or Kh-25ML laser-guided AGMs, Kh-31A active radar homing anti-shipping missiles, Kh-31P or Kh-25MP (AS-12 'Kegler') anti-radiation missiles, KAB-500KR TV-guided bombs, up to four B-13L rocket pods with 20 S-13 FFARs or B-8M1 rocket pods with 80 S-8 FFARs, and various free-fall bombs. The GSh-301 30-mm internal gun was retained but the ammo supply was reduced to 100 rounds. The smart bombs could be dropped singly or simultaneously.

The ESM suite included a Gardeniya-1FU (L203B) active jammer and two BVP-60-26 chaff/flare dispensers with sixty 26-mm rounds each – twice the capacity of the 'Fulcrum-A'. The dispensers were buried in the aft fuselage, the characteristic dorsal fin extensions of the 'Fulcrum-A/C' housing 30-round chaff/flare dispensers being deleted. The ECM aerials were ideally positioned at the wingtips under dielectric panels fore and aft, giving complete 360° coverage.

Normal TOW was 15,800 kg (34,832 lb) and MTOW 18,00 kg (39,682 lb). The MiG-29M had better combat efficiency than the F-16C, F/A-18C, Eurofighter EF.2000, Rafale and other Western fighters in the same class. Serviceability was much improved as compared to earlier versions; seven technicians needed 30 minutes to perform pre-flight checks and 15–25 minutes for a post-flight check. The airframe's service life was increased to 2,500 hours and could be extended to 4,000 hours. Mean time between failures (MTBF) was at least eight hours; overall maintenance labour intensity was 11.5 man-hours and mean repair time 1.2 hours. Maintenance was done at 200-hr intervals.

Six flying prototypes and a static test airframe were built. The first prototype, 151 Blue (i.e., *izdeliye* 9.15 No. 1), took to the air on 25 April 1986, piloted by Valeriy Ye. Menitskiy who superseded Aleksandr V. Fedotov as Mikoyan's CTP.[3] Unlike subsequent prototypes, it sported prominent T-shaped black and white phototheodolite calibration markings on the tail.

The aircraft (c/n 05551) was powered by standard RD-33s because the uprated RD-33K had not yet completed its trials programme. No radar was fitted, since 151 Blue was intended mainly for verifying the new structural components and for control system, handling and performance testing. According to Mikhail R. Val'denberg the aircraft originally flew with the FBW control system disengaged, using only the backup mechanical controls; FBW testing did not begin until November 1989. However, other sources in the Mikoyan OKB discount this, stating that the first prototype used FBW controls throughout.

The second prototype, 152 Blue (c/n 05552), also entered flight test with RD-33 engines but was retrofitted with RD-33Ks in 1989. It was also the first to be fitted with the N-010 radar, a HUD and two CRT displays, thus becoming the first MiG-29M in representative production configuration; conventional electromechanical flight instruments were retained as a backup. The aircraft was used for FBW testing, radar trials, handling, performance and field performance testing with and without external stores, powerplant and fuel system testing. The third aircraft, 153 Blue (c/n 05553) it was demonstrated to top-ranking industry and military officials at Kubinka AB on 23 June 1989 along with the other latest Soviet combat aircraft. This aircraft and the fourth and fifth prototypes, 154 Blue and 155 Blue (c/ns 05554 and 05555), were used for comprehensive powerplant, avionics and systems testing, live air-to-air and air-to-ground firing trials and cockpit ergonomics trials. The fourth aircraft was especially used to verify the new IRST/LR and the fifth prototype for performance and field performance testing.

Like 155 Blue, the final prototype, 156 Blue (c/n 05556), was built by MAPO at Moscow-Khodynka in the early '90s.[4] This aircraft did not participate in the State acceptance trials since it came after Stage 1 of the trials had been completed in September 1991. The fifth and sixth aircraft were used for avionics trials (including electromagnetic compatibility trials) and live weapons firing trials against both aerial and ground targets, featuring a complete avionics suite with modifications introduced after the third prototype's tests. The final prototype had a redesigned instrument panel with larger CRTs which meant some of the mechanical instruments had to be omitted and their functions transferred to the

---

[3] Fedotov lost his life in the crash of the third production MiG-31 'Foxhound' interceptor (201 Blue, f/n 0201) on 4 April 1984.

[4] Since the VVS product code is *izdeliye* 9, the full c/ns of the six prototypes could be 2960905551 through 2960905556 but this is unconfirmed. 156 Blue's c/n has also been quoted as 27585.

EFIS. In this shape the MiG-29M was recommended for production upon elimination of the shortcomings detected during trials.

Painting in airframe parts that are not there to confuse the enemy is nothing new; e.g., Canadian Air Force CF-18A Hornets have false canopies painted on the underside of the nose. Mikoyan, however, gave the idea a new twist. All MiG-29M prototypes except the last one had phoney dorsal air intakes painted on the LERXes which would show up on satellite imagery. The idea was to fool Western intelligence agencies into thinking these were ordinary 'Fulcrum-As' or - Cs. 156 Blue did not have this camouflage because in 1992 the MiG-29M began participating in Western airshows, giving observers a chance to examine it closely, and this elaborate deception became pointless.

Separate leading engineers were assigned to each of the MiG-29M prototypes for the duration of the flight test programme: Boris M. Chuck to 151 Blue, Vasiliy F. Shtykalo to 152 Blue and 155 Blue, Pavel G. Orlov to 153 Blue, Vladimir N. Trooshkov to 154 Blue and Sergey A. Revnov to 156 Blue.

Early test flights showed a marked improvement in manoeuvrability; pilots praised the MiG-29M's handling. The fighter had a maximum true airspeed (TAS) of 2,450 km/h (1,361 kts) or Mach 2.3, a maximum indicated airspeed (IAS) of 1,480 km/h (822 kts) and a 310 m/sec (1,017 ft/sec) rate of climb at 1,000 m (3,280 ft). Service ceiling was 17,000 m (55,774 ft), range on internal fuel 2,000–2,200 km (1,111–1,222 nm) and maximum ferry range with three drop tanks 3,200 km (1,777 nm). With a 3,500-kg (7716-lb) ordnance load the aircraft had a 20-minute on-station loiter time within 520 km (288 nm) from base. Combat radius was 1,250 km (694 nm) in dogfight mode (involving five 360° turns) with 2+2 short/medium-range AAMs and three drop tanks, 1,440 km (800 nm) in Mach 0.85 subsonic intercept mode with two medium-range AAMs and three drop tanks, and 1,190 km (661 nm) in strike mode with two AGMs, two short-range AAMs and three drop tanks. Normal and maximum TOW rose to 16,800 kg (37,037 lb) and 22,300 kg (49,162 lb) respectively. Still, this had almost no adverse effect on field performance. Take off run was 250–500 m (820–1,640 ft) depending on gross weight and landing run with brake chutes 500–600 m (1,640–1,968 ft).

The MiG-29M's G limits, rate of climb and acceleration were roughly the same as in the production MiG-29/MiG-29UB. The maximum AOA, however, was much higher, enabling the fighter to make brief 9 G manoeuvres with a full fuel load, which was a major improvement over production aircraft. The MiG-29M had an electronic alpha limiter; initially the AOA limit was set at 30° but chief project engineer Mikhail R. Val'denberg stated this would be increased when the aircraft completed flight tests. The new FOD protection screens were put to the test when one of the prototypes collided with a duck on take off. The bird went into an air intake and made a dent in the screen but the engine suffered no damage.

General Designer R. A. Belyakov claimed that the MiG-29M was 'the world's finest aircraft as regards stall and spin recovery. Even the [basic] MiG-29 was perfect in this respect; with the MiG-29M we took it even further.' According to the Soviet aerospace industry development plan, the MiG-29M was to supersede the 'Fulcrum-A/C' gradually on the MAPO production lines in the early '90s. The first 60 production aircraft would be built in parallel with first-generation 'Fulcrum' before the beginning of 1990; within the next decade the number of production MiG-29Ms would reach 300 or even 400. Still, these hopes were shattered. The trials programme was making slow progress; only the manufacturer's flight tests were completed by the early '90s. These were deemed to be successful, even though the first (and later the second) aircraft had to be grounded because of fatigue cracks. The State acceptance trials, however, were suspended after Stage 1 because of funding shortages. Still, the State commission recommended that the MiG-29M be launched into production upon elimination of certain shortcomings, mostly in the radar. The broad weapons range was not completely integrated with the WCS during Stage 1, and minimum safe range for missile launches was not determined.

The collapse of the Soviet Union and ensuing political and economic chaos certainly did not help; State funding, which had been a mere trickle until then, all but dried up completely. Besides, the Russian Air Force stopped MiG-29 purchases in 1991, as it could not afford to buy both the Su-27 and the MiG-29 when Russia was in the throes of a financial crisis. As a result, the factory airfield in Lookhovitsy soon became crammed with row upon row of new but unwanted 'Fulcrums' – a sorry sight indeed. The final flight under the State acceptance trials programme was made in May 1993. Between them the five prototypes participating in the programme made 1,068 flights.

On 13 February 1992 the fifth prototype was demonstrated to top-ranking military officials and the leaders of the CIS states at Machoolischchi AB near Minsk. A few weeks later the same aircraft was demonstrated to Russian Air Force C-in-C Col.-Gen. Pyotr S. Deynekin in Akhtoobinsk during his visit to NII VVS. Later 155 Blue participated in the Kubinka-93 (29 May 1993), MAKS-93 (31 August – 5 September 1993) and Farnborough International '94 airshows. Logically, the MiG-29M would have been 'Fulcrum-E' but, since the true designation was known, no NATO code name was allocated. The sixth prototype was also present in the static park at several airshows – FI'92, Le Bourget '93 and MAKS-95 (22-27 August 1995). For the latter occasion the aircraft had been re-coded 301 Blue but the original tactical code 156 on the dielectric fin caps (which no-one had apparently taken the trouble to change) gave it away. Another change at MAKS-95 was the Russian flag applied to the rudders.

According to MAPO-MiG estimates, the MiG-29M can match the performance of the Boeing/Lockheed F-22A Raptor fifth-generation fighter. Its combat potential is 1.5 times that of the 'Fulcrum-A/C' in the counter-air rôle and 3.4 times better in the strike rôle. The MiG-29M has evolved into a true multi-rôle combat aircraft. Russian popular press reported that the VVS planned to acquire 30 MiG-29Ms in 1996. However, the plan had to be shelved because the MoD had no money to fund the order.

Anatoliy A. Belosvet, Deputy General Director of ANPK 'MiG',[5] stated that virtually all technical problems associated with the fighter's WCS had been eliminated by 1997 and the State acceptance trials could be quickly completed, providing State funding was made available. The second, third, fourth and fifth prototypes are now operated by GLITs in Akhtoobinsk while the final aircraft is retained by LII for demonstration purposes.

MiG-29ME (MiG-33) export multi-rôle fighter

ANPK MiG is also working on a downgraded export version of the MiG-29M designated MiG-29ME or MiG-33. This will have a less capable WCS borrowed from the MiG-29SD/SE based on the N-019ME radar. Mikoyan engineers are also considering upgrades of the MiG-29M with enhanced manoeuvrability and greater range. Higher manoeuvrability could be achieved by fitting canards or thrust-vectoring engines. Provisional three-views of the MiG-33 released to date show unique canards with a dogtooth.

MiG-29UBM combat trainer project (*izdeliye* 9.61)

A trainer version of the MiG-29M similar to the MiG-29UB was under consideration for some time. To stress the similarity and 'generation change' from the MiG-29UB (*izdeliye* 9.51) the aircraft was designated MiG-29UBM or *izdeliye* 9.61. However, this remained a 'very paper airplane' because of the suspension of the MiG-29M programme.

MiG-29Sh attack aircraft (proposal)

After evaluating the MiG-29 in the strike rôle MAPO-MiG proposed a specialised attack version of the 'Fulcrum' designated MiG-29Sh (*shtoormovik* – attack aircraft). The aircraft featured enhanced survivability, (more than 1,000 kg/2,204 lb of armour plate), a 5,000-kg (11,022-lb) ordnance load and a wider weapons range which could include advanced air-to-surface missiles (e.g., anti-tank guided missiles) as they came along. Gross weight was 25,500 kg (56,217 lb). To ensure adequate performance despite the increased weight the MiG-29Sh was powered by new RD-43 engines rated at 9,900 kgp (21,825 lb st) in full afterburner.

MiG-29 (*izdeliye* 9.25) multi-rôle fighter project

The MiG-29M's lengthy trials programme and funding shortfalls led Mikoyan leaders to believe that the fighter would be obsolete by the time it finally completed its trials. This and the Russian Air Force's decision not to spend the limited money there was on two different fighters led ANPK MiG to develop an upgraded version of the MiG-29M at its own risk.[6] Development work had proceeded since the late '80s; the main objectives were to extend range, improve agility and integrate additional weapons.

The new fighter was designated *izdeliye* 9.25. It featured engines uprated to 10,000 kgp (22,045 lb st). The fuselage was stretched by moving the engines 910 mm (2 ft 11.82 in.) to make room for an additional integral fuel tank. Canard foreplanes were introduced to increase agility, and wing area was enlarged. A new weapons control system built around a new radar was fitted and the ordnance load was increased to 5,000 kg (11,023 lb); the weapons range included anti-tank guided missiles.

---

5 The Mikoyan OKB's new official name (ANPK = *Aviatseeonnyy naoochno-proizvodstvennyy kompleks* – Aviation Scientific & Production Complex).

6 The VVS suspended further purchases of the MiG-29 in the early '90s, opting for the Su-27, even though these were fighters of different classes and rôles. This has caused MiG-29 production effectively to come to a standstill.

Mikoyan planned to proceed with the upgrade programme in three stages; the aircraft was designated MiG-29M1, MiG-29M2 and MiG-29M3 at the respective stages. Stage 1 introduced the fuselage stretch which allowed fuel tank No. 3 to be enlarged and tank No. 4 to be added, increasing internal fuel volume 20% to 7,000 lit. (1,540 Imp. gal.). During Stage 2 the canards and increased-area wings were introduced, and fuel capacity was increased once again thanks to wing tanks of nearly double size.

Finally, Stage 3 was the installation of the new engines and new avionics suite, which would turn the MiG-29 into a fifth-generation fighter. Fuel tank No. 2 was enlarged and a further tank (No. 5) added, bringing the total to more than 8,000 lit. (1,760 Imp. gal.) – 40% more that the MiG-29M's and a whopping 90% more than the 'Fulcrum-A's'. A refuelling probe was also introduced. Thus the lightweight MiG-29M3 would equal the range of the much heavier Su-27 and Su-27M (Su-35) if drop tanks were carried.

Initial VVS reactions were positive. Later, however, interest waned and the programme was shelved along with the MiG-29M as funding dried up.

MiG-29 (*izdeliye* 9.35) multi-rôle fighter project

At a VPK MAPO press conference held on 21 August 1997 during the MAKS-97 airshow Mikoyan announced that an even more massive upgrade of the 'Fulcrum' referred to by the press as MiG-35 was in the making. This statement was not very far from the truth. Since it had become clear by the late '90s that no more money would be forthcoming for the MiG-29M, ANPK MiG decided to cheat the money from the stingy government by proposing an allegedly new-generation fighter.

Thus a new upgrade proposal was drawn up in 1997. The aircraft was based on the stillborn *izdeliye* 9.25 project and thus designated *izdeliye* 9.35; the MiG-35 designation which appeared in the popular press was pure fiction. The fighter incorporated the improvements proposed for *izdeliye* 9.25, albeit on a more modern technical level, and some ideas from the MFI programme – the famous fifth-generation multi-rôle fighter known as Project 1.42. Like its predecessor, *izdeliye* 9.35 featured uprated engines with revised air intakes and inlet ducts, a 910-mm fuselage stretch, a new radar and an increased ordnance load. Internal fuel capacity was increased to approximately that of the MiG-29SMT, giving an extra 1,500 kg (3,306 lb) of fuel. Besides the extra integral tank

ahead of the engines and larger wing tanks, two strap-on fuselage tanks (No. 4 and 4-A) and integral tanks in the fin roots were added. To further extend range *izdeliye* 9.35 had flight refuelling capability.

Because length and take off weight had grown, wing area was increased by increasing span and root chord; the result was quite similar to the MiG-25 'Foxbat' in planform, with lopped-off wingtips and a straight trailing edge (the kinked trailing edge *à la* F-15 depicted in Western drawings of the MiG-35 is totally incorrect). The landing gear was beefed up to absorb the extra weight, and 01420 Al-Li alloy gave way to more conventional D16 duralumin at some locations. Mikoyan claimed that structurally the new 'Fulcrum' had virtually nothing in common with the basic MiG-29. The increased internal fuel capacity doubled the new fighter's range as compared to the 'Fulcrum-A'. Contrary to Western allegations, no canards were planned (unlike *izdeliye* 9.25) but thrust-vectoring engines with axisymmetrical two-plane nozzles could be incorporated at a later stage.

Some Mikoyan representatives claimed that *izdeliye* 9.35 had a combat potential approaching that of the heavier and more costly Su-35 multi-rôle fighter. The type of radar was still to be decided but it could possibly be the Phazotron Zhuk-F phased-array radar capable of tracking 24 targets at a time while guiding missiles to eight priority threats. The aircraft had ten weapons hardpoints (possibly with two wingtip missile rails) and could carry a wide range of air-to-air weapons, including R-77 fire-and-forget AAMs. Yet this project seems to be suffering the same fate as previous MiG-29 upgrade programmes – the Russian MoD does not want it because it cannot afford to buy it. Mikoyan believes that attracting Western investors (i.e., possible customers) is a must if the project is to materialise. Some Western analysts believe the lightweight MiG-35 is nothing less than VPK MAPO's attempt to compensate for the delays with the heavy 1.42/1.44.

Trainer derivative of *izdeliye* 9.35 (proposal)

Concurrently with *izdeliye* 9.35 ANPK MiG submitted a proposal for a two-seat trainer version. The aircraft differed mainly in having a new forward fuselage (frames No. 1 through 7), retaining the improvements introduced on the single-seater; unlike the MiG-29UB, the new trainer retained the fire control radar. The instructor's seat was raised to improve visibility, creating a distinctive humpbacked silhouette strikingly similar to the Su-27UB

After several mid-life updates the range of weaponry that can be carried by the MiG-29 was expanded considerably. (Yefim Gordon)

The first prototype MiG-29M (151 Blue) accompanied by the first prototype MiG-29K (311 Blue) in a rare formation flight; note phototheodolite calibration markings. (Sergey and Dmitriy Komissarov archive)

'Flanker-C'. Like the single-seater, the trainer version of *izdeliye* 9.35 has been put on hold indefinitely.

MiG-29SMT Stage II upgrade project

Yet there is a Russian saying that new things are thoroughly forgotten old ones. In 1998 Mikoyan proposed an upgrade of the MiG-29SMT which would match the capabilities of *izdeliye* 9.35. The so-called Stage II upgrade would introduce RD-43 engines uprated to 10,000 kgp (22,045 lb st) with thrust vectoring both in the pitch and the yaw plane. The weapons control system would be built around an all-new Zhemchoog (Pearl) fire control radar with a detection range of 130 km (72 nm) and 180° scanning in azimuth. The radar will be capable

of tracking ten targets at a time while guiding missiles to four priority threats.

The aircraft would have new wings featuring four hardpoints each, enabling it to carry new K-37M long-range AAMs (to be designated R-37M on production form), K-77M (R-77M) advanced medium-range AAMs and K-30 (R-30) advanced short-range AAMs, as well as new air-to-surface missiles. The latter to include Kh-31AM/Kh-31AD and Kh-35 (Kh-35U) active radar homing AGMs, Kh-31PM/Kh-31PD anti-radiation missiles, Kh-36 semi-active radar homing (SARH) missiles, Kh-25MTV TV-guided AGMs, and Kh-29L and Kh-25ML laser-guided AGMs. The weapons range might also include the Kh-38 advanced AGM. This would make the MiG-29SMT's combat capabilities nearly twice as

An air-to-air study of the sixth prototype MiG-29M, 156 Blue. (Aviatsiya i Kosmonavtika)

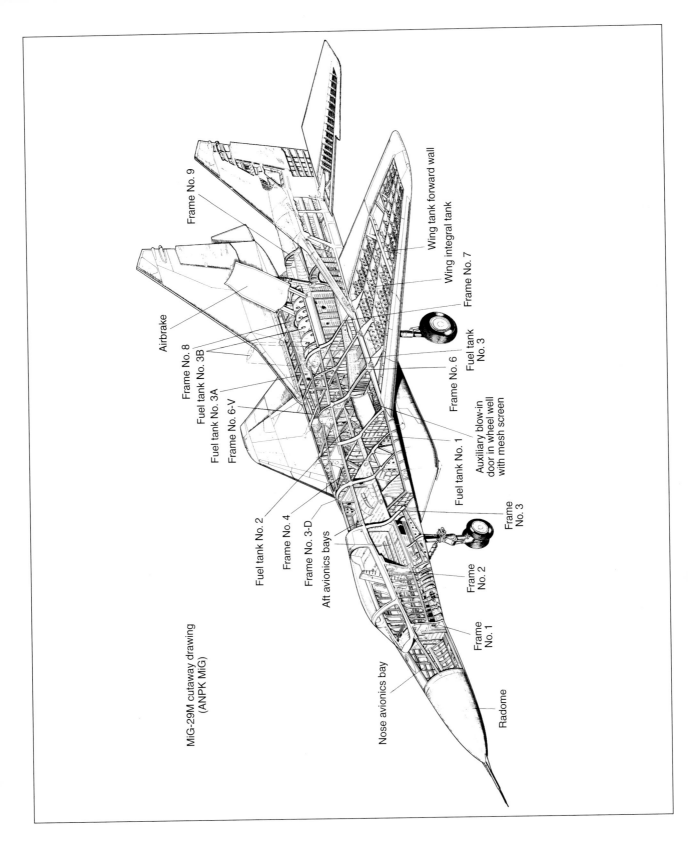

MiG-29M cutaway drawing (ANPK MiG)

Frame No. 9

Wing tank forward wall

Wing integral tank

Frame No. 7

Airbrake

Frame No. 8

Fuel tank No. 3B

Fuel tank No. 3A

Frame No. 6-V

Fuel tank No. 2

Frame No. 4

Frame No. 3-D

Aft avionics bays

Frame No. 6

Fuel tank No. 3

Fuel tank No. 1

Auxiliary blow-in door in wheel well with mesh screen

Frame No. 3

Frame No. 2

Frame No. 1

Nose avionics bay

Radome

78

good as those of the Su-27 in air-to-air combat and more than three times better in the strike rôle.

The Stage II upgrade would also introduce a new BINS-SP (*bortovaya inertseeahl'naya navigatseeonnaya sistema so spootnikovoy poprahvkoy*) navigation suite featuring ring laser gyros and correction via satellite link on board-INS with satellite correction. The MiG-29SMT would also feature a new 'Kedr-29' (Cedar) ESM suite comprising an RHAWS, active ECM, podded threat distinguishing system and chaff/flare dispensers.

To guide advanced AGNs to their targets the aircraft would carry an IKSPOZ pod (*infrakrahsnaya sistema poiska, opoznavahniya i zapominahniya* – IR search, [target] identification and memorization system) intended to . . . well . . . *expose* targets. The name is actually somewhat misleading, as, besides an IR seeker, the system would feature low light level TV and a laser rangefinder. A new data link system would enable the fighter to operate in concert with MiG-31 and Su-27 interceptors. Radar-absorbent materials and coatings would reduce the aircraft's radar cross-section to 0.5–1 m² (5.37–10.75 sq. ft), i.e., 15 to 30 times less than that of the current 'Fulcrum-C' which has an RCS of 15 m² (161.29 sq. ft).

The total internal fuel load would increase from 4,775 kg (10,526 lb) to 5,600 kg (12, 345 lb) and the TOW will rise from 16,850 kg (37,147 lb) to 18,000 kg (39,682 lb). Range at high altitude would increase from 2,200 km (1,222 nm) to 2,500 km (1,388 nm) on internal fuel only, from 2,800 km (1,555 nm) to 3,100 km (1,722 nm) and one drop tank on the centreline station and from 3,400 km (1,888 nm) to 3,700 km (2,055 nm) with these three drop tanks. What's more, this would be quite a cost-effective solution. According to Mikoyan estimates, the MiG-29SMT Stage II would cost only 25% more than the current 'Fulcrum-C' and not more than the Su-27 while giving a considerable boost in combat potential over both types.

As indicated earlier, the MiG-29SMT Stage II could fill the tactical reconnaissance, interceptor, attack and C³ (command, control and communications) roles. Experts estimate that it would be eight times more effective than today's 'Fulcrum' while being at least 35–40% cheaper to operate.

5

Pushing for The Navy

MiG-29K shipboard fighter (*izdeliye 9.31*), 'Fulcrum-D'

A s early as the '50s when the USA and their NATO allies began bolstering their naval power, especially aircraft carriers, Soviet military leaders realized the Soviet Navy needed aircraft carriers to deter potential adversaries at sea. However, creating a 'real' aircraft carrier equipped with conventional takeoff and landing (CTOL) jet fighters within a short time was impossible because, unlike the US and Great Britain, the Soviet Union had no prior experience with such ships. Therefore, as a first step in this direction, the Ministry of Defence initiated the development of anti-submarine warfare (ASW) carriers or large ASW ships, as they were officially called (BPK – *bol'shoy protivolodochnyy korahbl'*). For starters these would carry helicopters and then vertical takeoff and landing (VTOL) attack aircraft.

The first of these ships, 'Moskva' class (Project 1123) ASW carrier SNS[1] *Moskva*, was commissioned in 1967, followed by sister ship SNS *Leningrad* in 1969. They had a carrier Wing of 14 Kamov Ka-25 helicopters – mainly the Ka-25PL 'Hormone-A' version (PL = *protivolodochnyy* – ASW (attr.)) but also a couple of Ka-25PS (*poiskovo-spasahtel'nyy* – search and rescue (attr.)) 'Hormone-C' SAR choppers and Ka-25Ts (*tseleookazahtel'*) 'Hormone-B' over-the-horizon (OTH) targeting helicopters. The Soviet Navy's capability was further increased by the addition in 1975 and 1978 of the first true aircraft carriers – *Kiev* class (Project 1143) cruisers SNS *Kiev* and SNS *Minsk*. These featured an angled flight deck, rather like HMS *Invincible*, and had a carrier Wing comprising 16 Yak-36M (Yak-38) 'Forger-A' V/STOL fighters and 16 Ka-25 or Ka-27 'Helix' helicopters.

(It should be noted here that the Soviet (Russian) carriers were, and still are, referred to as heavy aircraft-carrying cruisers. The term was coined to circumvent an international treaty prohibiting the passage of aircraft carriers through the straits of Bosporus and Dardanelles. Since the carriers were built at the Black Sea shipyards, calling them by their proper name would mean they would be locked in the Black Sea, which of course was totally unacceptable.)

However, while being the Soviet Navy's only

operational V/STOL jet the Yak-38 was, putting it mildly, not a very capable combat aircraft. Its unusual combined powerplant comprising a Tumanskiy R-27V-300 lift/cruise engine and two Kolesov (RKBM) RD36-35FVR lift-jets was extremely thirsty in VTOL mode, meaning the 'Forger's combat radius even in clean condition was little more than 500 km (277 nm). With external stores it shrank to only 90–160 km (50–88 nm) – even choppers could do better than that. Besides, the subsonic Yak-38 was virtually no good in the air defence rôle since it lacked an internal gun, missile armament and radar and had inadequate speed, ceiling and range.

The obvious necessity to enhance the Soviet Navy's potential with a CTOL carrier led the Ministry of Shipbuilding to task one of its divisions, the Neva Design Bureau in Leningrad (NPKB – *Nevskoye proyektno-konstrooktorskoye byuro*), with developing such a ship. Initial research and feasibility studies were made as early as in 1968; however, the project was not included in the military shipbuilding plan for the 1971-1980 decade because CTOL shipboard aircraft projects on hand were still at a very early development stage.

Yet the SOR for the carrier was beginning to take shape. The 40,000–45,000-ton displacement and the carrier Wing consisting of 28 fighters and four helicopters outlined in the original project of 1968 were deemed to be insufficient; therefore, in 1972 the NPKB submitted a revised project. The carrier Wing now comprised navalized MiG-23ML 'Flogger-G' fighters with an arrester hook, a beefed-up landing gear and an uprated R-100 turbojet, navalized Su-25 'Frogfoot-A' ground-attack aircraft and Beriyev P-42 Garpoon (Harpoon) ASW aircraft. The latter was a chubby straight-wing aircraft powered by two Lotarev D-36 turbofans which bore a striking resemblance to the Lockheed S-3 Viking. This was the first time the Mikoyan, Sukhoi and Beriyev bureaux established direct links with the Ministry of Shipbuilding in order to prepare SORs jointly for the shipboard aircraft.[2]

Having reviewed the project, the Minister of Aircraft

---

[1] Soviet Navy ship.

[2] Of the three, only the second aircraft was to see production and service as the Su-25UTG (*oochebno-trenirovochnyy (samolyot) s gakom* – arrester hook-equipped trainer), a spinoff of the Su-25UB 'Frogfoot-B'. The Mikoyan and Beriyev projects were terminated at the advanced design stage.

312 Blue, the second prototype MiG-29K, sits on the deck of RNS Admiral Kuznetsov *(ex-Tbilisi) among 'rival' Su-27Ks. (Yefim Gordon archive)*

Industry, the Minister of Shipbuilding, the Air Force C-in-C and the Navy C-in-C submitted a joint report to the Central Committee of the Communist Party and the MoD in mid-1973, recommending that a nuclear-powered multi-rôle carrier displacing 80,000 tons be proceeded with. Besides missiles, the carrier was to be equipped with P-42 ASW aircraft and T10-K fighters. The latter was the manufacturer's designation of the future navalized Su-27K 'Flanker-D', the K denoting *korabel'nyy* (shipboard). However, a go-ahead at the highest level was needed to build the three carriers envisaged by the programme, and the Soviet leaders had said no.

As the next-best solution, Marshal Ustinov (then Defence Secretary[3] with the CC of the Communist Party) proposed modifying Project 1123 carriers. Rather than upgrading the two existing Project 1123 ships, SNS *Moskva* and SNS *Leningrad*, a third ship would be built with increased displacement and a carrier Wing comprising V/STOL fighters and helicopters. The next two carriers would be even more extensively modified, featuring steam catapults for launching MiG-23K fighters

[3] *Not* in the meaning attached to this phrase in the US. Ustinov was not yet Minister of Defence then but, speaking in US terms, chairman of a standing committee handling defence matters.

SNS Tbilisi, the Soviet Navy's first CTOL carrier, seen from astern. (Yefim Gordon archive)

and Su-25K attack aircraft.[4] This project was designated, somewhat enigmatically, large cruiser with aircraft armament, and the Ministry of Shipbuilding began finalising it with a view to commissioning two nuclear-powered carriers by 1985.

Since CTOL carriers were absolutely new to the Soviet Navy, the deck catapult, arrester wire installation and emergency barrier, optical and electronic landing aids and other things peculiar to carrier operation had to be perfected and mastered. To this end a special Research, Development and Training Complex (RDTC) was to be constructed at Novofyodorovka airbase near Saki. However, building the large cruisers called for an upgrade of the existing shipyards; Gosplan (the Soviet Union's economic planning and budget management organization) did not authorise extra funds for this, and the large cruisers were abandoned in favour of Project 1143 carriers. These would carry V/STOL aircraft, but the fifth

Project 1143 carrier would be suitably modified for operating CTOL aircraft.

As the Soviet aircraft carrier programme got under way the aircraft designers were immediately faced with the task of selecting the best takeoff mode; they had to choose between a deck catapult and a ski jump. The catapult launch technique is certainly more common. The aircraft is hooked up to the catapult shoe, and as the catapult fires it accelerates to some 300 km/h (166 kts) as it clears the flight deck. Then it dips below deck level, pitching up to normal takeoff angle of attack, and begins climbing normally.

The high launch speed is required because the aircraft's AOA on deck is close to zero and the launch trajectory is almost horizontal. Since the catapult track is only about 90 m (295 ft) long, the acceleration to 300 km/h is a violent experience; during launch the pilot is subjected to 4.5 Gs which often causes *G-loc* (G-induced loss of consciousness), impairing his ability to fly the aircraft.

Another peculiarity of catapult-launched aircraft is the necessity to increase the AOA (and thus lift) after

---

[4] This designation was subsequently reused for the export version of the single-seat 'Frogfoot-A'. In the *real* Su-25K the suffix means *kommehrcheskiy* (commercial, i.e., downgraded customer version), not *korabel'nyy*.

disengagement from the catapult shoe in order to permit takeoff with a full fuel and ordnance load. Therefore, catapult-launched aircraft are fitted with a so-called jump strut – a nose gear unit with an extra-extensible oleo which is extended forcibly to its full length. However, this requires the strut and forward fuselage to be reinforced, incurring a weight penalty and impairing performance.

Conversely, on a carrier equipped with a ski jump the aircraft is restrained by pop-up detents, allowing it to go to full afterburner before the detents are retracted. After leaving the ski jump the aircraft has a positive AOA and pitch angular speed; these increase as the aircraft accelerates, assisting climb. Thus, the pilot stays in control at all times, which enhances flight safety. The ski jump technique obviates the need for additional reinforcement of the nose gear and forward fuselage to absorb the extra loads generated by the catapult, saving weight and improving performance. On the other hand,

the speed at which the aircraft clears the ski jump (120–140 km/h or 66–77 kts) is approximately half of that during catapult launch, which means especially stringent requirements apply to the aircraft's stability and handling.

After carefully studying the catapult launch and ski jump options and analysing operational experience with shipboard fighters abroad, the Sukhoi and Mikoyan bureaux proposed that the future carrier should be equipped with a ski jump. This opinion was supported by LII, TsAGI, GosNIIAS and TsNII-30. In mid-1981 Marshal Ustinov, by then appointed Defence Minister, approved the proposal put forth by the Ministry of Aircraft Industry (MAP) and the VVS. This concerned ski jump takeoff research with the MiG-29 and Su-27 fourth-generation fighters, which implied the new carrier would be equipped with a ski jump. However, the carrier Wing was to consist mainly of Yak-41 (Yak-141) 'Freestyle' supersonic V/STOL fighters, the MiG-29 and Su-27 being

Another view of SNS Tbilisi from the ski jump. (Yefim Gordon archive)

regarded as a second choice in case the Yak-41 programme failed. Beriyev P-42 ASW aircraft and Antonov An-71 'Madcap' airborne early warning (AEW) aircraft [5] could also be included in the carrier Wing.

By mid-1982 the RDTC at Novofyodorovka AB in Saki was fully operational. The pompous and tongue-twisting official appellation NIUTK (*Naoochno-issledovatel'skiy i oochebno-trenirovochnyy kompleks* – RDTC) soon gave way to the easily pronounceable nickname Nitka (Thread) which soon found its way into official documents as well. The complex comprised the T-1 ski jump, a rather provisional deck catapult and the BS-P-1 arrester complex with two arrester systems (one with a cable, the other with a chain). The catapult, arrester hook, Svetlana-2 (S-2) [6] arrester wire installation and S-23N emergency barrier could be tested simultaneously; Ministry of Shipbuilding representatives tested all of this thoroughly before flight tests commenced. A weighted trolley fitted with an arrester hook was fired by the catapult, engaging the arrester wire immediately afterwards. If the arrester wire *and* the barrier failed, there was the chain arrester as a last resort.

Carrier compatibility trials began next. Since the navalized 'Flanker' and 'Fulcrum' prototypes were not yet available, LII experimentally fitted a MiG-27 'Flogger-D' ground-attack aircraft (03 Blue) with an arrester hook (the folding ventral fin had to be removed). This testbed flown by LII test pilots A. V. Krootov and S. N. Tresvyatskiy was used to study the influence of the aircraft's weight and speed on arrester wire engagement (both normal and offset) and the effect of G loads on the pilot's system. Practical work to adapt fourth-generation fighters to CTOL carriers began on 21 August 1982 when the MiG-29KVP research aircraft (18 Blue) made the first takeoff from the provisional T-1 ski jump at the hands of Mikoyan test pilot Aviard G. Fastovets.

Starting in 1983, the carrier (Project 1143.5) and the aircraft that were to operate from it were developed almost in parallel, the two ministries responsible for the programme (the Ministry of Shipbuilding and MAP) working in close cooperation. Yakovlev, Sukhoi and Mikoyan were all busy with naval fighter projects. It should be noted that initial studies of carrier-based versions of the MiG-29 and T-10 dated back to 1973.

Originally it was intended that the MiG-29K, as the naval version was designated, would fill the counter-air rôle for the carrier group, and it was with this fighter in mind that the carrier was designed.

Meanwhile, stage 1 of the trials at the Nitka RDTC necessitated a drastic redesign of the ski jump. The new T-2 ski jump completed in 1984 was 5.6 m (18 ft 4.47 in.) high, 53.5 m (175 ft 6.3 in.) long and 17.5 m (57 ft 5 in.) wide; it had a 14.3° incline and was an exact copy of the future carrier's bows. Sukhoi test pilot Nikolay F. Sadovnikov made the first takeoff from the restyled ski jump on 25 September 1984 with the T10-25 (25 Blue), an early-production 'Flanker-B' fitted with an arrester hook under the Su-27K programme. Mikoyan joined in with the MiG-29KVP on 1 October and the trials continued until 25 October.

Trials conducted in 1982-84 showed that building a CTOL carrier-borne fighter using a ski jump for takeoff and an arrester wire system for landing was indeed feasible. Hence the Central Committee of the Communist Party and the Council of Ministers issued a directive in 1984, ordering the Sukhoi and Mikoyan bureaux to develop such aircraft. Sukhoi were to design the T10-K (Su-27K) heavy fighter while Mikoyan were to work on the lighter multi-rôle MiG-29K, an air defence fighter with a secondary anti-shipping strike and ground-attack capability.

The carrier Wing of the Soviet Union's first CTOL carrier would be structured in a similar fashion to US Navy carriers which had Grumman F-14A Tomcat heavy fighters and lighter F/A-18 fighter/attack aircraft. The composition was finalised in 1978; the Project 1143.5 carrier would be armed with 18 Su-27Ks, 28 MiG-29Ks and 14 Ka-252 helicopters – eight Ka-252PL ASW choppers, two Ka-252PS SAR choppers and four Ka-252RLD AEW/OTH targeting helicopters. (Ka-252 was the manufacturer's designation of the Ka-27, reflecting its 'Hormone' heritage – i.e., Ka-25 Mk 2. In production form the helicopters were designated Ka-27PL 'Helix-A', Ka-27PS 'Helix-C' and Ka-31; RLD means *rahdiolokatseeonnyy dozor* – radar picket.)

The carrier's fixed-wing element was now tasked solely with the counter-air rôle and thus was not intended to carry air-to-surface weapons. The Su-25K attack aircraft and the P-42 ASW aircraft were abandoned. No bets were as yet placed on the Yak-41 because of the major engineering challenges associated with designing a supersonic V/STOL aircraft, but if everything worked the fighter could complement the Su-27K and MiG-29K

---

[5] A much-modified An-72 'Coaler' twin-turbofan tactical transport; two prototypes built to date.

[6] The most improbable code names were sometimes used for military hardware. Svetlana is a Russian woman's name.

aboard Project 1143.5 carriers, besides supplanting the Yak-38 on the Soviet Navy's three operational VTOL carriers – SNS *Kiev*, SNS *Minsk* and SNS *Novorossiysk*.

Full-scale development of the navalised 'Fulcrum' began in 1984. Actually two upgraded versions of the MiG-29 were being developed in parallel under General Designer Belyakov and Chief Project Engineer Val'denberg – the MiG-29M (*izdeliye* 9.15) for the VVS and the MiG-29K (*izdeliye* 9.31) for the AV-MF. The MiG-29K was to provide air defence for the carrier group day and night in any kind of weather at altitudes between 30 and 27,000 m (98–88,582 ft). Apart from air defence, it was to act as a hunter, destroying enemy ASW, transport and AWACS aircraft, make anti-shipping strikes, support marine landings, escort land-based aircraft, set up minefields (in short, kill everything in sight) and perform reconnaissance tasks.[7]

The MiG-29K was based on its land-based counterpart, the MiG-29M, and the airframe was likewise largely welded of Al-Li alloy. However, the MiG-29K was tailored to carrier operations and thus differed considerably from the MiG-29M. Special attention was given to corrosion protection to enable operation in the salty ocean air. More stringent requirements applied to structural materials, coatings, seals and gaskets. The fuselage (primarily the main fuel tank) was beefed up considerably to absorb the augmented loads during no-flare landings and arrester wire braking.

The aircraft was powered by RD-33K engines rated at 5,500 kgp (12,125 lb st) dry and 8,800 kgp (19,400 lb st) reheat, with duplex FADEC and automatic fuel flow management systems. Unlike the MiG-29M, however, the engines had a 9,400-kgp (20,723 lb st) takeoff contingency rating. The latter guaranteed the aircraft could take off from either of the two forward takeoff stations (105 m/344 ft from the bows) with a 17,700-kg (39,021-lb) TOW and from takeoff station 3 (195 m/640 ft from the bows) with a maximum 22,400-kg (49,382-lb) TOW. The added thrust enabled a safe go-around if the aircraft missed the arrester wires. The air intakes were borrowed straight from the MiG-29M, featuring FOD protection grids, auxiliary intakes in the mainwheel wells and movable lower lips.

To reduce approach speed, wingspan was increased to 12.0 m (39 ft 4.44 in.) and wing area to 43 m² (462.36 sq.

ft). The wings featured a modified TsAGI P-177M aerofoil instead of the basic P-177, double-slotted flaps inboard and flaperons outboard. The dorsal fin extensions housing the chaff/flare dispensers were deleted and the dispensers incorporated in the aft fuselage. As on the MiG-29M, stabilator chord was increased to improve pitch control at low speed, resulting in a characteristic dogtooth.

The outer wings folded hydraulically to a vertical position for hangar stowage, reducing span to 7.8 m (25 ft 7 in.). For better fatigue resistance the wings were of welded steel construction. The radome could also be folded upwards to decrease overall length from 17.27 m (56 ft 7.92 in.) to 15.1 m (49 ft 6.48 in.).

The landing gear struts were lengthened, featuring heavy-duty, increased-stroke, shock absorbers and tiedown shackles. Special links shortened the struts during retraction to make sure they would fit into standard wheel wells. The nose gear unit incorporated a modified steering mechanism allowing the nosewheels to turn through ±90° for deck handling. It also mounted approach lights resembling miniature traffic lights to inform the landing signals officer (LSO) of the aircraft's position and speed on final approach. All wheels were fitted with new higher-pressure (285 psi) tyres. The brake parachute was deleted; a quick-release flight data recorder (FDR) and the arrester hook attachment and rebound damper were installed where the brake chute canister had been. Like the MiG-29M, the naval version had a one-piece dorsal airbrake which was used to reduce approach speed.

Deletion of the dorsal auxiliary intakes made room for additional fuel in the LERXes, increasing the internal fuel capacity to 5,720 lit. (1,258.4 Imp. gal.) or 4,460 kg (9,832 lb) of usable fuel. The MiG-29K had single-point refuelling for both internal tanks and three drop tanks (1,520 lit./334.4 Imp. gal. on the centreline and 1,150 lit./253 Imp. gal. on the inner wing stations). The total fuel load with three drop tanks exceeded 6,500 kg (14,329 lb). A fuel jettison system was provided to lighten the aircraft to the 15,300-kg (33,730-lb) maximum landing weight in the event of an emergency landing. To further increase range the MiG-29K was fitted with a fully retractable L-shaped refuelling probe offset to port ahead of the windscreen; this allowed the fighter to receive fuel from any aircraft equipped with an UPAZ-1A podded hose drum unit (HDU).[8] For night refuelling the probe was

---

[7] The apparent contradiction as to the aircraft's rôle is explained by the constantly changing requirements. Dozens of directives appeared while the development programme was in progress, and each one contained new requirements!

[8] UPAZ = *oonifitseerovannyy podvesnoy agregaht zapravki* – standardized suspended (i.e., external) refuelling unit like, e.g., those of the VC-10 K. Mk 1/Mk 2. The standardized part of the name means it is fitted to Il-78/78M tankers but can also be used by fighters as a buddy refuelling pack.

illuminated by a special retractable light. The arrester hook was also illuminated during night landings. The MiG-29M's WCS was almost identical to that of the MiG-29M, comprising an RLPK-29UM radar targeting system and an OEPrNK-29M targeting/navigation complex. The N-010 Zhuk radar as fitted to the naval 'Fulcrum' incorporated modifications for better target definition over water.

The SUV-29K WCS enabled the MiG-29K to seek, detect, identify and destroy single and group targets above and below its own flight level, day and night, in any kind of weather and in an ECM environment. The dual targeting systems allowed it to attack covertly (without revealing itself by switching on the radar) and to use several kinds of weapons in a single pass. The radar could track ten targets while guiding missiles to four of them designated as priority threats. Close formations of enemy aircraft could also be attacked. An important feature of the WCS was automatic evasive action so as to avoid being hit by debris or fragments of the aircraft's own missiles.

The cockpit data presentation and weapons selection systems received a major upgrade. A single multi-function missile control panel allowed additional air-to-surface missile types to be integrated. The SOI-29K data presentation system (*sistema otobrazheniya informahtsii*) included a HUD and two CRTs on the instrument panel. The cockpit of the naval version was virtually identical to that of the MiG-29M, differing largely in navigation equipment. The MiG-29K was equipped with an SN-K Oozel (Knot) navigation suite for overwater flights and carrier approach. It included an INS-84 new-generation inertial navigation system, satellite navigation equipment, a Resistor SHORAN/ILS, an air data system and a digital processor. The SN-K navigation suite worked in concert with the carrier's VOR/localizer and glideslope beacons; it featured a jam-proof secure data link and automatic built-in test equipment (BITE). It was more accurate and had a higher navigation data feed rate than systems used hitherto.

Like the MiG-29M, the naval 'Fulcrum' was to have an ESM suite comprising a signals intelligence (SIGINT) pack, a Mak-F (Poppy) IR seeker to warn against missile attacks, a Gardeniya-1FU jammer and two BVP-60-26 chaff/flare dispensers. Like its land-based equivalent, the MiG-29K featured ECM aerials at the wingtips; however, the wingtips were characteristically bulged to accommodate the ECM gear, probably because the longer-span wings were thinner at the tips.

The MiG-29K had eight underwing weapons pylons and a centreline pylon. The ordnance load was increased to 4,500 kg (9,920 lb) and included eight combinations of AAMs and no less than 25 air-to-surface weapons options. Air-to-air weapons included up to four R-27R (R-27RE) or R-27T (R-27TE) medium-range IR-homing/SARH missiles, up to eight R-73 short-range missiles and up to eight R-77 (RVV-AE) medium-range active radar homing AAMs. Typical external stores in counter-air mode were four R-27s (or two R-27s plus drop tanks) and four R-73s. In strike mode the aircraft could carry up to six Kh-25ML or Kh-29L (Kh-29T) AGMs, up to four Kh-31A or Kh-35 ASMs, up to four Kh-31P or six Kh-25MP ARMs, up to four KAB-500KR TV-guided bombs. Unguided weapons included up to nine 500-kg (1,102-lb) or up to sixteen 250-kg (551-lb) dumb bombs, KMGU submunitions pods, two S-25 heavy rockets, four B-13L rocket pods with 20 S-13 FFARs or four B-8M1 rocket pods with 80 S-8 FFARs. Like the MiG-29M, the naval fighter had the GSh-301 gun with 100 rounds. Specified combat radius was 850 km (472 nm) on internal fuel, increasing to 1,050 km (583 nm) with one drop tank and 1,300 km (722 nm) with three drop tanks. On-station time during combat air patrol (CAP) missions within 250 km (138 nm) from the carrier was 1.6–2.3 hrs.

The naval fighter shared the MiG-29M's combined digital/analog FBW control system with multiple electronic backup in all three control channels and mechanical backup in the yaw and roll channels. The crew escape system had a feature unique to the naval version: the ejection seat trajectory was inclined 30° sideways so that the seat would go overboard instead of falling on the deck and give the pilot a few extra dozen feet of altitude. Naturally, the structural changes added to the aircraft's empty weight. In normal takeoff configuration with four missiles and internal fuel only the MiG-29K weighed 15,570 kg (34,325 lb); MTOW with four missiles and three drop tanks was 18,210 kg (40,145 lb).

The design effort led by Mikhail Val'denberg took four years to accomplish. In early 1988 the OKB's experimental shop and the Znamya truda factory began jointly manufacturing two prototypes. The first prototype (c/n 2016188?)[9] completed its ground systems tests by early June. Coded 311 Blue (i.e., *izdeliye* 9.31 No. 1), the aircraft took off for the first time on 23 June with Toktar O.

9 This number is stencilled on some airframe parts but obviously does not fit the 'Fulcrum's' construction number pattern.

311 Blue, the first prototype MiG-29K shipboard fighter. (Mikoyan OKB archive)

Aubakirov at the controls; he was to remain project test pilot throughout the trials programme which ended in 1991.

The first prototype did not utilise the specially developed navalised manufacturing technologies and was not fitted with a weapons control system. The aircraft was painted in standard two-tone grey camouflage and sported T-shaped black and white phototheodolite calibration markings on the nose and tail. A small Soviet Navy flag was painted on the port air intake next to the tactical code, with the Mikoyan OKB logo symmetrically on the starboard intake.

After making a few test flights at Zhukovskiy to evaluate its performance and handling 311 Blue was ferried to Novofyodorovka AB. There the aircraft was used for extensive trials on the 'unsinkable carrier' along with the MiG-29KVP testbed. By then the Nitka RDTC had been equipped with a representative S-2 arrester wire system and a Luna-3 (Moon, pronounced loonah) visual approach system. The results of these test flights confirmed the fighter's performance (especially field performance) and paved the way to actual carrier compatibility trials. Trials at Novofyodorovka included taxying (deck manoeuvrability) trials, verification of the aircraft's acceleration on takeoff and engine operation at the takeoff contingency rating. The

reliability of the pop-up detents restraining the aircraft until the engines went to full power was also tested. Special attention was paid to the no-flare landing technique demanding great accuracy; the glideslope angle during such landings was 3.5–4°. Mikoyan engineers calibrated the Luna-3 visual approach system so that the aircraft touched down in the required landing area, a 12-m (39-ft) circle painted on the deck, with a sink rate variance of no more than 0.5 m/sec (1.6 ft/sec).

A special naval simulator designed by TsAGI engineers Zakharov and Tkachenko came in extremely handy during the trials programme. After practising on this simulator, Mikoyan test pilots became proficient enough to maintain constant speed on final approach and catch the wire successfully even without engaging the autothrottle.

Construction of the carrier at the Black Sea Shipyard in Nikolayev (Ukraine), proceeded in parallel. Laid down as SNS *Riga*[10] on 1 April 1982 (some April Fool's Day joke, indeed), she was rechristened ***Leonid Brezhnev*** in November the same year after the Soviet Union's late

---

[10] The Soviet Navy seemed to have a tradition of naming aircraft carriers after cities. There were two 'Moskva'-class ASW helicopter carriers (SNS *Moskva* and SNS *Leningrad*) and three 'Kiev'-class aircraft carriers (SNS *Kiev*, SNS *Minsk* and SNS *Novorossiysk*).

leader and launched on 6 December 1985. In August 1987 the unfinished carrier was rechristened again, becoming SNS *Tbilisi*, and it was under this name that she was commissioned. While the carrier was undergoing completion and outfitting, a sister ship was laid down – again as SNS *Riga*, becoming SNS *Variag* in 1990.[11] The third CTOL carrier, SNS *Ul'yanovsk* (Project 1143.7), was to feature a nuclear powerplant and steam catapults.

SNS *Tbilisi* was a classic aircraft carrier with a straight-through flight deck, an island offset to starboard and an angled landing deck equipped with a four-wire S-2N arrester system. The central part of the ship was occupied by the hangar equipped with a turntable and conveyor belts for aircraft handling. For the first time in Soviet practice the deck lifts (which were large enough for two aircraft each) were placed on the starboard edge of the deck rather than in the middle of it and the hangar doors had watertight sliding shutters. Unlike most carriers in the same class, SNS *Tbilisi* had a ski jump on which two takeoff heading lines converged.

Takeoff station No. 1 was on the starboard side ahead of the forward deck lift, with station No. 2 located symmetrically to port; the takeoff run from either position was 105–110 m (344–360 ft). Station No. 3, located on the port takeoff line 195 m (640 ft) from the bows at the intersection with the angled deck axis, was used by CTOL aircraft for high gross weight takeoffs; alternatively it could be used by the Yak-41M for short (rolling) takeoffs from the angled deck. All three stations had hydraulically-actuated jet blast shields cooled by sea water to protect other aircraft waiting their turn for takeoff; at station No. 1 the shield also protected deck handling equipment and personnel assembled in the service area near the island. The takeoff stations also featured pop-up detents for the aircraft's mainwheels, which an operator retracted by pushing a button; the three operators sat in semi-enclosed cabins buried in the flight deck near the respective stations.

A white circle near the second arrester wire marked the normal touchdown point. The four wires were set at 12 m (39 ft) intervals and normally lay flush with the deck; they were raised before touchdown and kept from sagging by sprung supports. The gyrostabilized Luna-3 visual approach system was installed on an outrigger on the port side near the midship frame; in daytime the high-intensity

approach lights were visible at about 3 km (1.6 nm) range. The LSO sat in an enclosure on the stern, instructing the pilots by radio; it was his responsibility to authorise landing or call a go-around.

Carrier compatibility trials were scheduled to begin in the autumn of 1989, even though SNS *Tbilisi* still wasn't 100% complete by then. They would show if the carrier satisfied the aircraft designers' requirements and whether the naval pilot training techniques were correct. On 21 October 1989 the carrier put to sea for the first time under a joint directive of MAP, the Ministry of Shipbuilding, the VVS and the Navy, making a voyage from Nikolayev to the Navy base at Sevastopol' for the official handover to the Navy.

Seagoing trials commenced at the end of the month. Before a landing could be risked, however, a new series of test flights at Novofyodorovka had begun on 30 August; these quickly progressed into low passes over the carrier. On 27 October at about 11 a.m. the second prototype Su-27K (T10K-2, 39 Blue) piloted by Viktor G. Pugachov put in an appearance, flying over the ship at about 1,500 m (4,921 ft). The deck hands watched as the fighter circled, gradually descending, appearing suddenly out of the mist to thunder over the flight deck.

Toktar Aubakirov appeared next in the MiG-29K prototype, much to the joy of Mikoyan representatives standing on the deck. At first he flew along the carrier's port side, judging the effect of the carrier's wake turbulence to which the lighter MiG-29K was more susceptible. During one such flypast Eduard Yelian, acting chief of Mikoyan's flight operations section, ignored orders from the bridge and rushed out to the edge of the deck to greet the pilot. Seeing his salute, Aubakirov got high spirits and made a steep turn to starboard, passing over the carrier's bows.

Flights continued next day. Pugachov passed lower and lower, even making an unscheduled touch-and-go. Aubakirov, on the other hand, was wary, not risking a touchdown but making repeated passes about 1 m (3 ft) over the deck. The flight plan for both pilots contained a rather vague phrase, practising carrier landing techniques; no one could tell if this implied making an actual landing or not, so each pilot picked the technique he considered appropriate and safe. At the same time the carrier's crew made phototheodolite measurements, calibrated the approach radar, beacons etc. Initially the flights progressed with the *Tbilisi* standing at anchor with her bows to the wind; later flights were made while the carrier moving at 10–13 kts on various headings.

Before making a real landing Mikoyan, Sukhoi and NII

---

[11] Variag is an archaic Russian word for the vikings. The name has an honourable connotation in the Russian navy; in the Russo-Japanese war of 1905 a cruiser of the same name was scuttled by her crew when capture was imminent and went down with all hands rather than face the ignominy of surrender.

Aircraft 918 making a low-level training pass over SNS Tbilisi's *deck. (Yefim Gordon archive)*

VVS pilots trained day after day, mastering the unfamiliar no-flare landing technique. It was hard to get rid of the habit of hauling back on the stick before touchdown. Each pilot was to make some 400 landings on the 'unsinkable carrier' before he was cleared for real-life carrier landings.

The flights resumed on the morning of 1 November. For safety's sake the air traffic was organized so that when one aircraft was on short finals the other was halfway through the landing pattern. Mikoyan and Sukhoi representatives, L. V. Belov (the *Tbilisi's* chief designer) and his deputy Yuriy D. Sergeyev, shipyard director Yuriy I. Makarov, Mikoyan, LII and TsAGI specialists, ship's officers and members of the State commission gathered in the ATC room. The approaching fighters were plainly visible

through the large windows, but only the ATC officer could see the actual moment of touchdown. For more than an hour and a half the fighters circled while the commission watched; finally, at 1:46 p.m. local time the T10K-2 touched down, catching the second wire, and came to a halt after a landing run of about 90 m (295 ft). The first conventional carrier landing in the Soviet Union was successfully accomplished. At 3:12 p.m. the MiG-29K followed suit, touching down somewhat more roughly; in fact, it appeared to onlookers that the aircraft dropped onto the deck like a gliding brick.

The rival Sukhoi OKB had claimed the first carrier landing. Not to be outdone, Mikoyan decided to beat them to the first takeoff which was slated for the very next day. However, the weather turned out to be worse than

TOP: *Aircraft 918 making a simulated landing approach. (Yefim Gordon archive)*

ABOVE: *The first prototype MiG-29K makes a training pass over SNS Tbilisi. (ITAR-TASS)*

TOP: *Toktar Aubakirov made several touch-and-gos before the first real deck landing. (Yefim Gordon archive)*

ABOVE: *We did it! The picture was taken immediately after the first deck landing. (Yefim Gordon archive)*

311 Blue being readied for loading into SNS Tbilisi's hangar. (Yefim Gordon archive)

expected; it was all Mikoyan reps could do, sitting there and waiting while dusk drew steadily nearer. Yelian and the carrier's ATC supervisor had an argument on whether the MiG should be authorised to take off, and tempers mounted on both sides. The ATC's verdict was no, and with good reason . The Su-25UTG trainer prototype which was in the air at the moment was running low on fuel and the ship was heading away from the shore. The trainer had to land before nightfall; landing in the dark was out of the question. Still, Yelian managed to get the go-ahead and a few minutes later got a deck handling tractor to position the MiG-29K on takeoff station No. 3 affording the longest takeoff run. Aubakirov started the engines, engaged normal afterburner, then contingency mode and took off, making straight for Saki so as to clear the area for the Su-25UTG. This hurried takeoff demanded no smaller skill than the preceding landing because the aircraft was light and tried to become airborne prematurely; the pilot had to keep it on the deck forcibly to avoid crashing into the ski jump which rose up ahead like a wall. Still, this

was the most spectacular takeoff of the trials programme.

Pictures of the first prototype aboard the carrier taken by A. Kremko, a correspondent of the TASS information agency, were circulated in November 1989, whereupon the MiG-29K received the NATO code name 'Fulcrum-D'. The first successful carrier landings and takeoffs were followed by a period of intensive test flights both on SNS *Tbilisi* and on the Nitka RDTC which lasted until 17 October 1991. Landing was possible in automatic, directed (command link) and manual mode. To this end the carrier was equipped with VOR/localizer and glideslope beacons, approach radar and the Luna-3 visual approach system. The fighter approached the carrier on a 4° glideslope, touching down without flaring out, and the arrester hook caught one of the arrester wires raised 10–15 cm (4–6 in.) above the deck, bringing the aircraft to a standstill. If the aircraft missed the wires the pilot could apply full throttle and make a go-around. An emergency barrier could be erected if a damaged aircraft was coming in or if the pilot was wounded. Touchdown speed was 230 km/h (127 kts) and the dynamic load limit during deceleration was 4.5 G.

Trials held in 1990 were concerned mainly with autolanding system testing and aircraft-to-carrier avionics compatibility tests. SNS *Tbilisi* completed her seagoing trials the same year. On 4 October she was rechristened once again, becoming SNS *Admiral Kuznetsov*.[12] In the same year Mikoyan test pilot Anatoliy N. Kvochur made the first night carrier landing and the first night takeoff from the carrier. Until then the MiG-29K had operated from the carrier strictly in 'clean' condition but, also in 1990, Kvochur made the first takeoff (in daytime) with a typical ordnance load of four missiles. One takeoff was rather unusual. Post-flight inspection revealed a fatigue crack in one of the main gear oleos, which meant the aircraft had to be removed from the carrier for repairs. However, the carrier was at sea and waiting for it to return to base would take too long, so Kvochur was authorised to take off at night with a reduced fuel load to ease the strain on the gear. The takeoff and the subsequent landing went

well and the aircraft rejoined the trials programme after the damaged unit had been replaced.

In August 1991 the MiG-29K commenced its State acceptance trials. Besides Aubakirov and Kvochur, Mikoyan test pilot Taskayev was now flying the aircraft. He soon mastered carrier operations, including takeoffs with external stores. On several occasions Taskayev took off from station No. 1 with a full load of four dummy AAMs and three drop tanks amounting to a TOW of 22 tons (48,500 lb); such high gross weight takeoffs were usually made from the far station No. 3.

The second prototype, 312 Blue, joined the flight test programme at its final stage. Unlike the first prototype, this aircraft (c/n 27579) wore a naval colour scheme with dark bluish grey upper surfaces and light grey undersurfaces; it lacked calibration markings and wore the Soviet Navy flag on the fins rather than on the intakes. On 312 Blue the refuelling probe had been completely enclosed when retracted, with a rear door segment attached to the probe and a downward-hinging forward segment; however, the latter was dispensed with on the second aircraft. 312 Blue was intended mainly for avionics testing and featured a complete WCS and weapons selection system. The aircraft

---

[12] The full official name is SNS *Admiral Flota Sovetskovo Soyuza Nikolay Kuznetsov* (Fleet Admiral Nikolay Kuznetsov).

The MiG-29K on SNS Tbilisi's *deck elevator. (Yefim Gordon archive)*

had minor external differences from the first prototype: the refuelling probe was not completely faired (and therefore plainly visible even when retracted) and the IRST 'ball' was black, not white.

Besides flying, the final stage of the carrier's State acceptance trials included aerodynamic trials of the jet blast deflectors. The deflectors were a constant source of annoyance. Not least because their water cooling system had a propensity to explode when overheated, as demonstrated by the Su-27K on two occasions. A lot of aircraft was involved in the trials: two MiG-29Ks, three Su-27K prototypes, the prototype Su-25UTG (08 Blue), a Ka-27PS (this always took off before the fixed-wing aircraft did, ready to pick up ditched pilots in the event of

A close-up of the arrester hook on Aircraft 918. (Andrey Yurgenson)

an accident), Ka-29 'Helix-B' naval assault choppers and the second prototype Ka-31 (032 Black). Curiously, the latter sported the Soviet flag and *Gidromettsentr* titles, masquerading as a civil weather research aircraft!

Sukhoi test pilots Mel'nikov and Aver'yanov and Mikoyan test pilot Taskayev did a lot of flying at this stage (Taskayev had superseded Aubakirov who had begun training for a space mission). However, the political situation in the USSR was rapidly turning into chaos. Shortages of jet fuel and fuel oil for the carrier and, more importantly, the necessity to urgently prepare the ship for transition to the Northern Fleet forced a premature termination of the trials. The flights were suspended and SNS *Admiral Kuznetsov* was firmly anchored at the Navy base in Novorossiysk.

Thus the 'Fulcrum-D' never got the chance to complete its State acceptance trials. Another reason for this was a

rather absurd accident. In the 13th flight of the State acceptance trials programme NII VVS test pilot Kandaoorov landed normally after a 1.5-hour sortie and inadvertently worked the landing gear control switch, selecting gear up. Realizing his mistake, he immediately selected gear down but too late. The retraction jacks and hydraulic lines burst and aircraft sank down on its belly, suffering serious damage. While 311 Blue was undergoing repairs the carrier departed for Novorossiysk.

The first prototype made a total of 313 flights, including 13 under the State acceptance trials programme. Between them Mikoyan and NII VVS test pilots made 74 carrier landings and a number of aerial refuellings. After the accident described above 311 Blue made another seven flights, bringing its total score to 320. The second prototype was grounded after only six flights. The uprated RD-33K engines behaved well throughout the trials programme. The State acceptance trials were suspended in early 1992.

The Sukhoi OKB had better luck with the Su-27K. This aircraft began its State acceptance trials earlier and managed to complete them successfully; in fact, the 'Flanker-D' was selected as the prime contender for the carrier-based fighter after the trials commenced. True, the Su-27K suffered from payload restrictions because of its high gross weight; besides, the MiG-29K had a broader weapons range. However, the Sukhoi fighter had longer range, high manoeuvrability, state-of-the-art avionics, ten hardpoints for assorted AAMs and, most importantly, a higher thrust-to-weight ratio. This allowed the Su-27K to emerge as the winner, entering production in 1989 and becoming the Soviet Union's first operational CTOL shipboard fighter.

As noted earlier, the MiG-29M was to supersede the 'Fulcrum-A/C' gradually on the production lines in the early '90s. Plans also included the production of 27 MiG-29Ks between 1986 and 1995. However, Mikoyan's gamble on advanced weapons systems did not pay off. Defence spending cuts and the subsequent complete termination of State support for the programme prevented the MiG-29K from reaching maturity in time.

Besides, the collapse of the Soviet Union and lack of funding has caused construction of further aircraft carriers to be put on hold indefinitely. When the Black Sea Shipyard in Nikolayev became property of the newly-independent Ukraine in early 1992, construction of the 70% complete SNS *Variag* was suspended and finally abandoned. SNS *Ul'yanovsk*, laid down in November 1988, fared even worse – starting in February 1992 the

ABOVE: *Between flights the aircraft was tied down with chains. (Yefim Gordon archive)*

BELOW: *The second prototype climbs away after clearing the ski jump. (Yefim Gordon archive)*

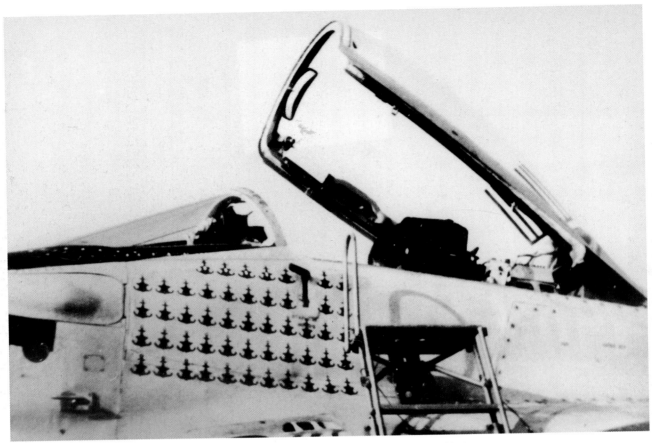

Mission markings on the fuselage of 311 Blue indicating the number of deck landings. (Yefim Gordon archive)

20% complete hull was gradually broken up. Given all this, continuing work on a second CTOL shipboard fighter was pointless: the Carrier Wing of Russia's so far only CTOL carrier, RNS (Russian Navy ship) *Admiral Kuznetsov,* could manage with the Su-27K.

Operational experience with the 'Flanker-D' and the *Admiral Kuznetsov's* first Mediterranean cruise from December 1995 to March 1996 made the Russian Navy give some serious thought to reviving the MiG-29K programme. According to Anatoliy A. Belosvet, Deputy General Director of ANPK MiG, the time elapsed since the State acceptance trials has been sufficient to eliminate the fighter's main bugs which affected its mission avionics suite; now the company hopes to refine the MiG-29K to production standard.

The MiG-29K had its airshow début on 13 February 1992 when the second prototype was demonstrated to top-ranking military officials and the leaders of the CIS States at Machoolischchi AB with two red star mission markers

below the cockpit denoting arrester wire engagements. On 11–16 August the same year 312 Blue was demonstrated to the general public for the first time at MosAeroShow '92 in Zhukovskiy. The same aircraft was present again in the static park at the MAKS-93 and MAKS-95 airshows, displaying the newly-readopted St. Andrew's flag (Russian Navy flag) instead of the earlier Soviet Navy flag and six mission markers. In September 1996 312 Blue participated in the first hydro aviation show in Ghelendzhik on the Black Sea. Later the aircraft went to Akhtoobinsk for use in the MiG-29M's weapons system trials. Since the second prototype was unavailable for display purposes, the static park at MAKS-97 (19-24 August 1997) featured the hastily polished-up first prototype proudly displaying its 50 mission markers and carrying Kh-31A and Kh-35 anti-shipping missiles. The same aircraft was displayed with a full ordnance load alongside the MiG-29SMT mockup when the latter version was officially unveiled at LII on 29 November 1997.

ABOVE: *312 Blue was present again at MAKS-93 in Zhukovskiy, armed with two Kh-25 ASMs, two R-77s and four short-range AAMs (two R-60Ms and two R-73s).* (Yefim Gordon)

BELOW: *The MiG-29K had its public début in August 1992 when 312 Blue was in the static park at MosAeroShow '92 in Zhukovskiy.* (Yefim Gordon)

MiG-29KU shipboard trainer project (*izdeliye* 9.62)

It is no secret that training shipboard aircraft crews, especially fighter pilots, is an extremely complex affair. Pilot error on takeoff or landing almost inevitably ends in disaster. To facilitate conversion training the Mikoyan OKB developed a projected two-seater version of the 'Fulcrum-D' designated MiG-29KU (*korabel'nyy oochebnyy (samolyot)* – shipboard trainer). Curiously, the manufacturer's designation was *izdeliye* 9.62 – i.e.,

izdeliye 9.31 times two because this was a two-seater!

Experiments with the MiG-29UB quickly showed that the standard 'Fulcrum-B' was no good for training naval pilots, as visibility from the rear seat was totally inadequate for carrier landings. Therefore, unlike the MiG-29UBM project (*izdeliye* 9.61), the MiG-29KU's forward fuselage was totally redesigned, featuring separate cockpits for the trainee and instructor in a stepped-tandem arrangement *à la* MiG-25PU/RU 'Foxbat-C'. This arrangement afforded both crew members an excellent

ABOVE: *In due time the Soviet Navy flag on the fins of the second prototype gave way to St. Andrew's flag of the Russian Navy (Yefim Gordon)*

BELOW: *The second prototype with representative armament (left to right, Kh-25ML, Kh-29T and Kh-25MP). Note wing restraining braces. (Yefim Gordon)*

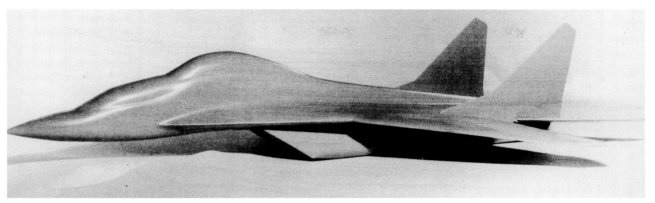

ABOVE: A model of the proposed MiG-29KU shipboard trainer. (Mikoyan OKB archive)
BELOW: The MiG-29KU forward fuselage mockup as a teaching aid at the Air Force Academy in Monino. (Aleksey Mikheyev)

(and identical) field of view at high alpha. Like the single-seat MiG-29K, the MiG-29KU would be powered by uprated RD-33K engines and feature restyled air intakes, wing folding and arrester hook.

However, the project was terminated at an early stage when the MiG-29K programme was suspended. Only a full-scale mockup of the new forward fuselage was built, and this currently survives as a teaching aid at the Yuriy A. Gagarin Air Force Academy in Monino.

MiG-29SMT (*izdeliye* 9.17K) shipboard fighter project

In late 1997 ANPK MiG proposed a navalised version of

the MiG-29SMT to Russia's Ministry of Defence. The principal differences from the existing MiG-29K were increased range on internal fuel and a revamped cockpit with an EFIS identical to that of the MiG-29SMT. By February 1998 the project was still at the preliminary development stage.

If *izdeliye* 9.17k did not find its way aboard Russian Navy carriers, Mikoyan considered offering the aircraft to the Indian Navy. Alternatively, the aircraft could be purchased by the air force (!) since the STOL capability, beefed-up landing gear and arrester hook could enable it to operate from short tactical airstrips equipped with ski jumps and arrester systems.

6

In Action

Typically of the VVS, the MiG-29 achieved initial operational capability (IOC) several months before the State commission signed the act of acceptance formally clearing the fighter for service. In July 1983 some 20 initial production aircraft were handed over with great ceremony to the 234th Proskoorovskiy GvIAP[1] (*gvardeyskiy istrebeetel'nyy aviapolk* – Guards fighter regiment = fighter Wing) at Kubinka AB near Moscow. This unit which can trace its history back to 1938 was traditionally the first to receive new types of fighters and was thus something of a showcase unit.

To complicate the situation, there were as yet no production MiG-29UB trainers and the prototype (51 Blue) was still under test at the time. Still, somebody obviously pulled strings because 51 Blue was flown to Kubinka – and promptly went unserviceable. Chief Marshal (Air Force) Pavel S. Kutakhov, who was Soviet Air Force C-in-C at the time, ordered his first deputy, Marshal A. N. Yefimov, to personally check on the progress of the 234th GvIAP's conversion to the MiG-29. The Mikoyan OKB sent Chief Project Engineer Mikhail R. Val'denberg, chief test pilot Aleksandr V. Fedotov and several other employees to Kubinka to monitor the conversion process and aid VVS pilots if necessary. The chief of the VVS' flight safety section was also there. The Mikoyan delegates didn't believe that a trainer version of the 'Fulcrum' was really necessary, claiming that a service pilot flying the MiG-21 could go straight on to the MiG-29 without any trouble.

Val'denberg began pursuing this point, urging Yefimov to authorise VVS pilots to convert to the new fighter. He was supported by Dmitriyev (Commander of the Air Force of the Moscow Defence District), Fedotov and the general responsible for flight safety. Yefimov resisted for a long time and eventually left without giving a definitive yes or no. It was up to the remaining top brass to resolve the matter now; the answer, of course, was a thumbs-up and the 234th GvIAP re-equipped with the MiG-29 without having a single trainer.

However, the MiG-29 first came to Kubinka a while earlier. Since the 234th was a showcase unit, it was often used to demonstrate new military aircraft to Soviet government and military leaders and various foreign delegations.[2] It was there that the 'Fulcrum' was demonstrated officially for the first time (to Defence Minister Marshal Ustinov) on 7 April 1981. Mikoyan test pilot Orlov gave a brief five-minute flying display to show Ustinov & Co. what the new fighter could do.

'I engaged full 'burner,' – Orlov reminisced, – 'and the nearly 16 tons (35,264 lb) of thrust pressed the aircraft's nose down. At a weight of 13 tons metric (25,652 lb) the brakes could not hold the fighter and it crawled forward, tyres squealing against the runway. I let go the brakes and the aircraft rushed forward like a dog which has burst its leash. The speed grew quickly... NOW! I pulled back on the stick and the aircraft became airborne immediately. I continued hauling back to put it into a vertical climb as I retracted the gear. Now, climbing vertically at 400 km/h (222 kts), I checked the altitude – 1,200 m (3,937 ft), made a barrel roll and put the nose down. At low altitude I checked my position and made a skewed loop, then a wingover, a turn, a three-quarters loop, putting the fighter into a vertical dive, then a half roll in the dive before pulling out. Finally, I passed over the runway, making a barrel roll over the middle of it, and broke to land.'

Along with the MiG-29 Marshal Ustinov examined other advanced combat aircraft, including an early Su-27 prototype (one of the original ogival-winged 'Flanker-As'). The latter also made a demonstration flight at the hands of Sukhoi test pilot Vladimir S. Ilyushin. The MiG-29, however, stole the show thanks to its high manoeuvrability and the pilot's skill.

The 4th Combat and Conversion Training Centre (TsBP i PLS – *tsentr boyevoy podgotovki i pereoochivaniya lyotnovo sostahva*) in Lipetsk was one of the first VVS units to receive the MiG-29. As early as the mid-80s the centre began developing operational recommendations and tactics for the type. The Lipetsk centre's pilots performed mock combat between the MiG-29 and the production Su-27 ('Flanker-B') to evaluate their respective

---

[1] The honorary Proskoorovskiy appellation was given to mark the unit's part in liberating the town of Proskoorovo during WW II. The Guards units are the elite of the Soviet (Russian) armed forces and the Guards appellation was given for gallantry in combat, thus being another indication that this is a WW II-vintage unit.

[2] Kubinka now hosts the 237th TsPAT (*tsentr pokahzov aviatseeonnoy tekhniki* – Aircraft Display Centre) named after WW II ace Ivan N. Kozhedoob.

merits and drawbacks. The pilots' opinion was that, despite the Su-27's FBW controls, pilot workload was greater than in the MiG-29. Currently No. 1 Squadron of the centre's mixed air regiment is equipped with 'Fulcrum-A/B/Cs'. By the end of 1991 MAPO's divisions at Moscow-Khodynka and in Lookhovitsy had built about 1,200 single-seat MiG-29s between them, and nearly 200 MiG-29UB trainers had been assembled in Gor'kiy. More and more VVS units re-equipped with the new fighter as production increased.

(**Note:** All data on the location, strength and numeration of VVS units given below come from published sections of the Information Exchange Protocol on Combat Aircraft and Helicopters submitted by the Soviet Union during preparation of the Conventional Forces in Europe (CFE) reduction treaty and from popular press.)

By 1991 the VVS had some 800 'Fulcrums' on strength. They were operated by 25 fighter regiments, usually with 32 fighters to a unit (though some units had as many as 48 or 54 aircraft). Nearly 800 MiG-29s were permanently deployed abroad (in East Germany, Hungary and Czechoslovakia); the reason for this was the fighter's ability to deliver tactical nuclear weapons. The biggest 'Fulcrum' contingent was stationed in East Germany with the Western Group of Forces (ZGV – *Zahpadnaya grooppa voysk*).[3] This included eight fighter regiments equipped with MiG-29s, united into three fighter divisions which in turn were part of the 16th VA with headquarters at Wünsdorf (*vozdooshnaya armiya* – air army = air force).

The first MiG-29s came to East Germany in 1986,

replacing MiG-23M 'Flogger-Bs' with the 33rd IAP based at Wittstock. This was actually the fourth VVS unit to fly the 'Fulcrum', following the units at Kubinka, Ros' and Tskhakaya. The 733rd IAP at Pütnitz (Damgarten),[4] a previous MiG-23MLD 'Flogger-K' operator, followed in 1987. In late 1987 and early 1988 another MiG-23M unit, the 35th IAP at Zerbst, converted to the MiG-29. Re-equipment was slow and MiG-29UB trainers were scarce at first, forcing ZGV fighter units to retain their original MiG-23UB 'Flogger-C' trainers. The first MiG-29s deployed to East Germany were 'Fulcrum-As', including some very early-production aircraft with ventral fins; these were later supplemented with 'fatback' 'Fulcrum-Cs'. By the late '80s the ZGV operated a mix of early and late MiG-29s and some MiG-23s. Re-equipment proceeded apace; the 85th GvIAP at Merseburg and the 73rd GvIAP at Köthen said goodbye to their MiG-23Ms and 'MLDs respectively in 1988. Next year the MiG-29 became operational with three more units – the 968th IAP at Altenburg (Nöbitz), the 31st GvIAP at Alt Lönnewitz (Falkenberg)[5] and the 787th IAP at Eberswalde (Finow).

By 1990 nearly 250 MiG-29s were stationed in East Germany, apart from MiG-29UBs and the East German Air Force's own 'Fulcrums'. Details of the ZGV's MiG-29 fleet are given in **Table A** below; MiG-23UBs used as a stand-in for the MiG-29UB are also listed for the sake of

---

[3] Also called GSVG (*Groppa sovetskikh voysk v Ghermahnii* – Group of Soviet Forces in Germany)

[4] NATO and the VVS often used different names for the same East German airbases. In such cases the NATO name comes first with the Soviet name following in parentheses.

[5] There have been variations in the spelling of two East German airbases: Falkenberg and Falkenburg, Sperenberg and Sperenburg. The former version is probably correct in both cases.

TABLE A

Unit	Base	Type	Known tactical codes
6th GvIAD/ **31st GvIAP**	Alt Lönnewitz (Falkenberg)	MiG-23UB	60 Red, 61 Blue, 63 Red, 64 Red
		MiG-29 'Fulcrum-A' (all codes red)	01, 12, 21, 22, 23, 35
		MiG-29 'Fulcrum-C' (all codes red)	02, 03, 04, 06, 07, 08, 10, 11, 20, 24, 25, 27, 28, 29, 30, 31, 32, 33, 34, 35, 36, 37, 38, 40, 45, 46; 54?
		MiG-29UB	60 Red, 61 Blue, 63 Red, 64 Red

continued

Unit	Base	Type	Known tactical codes
6th GvIAD/ **85th GvIAP**	Merseburg	MiG-23UB	71 Blue
		MiG-29 'Fulcrum-A' (all codes blue)	01, 02, 03, 04, 06, 07, 08, 10, 14, 22, 23, 24, 25, 26, 27, 29, 30, 32, 33, 34
		MiG-29 'Fulcrum-C'	31 Blue, 38 Blue, 39 Blue, 40 Blue
		MiG-29UB	71 Blue, 76 Blue
6th GvIAD/ **968th IAP**	Nöbitz (Altenburg)	MiG-23UB	91 Red, 96 Orange, 97 Yellow
		MiG-29 'Fulcrum-A' (all codes yellow)	*07, 15, 16, 34, 41, 42, 43, 46, 49, 50, 52, 57, 58, 59*
		MiG-29 'Fulcrum-C' (all codes red)	01, 03, 05, 06, 09, 21, 22, 25, 26, 35, 36, 38, 39
		MiG-29UB	64 Yellow, 65 Yellow
16th GvIAD/ **33rd IAP**	Wittstock	MiG-23UB (all codes low-viz)	66 White, 68 White, 69 White
		MiG-29 'Fulcrum-A'	01 White, 02 White, 03 White, 05 White, 06 White, 07 White, 08 White, 09 White, 10 White, 11 White, 12 White, 20 White, 21 Blue, 22 White, 23 White, 24 Blue, 26 Blue, 27 Blue, 28 Blue, 29 White, 30 White, 31 White, 33 White, 34 White, 36 White, 37 White
		MiG-29 'Fulcrum-C'	38 White, 39 White
		MiG-29UB	55 White, 64 White outline, 71 White, 72 White, 91 Red
16th GvIAD/ **733rd IAP**	Pütnitz (Damgarten)	MiG-23UB	50 Yellow, 60 White, 90 White, 96 Blue
		MiG-29 'Fulcrum-A' (all codes white)	20, 21, 22, *23, 24, 25, 26,* 32, 34
		MiG-29 'Fulcrum-C' (all codes white)	01, 02, 04, 05, 06, 07, 08, 09, 10, 11, 12, 41, 42, 44, 45, 49, 51, 52, 53, 54
		MiG-29UB	66 Blue, 74 White, 80 White
16th GvIAD/ **787th IAP**	Eberswalde (Finow)	MiG-23UB	20 Red, 22 Red, 52 Red, 62 Blue, 65 Red
		MiG-29 'Fulcrum-C' (all codes white)	01, 02, 03, 04, 05, 06, 07, 08, 09, 10, 68, 69, 70, 71, 73, 74, 75, 76, 77, 78, 79, 80, 82, 83, 84, 85, 87, 89
		MiG-29UB	11 White, 33 White, 72 White
126th GvIAD/ **35th IAP**	Zerbst	MiG-23UB (all codes red)	64, 90, 91, 92, 93, 94, 96, 97
		MiG-29 'Fulcrum-A' (all codes red)	*09, 10, 11, 12, 20, 21, 22, 23, 24, 26, 27, 28, 29*
		MiG-29 'Fulcrum-C' (all codes blue??)	01, 02, 03, 04, 05, 06, 07, 08, 34, 40, 41, 42, 43, 44, 45, 46, 47, 49
		MiG-29UB	60 Red, 70 Red, 91 Red ***continued***

Unit	Base	Type	Known tactical codes
126th GvIAD/ **73rd GvIAP**	Köthen	MiG-23UB	89 Blue, 90 Blue, 93 Red
		MiG-29 'Fulcrum-A' (all codes red)	21, 22, 23, 24, 28, 29, 30, 43, 44, 45, 46, 47, 48, 54
		MiG-29 'Fulcrum-C' (all codes red)	01, 02, 03, 04, 05, 06, 07, 08, 09, 10, 11, 12, 13, 14, 20, 40, 41, 42
		MiG-29UB	70 Red, 91 Red

Notes:
- 'Fulcrum-A' tactical codes given ***in bold italics*** indicate early-production aircraft with ventral fins.
- The 31st GvIAP bore the honorary appellation *Nikopol'skiy* for its part in the liberation of the Ukrainian city of Nikopol' during WW II.
- The 73rd GvIAP bore the honorary appellation *Sevastopol'skiy* for its part in the liberation of Sevastopol', a major Black Sea port and Soviet Navy base, during WW II.
- The 16th GvIAD (***gvardeyskaya istrebeetel'naya aviadiveeziya*** – Guards fighter division) bore the honorary appellation *Sveerskaya* for its part in the liberation of the town of Sveer' during WW II and was decorated with the Order of the Red Banner of Combat.

completeness.

Most aircraft wore standard two-tone grey camouflage. Some, however, had non-standard paint schemes. E.g., two 733rd IAP single-seaters – 'Fulcrum-A' 21 White and 'Fulcrum-C' 44 White – wore the Soviet equivalent to the USAF's Vietnam War-era wraparound SEA scheme, being painted olive drab and grey-green overall, i.e., without the usual light grey undersurfaces. This wraparound ZGV scheme was probably associated with the squadron's ground-attack rôle. One 73rd GvIAP aircraft was said to have a desert camouflage scheme.

Many early 'Fulcrum-As' had a very weathered finish which the technical staff refreshed on site, painting up battered areas without worrying about an exact colour match. The result could be rather messy, giving the aircraft a patchwork appearance. Moreover, since the tactical codes of VVS aircraft are usually simply the aircraft's number in the regiment (as noted earlier), they are changed when an aircraft is transferred to another unit. Many ZGV MiG-29s showed obvious signs of such re-coding: the old code on the air intakes was overpainted (often with whatever colour was within reach) and the new code applied over the resulting blotch. The old code, however, remained on the fins.

In keeping with a WW II tradition, most 31st, 73rd and 85th GvIAP MiG-29s wore the Guards badge on the port side of the nose or on the port intake (the former was more common). Moreover, many aircraft stationed in East Germany sported colourful unit badges – which was

rather uncommon and not encouraged in the VVS (the proximity of the West was probably beginning to rub off!), and the MiG-29s were no exception. E.g., the fins of some 33rd IAP 'Fulcrums' featured white circles edged with blue and red (an obvious allusion to pre-1917 Russian AF roundels) with a red bison, a red wing and a blue MiG-29 silhouette on white. Many 968th IAP aircraft had a red star with blue trim and wing on the port side of the nose; a similar badge had been worn by 3rd Independent Air Corps fighters during WW II.

The MiG-29 was also stationed in other Warsaw Pact states, though in much smaller numbers. A single regiment with 34 'Fulcrums' (part of the 36th VA based in Budapest) operated from Kiskunlaháza, Sarmellek and Tokól airbases in Hungary. The 131st SAD (*smeshannaya aviadiveeziya* – mixed air division) included a fighter regiment operating ten MiG-29s and 26 MiG-23s from Milovice AB in Czechoslovakia. Back at home, ten MiG-29 regiments totalling some 350 aircraft were based in the European part of the Soviet Union. Two thirds of these units were stationed outside Russia. The Ukraine had three units – in Mukachovo, Ivano-Frankovsk (both reporting to the 14th VA in L'vov) and at Martynovka AB. The latter unit, part of the 5th VA (Odessa), operated a mixed bag of 'Fulcrum-Cs', MiG-29UBs and MiG-23UBs and was the only 'Fulcrum' unit to be transferred to the Soviet Air Force's fighter-bomber arm.

This naturally brought about a change in priorities

(training was centred on strike missions). Unlike other units flying the type, the main armament consisted of large-calibre bombs (FAB-500ShN etc.), S-24 heavy unguided rockets and S-8 FFARs rather that air-to-air missiles. Versions armed with guided air-to-surface weapons did not exist at the time, and the MiG-29's efficiency in the strike rôle was far lower than that of the older MiG-27 and Su-17 which were dedicated fighter-bombers (especially the latest MiG-27K 'Flogger-J2' and Su-17M4 'Fitter-K'). In 1990 the Martynovka unit briefly deployed to Tiraspol' in Moldavia but returned home just in time to avoid being embroiled in a civil war when the republic's Transdniestrian region declared independence.

In Belorussia a fighter unit with 51 aircraft (part of the 26th VA in Minsk) operated from Beryoza AB. Another unit with 35 'Fulcrums' (the 176th IAP, part of the 34th VA in Tbilisi) was based at Tskhakaya AB in the Georgian Soviet Socialist Republic. This unit's name has come to be connected with a very unfortunate and widely publicised incident when one of its pilots defected to Turkey on 20 May 1989. Capt. Aleksandr M. Zooyev was a first-class fighter pilot but a thoroughly rotten person; he was known as a pocket Napoleon, extremely vain and egotistical. At one time he was a candidate for the VVS' Test Pilots School but this did not materialise. Moreover, Zooyev had been suspended from active duty some time before the incident because of poor discipline; indeed, his track record was so poor that his superiors were considering a dishonourable discharge. Obviously resentment at this, coupled with his personality, led him to commit treason. After sedating the pilots and ground crew of the quick reaction alert flight and cutting the telephone cables to prevent anyone from raising the alarm he shot and seriously wounded a sentry on the parking ramp who tried to stop him. Then he took off in one of the QRA MiG-29s despite also being wounded in the shootout. Subsequent analysis of flight data recorder readouts showed that Zooyev had twice attempted to strafe the airfield before making for the border but a safety feature of the internal gun foiled his plan.

The Turkish border was a mere ten minutes' flight from Tskhakaya AB. Another 176th IAP MiG-29 scrambled to intercept the defector seven minutes later but could not get within firing range before the target entered Turkish airspace. Two fighters from a neighbouring base took even longer (12 minutes) to get airborne. Surface-to-air missile sites in the area were alerted but failed to detect the target because Zooyev was flying at ultra-low level to avoid radar detection. Thus Zooyev was able to cross the border

unscathed, landing at the civil airport in Trabzon. The stolen fighter was returned the very next day pursuant to an agreement between the Soviet Union and Turkey. The defector's fate is unknown; despite insistent demands from the Soviet government, Zooyev was not extradited by whatever country he ended up in.

131 'Fulcrums' were based in the European part of the Russian Federation in 1990; most of them, however, were operated by training units and the Air Force's R&D establishments. Of these, the Lipetsk Conversion Training Centre's 968th IIIAP (*instrooktorskiy issledovatel'skiy istrebeetel'nyy aviapolk* – instructional and research fighter regiment) and IIAPIB (*instrooktorskiy issledovatel'skiy aviapolk istrebeeteley-bombardirovschchikov* – instructional and research fighter-bomber regiment) had 37 aircraft between them.[6]

No less than 79 MiG-29s belonged to two instructional fighter regiments of the 1080th Flight Conversion Training Centre (UATs PLS – *oochebnyy aviatseonnyy tsentr pereoochivaniya lyotnovo sostahva*) in Borisoglebsk. Finally, fifteen 'Fulcrums' were operated by the 234th SAP (*smeshannyy istrebeetel'nyy aviapolk* – mixed fighter regiment) at Kubinka AB. The above units were part of the Moscow Defence District in the late '80s. Another MiG-29 unit with 40 aircraft operated from Orlovka AB in the Far East, reporting to the 1st VA (Khabarovsk). Some 'Fulcrums' were stationed in the Central Asian republics of the Soviet Union, including 22 aircraft in Turkmenia (Maryy AB),[7] 30 in Uzbekistan and an unknown number in Kirghizia where Loogovaya AB near the capital, Frunze, served as a training centre for foreign MiG-29 pilots and ground crews.

Sqn 1 of the Combat Training Centre located at Maryy AB was the first VVS unit in Soviet Central Asia to master the 'Fulcrum'. This was an 'aggressor' unit which previously operated MiG-21*bis* 'Fishbed-Ns' and various versions of the MiG-23, often sporting sharkmouths and other gaudy nose art supposedly characteristic of the 'potential adversary'. (Incidentally, such artwork was not worn by the unit's MiG-29s but did appear on 'Fulcrums' operated by some other units – e.g., the 120th IAP based at Domna AB 30km (18.6 mi.) southwest of Chita in the Transbaikalian Defence District.)

Originally the unit's MiG-29s retained their factory finish and red tactical codes outlined in white. However,

---

6 The Lipetsk centre's complement of MiG-29s has been reduced to 14 aircraft operated by the 968th IIIAP's 2 Sqn as of this writing.

7 Pronounced like the French name Marie.

as regular units operating the 'Fulcrum' began visiting Maryy for a tussle with the 'aggressors', telling the 'good guys' from the 'bad guys' became a problem, especially when air-to-air combat between groups of aircraft was planned. The problem was solved by applying special markings to the upper wing surfaces and fuselages of aggressor aircraft; these were known locally as brandy stripes. Additionally, the tactical code was repeated on the fins in white characters 15–20 cm (approx. 6–8 in.) high, making it easier to find the right aircraft in a line of parked fighters; this soon became a common feature in MiG-29 units.

The 'Fulcrum' was also operated by the AV-MF. In 1989 a complete fighter division comprising two MiG-29 regiments and a MiG-23 regiment was transferred to the Black Sea Fleet's air arm. One of the 'Fulcrum' units (the 161st IAP) operated from Limanskoye AB near Odessa while the other (the 86th IAP) was based at Markuleshty AB in Moldavia. In the early '90s one squadron of MiG-29s (12 aircraft) was assigned to the Air Defence Command (PVO – *protivovozdooshnaya oborona*). The squadron was part of a fighter unit reporting to the 19th Independent PVO Army and operated from Privolzhskiy AB near Astrakhan' on the Volga river.

The political developments of the late '80s in Eastern Europe and the subsequent collapse of the Soviet Union affected the fate of MiG-29 units a good deal. Tensions between East and West were relaxing. On 6 July 1990 NATO's London summit passed a declaration on impending German reunification (which formally took place on 3 October 1990). Hence on 12 September a truly historic treaty was signed in Moscow under which the Soviet Union pledged to gradually withdraw its troops from Germany. Other East European states plunged eagerly into capitalism, breaking away from their socialist past and the bullying and patronising Big Brother personified by the Soviet Union. The end of the Cold War rendered the Warsaw pact unnecessary; brotherhood gave place to estrangement and the military bloc designed to oppose NATO aggression quietly died a natural death.

Keeping Soviet troops in Eastern Europe was no longer justified. The Soviet MoD found itself facing the Herculean task of relocating numerous Soviet Army and VVS units back home. These included the ten MiG-29 regiments stationed in the former East Germany, Hungary and Czechoslovakia; some of them had to be reorganized or disbanded entirely. The first 'Fulcrums' began pulling out of Germany in the spring of 1991 when the 85th GvIAP from Merseburg and the 73rd Sevastopol'skiy

GvIAP from Köthen moved to Starokonstantinov AB in the Ukraine and Shaykovka AB in the Moscow Defence District. Next year the 968th IAP from Nöbitz (Altenburg), the 35th IAP from Zerbst and the 787th IAP from Eberswalde (Finow) relocated to Lipetsk and to Ros' in Belorussia. The 31st Nikopol'skiy GvIAP from Alt Lönnewitz (Falkenberg) followed in 1993, moving to Zernograd in the North-Caucasian Defence District. The 33rd IAP at Wittstock and the 733rd IAP at Pütnitz (Damgarten) came last, departing for Andreapol' in the Moscow Defence District in April 1994. The neighbouring Zherdyovka AB became home to 'Fulcrums' returning from Hungary (Kiskunlaháza AB closed on 20 May 1990, followed by Sarmellek exactly five months later and Tokól on 5 June 1991), while the aircraft based at Milovice in Czechoslovakia moved to Ivano-Frankovsk in the western part of the Ukraine.

1991 brought even more dramatic changes than the need to withdraw from Eastern Europe. Torn apart by political unrest and economic problems, the 'unbreakable union of free republics' (to quote the opening lines of the Soviet State anthem) turned into a Soviet Disunion, fifteen new states bickering with each other over who owned what. (12 of these eventually got organized into the Commonwealth of Independent States, which helped sort things out.)

One of the most sore problems was the division of the armed forces. Though Russia had become the Soviet Union's legal successor and accepted the latter's international obligations, much of the Soviet armed forces' weaponry and military bases remained outside the Russian Federation – in the 'nearby foreign countries', as the other CIS states are wont to be called in Russia. This applied to the tactical arm of the VVS (FA – *frontovaya aviatsiya*) as well, since many FA units were stationed along the borders of the former Soviet Union. The CIS leaders agreed that such units based in Belorussia (Belarus), Turkmenistan, Uzbekistan and the Ukraine would remain there, becoming the basis of the air forces of these respective states. The fighter force of the Black Sea Fleet's air arm, on the other hand, effectively ceased to exist. The fleet's fighter division was disbanded; one of the MiG-29 regiments (the 161st IAP) became part of the Ukrainian Air Force while the other (the 86th IAP) was included in the Moldovan Air Force.

By early 1992 the Russian Air Force (now referred to as VVS RF – *voyenno-vozdooshnyye seely Rosseeyskoy Federahtsii*) had some 300 MiG-29s on strength; more than half of them were still in Germany, awaiting redeployment to Russian airbases. In 1992–93 the 'Fulcrum' fleet was augmented by the addition of the 176th IAP which moved from Tskhakaya AB in Georgia to the Transbaikalian Defence District in Eastern Siberia. Also in 1993, some of the 16th VA units withdrawn from Germany, MiG-29 units from Hungary and Czechoslovakia, and the Moscow Defence District's Air Force units were organized into a new formation which inherited the 16th VA name and has its headquarters at Kubinka AB. Currently 16th VA 'Fulcrums' equip the formation's fighter division, the Lipetsk training centre and the Kubinka display centre.

MiG-29s are also operated by a fighter regiment and the Borisoglebsk training centre reporting to the 34th VA (headquartered at Rostov-on-Don), by the Krasnodar Military Combined Flying and Technical School[8] of the Air Force's Reserve and Personnel Command, and by fighter units based at Domna AB and Orlovka AB (Khabarovsk region). According to press reports, about 460 'Fulcrums' were in service with VVS RF in 1997.

In 1994 the best pilots of several Russian AF air armies participated in a combat skill contest (rather like the USAF's William Tell contest). MiG-29 pilots from the Shaykovka unit commanded by Col. Vasiliy Podkorytov walked away with all the prizes. The flight led by Maj. Leonid Gaponov excelled in piloting techniques. Gaponov Roomyantsev were also unequalled in air-to-air combat.

From its first days of MiG-29 operations the 234th GvIAP started forming a display team flying the type. It was not until mid-1990, however, that the team was officially organized as the unit's Sqn 2 under the name Strizhi (Swifts; pronounced streezhee).[9] It was staffed with the unit's best 'Fulcrum' pilots; Col. Aleksandr N. Kutuzov, a distinguished military pilot, led the team since its founding day. The team had ten single-seat 'Fulcrum-As' coded 33 White and 40 White to 48 White, as well as three MiG-29UBs (32 White, 34 White and 35 White). All of them wore an eye-catching colour scheme with bright blue tails, blue/white wings, white engine nacelles and a white fuselage with a black spine and blue lightning flash punctuated by the Mikoyan logo below the windscreen. The tactical code was applied to the fins because its usual position on the air intakes was occupied by the team's badge, a stylised black swift on an orange disc. Originally

8 I.e., preparing both pilots and tech staff.

9 Sqn 1 is the *Roosskiye Vityazi* (Russian Knights) team flying the Su-27/Su-27UB 'Flanker-B/C'. There was also Sqn 3, the *Nebesnyye Gusahry* (Celestial Hussars) team flying the Su-25 'Frogfoot-A', but this was disbanded in 1996 for financial reasons.

'Why on earth don't all Russian fighters have cockpits like this one?' That's what President Boris Yeltsin is probably thinking as current MiG-29 project chief Valeriy Novikov shows him the MiG-29SMT's 'glass cockpit' at the MAKS-97 airshow, 19 August 1997. (ITAR-TASS)

ABOVE: *This picture shows how the upper surfaces of the Strizhi aircraft are painted.* *(Yefim Gordon)*
BELOW: *Pre-flight checks on a MiG-29UB.* *(Yefim Gordon)*

the Strizhi performed on four aircraft piloted by Lt.-Col. Kutuzov (leader), Maj. Aleksandr Katashinskiy (left wingman), Maj. Andrey Makarenko (right wingman) and Lt.-Col. Aleksandr Zakharov. Later they were joined by Maj. Aleksandr Sherstnyov and Maj. Vladimir Galoonenko. The team perfected the six-aircraft display technique in close formation, the aircraft flying within 3 m (10 ft) of each other.

Each new aerobatics element is checked on a computer by mathematical analysis and polished to perfection in training sorties before being included in the display programme. Sometimes even pilot error provided fresh ideas. On one occasion a pilot forgot to retract the landing gear before making a loop straight after takeoff as planned and was very surprised that the aircraft had let that pass. This led to the introduction of a new element when a six-aircraft formation made a loop with the gear down and landing lights on.

The Strizhi had its début in France on 13 May 1991, performing at Reims-Champagne airbase (BA112), home of ECTT2/30 Normandie-Niémen. The latter unit (which had flown Yak-3 fighters as part of the Soviet Air Force during WW II) had made a goodwill visit to Kubinka in 1990; now the 234th GvIAP repaid the visit, marking the 50th anniversary of the Normandie-Niémen squadron. Four single-seaters (including 43 White, 44 White and 46 White) and two MiG-29UBs (32 White and 34 White) went to Reims, accompanied by an Il-76MD 'Candid' support aircraft (01 Red, ex SSSR-78837, c/n 1003401024). The six fighters performed virtually every aerobatics element, constantly changing formation – echelon, diamond, wedge, star etc. The show was concluded by an element known as the tulip (similar to the Bomb Burst but initiated in level flight, not a vertical dive); the aircraft let loose a salvo of IRCM flares as they parted, making the finale very impressive indeed.

The Strizhi has displayed its skill around the world, performing at airshows in Belgium, Germany, Thailand, Malaysia, Finland, Sweden, Norway, Mongolia, Vietnam, Laos and the Philippines. Of course, the team has also performed on its home ground. This included the open days at Kubinka AB on 11 April 1992, 29 May 1993, 14 May 1994 and the grand military parade at Poklonnaya Gora in Moscow on 9 May 1995 marking the 50th anniversary of VE-Day. The Strizhi has also become a regular participant of the Aviation Day flypasts at Moscow-Tushino airfield and the biennial international airshows at Zhukovskiy – MAKS-93, MAKS-95 and

A Strizhi MiG-29 shares the apron with a Su-27 of the Russkiye Vityazi (Russian Knights) team also based at Kubinka. (Yefim Gordon)

MAKS-97. On 8 August 1997 the Strizhi excelled again at the Kubinka air fest staged to celebrate the 16th VA's 50th anniversary. First, four of the team's aircraft performed group aerobatics, followed by a solo display by Nikolay Dyatel. After that, Col. Aleksandr Gornov and Lt.-Col. Aleksandr Katashinskiy performed in a pair on 'Fulcrum-Cs'.

Unfortunately, the MiG-29 has had its share of accidents. Forty-five 'Fulcrums' had crashed by 1 April 1998, with the loss of 23 pilots. The highest attrition was recorded in 1993: 22 of the 31 VVS RF aircraft lost that year were MiG-29s. However, only six crashes were caused by design and manufacturing defects. Over the years, the MiG-29 has become an extremely reliable aircraft; this goes for both airframe and engines (only four accidents were attributed to engine failure). In 90 per cent of the cases pilot error was the cause of the accident. Still, the pilots can hardly be blamed, since the fuel shortages and budget cuts that followed the collapse of the Soviet Union inevitably caused a drastic fall-off in the number of flight hours. And staying on the ground certainly does not improve flying skills!

In early February 1984 two experienced pilots – senior inspector pilot Col. A. A. Koreshkov and NII VVS test pilot Col. V. A. Lotkov – were killed in identical circumstances within a few days, encountering reverse roll reaction to rudder input and losing control of the aircraft in a steep turn. Both crashed while practising for a display session at Kubinka AB when the MiG-29 was due to be demonstrated to government officials. Operational experience with the type was still scarce then and operational procedures had not yet been perfected.

On 14 December 1987 a early-production MiG-29 (f/n 0203) suffered an engine fire and crashed near Ivano-Frankovsk in the Ukraine, killing the pilot. A mid-air collision between a 'Fulcrum-A' and a MiG-29UB occurred in the same parts (the date is unknown). The trainer crashed, killing both pilots; the single-seater managed to make it back to base.

On 7 February 1992 the Lipetsk training centre suffered the loss of its chief, Gen. Sulambek S. Oskanov. During a night intercept training sortie his MiG-29 suffered a control system failure at low altitude and started rolling. Repeated attempts to stabilise the aircraft were unsuccessful, still the pilot did not eject because the fighter would drop on a major railway station and the death toll would be immense. When the aircraft was clear of the area it was too late for ejection. The MiG-29 crashed in a field near the village of Kozel'ki, killing the pilot.

The most famous accident was at the 38th Paris-Le Bourget airshow where a single-seat MiG-29 (303 Blue, ex 10 Blue, c/n 2960516767) and a MiG-29UB (304 Blue, ex 53 Blue, c/n 4029692486) were among the Soviet exhibits. On opening day (8 June 1989) Mikoyan test pilot Anatoliy N. Kvochur was making a demonstration flight in 303 Blue. During a high-alpha/low-speed pass at 160 m (525 ft) concluding the 'Fulcrum's' aerobatics display, a flash of flame belched from the starboard engine's nozzle as the engine surged. Kvochur immediately selected full afterburner for the good engine, but at 180 km/h (100 kts) he had insufficient rudder and aileron authority to counter the thrust asymmetry and the result was inevitably an irrecoverable departure. The engine failed at 13 hrs 44 min 57 sec; the stricken fighter immediately yawed and rolled to starboard, the nose 'falling through' until the aircraft entered a vertical dive at 13:45.01. Two and a half seconds later Kvochur ejected at 92 m (302 ft) after making sure the aircraft would not hit the spectators. At 13:45.05 the fighter impacted beside the runway, erupting in a tremendous fireball. The pilot landed a mere 30 m (98 ft) from the wreckage, the ejection seat bouncing right next to him.

To give credit where credit is due, the airport's rescue and firefighting team was on the scene 55 seconds after the crash. Kvochur was rushed to a hospital but released the same day with nothing worse than bruises and a cut above his right eyebrow from the oxygen mask. Indeed, he had been extremely lucky, as he had ejected outside the seat's operating envelope, not to mention the proximity of the fireball and the falling seat. Yet the incident spoke a lot for the design of the Zvezda K-36DM ejection seat. As observers noted, the MiG-29 demonstrated its structural integrity (as well as the soft nature of the ground at Le Bourget) by burying its entire forward fuselage, including the cockpit, in the ground before blowing up. Naturally, there was a good deal of speculation as to the cause of the crash. Video footage showed that the MiG had suffered at least two lightning strikes immediately before the accident. However, examination of the wreckage and FDR analysis revealed that the starboard engine had been critically damaged by multiple birdstrike.

On 3 June 1993 two MiG-29s from Domna AB were flying a night intercept training sortie; one of the fighters was the hunter and the other acted as the target for a simulated missile launch. The attacking aircraft was closing in on the target much too fast and the two fighters collided, crashing in an unpopulated area. The attacking pilot was killed, the other pilot ejected safely. In the same month a MiG-29 from Maryy AB suffered an uncontained engine failure during an aerobatics session. As a fire warning sounded at the top of a loop the pilot activated the fire extinguishers and requested an emergency landing. However, the brake parachute did not deploy and the wheel brakes operated inefficiently (probably because of shrapnel and/or fire damage to wiring and hydraulic lines). Realizing he could not stop the aircraft in time, the pilot ejected; the fighter overran, colliding with the localizer beyond the runway threshold, and exploded.

Unfortunately, the Paris accident was not the only one of the kind. Participants of the 1993 Royal International Air Tattoo (RIAT) at RAF Fairford marking the Royal Air Force's 75-year jubilee included a display team from LII – two single-seat MiG-29s flown by test pilots Sergey Tresvyatskiy and Aleksandr Beschastnov and a Tu-134AK support aircraft. The visit was sponsored by the Aviatika production association affiliated with MAPO (it manufactures the MAI-890 ultralight aircraft at MAPO's Moscow-Khodynka plant). The team had arrived on 21 July from Prague where the 'Fulcrums', coded 526 Black (c/n 2960525887) and 926 Black (c/n 2960515564) and painted in a blue/yellow display colour scheme, had performed at the Czech AF's 75-year anniversary show.

For the next two days the pilots were busy practising. However, the 'real thing' on 24 July ended in a spectacular collision at 200–250 m (656–820 ft) in which Beschastnov's aircraft was virtually cut in two aft of the cockpit and burst into flames. Incredibly, both pilots escaped without a scratch, even though one of them had to eject from an inverted position; a BBC announcer said that the pilots had 'jumped out from under the coffin's lid'. The accident information message released by the RAF Inspectorate of Flight Safety (IFS) went as follows:

'1. On 24 July 93 at 1527 hrs (local), a pair of MiG-29s of the Russian Flight Research Institute took off in close formation to commence their display at the RAF Fairford International Air Tattoo (IAT). The cloud was scattered at 3,000 ft (914 m – Auth.), visibility excellent and surface wind down runway at 8 kts (4 m/sec). The display was normal until the final manoeuvre which was simultaneous loops commenced from long line astern, prior to a break to land. The leader, who pulled up first, carried out a normal loop. The aircraft entered cloud at the top. The Number 2 commenced his loop with some lead

on the first aircraft, executed a slightly tighter loop and experienced difficulties with the cloud. At some stage during the manoeuvre, both pilots lost visual contact with each other and called it. As a result of the Number 2's tighter loop, the leader was lower and not as far in front of the Number 2 as he expected. Although still unsighted, the lead pilot decided to carry out his break to downwind, believing it would take him out of the flight path of the other aircraft. Shortly after commencing his break, the left wing of the lead aircraft impacted the fuselage of the number 2 aircraft. Both aircraft immediately became uncontrollable. Both pilots ejected successfully and were uninjured. The aircraft impacted to the NE of the airfield 700 m (2,300 ft) from the crowd line. One aircraft crashed on the perimeter fence and the other about 600 m (1,968 ft) beyond. Remarkably, only one person on the ground received minor injuries. A Belgian C-130, an Italian Air Force (Aeritalia) G222 and a French Air Force Alpha Jet were slightly damaged.

2. An RAF BoI (Board of Investigation) was convened to investigate the circumstances of the accident. Preliminary assessment is that the cause of the collision involved the following factors: flight into cloud, the tighter loop by the Number 2, and the leader's break without visual contact with his Number 2. Both pilots stated that their aircraft were serviceable prior to the impact.

3. Service and IAT orders and instructions appear valid. It is not clear whether the Russian Research Institute MiG-29s were civilian or military.

4. There are no recommendations at this stage.'

The British reaction to the crash was something like 'don't worry too much; you're not the first, you're not the last'. The RAF accepted costs of recultivating the soil at the crash site while the Russian party paid for the damage to the parked aircraft. The pilots returned to active duty on 2 August.

On 15 September the same year a 33rd IAP MiG-29 from Wittstock AB (20 White, c/n 2960520565, f/n 1817) was accidentally shot down by his wingman, another MiG-29 (tactical code unknown, c/n 18454). A British reference book, *Euromil – Military Air Arms in Europe*, states the date of the crash as 14 September 1992. The two pilots were scheduled to practise gun firing that day with one aircraft acting as the target; however, the wingman's own 'Fulcrum' went unserviceable immediately before the sortie and the pilot was ordered to take off in another aircraft. The pilot was unaware that the training mode had not been selected on this aircraft's gun and pushed the fire button, honestly believing that nothing would happen. Instead, he inadvertently made a few holes in his flight leader and debris from the lead aircraft apparently damaged the other MiG as well, forcing both pilots to eject; luckily, there were no casualties.

In the summer of 1995 MAPO test pilot S. N. Shaposhnikov was killed while practising aerobatics over the factory airfield in Lookhovitsy prior to an airshow in South Africa. Pilot error was cited as the cause of the crash. In August 1995 120th IAP (23rd VA) pilots were practising for their performance over Chita at the celebrations marking 50 years of victory in WW II. The unit had seen action in the Afghan war and had been the best in the Russian Air Force's fighter arm for several years running. On 22 August six 120th IAP MiG-29s were practising over the Chita airport in close formation. The aerobatics display included numerous elements in quick succession, the aircraft pulling out of a dive at just 200 m (656 ft). Locals watching the practice session from the balconies of apartment buildings surrounding the airport said that the six-ship formation climbed vertically, then turned sharply and went into a vertical dive (probably preparing for a Bomb Burst). As it did so the rearmost aircraft coded 30 and piloted by Capt. A. Siplivets hit wake turbulence from another MiG-29. Rolling uncontrollably, the fighter dived into the ground near the runway threshold and exploded, disintegrating utterly; only the engines and pieces of the tail unit remained in the crater.

The Tester-UZLK FDR was salvaged and promptly sent to the Aircraft Operations and Repair Techniques Institute in Lyubertsy, one of Moscow's satellite cities (NII ERAT – *Naoochno-issledovatel'skiy institooteks pluatahtsii i remonta aviatseeonnoy tekhniki*). It turned out that the pilot never tried to eject, attempting to regain control of the aircraft till the end. However, at low altitude there was just too little time for recovery. Reprisal was swift. The unit's CO and chief of staff got a severe dressing-down 'for inadequate control'; the technical staff was disciplined for offences having nothing to do with the crash. The flight leader, Capt. Shapka, got the main

blame; the investigators accused him of 'negligent training of personnel', implying that the pilots were not trained to keep formation properly. The highly skilled pilot was ignominiously fired from the Air Force. As if that weren't enough, the 120th IAP suffered another loss the same day. Lt.-Col. Svetlichnyy, the unit's executive officer, who had served his country with distinction and earned two Orders of the Red Star in Afghanistan, did not wait for the ruling of the investigation board and pronounced his own verdict and shot himself in his study . . .

On 4 March 1996 two MiG-29s collided over the vast expanse of taiga near Chita during a training sortie. The pilots, Yershov and Tyapkin, probably had no chance to take evasive action and ejected seconds before the impact. A brand-new MiG-29UB was lost in Gor'kiy when 234th GvIAP pilots lost control of the aircraft during the pre-delivery checkout flight; both pilots ejected safely. Another 'Fulcrum-B' crashed in Gor'kiy after repeated but unsuccessful attempts to recover from a spin, killing factory test pilot Kherodinov and VVS pilot Bespalov. VVS pilots Larionov and Mazur lost their lives in a MiG-29UB in similar circumstances. A 'Fulcrum-A' operated by LII (f/n 0802) crashed towards the end of the trials programme when LII test pilot Rimas A. A. Stankiavicius failed to recover ffrom a flat spin initiated at 11,000 m (36, 089 ft). The aircraft was equipped with spin recovery rockets but one of them had been connected incorrectly and the fighter became uncontrollable when the rockets fired, forcing Stankiavicius to eject at 1,800 m (5,905 ft).

Not all accidents were in-flight ones. A single-seat MiG-29 and a MiG-29UB were destroyed by fire on the ground at the Air Force aircraft overhaul plant No. 121 at Kubinka AB. Another single-seater burned out at Tskhakaya AB (no dates are known). Yet in spite of these accidents the MiG-29 has a far better safety record than many Western fighters. The 'Fulcrum' is well liked by service pilots of the Russian Air Force.

The first reports of new-generation fighters under development in the Soviet Union appeared in the Western press in the mid-70s. In August 1977 the *International Defence Review* (*IDR*) magazine revealed that a new Soviet fighter designated MiG-29 was undergoing trials in the Ramenskoye flight test centre (which, as mentioned earlier, was the erroneous name of LII in Zhukovskiy). The designation was based on educated guesswork, as Soviet fighters get odd-number designations and the MiG-27 was bound to be followed by the MiG-29. However, the author was mistaken, as the MiG-29 had not yet flown at the time; the aircraft in question was almost certainly the first prototype Su-27 (T10-1) which entered flight test on 20 May 1977.

The **IDR** feature was presaged by photos of the ramp at LII made by a US surveillance satellite. These depicted several new combat aircraft of as yet unknown origin, including two fighters which received the temporary ASCC reporting names 'Ram-K' and 'Ram-L'. As mentioned earlier, such names were allocated instead of the usual by class reporting names (F for fighter, B for bomber, M for miscellaneous etc.) until the aircraft's manufacturer and rôle had been positively identified. E.g., the Su-25 'Frogfoot' attack aircraft was initially referred to as 'Ram-J', the Tu-160 'Blackjack' strategic bomber as the 'Ram-P' and the Myasischev M-17 /M-55 'Mystic' high-altitude reconnaissance aircraft as the 'Ram-M'. In due course the 'Ram-K' and 'Ram-L' were identified as the T10-1 and the first prototype MiG-29 (aircraft 901) respectively, becoming the 'Flanker' and 'Fulcrum'.

Yet the USA were reticent about their findings at LII and took their time publishing data on and photos of the MiG-29. The first information about the fighter's existence was released by the Pentagon two years later, in March 1979. As for the satellite imagery, it was not published until November 1983 when the 'Fulcrum' had achieved IOC and the Central Intelligence Agency got a much better idea of the new fighter's design and combat potential. The photos released for publication were of extremely poor quality, showing only a blurred shape vaguely reminiscent of the F-15; there have been persistent reports, however, that the photos have purposefully been 'coarsened' considerably and that the Pentagon has kept the good-quality originals to itself!

The Western world got its first good look at the MiG-29 on 1 July 1986 when six 'Fulcrum-As' from Kubinka AB accompanied by an Antonov An-12BP 'Cub' support aircraft came to Kuopio-Rissala AB in Finland, home to the 31st fighter squadron/Karelian Air Wing (31 HLeLv/Karjalan Lennosto) on a four-day friendly visit. The fighters (01 Blue, 02 Blue, 03 Blue, 07 Blue, 08 Blue and 12 Blue) were flown by Col. V. V. Longinenko (sic)[10] who headed the delegation, Col. V. Yashin, Maj. V. Solovyov, Maj. V. Kravets, Maj. V. Chilin and Maj. A. Arastov. Finland was very probably chosen because the Finnish Air Force (*Ilmavoimat*) traditionally operated aircraft from East and West alike and could well order the MiG-29 as a MiG-21 replacement.

Such visits were nothing new; however, this was the first occasion when the latest Soviet military hardware was displayed in the West, and of course the interest generated by the visit was immense. Western specialists and photographers were not allowed to inspect the MiG-29 at close range, yet some good-quality photos were taken and the observers got the first taste of the fighter's high manoeuvrability. This triggered a wave of publications whose authors conjectured on the 'Fulcrum's' design features, performance and combat potential. Typically on such visits Soviet military aircraft had sensitive equipment items removed. The MiG-29s at Kuopio-Rissala were no exception, lacking pylons so as to avoid revealing how many missiles the aircraft could actually carry.

Despite the new Soviet policy of *glasnost'* (openness) and the fact that the MiG-29 had been displayed abroad, the Soviet media were tight as a clam about the fighter's existence. It was not until 19 March 1987 that *Krasnaya Zvezda (Red Star)*, the Soviet armed forces' newspaper, published a poor-quality photo of a four-ship formation of MiG-29s from Kubinka. By then, exports had also begun, India taking delivery of the first aircraft in 1986 and Iraq and Yugoslavia the next year. *Glasnost'* obviously took some time coming! Since there was no point in keeping the fighter veiled in secrecy any more, the Soviet government made an unprecedented decision to demonstrate the MiG-29 at the 1988 SBAC airshow at Farnborough. Until then, Soviet participation in international airshows had been strictly (one might even say ostensibly) civilian. Mikoyan dispatched two 'Fulcrums' to Farnborough – the ill-fated single-seater 10 Blue mentioned earlier and the third prototype MiG-29UB (53 Blue).

The single-seater was flown by Mikoyan test pilot Anatoliy N. Kvochur and the trainer by Roman P. Taskayev. The MiG-29s landed at Farnborough after making a refuelling stopover at Wittstock AB in East Germany. In British aerospace they were escorted by two RAF Panavia Tornado F. Mk 3 interceptors of No. 5 Sqn (XT736/'CK' was one) and a BAe VC10 K. Mk 3 tanker acting as a camera ship for journalists. Curiously, the fighters arrived without pylons but when the airshow opened on 4 September, 10 Blue had four underwing pylons. These were delivered, along with other equipment and spares, by the An-124 Ruslan ('Condor') widebody freighter registered SSSR-82007 (c/n 19530501005, f/n 01-05) which was one of the Soviet exhibits.

The appeerance of two Soviet fighters created a veritable sensation; as David A. Brown (*Aviation Week &*

---

10 This was how the name was spelled by *Air International* but it sounds doubtful; the correct name was almost certainly Logvinenko.

ABOVE: *The cockpit canopy of a 'Fulcrum-A' operated by the Strizhi team. (Aleksey Mikheyev)*

LEFT: *The cockpit canopy of a MiG-29UB. (Aleksey Mikheyev)*

Space Technology) put it, 'there also was a large dose of **udivlenye** – with Western observers expressing amazement that Soviet air force (sic) MiG-29s and Royal Air Force Tornado F.3s could be seen flying in a graceful formation at Farnborough'. The 'Fulcrum' quickly demonstrated its superiority to Western fighters present at the show; to quote Menitskiy (then Mikoyan CTP) who was present at the show, 'the joint practice sessions put everything into its proper place. The top of a loop executed on the MiG-29 is some 100 m (328 ft) lower than on the F-16C or (Dassault) Rafale. Turning time is better than the Rafale's, to say nothing of the Mirage 2000. The F-16's time is very close, being only 0.8–1.5 seconds worse (than the MiG-29's). The MiG-29 has an advantage during takeoff as well – it gets unstuck and starts climbing quicker than the others. The Rafale and Mirage 2000 have a slightly better roll rate but they don't have any advantage at high alpha and during the so-called "special rolls" (a test manoeuvre developed to identify AOA limits).'

The MiG-29's tailslide manoeuvre performed by

ABOVE: *The twist-cassegrain radar bin of the 'Fulcrum-A's' Phazotron N-019 'Topaz' fire control radar. (Yefim Gordon)*

BELOW: *The N-019M seen beside the MiG-29's forward fuselage shows how much space the radar actually occupies. (MAPO)*

The engine bays and brake parachute container of a MiG-29 with the engines removed. (MAPO – Artur Sarkisyan)

Kvochur and Taskayev was a true show-stopper, as it had been performed previously on competition aerobatic aircraft only, not on fast jets. The tailslide was included in the display programme at Farnborough to give the spectators a better idea of the fighter's capabilities. Firstly, it showed that the controls remained effective at ultra-low speeds (trajectory control was retained at zero and even negative airspeed when the aircraft briefly moved tail-first before exiting the manoeuvre in a dive). Secondly, it demonstrated the fighter's high thrust-to-weight ratio and smooth engine operation throughout the flight envelope.

There have been discussions as to whether the tailslide could be used as an element of dogfight tactics. Some observers have dismissed it as a flashy airshow stunt and nothing else but others believe this is not so. The fighter's unconventional trajectory may cause the enemy to lose target lock-on because the Doppler effect disappears when the MiG-29 literally stands still on its tail for a few seconds. Present-day fire control radars have a memory feature and if target lock-on is lost they will recall the target's direction of flight and try to locate it in that direction. However, after making a tailslide the MiG-29

pops up where the enemy's radar least expects it to be. On the other hand, pilots were wary of the manoeuvre because it implies a loss of speed; regaining speed would take a lot of time and any advantage gained by means of the tailslide could be lost. The distrust of Western observers was partly due to the fact that no other production fighter was capable of performing the tailslide at the time. The proof of the pudding is in the eating, and new things are always treated warily. Anyway, the 'Fulcrum' overshadowed everything else at FI'88, including fighters traditionally in demand with weapons-importing countries. Features in aviation magazines describing the airshow appeared with headlines such as 'Soviet MiG-29 Fighter Sparks Farnborough Opening' *(AW&ST)*, 'Glasnost on the Wing' *(Flight International)*, 'The Show-Stopper: MiG-29 at Farnborough' *(IDR)* etc.

While traditionally supplying combat aircraft to a number of friendly nations, the Soviet Union had been unwilling to be advertised as a weapons exporter. The *perestroika* and *glasnost'* policies which were the beginning of democratic reforms in the country changed all that. The Soviet Union was becoming increasingly more open to the outside world, the Cold War and the arms race were winding down. Gradually people in the Western world began shedding the old Soviet threat myth, though this took some time to accomplish. To quote the famous biologist Gerald Durrell, 'reputations, whether true or false, die hard, and for some reasons a bad reputation dies hardest of all.'

Openly demonstrating the latest Soviet military hardware in the West was an important way of getting rid of the Cold War heritage. Besides, by entering the world weapons market the Soviet Union could earn sizeable profits. (In the past Soviet weapons exports had been a purely political matter and usually did not generate any profits – indeed, many third-world countries never paid for the weapons at all or got them for the proverbial

10,000 goatskins!) Participating in various international airshows and trade fairs would be the best way to advertise the aircraft. It so happened that the MiG-29 was the first Soviet (Russian) combat aircraft openly demonstrated abroad with a view to attracting export orders. This was the beginning of Russia's cooperation with the outside world in the field of military technology.

FI'88 was but the first of the 'Fulcrum's' numerous airshow appearences and the fighter was invariably a success with the visitors. In June 1989 the same two aircraft – MiG-29 10 Blue and MiG-29UB 53 Blue – were displayed at the Le Bourget airshow. These had been recoded 303 Blue and 304 Blue respectively for the occasion; the new tactical codes were in fact Le Bourget exhibit numbers. The Soviet delegation included chief

The wingtip of a 'Fulcrum-C', showing ECM antennas. (Viktor Drooshlyakov)

The fin fillets and chaff/flare dispensers on MAPO demonstrator 333 White; note c/n (29605)36093. (Andrey Yurgenson)

project engineer Mikhail R. Val'denberg, pilots Menitskiy, Kvochur and Taskayev, MiG-29 leading engineer Ootkin, flight operations engineer Belov, a ground crew and the chiefs of some Mikoyan divisions (e.g., flight test facility chief Troitskiy). As noted previously, the single-seater was lost on 8 June when the starboard engine failed after a birdstrike.

In August 1989 MiG-29 315 Blue (c/n 2960513315?) and MiG-29UB 304 Blue arrived in Abbotsford (British Columbia) via Elmendorf AFB (Alaska) to participate in an airshow. Once again, they were flown by Menitskiy, Kvochur and Taskayev. A Canadian Air Force CF-18A escorted the MiGs in Canadian airspace. Also in August 1989 a group of MiG-29s from Kubinka visited Kuopio-Rissala AB again. This time the 'Fulcrums' display was marred by an incident on 2 August when 02 Blue piloted by Col. Viktor Bytskov overran on landing after making a solo aerobatics display. The aircraft landed too fast and the brake parachute was torn off; the wheel brakes could

not halt the aircraft in time and it entered the emergency barrier at the runway's end at about 10 kts, suffering minor damage.

315 Blue and 304 Blue became Mikoyan's display hacks. 1990 was a busy year for them: piloted by Taskayev and Marat R. Alykov, the two 'Fulcrums' participated in airshows in Hannover, Le Havre, and Geneva followed by a tour of Canada and the USA. During the latter Menitskiy flew as co-pilot of the Il-76MD support aircraft captained by test pilot Bliznyuk. The route of the North American tour went as follows: Zhukovskiy, Novyy Urengoy, Tiksi, Anadyr', Elmendorf AFB (Alaska), Comox (British Columbia), Ottawa, Winnipeg, Kalamazoo (Michigan), Rockford (Illinois), Wright-Patterson AFB (Dayton, Ohio), Winnipeg, Comox, Elmendorf, Anadyr', Tiksi, Novyy Urengoy, Zhukovskiy. The fighters performed in Ottawa, Kalamazoo, Rockford and Dayton; the other stops *en route* were just refuelling stopovers. On the return journey the group flew from

Comox to Zhukovskiy in a single light day lasting 31 hours because it was following the sun.

Next year the MiG-29S prototype (407 Blue) and a MiG-29UB were demonstrated at airshows in the Philippines and China. The route of the tour was: Zhukovskiy, Omsk, Irkutsk, Peking, Guangchow, Manila and back home. Again Taskayev and Alykov were flying the fighters; the group also included MiG-29 leading engineer S. V. Shal'nyov, flight operations engineer N. A. Belov, a ground crew and deputy project chief V. V. Novikov.

In the same year the MiG-29 was present at airshows in Cleveland (Ohio), and Harrisburg (Pennsylvania). Alykov and Garnayev did the flying but Menitskiy was also included in the group as a backup pilot. Both versions of the 'Fulcrum' were also on display at the IDEX'90 international defence exhibition in Dubai (United Arab Emirates).

In 1992 a Russian Air Force An-124 airlifted a 'Fulcrum-A' and a 'Fulcrum-B' to Malaysia for display and training purposes, since the Royal Malaysian Air Force had ordered the type. The Russian delegation demonstrating the fighters included pilots Menitskiy and Gorboonov, MiG-29 leading engineer Belyasnik, flight operations engineer Belov, a ground crew and deputy project chief Slobodskoy. Also in 1992, MiG-29S 407 Blue and the sixth MiG-29M prototype (156 Blue) piloted by Pavel N. Vlasov and Roman P. Taskayev were on display at FI'92. Next year the same pilots demonstrated the Malaysian version of the 'Fulcrum-A' and the MiG-29M at Le Bourget.

In 1994 a single-seater (f/n 5211) and a MiG-29UB were present at a defence exhibition in Santiago de Chile. Apart from Taskayev, the fighters were flown by MAPO test pilots Pelekh and Shaposhnikov. The Russian delegation also included Belyasnik, project chief Sedov and deputy project chief Slobodskoy.

In the summer of 1994 MiG-29 506 Blue (c/n 2960535121; f/n 5006?) was demonstrated at the ILA'94 airshow at Berlin-Schönefeld by Taskayev and Vlasov. Shortly afterwards, in September 1994, another MiG-29M prototype (155 Blue) put in an appearance at the Farnborough airshow along with a production MiG-29. By then the false dorsal auxiliary intakes originally painted on the LERXes of 155 Blue had been painted out because this camouflage was no longer needed. Taskayev and Alykov flew the 'Fulcrums' at FI'94 and the Mikoyan delegation was headed by Shal'nyov who had been promoted to deputy project chief.

The static display at ILA'96 included a 'Fulcrum-A' (357 Blue) fitted experimentally with the semi-retractable refuelling probe designed to meet the Malaysian requirement. The same aircraft was presented at FI'96 as the MiG-29SM with an enhanced strike capability. Of course the MiG-29 inevitably participated in the airshows in Zhukovskiy. Besides the Strizhi aerobatic team, the flying display included LII's own MiG-29UB 86 Blue and MiG-29S 506 Blue; the latter (like 407 Blue) had thin stripes of Russia's national colours of white, blue and red running across the fins above the tactical code. Four 'Fulcrum-As' based at Lookhovitsy were painted in a non-standard metallic blue/metallic green/silver camouflage

ABOVE: *The MiG-29M's dorsal airbrake. (Yefim Gordon)*
OPPOSITE: *The starboard fin of 999 White. (Yefim Gordon)*

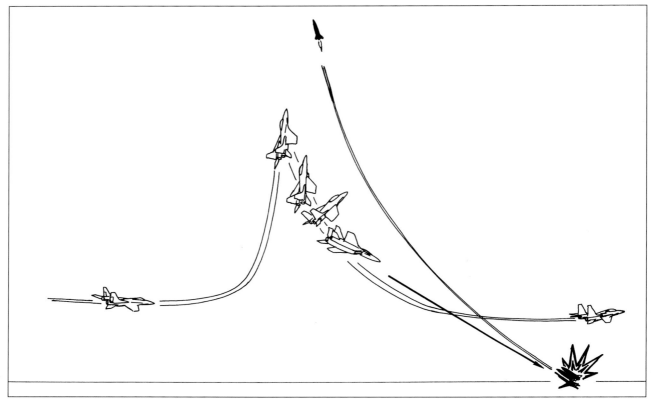

The MiG-29 was the first jet fighter to perform the tailslide manoeuvre.

with MAPO and Mikoyan logos for display purposes, including demonstration to foreign delegations. These aircraft coded 333 White, 555 White (c/n 2960540517), 777 White and 999 White (c/n 2960536591) were sometimes referred to as MiG-29SE or MiG-29SM but this is obviously incorrect.

A big day in the MiG-29's history was 26 April 1995. That day Roman P. Taskayev (who has been awarded the Hero of Russia title) set an altitude record in the 12–16-ton (26,455–35,273-lb) gross weight class, climbing to 27,460 m (90,091 ft) in a standard MiG-29. In May the same year a 'Fulcrum' set another record, climbing to an altitude in excess of 25,000 m (82,020 ft) with a 1,000-kg (2,204-lb) payload. These records were officially recognised by the FAI at the year's end, substantiating the MiG-29's excellent reputation and proving the potential of the Russian aerospace industry and the Mikoyan design bureau.

Apart from the Gulf War when Iraq made no real effort to oppose the Allies, the MiG-29 has never been in real combat. According to the US Department of Defense, three Iraqi MiG-29s were shot down on 17 January 1991 and two more on 19 January. It could hardly have been different, considering that in modern warfare the outcome of a battle depends on pilot skill and adequate information support as much as on the aircraft's capabilities; and the Iraqi pilots were definitely lacking in the first and second. Speaking of information support, German reunification gave NATO a chance to evaluate the MiG-29 in mock combat with the F-15 and F-16, which was especially welcome because Operation *Desert Storm* was already brewing at the time. The verdict was that the 'Fulcrum' was an excellent weapons system if used properly. But, as a saying goes, equipment is but a piece of metal in the hands of a savage.

In keeping with the openness policy the Soviet Union offered foreign pilots a chance to fly the MiG-29, and many jumped at the opportunity. These included Maj. Robert Wade (a CAF Hornet pilot), David M. North (managing editor of *AW&ST*), John Farley (former project test pilot of the British Aerospace Harrier) and Benjamin Lambeth, a Sovietologist and tactical aircraft specialist with the Rand Corporation. 'I have piloted the MiG-29 and consider it an honour and good luck', Gen. Bernard Norlen, commander of the *Armée de l'Air*'s Tactical Air Command, said in February 1992 after flying the 'Fulcrum' at Kubinka AB. 'We are satisfied that the MiG-29 meets our requirements. We have compared it to other types and gave preference to the aircraft powered by two engines with reference to the aircraft powered by one engine', said Lt.-Gen. Haji Abdul Ghani Aziz, Royal Malaysian Air Force C-in-C, during his Moscow visit in November 1994.

'The MiG-29 is a very special aircraft. It is a superb fighter for close combat. In a lot of areas it is superior to a lot of jets in the West – it turns better in a dogfight', said Johan Köck, commander of 2/JG 73, the *Luftwaffe* unit operating the type, in an interview to *The Scotsman*. 'It is a pilot's aircraft. It is easily controllable and highly responsive . . . In general the cockpit and ejection seat are comfortable, and the view from the cockpit is good as

well . . . The helmet-mounted target designation system is impressive', said Austrian Air Force C-in-C Gen. Erich Wolf after trying out the aircraft at Zhukovskiy.

Trade magazines were equally enthusiastic. 'The MiG-29 is one of the premier light tactical fighters having up-to-date weapons and a relatively low fly-away cost', wrote *Asian-Pacific Defence Reporter* No. 3–4, 1995. 'The participation of the MiG-29 in the NATO "Tactical Air Meet '95" caused something of a sensation . . . The main lesson stemming from the TAM'95 exercises has been the final confirmation (if such was needed) of the overwhelming superiority of the Russian air-to-air weapon system installed on the MiG-29', wrote *Military Technology* No. 12, 1995.

What's more, in its 26 February 1990 issue *AW&ST* urged NATO to let Soviet pilots fly US fighters: 'The Soviet Union has now allowed three North American pilots to fly the Mikoyan MiG-29 and an Australian to fly

The vectoring nozzle developed for the new Klimov afterburning turbofans (RD-43, RD-133 and VKS-10) which may be fitted to future versions of the MiG-29. (Yefim Gordon)

the Sukhoi Su-27 from the front seat. It is time for reciprocity', the editorial said.

The MiG-29 has become recognised as one of the best fourth-generation fighters. Its high thrust-to-weight ratio and refined aerodynamics give it an excellent rate of climb, acceleration and turning radius, enabling prolonged high-G manoeuvring. It has proved to be a robust fighter which can take a lot of punishment; e.g., only a single case of vertical tail deformation due to G loads has been recorded over the years. The capable weapons control system and wide choice of armament enable the fighter to destroy aerial and ground targets day and night in all weather conditions and in an ECM environment.

Mikoyan engineers believed in the 'Fulcrum', and their trust was rewarded. The MiG-29 has earned a good reputation for its reliability and maintainability. The aircraft is designed to be compatible with civil airfields meeting ICAO standards as well as with military bases. The fuel and power connectors etc. are standardised, enabling the aircraft to use both Russian and Western ground support equipment (though in past years Western observers used to phrase this a bit differently: 'designed to be compatible with captured NATO equipment'!). The connectors and access panels are conveniently located so that virtually all maintenance is done from ground level, with no need for stepladders. The modular structure of the aircraft's systems and high degree of systems component interchangeability have eased maintenance and repair. Easy access to the engines facilitates engine maintenance and change. The built-in test equipment monitors more than 80 per cent of the aircraft's systems.

The main problem facing the MiG-29's manufacturer and the principal customer (the Russian Air Force) is not of a technical but of a purely financial nature. Production of the 'Fulcrum' virtually ground to a halt in 1991 because no funding was available. This left the VVS short of a considerable number of fighters and MAPO without money. The much more capable MiG-29M is now facing an uncertain future. So is the MiG-29K naval fighter, even though the very first cruise of the carrier RNS *Admiral Kuznetsov* showed clearly that the decision to cancel the MiG-29K was a mistake. However, while there's life there's hope: the programme may still be revived.

The most recent conflict in which the MiG-29 participated is the war in Yugoslavia. When NATO launched Operation *Allied Force* on 24 March 1999, JRV MiG-29s were brought into play against the attackers. At first things did not look too good for the 'Fulcrums'. One

aircraft was destroyed on the ground at Batajnica AB by the direct hit of a cruise missile targeted from a surveillance aircraft; three more (some sources even claimed five more) were shot down, including one on the very first day by a Royal Dutch Air Force/322 Sqn Lockheed Martin F-16C (J-063).

Three days later, however, the MiGs – and the Serbs in general – were avenged in spectacular fashion when a USAF/49th FW/8th FS Lockheed F-117A Nighthawk fighter-bomber (82-0806 'HO') operating out of Aviano AB in Italy was shot down about 30 km (25 mi) north-west of Belgrade. The pilot, Capt. Ken Dwilli, ejected and was rescued by a USAF CSAR team. The cause of the loss was immediately the subject of much speculation. NATO spokesmen claimed the crash had been due to poor weather or mechanical malfunctions.

In Russia, the initial theory was that the supposedly invulnerable stealth aircraft had been downed by a Kvadraht (Square; NATO SA-4 *Ganef*) surface-to-air missile. However, in late May the Russian MoD daily *Krasnaya Zveda* (Red Star) stated that the F-117A had been destroyed by a MiG-29 flown by Lt.-Col. Gvozden Djukić. According to Djukić, he had spotted the lone enemy aircraft at dusk 1.5 km (0.9 mi.) ahead while flying a combat air patrol mission on Serbia's western border, recognizing it instantly as an F-117 by its distinctive shape. The fighter-bomber started disintegrating after being hit by the first missile and the pilot ejected right away. It should be noted that the pilot very probably did not switch on the radar, using either the IRST or the HMS to guide the missile, otherwise the F-117 pilot would have had ample warning from his RHAWS.

'I felt as pleased as an Indian that had just taken a scalp, or even more,' Djukić recounted. 'Capt. Ken Dwilli probably didn't know we were hunting for him when he flew to wreak death and destruction on our cities. He also hadn't heard of our proverb, "A black sheep is a bad sheep," and Mr Dwilli's squadron was named "Black Sheep". Perhaps the name had played a dirty trick on him!' For this 'kill' Djukić was awarded a medal, receiving it from the Yugoslav President Slobodan Milośević.

However, it has to be said that the JRV tried to use its aircraft as little as possible in an attempt to conserve them, relying mainly on anti-aircraft artillery and missiles. The Yugoslavs were clearly learning from Iraqi mistakes in the Gulf War when Saddam Hussein had thrust all his assets into the battle and lost a lot of aircraft. Waging an all-out war with a handful of fighters against NATO bomber armadas was pointless.

7

Foreign 'Fulcrums'

By mid-1994, some 500 MiG-29s had been delivered to or ordered by the air forces of 16 nations. By 1997 the 'Fulcrum' was in service in 23 states, including the CIS. Known operators of the type are dealt with in this chapter.

Belorussia

The Belorussian Republic was the third-largest operator of the type in the CIS (Russia and the Ukraine take first and second place), with 47 aircraft on strength. However, economic problems and the inability to keep a large air force led Belorussia to put the 'Fulcrums' up for sale. Eventually Beltechexport, a government company, signed a contract with the Peruvian Government for the delivery of 18 MiG-29s to the Peruvian Air Force; the first four aircraft were shipped to Peru shortly afterwards. Some sources stated that the fighters were sold for US$ 11–14 mln apiece, i.e., half the real market price; there have been rumours, however, that the price was as low as US$ 4.0–4.5 mln apiece.[1]

In an attempt to solve the maintenance problem the Belorussian AF assigned its MiG-29s to the military aircraft overhaul plant in Baranovichi. Still, without cooperation with Mikoyan and MAPO, the results remain unsatisfactory.

Bulgaria

In 1990 the Bulgarian Air Force (*Voyenno Vozdooshni Seeli*) took delivery of 12 MiG-29s – ten single-seaters (*izdeliye* 9.12A standard) and two MiG-29UBs. Currently Bulgaria is reported to have 21 or 22 on strength. As in the CIS, Bulgarian AF fighters usually wear two-digit tactical codes making positive identification all but impossible. Known 'Fulcrums' are 20 White, 22 White, 23 White and 29 White (all single-seaters) and MiG-29UBs 02 White and 05 White. On 29–30 June 1996 Bulgarian MiG-29 15 White and MiG-29UB 02 White participated in the Czech International Air Fest (CIAF'96) at Hradec Kralové airbase.

In 1996 Russia and Bulgaria began negotiations on new military aircraft purchases. The Bulgarian Telegraph Agency, BTA, reported that Russia offered Bulgaria a US$ 450 million target-oriented credit with a three-year zero-interest period. Part of the money would pay for 14 MiG-29SM fighters and two MiG-AT advanced trainers, while the rest would be used to reconstruct the aircraft overhaul facility in Plovdiv, creating 1,000 jobs. Bulgaria would also receive the right to overhaul Mikoyan aircraft operated by European, Asian, Middle Eastern and North African states. This is a huge market, with some 1,200 MiG-21s, 750 MiG-23s and 350 MiG-29s in service in the above regions, and the overhaul business can generate sizeable profits.

VPK MAPO[2] led the negotiations as the Russian party. These culminated in the Moscow meeting of Russian Prime Minister Chernomyrdin and Bulgarian Prime Minister Sofiyanskiy where the two government leaders voiced agreement to sign a deal. This issue is all the more important because the MiG-29 currently forms the backbone of Bulgaria's air arm. The Bulgarian Air Force had accumulated a wealth of experience with the type and had well-equipped maintenance facilities and highly qualified personnel. However, the country's recent economic problems had taken their toll on the air force as well; the fighter force needed new and more modern hardware.

For the first time since the fall of communism in Bulgaria, economic ties with Russia made the headlines in the country's newspapers. The main debates raged around the possible deliveries of new MiG-29s; opinions varied from utter denouncement to claims that the deal was the air force's only chance of survival. Bulgarian AF C-in-C Mikho Mikhov was one of the supporters of the deal, stating that the MiG-29 was the most cost-effective solution.

Opponents in the government claimed that buying Russian weapons would increase the country's

---

1 The export price quoted by Aviaexport in 1989 was US$ 23 mln for the single-seater and US$ 28 mln for the MiG-29UB.

2 VPK = *voyenno-promyshlennyy kompleks* – military industrial complex. VPK MAPO is an aerospace industry amalgamation including, besides Mikoyan, the Kamov helicopter company, the Klimov engine design bureau and some avionics manufacturers. Still, the use of the VPK abbreviation in this context looks somewhat pretentious and out of place, as VPK usually denotes the defence industry **in general** and not just a single consortium in it, large and important though it be.

dependence on Russia and prevent NATO membership which Bulgaria is striving to attain. Mikhov's counter-argument was that a decision to follow Poland's or Czechia's example and re-equip with Western fighters would mean paying exorbitant sums for second-hand F-16s or F/A-18s; besides, this would require a complete replacement of ground support equipment, which meant further expenditures. Russia, on the other hand, offered the latest version of the 'Fulcrum' on extremely favourable terms. Also, the MiG-29 could be fitted with Western avionics compatible with NATO standards at customer request. Westernised MiG-29s are successfully used operationally, e.g., by the *Luftwaffe*.

Meanwhile, the ballyhoo in the Bulgarian media continued as proponents and opponents of the deal tried to win public support. The anti-'Fulcrum' papers either coyly referred to 'information from reliable sources' or launched obvious canards, such as Western businessmen allegedly expressing an interest in the Plovdiv aircraft overhaul facility with a view to upgrading it to overhaul US military transport aircraft. Another rumour circulated by the press was that the Su-25TK attack aircraft was regarded as a possible competitor to the MiG-29. Imagine a subsonic tank killer competing with a high-manoeuvrability supersonic fighter! Still, the deal did not materialise in the end. President Stoyanov did not authorise the purchase of new warplanes because of Bulgaria's difficult economic situation.

Cuba

Cuba is traditionally a Soviet ally and still enjoys friendly nation status with Russia. Hence the Cuban Air Force (FAR – *Fuerza Aérea Revolucionaria*) received the state-of-the-art MiG-29 even before the collapse of the Soviet Union. The first aircraft arrived at San Antonio de los Baños airbase in October 1989 and made its checkout flight following reassembly on 19 April 1990. There have been unconfirmed reports that the FAR currently has one squadron of MiG-29s (twelve single-seaters and two MiG-29UBs) on strength. Unlike FAR MiG-21s and MiG-23s, which wear a rather shocking 'bluebottle fly' camouflage, the 'Fulcrums' retain their two-tone grey factory finish. Two of the single-seaters have been identified so far, serialled 910 and 911.

Czech Republic

The country then known as Czechoslovakia was one of the first socialist states to receive the MiG-29 (*izdeliye* 9.12A) and MiG-29UB. In 1988 fifteen carefully selected Czechoslovak Air Force (ČVL – *Československé Vojenské Létectvo*) pilots were sent to Loogovaya airbase near Frunze, the capital of the Kirghiz Soviet Socialist Republic, for their training. Deliveries to 11SLP (*stíhací létecky pluk* – fighter regiment) based at Žatec in north-western Czechia began in the spring of 1989. The first aircraft to arrive was MiG-29UB 4401 test flown by Col. Vašek and Lt.-Col. Hackel on 24 April 1989. This was followed by the first nine single-seaters serialled 7501, 7702, 8003, 8304, 8605, 8906, 9207, 9308 and 3709 in June.[3]

Nine more MiG-29s (3810, 3911, 4012, 5113, 5414, 5515, 5616, 5817, 5918) and a single MiG-29UB (4402) were delivered in September, increasing the total to 20. And that was it; Defence Minister Miroslav Vacek announced in January 1990 that no further MiG-29 purchases were planned.

11SLP comprised two squadrons; the first of these was known as *Tigrí létka* (Tiger squadron) because some of its aircraft sported tiger stripes on the fins and stabilators and participated in Tiger Meets. Unlike most 'Fulcrums', Czech MiG-29s were painted in a so-called East European tactical camouflage (dark green/foliage green/dark earth/tan upper surfaces and light grey undersurfaces). The MiG-29s were used primarily in the air defence rôle. In 1991 CzAF pilots flew to Akhtoobinsk to train at the NII VVS firing range.

In 1992 the gentle revolution of 1989 which put an end to socialism in Czechoslovakia was followed by an equally gentle divorce. Quietly and without fuss the Federal Republic of Czechoslovakia split into the Czech Republic and Slovakia, and the 'Fulcrum' fleet was divided equally between the two. With two exceptions, odd-numbered aircraft went to Slovakia and even-numbered ones to Czechia. Consequently 11SLP at Žatec was disbanded and the aircraft of 1 Sqn went to 2 Sqn of 1SLP at České Budějovice which previously operated the MiG-23MF 'Flogger'-Bs. In late June 1994 1SLP MiG-29s engaged in

---

3 Generally the serials of Czechoslovak Air Force (CzAF) aircraft coincide with the last four digits of the c/n. However, there are exceptions. With the PZL Swidnik (Mil) Mi-2 'Hoplite' helicopter, for one, the serial matches the last two digits of the batch number and the number in the batch, which are *not* the last four digits. E.g., Mi-2T 8746 is c/n 518746074, i.e., utility version (coded 51 by the manufacturer), batch 87, 46th aircraft in batch of 50, completed in (07) July 1984.

MiG-29 serials are one of the exceptions, being in fact the last *two* digits of the c/n plus the fleet number of the respective version. E.g., MiG-29 8003 = c/n 2960526380, third 'Fulcrum-A' delivered. The reason for this is obscure.

ABOVE: *Czech Air Force MiG-29s (izdeliye 9.12A) escorting a pair of visiting USAF F-111s en route to an airshow. (Létectví a Kosmonautika)*

BELOW: *A Czech AF MiG-29UB trainer. Czechoslovakia's fleet of 'Fulcrums' was divided equally between the Czech Republic and Slovakia when the country split up; the Czech aircraft were later handed over to the Polish AF as a trade-in for new PZL W-3 Sokół helicopters. (Létectví a Kosmonautika)*

TOP: *With the exception of a single MiG-29UB trainer, all Moldovan MiG-29s acquired by the USAF wore a crudely applied non-standard green camouflage. Not all had the gaudy Moldovan insignia, as illustrated by these 'Fulcrum-C's. (AFM)*

ABOVE: *MiG-29UB 61 White being loaded into a USAF C-17A at Markuleshty. (AFM)*

mock combat with visiting *Armée de l'Air* Mirage 2000s, demonstrating the Russian fighter's superiority. Yet a few days later, on 30 June the unit was disbanded as well and the aircraft were grounded. The big question remained: what to do with them?

Having decided to join NATO, the Czech government was eager to dispose of Soviet equipment which did not conform to NATO standards and re-equip the CzAF with US aircraft. Thus on 22 December 1995 a contract was signed with Poland and all ten Czech MiG-29s were transferred to the Polish Air Force in exchange for new PZL Swidnik W-3 *Sokól* (Falcon) utility helicopters – which, incidentally, saved the 'Fulcrums' from the torch. The fighters had been in open storage, with a consequent deterioration in their condition, and there was no point in spending money on repairing aircraft which were phased out.

The ten aircraft taken over by the Czech Air Force (*České Vojenské Létectvo*) are listed below.

Serial	Model	C/n	Remarks
4402	MiG-29UB	N50903014528*	To PWL 28
3810	MiG-29	2960532038	To PWL 38
4012	MiG-29	2960532040	To PWL 40
5414	MiG-29	2960532354	To PWL 54
5616	MiG-29	2960532356	To PWL 56
5918	MiG-29	2960532359	To PWL 59
7702	MiG-29	2960526377	To PWL 77
8304	MiG-29	2960526383	To PWL 83
8906*	MiG-29	2960526389**	To PWL 86
9207	MiG-29	2960526392	To PWL 92

Notes:

* The c/n is doubtful, as the last two digits do not match the first two digits of the serial.

** Possibly the c/n is actually 2960526386 and hence the serial should have been 8606. (See Polish section.)

Germany

East Germany was the first of the Warsaw Pact countries to re-equip with the 'Fulcrum'. The first indication of this came in 1984 when East German Minister of Defence Gen. Heinz Hoffmann announced his intention to order the MiG-29 to his Swedish colleague visiting the Peenemünde airbase. Between March 1988 and May 1989 the East German Air Force (LSK/LV – *Luftstreitkräfte und Luftverteidigung der Deutschen Demokratischen Republik* – Air Force and Air Defence Force of the German Democratic Republic) received 20 MiG-29s (*izdeliye* 9.12A standard) and four MiG-29UBs. LSK/LV pilots had taken their conversion training in the Soviet Union in 1987. Contract worth was stated as one billion East German Marks.

The aircraft were operated by JG 3 (*Jagdfliegergeschwader* – fighter Wing) 'Wladimir Komarow' at Preschen AB near Forst, Cottbus. The unit was named after Soviet cosmonaut Vladimir Komarov who died when his spacecraft's heat shield failed during re-entry. The first of two squadrons (*Staffeln*) of JG 3 became operational in May 1988 (some sources state 5 April). Some sources, however, say that service entry was slow because of the need to upgrade the airbases from which the 'Fulcrums' would operate. Operations from

East German Air Force MiG-29s wore three-digit red serials on the air intakes. (Flieger Revue)

Preschen had a quirk: the base was located so close to the Polish border that the aircraft had to enter Polish airspace during their landing pattern. This was made possible by an agreement between East Germany and Poland under which Polish military aircraft could also fly into German airspace when operating from bases at Sczecin and Jelenia Góra.

Additional MiG-29 purchases were contemplated to re-equip, e.g., JG 1 at Holzdorf AB but they never materialised because of East Germany's inflexible state-planned economy. However, JG 3 'Fulcrums' occasionally deployed to Holzdorf. A MiG-29 flight simulator was also bought but never became operational because the building at Preschen intended for it was not yet built; trainees had to make do with a full-scale cockpit mockup which could be opened up for inspection. Some sources state that LSK/LV MiG-29s had some locally produced avionics components developed by the Militärtechnisches Institut at Wuhlheide near Dresden. These included parts of the radar set and the entire IFF system.

East German 'Fulcrum-As' also wore East European tactical camouflage and (typically of East German

fighters) red serials. Conversely, the trainers had standard two-tone grey camouflage and, like all other LSK/LV aircraft, black serials. These were not allocated consecutively, presumably so as to confuse spies. E.g., 181 and 185 were MiG-29UBs while the intervening serials 182 through 184 belonged to Tu-134AK VIP aircraft, ex DM-SCL, DM-SCK and DDR-SDS respectively, operated by TFG 44 (*Transportfliegergeschwader* – air transport Wing) at Marxwalde AB. Curiously, the serial 181 originally belonged to another TFG 44 Tu-134AK (c/n 35180, f/n 3006) and was reallocated to MiG-29UB c/n N50903006604 after the airliner was registered DDR-SDC on 9 March 1982. Additionally, for security reasons the serials were often changed on aircraft intended for public view. There are publicity photos of East German 'Fulcrum-As' 28 and 70 – actually 628 and 670 with the first digit of the serial overpainted.

When Germany reunited on 3 October 1990 the LSK/LV and the West German Air Force (*Luftwaffe der Bundesrepublik Deutschland*) merged into a single air

RIGHT: *FAP 045, one of two Peruvian Air Force MiG-29UBs. (AFM)*

BELOW: *Cuba's MiG-29s were delivered in 1989 and the FAR is believed to operate 10 'Fulcrum-A's and two MiG-29UB 'Fulcrum-B's. (World Air Power Journal)*

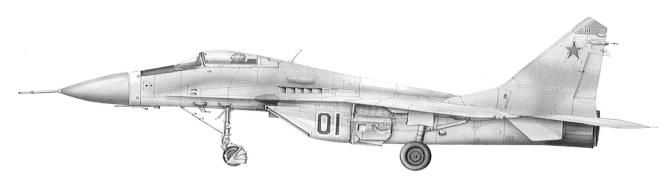

Aircraft 901 (01 Blue), the first prototype.

One of the early prototypes (tactical number unknown).

Aircraft 951, the prototype MiG-29UB 'Fulcrum-B'.

ABOVE & OPPOSITE: *A MiG-29 (izdeliye 9.12/'Fulcrum-A') in standard VVS camouflage with a typical weapons load.*

12 Blue, a standard 'Fulcrum-A' in Russian AF colours.

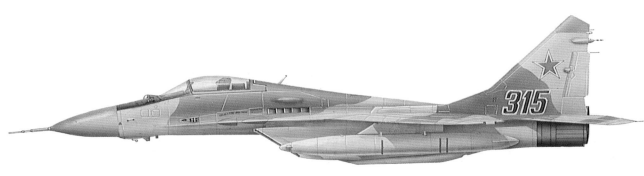

315 Blue, a company demonstrator with three drop tanks for ferry flights.

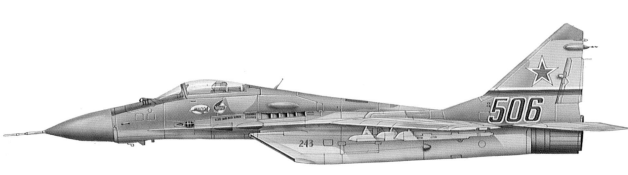

506 Blue, another company demonstrator with late-style MAPO and MiG stickers below the cockpit.

92 Red, one of the few MiG-29s operated by Russia's naval air arm (AV-MF).

46 Blue, a 'fatback' MiG-29 'Fulcrum-C' (izdeliye 9.13).

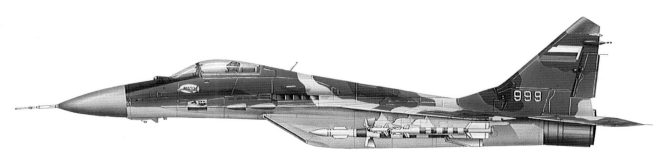

999 White, one of four MAPO-MiG demonstrators sporting a rather bizarre colour scheme.

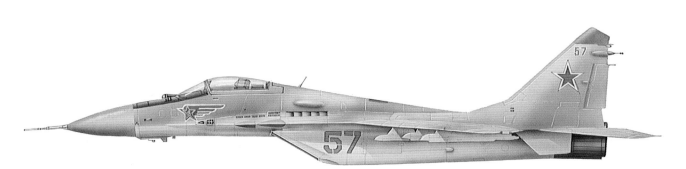

57 Yellow, a 968th IAP MiG-29 operating from Nöbitz in Germany; this was an early aircraft with ventral fins.

07 Blue, a 'Fulcrum-A' wearing the Guards badge.

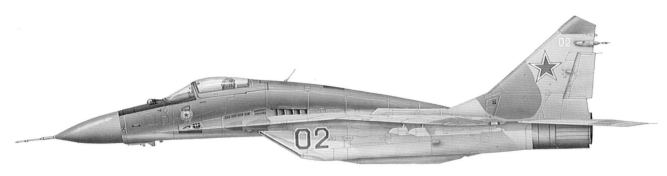

02 Red, a 'Fulcrum-C' operated by a Guards unit, with centreline drop tank.

Sharkmouthed 47 White with the Russian double eagle on the fins. Unusually, the tactical code is repeated on the insides of the fins; this aircraft was operated by the 120th IAP based at Domna AB.

08 Red, a 'Fulcrum-C' operated by a Guards unit, in non-standard dark green/dark earth/sand camouflage.

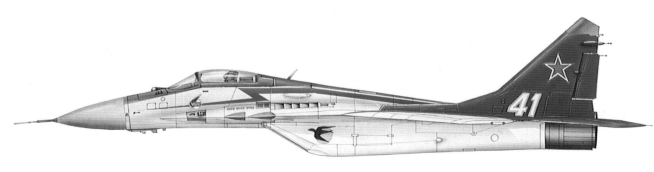

41 White, one of the single-seaters belonging to the Strizhi (Swifts) aerobatic team.

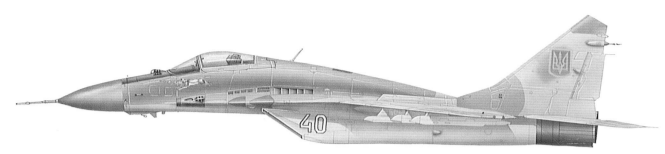

40 White, one of the Ukrainian Air Force 'Fulcrum-C's sporting the contemporary shield insignia and squadron markings.

102 White, a MiG-29 flown by the UAF's Ookrains'ki Sokoly/Ukrainian Falcons display team.

53 Blue, the company-owned MiG-29UB demonstrator which made the type's first appearance in the West at Farnborough International '88.

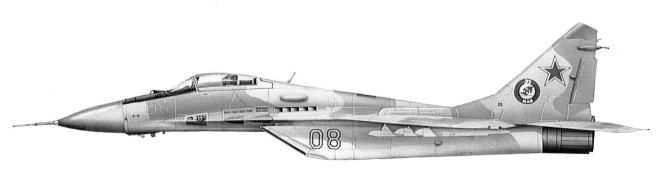

08 White, a 33th IAP 'Fulcrum-A' based at Püttnitz in Germany, with fin badge.

108 White (18108), a Jugoslovenske Ratne Vazduhoplovstvo *(Yugoslav AF) MiG-29 (izdeliye 9.12A).*

7501, a Slovak Air Force MiG-29 (izdeliye 9.12A).

7702, a Czech Air Force MiG-29 (izdeliye 9.12A). This aircraft was later sold to Poland.

679, an LSK/LV (East German AF) MiG-29 (izdeliye 9.12A) which later became Luftwaffe *29+12.*

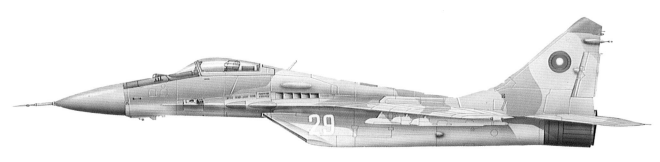

29 White, a Bulgarian Air Force MiG-29 (izdeliye 9.12A).

KB703, a 47 Sqn Archers MiG-29 (izdeliye 9.12B) of the Indian Air Force.

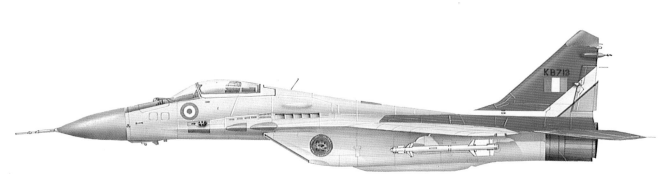

KB713, a 28 Sqn First Supersonics MiG-29 (izdeliye 9.12B) of the IAF.

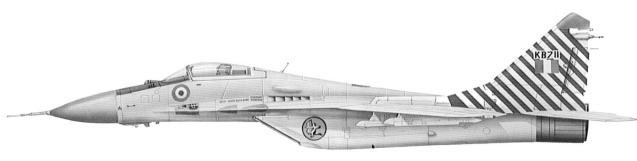

KB711, another 47 Sqn aircraft in a different colour scheme probably associated with war games.

LSK/LV MiG-29 No 604 with special markings to commemorate the last flight in East German service on 27 September, 1990.

15 Red, a MiG-29UB operated by the Polish Air Force's 1 PLM 'Warszawa'.

29+20, a Luftwaffe MiG-29.

27 Red, a Hungarian Air Force MiG-29UB.

49 Red, a Romanian AF MiG-29 (izdeliye 9.12A).

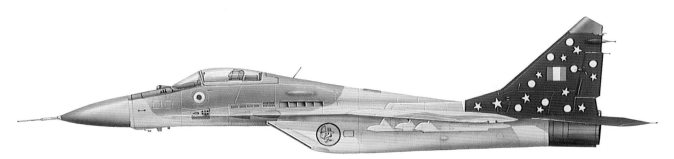

Another IAF 47 Sqn 'Fulcrum' with star-spangled fins.

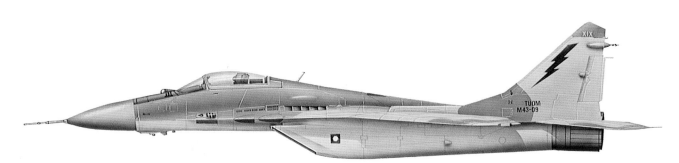

A Malaysian Air Force (TUDM) 'Fulcrum' obstinately misidentified by Western sources as 'MiG-29N'.

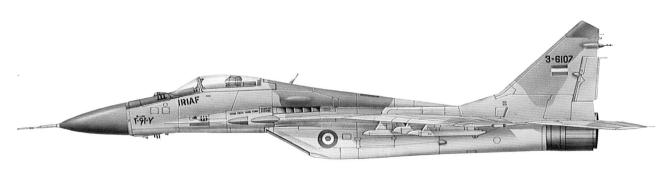

3-6107, an Islamic Republic of Iran Air Force (IRIAF) MiG-29 (izdeliye 9.12B).

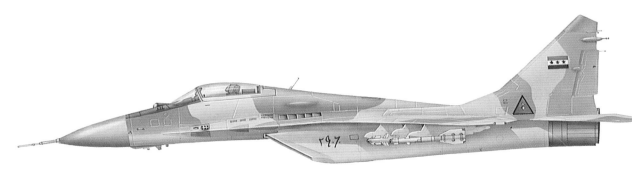

29060, an Iraqi Air Force MiG-29 (izdeliye 9.12B).

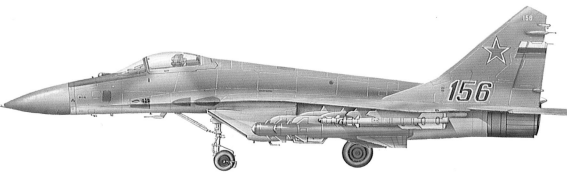

156 Blue, the sixth prototype MiG-29M/izdeliye 9.15 (later recoded 301 Blue) with four Kh-29T AGMs and four R-73 AAMs.

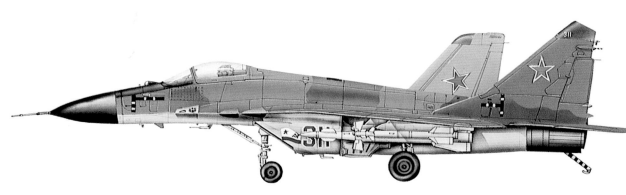

311 Blue, the first prototype naval MiG-29K (izdeliye 9.31).

312 Blue, the second prototype MiG-29K, with four Kh-31A anti-shipping missiles and four R-73 AAMs.

ABOVE: Luftwaffe MiG-29 29+20, still in Central European tactical camouflage. (Yefim Gordon archive)

BELOW: Luftwaffe MiG-29 29+20 operated by JG 73. The original LSK/LV serial 785 is still painted in white on the dielectric fin tip. (Yefim Gordon archive)

Mikoyan engineers discussing modifications to the MiG-29 with Luftwaffe *technical staff. Mikhail Waldenberg is fourth from the right. (Mikhail Waldenberg archive)*

arm with the somewhat less cumbersome name of *Luftwaffe*. Thus most East German military aircraft were temporarily taken on strength by the united armed forces (*Bundeswehr*) and received four-digit *Luftwaffe* serials. It should be noted here that the first two digits denote the type (e.g., 43 through 46 = Panavia Tornado IDS, 50 and 51 = Transall C.160 etc.). The MiG-29s were conveniently allocated serials in the 29+... block. Incidentally, the serials 29+01 through 29+21 were re-used, having been previously allocated to Lockheed F-104G Starfighters.

One of the single-seaters, 604, was painted in special markings to commemorate the type's last flight in East German service on 27 September 1990 at the hands of *Oberstleutnant* (Lt.-Col.) Günther Fichte. It was also the first MiG-29 to be repainted in *Luftwaffe* markings and the inscription 27.09.1990 below the cockpit was duly changed to 19.10.1990 to mark the first flight in united Germany. This particular 'Fulcrum' was referred to as die

Traditionsmaschine (the traditional aircraft)!

The old and new identities of the German 'Fulcrums' are given in the following **Table B**.

Euromil quoted a 'MiG-29 serialled 29+13 (ex LSK/LV 680)' – an aircraft which never existed. The 'baker's dozen' serial was not allocated to any aircraft for superstitious reasons;[4] instead, it was applied to a blue IFA Trabant 601S car owned by the unit and nicknamed 'Rudi'. Guests of honour were given a ride in this tiny, farting and smoky vehicle, finally signing their name on the inside of the passenger door!

After the reunification there was much debate as to whether Soviet aircraft should be retained. Since the MiG-29 was the most modern of these the German government decided to evaluate the type. To this end two

---

4 Purely LSK/LV superstition, it should be noted. The 'old' *Luftwaffe* had no reservations about using 13 as the final two digits.

TABLE B

Luftwaffe serial	Former LSK/LV serial	Model	C/n	Delivery date	Total time as of 3-10-90	Remaining time
29+01	604 Red	MiG-29	2960525106	Apr 88	216 hr	584 hr
29+02	607 Red	MiG-29	2960525108	Apr 88	380 hr	420 hr
29+03	615 Red	MiG-29	2960525110	Mar 88	227 hr	573 hr
29+04	628 Red	MiG-29	2960525111	Mar 88	252 hr	575 hr
29+05	635 Red	MiG-29	2960525113	Jun 88	241 hr	559 hr
29+06	661 Red	MiG-29	2960525114	Apr 88	271 hr	529 hr
29+07	668 Red	MiG-29	2960525115	Apr 88	280 hr	520 hr
29+08	669 Red	MiG-29	2960525118	Apr 88	214 hr	586 hr
29+09	670 Red	MiG-29	2960525121	Apr 88	244 hr	556 hr
29+10	676 Red	MiG-29	2960525124	Apr 88	294 hr	506 hr
29+11	677 Red	MiG-29	2960525188	Aug 88	212 hr	588 hr
29+12	679 Red	MiG-29	2960525132	May 88	240 hr	560 hr
29+14	684 Red	MiG-29	2960525800	Nov 88	213 hr	587 hr
29+15	693 Red	MiG-29	2960526300	Nov 88	214 hr	586 hr
29+16	699 Red	MiG-29	2960526301	Jan 89	194 hr	606 hr
29+17	745 Red	MiG-29	2960526302	Jan 89	204 hr	596 hr
29+18	777 Red	MiG-29	2960526310	Jan 89	184 hr	616 hr
29+19	778 Red	MiG-29	2960526314	May 89	157 hr	643 hr
29+20	785 Red	MiG-29	2960526315	Jan 89	210 hr	590 hr
29+21	686 Red	MiG-29	2960526319	Jan 89	190 hr	610 hr
29+22	148 Black	MiG-29UB	N50903006448	Apr 88	330 hr	470 hr
29+23	179 Black	MiG-29UB	N50903006526	Apr 88	328 hr	482 hr
29+24	181 Black	MiG-29UB	N50903006604	Apr 88	328 hr	482 hr
29+25	185 Black	MiG-29UB	N50903011408	Nov 88	220 hr	580 hr

single-seaters (29+20 and 29+21) and two trainers (29+22 and 29+25) were transferred in late October to WTD 61 (*Wehrtechnische Dienststelle 61 für Luftfahrzeuge* – military technical support unit, or rather Aircraft Test Centre No. 61) at Manching AB near Ingolstadt, Bayern, which also evaluated other Soviet military aircraft.[5] The others remained at Preschen with JG 3, which was transformed into *Erprobungsgeschwader* (test Wing) *MiG-29* in early 1991; this was to support the trials at Manching and perform proficiency training.

The trials programme comprising nearly 200 items was jointly developed by the *Luftwaffe* and the Federal Military Equipment Procurement Office. Performance, operational flexibility and reliability of the weapons system as a whole and its various components were investigated. Operating and maintenance/overhaul costs were calculated. Equally important was how the MiG-29

---

5 *Euromil* managed to make a mistake here as well, misidentifying the single-seaters operated by WTD 61 as 98+06 (ex 29+13) and 98+08 (ex 29+19)!

A Luftwaffe MiG-29 on display at ILA'96. (Yefim Gordon)

would fare against NATO fighters in air-to-air combat. The latter came as a considerable shock for USAF F-15 and F-16 pilots who often found themselves 'shot down' in mock combat before they even got the 'Fulcrum' on their radar screen! This was partly due to the MiG-29's agility and partly because the fighter's N-019 radar proved to be far more capable and resistant to ECM than expected. To ensure adequate flight safety during trials Rheine-Hopsten, Wittmund and Manching airbases were equipped with Soviet RSBN (*rahdiotekhneecheskaya sistema blizhney nahvigahtsii* – SHORAN) beacons used by the LSK/LV. East German emergency arrester barriers typical of LSK/LV bases were also installed at both ends of the runway at the latter two locations.

Meanwhile, the German government addressed the Soviet Union, seeking aid in modifying the MiG-29s to make them compatible with NATO standards. The Soviet government authorised the Mikoyan OKB to do the job. The *Luftwaffe* proposed that Mikoyan check and authorise all the changes, and so they did. The fighters

were fitted with new identification friend-or-foe (IFF), communications and tactical navigation (TACAN) equipment, flight instruments marked in feet and knots, an 'English-speaking' version of the Ekran (Screen) ground test system, anti-collision strobe lights etc., even the colours of the artificial horizon changed to suit NATO requirements. The instruments were altered in Moscow and delivered to Germany for installation, the rest of the changes were made on site. Curiously, the Danish aviation magazine *Flyv* referred to the modified aircraft as MiG-29G (the G probably standing for Germany) and MiG-29GT (German trainer?); however, no such designations ever existed.

Post-modification trials were held in April and May 1991 in Italy at the Air Combat Manoeuvring Installation (ACMI) at Decimomannu AB, Sardinia. The 'Fulcrums' won in all sessions of mock combat against various NATO fighters. As part of the evaluation programme four MiG-29s were detached to Wittmund AB near Wilhelmshaven, Niedersachsen (home of JG 71

TOP: *Luftwaffe/JG 73 MiG-29 29+05 (ex LSK/LV 635 Red) taxying at Laage AB near Rostock. (Henrik Glienke)*
ABOVE: *Another JG 73 'Fulcrum', MiG-29UB 29+23 (ex 179 Black), at the same location. (Henrik Glienke)*

MiG-29 29+22 at its original base at Preschen. (AFM)

Richthofen) on 4-27 March 1991. Evaluation was completed in June 1991 and on 25 July Minister of Defence Dr. Gerhard Stoltenberg ruled that the MiG-29 would remain in service for a 12-year period. Thus the 'Fulcrum' gained the distinction of being the only Soviet type to continue service with the *Luftwaffe* after German reunification; all other ex-LSK/LV aircraft were promptly sold (mostly to East European air forces), donated to museums or scrapped.

After this, *Erprobungsgeschwader* MiG-29 was reorganized once again, becoming 2/JG 73 and moving to Laage AB. (1/JG 73 operates McDonnell Douglas F-4F Phantom IIs and is based at Pferdsfeld AB.) Initially the aircraft retained their Central European tactical camouflage (and the former LSK/LV serial on the dielectric fin caps). In 1992, however, they received the new overall light grey air superiority finish introduced on the F-4F. MiG-29 29+11 was the first to be repainted in this fashion, attracting considerable attention from photographers when it appeared in the static park at the ILA'92 airshow at Berlin-Schönefeld airport on 15-21 June 1992.

Col. Manfred Menge, commander of JG 73, went to great lengths to praise the aircraft. Val'denberg, who was still MiG-29 project chief at the time, recalls that the German pilots demonstrated perfect landings of two aircraft at a time; the flight leader would touch down in the middle of the runway and his wingman at the beginning of the runway. When asked about this, Col. Menge commented that a good commander has to teach his men everything the aircraft allows them to do. The evaluation programme was taking rather long, and Menge told Val'denberg he would write an open letter to Chancellor Helmuth Kohl if the MiG-29 was rejected.

The 'Fulcrum' is expected to stay in service with the *Luftwaffe* until around 2002. Besides filling the air defence rôle, German MiG-29s are sometimes used as aggressor aircraft during NATO exercises (*Red Flag* etc.). Since mid-1995 two MiG-29s are on ready alert as part of NATO's quick-reaction forces. Currently the fighters are flown mostly by former LSK/LV pilots. Only six 'Fulcrum' drivers' have converted to the MiG-29 from Western types, coming from JG 71 Richthofen, JG 72 Westfalen and JG 74 Mölders. Col. Menge, commander of JG 73, is likewise an officer of the 'old' *Luftwaffe*, having formerly commanded JG 72 at Rheine-Hopsten AB, while his next in command is a former East German officer. The MiG-29 pilots are, in fact, among the very small portion of East German personnel to be employed by the united *Bundeswehr* – the military standards and doctrines of East and West Germany were just all too different. Training the East German personnel to new standards would be excessively costly and unnecessary, as the *Bundeswehr* would be overstaffed.

Since there were debates in Germany as to what aircraft would be the backbone of the *Luftwaffe's* fighter force in the near future, Russia suggested that the *Luftwaffe* purchase additional MiG-29s. The offer sounded attractive; an analysis by Germany's Federal Accounting Office (BRH – *Bundesrechnungshof*) which had leaked into the press showed that buying additional MiGs would be a better solution than building the Eurofighter EF2000.

Some Western observers believed that Russia would offer the MiG-29 for about DM 20 mln, which is three to five times less than the Eurofighter's selling price. Thus a possible contract for the delivery of 'Fulcrums' would cost DM 2 bln, decreasing Russia's DM 80 bln foreign debt to Germany. Yet a decision to rely on MiGs could make the *Luftwaffe* dependent on spares deliveries and maintenance, which Western experts deemed to be unreliable; to quote *Luftwaffe* C-in-C *Generalleutnant* Hans-Jörg Kuebart who had made a single flight in a MiG-29UB and was generally pleased with the aircraft, 'it's hard to understand who is responsible for the production and sales of spares for these aircraft in Russia'.

Another argument against buying more 'Fulcrums' was the relatively low engine and airframe life. The RD-33 engines of early-model MiG-29s had an MTBO of only 350–400 hrs and a service life not exceeding 600 hrs. Combat readiness was low at first; only six of the *Luftwaffe's* 24 MiG-29s were fully operational in early 1991 but this increased to 12 by January 1992. Russia sent a group of specialists from an overhaul plant dealing with the RD-33 and measures were developed to extend engine life by 50–100 hrs. Last but not least, buying Russian military aircraft was not very acceptable politically. Therefore the German government finally selected the EF2000 after all. This was probably primarily a political decision; among other things, it would create jobs in the German aerospace industry since DASA (Deutsche Aerospace) participates in the Eurofighter consortium.

In early 1997 the *Luftwaffe* successfully tested a modification enabling the German MiG-29s to carry three drop tanks – a feature until now found only on the 'fatback' 'Fulcrum-C'. As originally delivered the 'Fulcrum-A/Bs' could only carry a single centreline drop tank. The upgrade extended the fighter's range to 2,900 km (1,611 nm), amounting to a 800-km (444-nm) increase. Prototype modification work was performed by the Russian-German joint venture MAPS (MiG Aircraft Product Support GmbH) based at Manching AB, as agreed

Still wearing LSK/LV insignia, this MiG-29 was photographed after its inclusion into the Luftwaffe *inventory. (Yefim Gordon archive)*

to by MAPO-MiG. 11 more aircraft are to be brought up to this standard later on.

In late 1997 JG 73 detached four MiG-29s – three single-seaters (29+05, 29+20 and 29+21) and MiG-29UB 29+23 – to Decimomannu AB for a session of dissimilar aerial combat training (DACT) against four Panavia Tornado F.3s from the RAF's XI(F) Squadron from RAF Leeming, including ZE763 DG and ZE780. The Tornados flew a simulated strike profile while the MiGs flew defensive combat air patrol (CAP).

During air-to-air combat sessions the Tornados tried to pick off the 'Fulcrums' at long range, using their beyond visual range (BVR) attack capability. According to *Air Forces Monthly*, German pilots found the Tornado a difficult opponent to get to grips with, thanks to the tri-national fighter's superior avionics (primarily the powerful Ferranti Blue Fox radar) and the aggressive tactics employed by the British pilots.

This accounts for the 2 to 1 kill ratio in favour of the Tornados. E.g., on one occasion when a Tornado pilot saw a MiG-29 going for him with a firm intention to make a stern attack, 'the decision to retreat bravely was taken, with the F.3 flying at Mach 1.5 and trying to shake off the 'Fulcrum'. The MiG-29 took up the pursuit, only to be shot down by a second Tornado that had joined the chase'. (It should be noted that the *Luftwaffe* did not inform the Mikoyan OKB of the reasons of this apparent defeat.)

However, the British pilots also found the MiG-29 a formidable adversary up close because, unlike the Tornado F.3, the 'Fulcrum' was designed as a dogfighter, not a low-speed penetrator adapted for the air defence rôle. On one occasion when a Tornado was at its turning limits trying to stay behind the MiG, 'the German fighter rolled its wings level, pulled into a vertical climb, went over the top of the Tornado and dropped in behind for a perfect Archer kill'.

Luftwaffe MiG-29s had their share of accidents as well. JG 73 lost two single-seaters in 1996-97 (29+09 was one). One aircraft crashed on 25 June 1996. The other aircraft was lost in a fatal crash caused by pilot error (the aircraft entered a spin because of reverse roll reaction to rudder input from and the pilot could not recover because his corrective actions were wrong).

Hungary

The Hungarian Air Force (MHRC – *Magyar Honvedseg Repülö Csapatai*) had 22 single-seaters (*izdeliye* 9.12B standard) and six MiG-29UB trainers delivered by Russia as foreign debt payment. They were operated by the 59th fighter regiment at Kecskemet. Originally it consisted of two squadrons named Puma and Dongó (Bee) respectively; the latter got its aircraft in October 1993. A third squadron was added later and the unit was transformed into the 9th fighter regiment.

A landing study of a Hungarian MiG-29UB. (Ryszard Jaxa-Malachowski)

On 22 September 1997 a group of young American businessmen, members of the Young Businessmen Association, was given a ride in a MiG-29UB at Kecskemet in what was described as 'the first and last chance to fly the "Fulcrum"' before Hungary joined NATO (implying the type would be phased out thereafter). The ride was no cheap experience, the fee being US$ 5,000 per person per hour. A Hungarian MoD spokesman said the money raised in this fashion would be used to develop the Air Force. It said a lot for the current plight of the MHRC!

A Hungarian MiG-29 was reported to have crashed, but this is unconfirmed and no details of the crash are available.

Tactical code	Model	C/n	Remarks
01 Red	MiG-29	2960535116	
02 Red	MiG-29	2960535117	
03 Red	MiG-29	2960535124	
04 Red	MiG-29	2960535127	
05 Red	MiG-29	2960535148	
06 Red	MiG-29		
07 Red	MiG-29	2960535120	
08 Red	MiG-29		
09 Red	MiG-29		
10 Red	MiG-29	2960535158	
11 Red	MiG-29		
12 Red	MiG-29		
14 Red	MiG-29		
15 Red	MiG-29	2960535182	
16 Red	MiG-29	2960535184	
17 Red	MiG-29		
18 Red	MiG-29	2960535189	
19 Red	MiG-29		
20 Red	MiG-29	2960535191	
21 Red	MiG-29		
22 Red	MiG-29	2960535193	
23 Red	MiG-29		Crashed?
24 Red	MiG-29UB		
25 Red	MiG-29UB	N50903027146	
26 Red	MiG-29UB		
27 Red	MiG-29UB	N50903027268	
28 Red	MiG-29UB		
29 Red	MiG-29UB		

India

The Indian Air Force (IAF) was the first foreign operator of the MiG-29. India, which was traditionally on friendly terms with the Soviet Union (and at odds with neighboring Pakistan), contacted the Soviet government in the early '80s, requesting the delivery of the latest Soviet fighters. The reason was the delivery of F-16s to the Pakistani Air Force which could disrupt the balance of power in the region.

When Soviet Minister of Defence Marshal Ustinov visited India in February 1984 he agreed that the Soviet Union would supply India with 44 MiG-29s (40 'Fulcrum-As' and four 'Fulcrum-Bs') at US$ 11 mln apiece. Licence production of a further 110 aircraft was also discussed. HAL had some experience with Mikoyan designs by then, having built the MiG-21FL/M/*bis* 'Fishbed-D/J/N' under licence for the IAF at its Nasik, Maharashtra facility since 1966 and the MiG-27 'Flogger-J' since 1984.

Indian MiG-29 pilots were trained at Loogovaya AB near Frunze. In December 1986 the first 12 aircraft were delivered in the form of semi-knocked-down (SKD) kits to HAL's Nasik factory. Assembly was completed in May 1987 and the aircraft were delivered to two squadrons previously operating the MiG-21*bis* – 28 Sqn 'First Supersonics' and 47 Sqn 'Archers' at Poona (Pune) AB near Bombay, Maharashtra. The official handover ceremony took place at Poona on 6 December 1987, thus marking the beginning of the 'Fulcrum's career with the IAF. By early 1997 the IAF had taken delivery of 72 single-seat MiG-29s (*izdeliye* 9.12B standard) and eight MiG-29UBs. (There have been allegations, however, that India refused to accept the downgraded export version and managed to persuade the Soviet Union to deliver the fully-capable *izdeliye* 9.12!) Known serials are KB703, KB707, KB711, KB713, KB716, KB720, KB724, KB728, KB729, KB736, KB738, KB3110 and KB3126 (single-seaters) and KS903 (MiG-29UB). These were in service with three units as detailed overleaf.

Unit	Base	Quantity MiG-29	MiG-29UB	Delivery date
TABLE C				
47 Sqn Black Archers	Poona	46	4	1986
28 Sqn First Supersonics	Poona	18	2	1989
223 Sqn Tridents	Adampur	8	2	1995 (1996?)

Indian Air Force MiG-29 (izdeliye 9.12B). (World Air Power)

The aircraft were delivered in standard Soviet two-tone grey camouflage. Soon after service entry squadron badges appeared on the air intakes. Later some IAF 'Fulcrums' got some non-standard paint schemes with highly colourful tails, presumably for participation in war games.

Indian pilots praised the MiG-29, especially the ten aircraft of an unspecified new version delivered in 1995 (some sources say 1996). These aircraft had increased airframe and engine life, improved armament and an upgraded fire control radar which could track ten targets at a time while guiding missiles to two priority threats. The IAF is now considering upgrading the earlier aircraft to this standard.

The IAF has a habit of giving indigenous names to aircraft it operates – even though they may have a popular name already. E.g., the Aérospatiale SA 316B Alouette III was built under licence in Bangalore as the HAL Chetak, the MiG-27 was called Bahadur (Valiant in Hindi) and the Il-76MD was named Gajraj (King elephant). The MiG-29 was known locally as the Baaz (Eagle).

In 1997 there were reports that India plans to increase its 'Fulcrum' fleet to 120. India also discussed possible MiG-29M deliveries and retrofitting existing aircraft with refuelling probes. General Designer Rostislav A. Belyakov told the engineers to make the probe non-retractable and install it on the starboard side, as is customary in the West, rather than on the port side, as on

Soviet aircraft. A mockup of the fixed probe installation was actually built, but a contract was never signed and the idea was abandoned.

Over the years the IAF lost four MiG-29s in accidents. Two aircraft were lost in a mid-air collision in 1994. The IAF never acknowledged the fact of the collision, stating to Mikoyan that one of the fighters 'lost a fin in mid-air'. This was nothing short of an accusation of defective workmanship. However, Mikoyan experts analysing the flight data recorder (FDR) readouts proved this was not so. The FDR showed unambiguously that the fighter was pulling 0.8 Gs immediately before the fin disintegrated; then the G force abruptly increased to 2.0 and then fell back to 0.8 one tenth of a second later. The side force likewise increased abruptly from 4 to 8 Gs, going back to 4 Gs immediately afterwards. This cannot be achieved by applying full throttle or making a sharp manoeuvre; the only possible explanation was that the fighter had been hit by another aircraft. Still, the Indians have stuck rigidly to their story of structural failure. Perhaps they were simply too ashamed to admit the crash had been caused by pilot error.

The latest crash was at Poona AB on 21 January 1997. The base commander was making a training sortie in one of the single-seaters (KB738) when an engine fire warning lamp lit up. The aircraft headed back to base for an emergency landing but overran, killing the pilot.

Iran

When the eight-year-long and bloody war with Iraq ended in 1988, Iran decided to follow the example of its warlike neighbour and order the MiG-29. The Islamic Republic of Iran Air Force (IRIAF)[6] took delivery of the first batch of 'Fulcrums' in the year President Hashemi Rafsanjani visited Moscow. The aircraft were declared operational on 7 October 1990. The exact quantity is unknown; there have been unconfirmed reports that the IRIAF operates 14 MiG-29s (*izdeliye* 9.12B standard), but MAPO-MiG stated unofficially that several dozen were delivered in all. The aircraft are said to be painted in desert camouflage. Only one has been identified so far (3-6107). According to ANPK MiG, Iran retained nine ex-Iraqi MiG-29s flown to Iran during the Gulf War to get them out of harm's way.

One aircraft was lost on the ferry flight when the Soviet pilot lost his way, ejecting when the aircraft ran out of fuel. Another Iranian 'Fulcrum' crashed when the pilot got disoriented at low altitude. The IRIAF tried to blame the crash on a mechanical failure but MAPO-MiG experts proved the aircraft was OK; the cause was obviously controlled flight into terrain (CFIT); or, more plainly, pilot error. On 1-10 February 1996 the IRIAF displayed its

---

6 Formerly IIAF (Imperial Iranian Air Force, *Nirou Havai Shahanshahiye Iran*)

Iraqi MiG-29 (izdeliye 9.12B). (World Air Power)

aircraft at Mehrabad airport which is also a major air force base. The static park included a MiG-29.

Iraq

Iraq was the second Middle Eastern state to express an interest in the MiG-29, ordering 48 of the type in 1987. The first 18 aircraft (*izdeliye* 9.12B standard single-seaters and some MiG-29UBs) were delivered late the same year. Iraqi Air Force 'Fulcrums' were used in the air defence rôle, operating mostly from bases around Baghdad. It is thought that they were controlled and directed by three AWACS aircraft named Baghdad-1, Adnan-1 (ex Baghdad-2) and Adnan-2 and operating from Baghdad-Saddam Hussein International airport.[7]

There is no reliable information as to how many MiG-29s were actually operated by the Iraqi Air Force (*al Quwwat al-Jawwiya al-Iraqiya*). Unconfirmed reports state that 35 'Fulcrum-As' and six 'Fulcrum-Bs' were on strength in August 1990. Only one single-seater serialled 29060 has been positively identified so far (this aircraft was on display at Baghdad-Saddam Hussein International airport in early 1990). The first 18 aircraft reportedly wore desert camouflage; the rest, including 29060, were delivered in standard Soviet two-tone grey camouflage.

Iraqi 'Fulcrums' were just about the only ones to fire in anger, being used operationally in the Gulf War that followed Iraq's invasion of Kuwait on 2 August 1990. At least eight were reportedly shot down in dogfights by USAF F-15s and US Navy F/A-18s during Operation *Desert Storm* which began in February 1991 (ANPK MiG confirms two aircraft shot down at long range). Also, Allied pilots reported an incident in the opening stage of the war when an Iraqi MiG-29 flight leader accidentally shot down his wingman, then became disoriented and crashed into the desert.

When Saddam Hussein realised he was losing the war, nine MiG-29s, along with many other Iraqi Air Force aircraft, were reportedly flown to neighboring Iran (with which Iraq had conveniently entered a truce in 1988) to save them from being destroyed by the Allies. This was logical enough, since Iraqi fighter pilots were no match for the Allied pilots. There the aircraft and pilots were

interned and the 'Fulcrums' were retained by Iran a reparations for damage done during the Iran-Iraq war Still, some Western observers believed that if Iraq had actively used its MiG-29 fleet in the war it would have complicated things for the Allies a good deal and caused heavy losses of Allied aircraft.

Israel

Western information agencies reported that severa MiG-29s landed at Sedom airbase in the Negev desert in southern Israel sometime in 1997. Their origin is unknown; nor is there any information as to whether the aircraft had actually been sold to Israel or simply leased for evaluation purposes. An Israeli military spokesman has been quoted as saying that the Israeli Defence Force/Air Force (*Heyl Ha'Avir*) was not planning to buy the type; the objective was to consider upgrade possibilities by Israeli Aircraft Industries (IAI). Elbi Electronics, a division of IAI, had some experience with Soviet/CIS aircraft by then, having successfully upgraded the MiG-21MF 'Fishbed-J' for Romania (known as Lancer in upgraded form) and the An-72P 'Coaler-C' border patrol aircraft.

Israeli experts believe that the MiG-29 is at least as good as, and in some respects better than, the F-15 and F-16 (both of which are operated by the IDF/AF) as far as aerodynamics and performance are concerned. The avionics suite, on the other hand, is less capable than that of Western fighters. IAI is said to be discussing possible upgrade programmes with many MiG-29 operators, including Poland, Romania, Slovakia and the Ukraine There have also been unconfirmed reports that in 1990 Israel took possession of a Syrian Air Force MiG-29 whose pilot defected.

Kazakhstan (Kazakstan)

Kazakhstan, or Kazakstan, as this CIS republic has been called of late, has taken over a few ex-VVS MiG-29s based there. Unfortunately, the number operated by the Kazakh Air Force is unknown.

Malaysia

On 7 June 1994 Russia and Malaysia signed a US$ 560 million contract for the delivery of 16 single-seat MiG-29s and two MiG-29UB trainers to the Royal Malaysian Air Force (TUDM – *Tentera Udara Diraja Malaysia*). The

---

7 These were three Iraqi AF Il-76MD transports converted locally with the Thomson-CSF Tigre surveillance radar built under licence in Iraq. The *Baghdad-1* had the radar antenna in a large fairing supplanting the cargo doors while the other two had a more conventional rotodome on two pylons aft of the wings *à la* Ilyushin/Beriyev A-50 'Mainstay'. These were named after Defence Minister Adnan Khajrallah Talfah was killed in a helicopter crash in May 1988.

Malaysian MiG-29Ns being loaded into a Russian AF Antonov An-124 'Ruslan' freighter. (Viktor Drushlyakov)

contract stated that the aircraft were to be delivered with a higher gross weight (increased ordnance load) and more capable avionics, including radar; after delivery the single-seaters were to be retrofitted with refuelling probes. In the Western press the aircraft are sometimes referred to as MiG-29N and MiG-29NUB; however, these designations have **not** been confirmed by Mikoyan or by the TUDM.

The Malaysian 'Fulcrums' were not purpose-built under the contract; they were, to use a commercial aviation term, white-tails i.e. aircraft not ordered by any customer. For years these fighters manufactured in 1988–1990 (mostly Batch 52 aircraft) had been languishing at the factory airfield in Lookhovitsy, unclaimed and unpaid for by the Soviet (and since Russian) Air Force. Thus there was no need to wait for the aircraft to be built and the deliveries were made on schedule. The fighters were airlifted to Langkawi airbase near Kuala Lumpur by An-124-100 freighters owned by the Russian cargo airline Volga-Dnepr and jointly operated with the British cargo carrier HeavyLift.

In the spring of 1996 the MiG-29s participated in a TUDM exercise under the code name Jaguh earning high praise from military experts. On 22–30 June the same year one of the single-seaters serialled M43-05 was displayed at an airshow at Soekarno-Hatta International airport, Jakarta, Indonesia. The 'Fulcrum-As' appear to be serialled M43-01 through M43-16.

On 12–30 April 1997 the Flying Fish '97 exercise was staged in the South China Sea by the navies and air forces of the UK, Australia, New Zealand, Singapore and Malaysia. This was the largest single exercise in the history of the SEATO military block, involving more than 12,000 men and officers, 39 warships and 164 aircraft, including TUDM MiG-29s and Northrop F-5E Tigers. The scenario of the exercise was joint action by the five states to repel an attack on Malaysia and Singapore, including concerted action by various aircraft types and aerial refuelling. Observers at the exercise were particularly impressed by the MiG-29's performance. TUDM pilots and technical staff were quite pleased with the fighter's performance, handling and serviceability, stating that the aircraft had fulfilled its objectives completely. 14 of the TUDM's 16 'Fulcrum-As' were ready for action at the time of the exercise. At the debriefing the commanders of 17 Sqn and 19 Sqn operating the MiGs thanked the Russian specialists from VPK MAPO who provided support and maintenance during the exercise.

The rear fuselage and tail unit of Royal Malaysian Air Force MiG-29 M43-14. (Viktor Drooshlyakov)

Moldova

After the collapse of the Soviet Union a good deal of military equipment was left behind in the now-independent CIS states. Moldova (the former Moldavian Soviet Socialist Republic) inherited a MiG-29 unit (the 86th IAP) based at Markuleshty. The 31 (some sources say 33) aircraft included seven very early aircraft with ventral fins and at least one MiG-29UB.

However, the republic was just too small for the MiG-29s and there was always the danger of intruding inadvertently into foreign airspace. Therefore the

Moldovan government tried to sell the fighters via third parties. Four aircraft were sold to South Yemen in this fashion. However, Yemen soon dropped Moldova as an arms supplier because the aircraft came incomplete and without adequate technical support they were just costly but useless pieces of metal.[8] Yet, on 6 September 1997 Russian media announced that the USA had bought 21 ex-Moldovan 'Fulcrums' – six 'Fulcrum-As', 14 'Fulcrum-Cs' and a single MiG-29UB. The reason for this deal is noteworthy. Moldova kept looking for customers and, among other countries, approached Iran which already operated the type. This was the least desirable customer as far as the USA was concerned because the Iranian government, putting it mildly, was not exactly pro-American. The 'Fulcrum-C' has tactical nuclear strike capability, which is why the USA offered to buy the 'Fulcrums' wholesale in order to prevent them from going to 'rogue states' such as Iran.

There have been unconfirmed reports that the deal was worth US$ 80 million. If this is true, Moldova sold the fighters dirt-cheap – at about US$ 4 million apiece.

TV footage showed that the fighters wore a non-standard crudely applied two-tone green camouflage (which was partly removed by rain on some aircraft, revealing the original grey finish) and gaudy Moldovan insignia – a red/yellow/blue eight-rayed star on a white roundel. At least one aircraft, however (MiG-29UB 61 White), wore a conspicuous dark blue/pale blue colour scheme, suggesting it was used for display purposes. All the aircraft were sold in semi-dismantled condition ready for shipment.

North Korea (Korean People's Democratic Republic)

North Korea became the second Asian state to order the MiG-29. The type was purchased in response to the threat posed by South Korea's new F-16C/Ds. North Korea is unique among foreign MiG-29 operators in two respects. Firstly, it is the only country to have purchased licence manufacturing rights, and secondly, it is the only country outside the Soviet Union/CIS to operate five or six 'Fulcrum-Cs'. These were delivered as SKD kits and assembled on site. Unlike Soviet Air Force 'Fulcrum-Cs', the North Korean aircraft do not have the L203B Gardeniya-1FU active jammer. The first fighters were

---

8 According to ANPK MiG, five were actually sold to South Yemen and one more to Romania.

assembled in May-June 1988 and delivery of the entire order was completed by the end of the year. (Some sources state that the initial batch contained 12 aircraft and the total did not exceed 20.)

Peru

After losing in a border conflict with Ecuador in 1996 Peru decided to bolster its military power with MiG-29 fighters. Initially the Peruvian government approached Russia on this subject, but then the Peruvian Air Force (FAP – *Fuerza Aérea del Peru*) unexpectedly bought sixteen ex-Belorussian 'Fulcrums', 14 single-seaters and two MiG-29UBs, together with a load of R-27, R-60 and R-73 AAMs, 80-mm S-8 unguided rockets, incendiary bombs and support equipment. Press reports said Peru was to buy twelve aircraft at US$ 11–14 mln apiece; however, President Alberto Fujimori speaking on Peruvian television said the quantity and the price was a state secret.

There have been press reports that the contract was worth about US$ 80 million. If this is true the 'Fulcrums' were sold at about US$ 4 million apiece, which is

extremely cheap for a fighter in this class, even considering their far-from-perfect condition. The first four aircraft were delivered soon after the contract was signed. The FAP officially accepted the fighters at Las Palmas AB near Lima on 29 July 1997 which is a national holiday in Peru (Fatherland Day).

However, Belorussia was unable to supply spares and ammunition, provide maintenance etc. The ensuing scandal led to the removal of the Peruvian Minister of Defence; still, surprisingly perhaps, the deal was not cancelled. The FAP now found itself in a tight spot, as Russia (probably annoyed at being bypassed by 'little brother' Belorussia) had warned in advance that it would not service aircraft sold by third parties. Only four of the FAP's MiG-29s remained operational in the autumn of 1997.

Poland

The Polish Air Force (PWL – *Polskie Wojsko Lotnicze*) ordered 12 'Fulcrums', and deliveries began in 1989 after a group of PWL pilots took their training in the Soviet Union the preceding year. The first four single-seat MiG-29s (*izdeliye* 9.12A standard) serialled 65, 66, 67 and 70

Poland was one of the first Warsaw Pact countries to take delivery of the MiG-29. (Waclaw Holys)

arrived at Minsk-Mazowiecki airbase late in July, though some sources say June. They were followed by three MiG-29UBs (15, 42 and 64) on 1 August 1989 and five more 'Fulcrum-As' (105, 108, 111, 114 and 115) on 30 October 1990.[9]

The aircraft were operated by 1 Squadron of 1PLM (*Pułk Lotniczy Mysliwski* – fighter regiment) based at Minsk-Mazowiecki near the Polish capital of Warsaw. This unit traditionally was the first to operate new fighter types. 1PLM is assigned to the air defence of Warsaw; thus: the city's crest (known as Syrenka) was adopted as the unit badge. Its colour denotes squadron number (1 Sqn, yellow; 2 Sqn, red; 3 Sqn, blue).

After the dissolution of the Warsaw Pact, Poland began pushing for NATO membership. This involved switching to NATO standards and Poland decided not to buy

Russian equipment any more, including aircraft. Thus the 'Fulcrum' would be gradually phased out; the F-16, F/A-18 and Mirage 2000 were considered as possible replacements. This was undoubtedly a political decision; partly at least. Historically there have always been tensions between Poland and Russia. A Cold War-era survey of the Soviet Union's allies named East Germany as the best and Poland as the worst: the Soviets could never be quite sure which side they would take in a conflict. Yet economics outweigh politics, and Czechia's decision to phase out the MiG-29 came as a real, and probably unexpected, gift to the PWL. The ten CzAF aircraft were traded profitably for W-3 Sokół helicopters, bringing the total in PWL service to 22, and the Polish government was quite happy to strike the deal, NATO membership plans notwithstanding. Thus the 'Fulcrum' got a new lease of life.

The contract for the acquisition of nine single-seaters and a single trainer was signed on 20 December 1995 by a civilian Polish-Czech trade company. The first five ex-Czech aircraft (MiG-29s 7702, 9207, 3810, 5918 and MiG-29UB 4402) were ferried to Minsk-Mazowiecki AB by Polish pilots two days later, still wearing CzAF

---

9 PWL aircraft of Soviet origin often have four-digit serials tying in with the aircraft's batch number and its number in the batch. E.g., PZL Mielec (Antonov) An-2TD 0851, c/n 1G108-51 – i.e., An-2 (manufacturer's product code 1G), batch 108, 51st in batch. With some types, however, including the 'Fulcrum', simply the last two or three digits of the c/n were used as the serial. This is perfectly logical with Western types where production is not split into batches; with the MiG-29 it would be more logical to use the fuselage numbers but these were probably unknown to the Poles.

A Polish MiG-29 (izdeliye 9.12A) taking off. (Waclaw Holys)

roundels and serials. Another aircraft arrived on 29 December; the remainder were to follow on 8 January 1996. The Czech MiGs had been in open storage and water had leaked into the equipment, rendering it unserviceable. Hence some electrics components had to be 'borrowed' from the PWL's own 'Fulcrums' and installed on the Czech aircraft for the delivery flight. The aircraft needed an overhaul but Russia demanded sky-high prices for spares; therefore it was decided to buy only top-priority components which had to be replaced and repair the rest in-house. Repair costs were estimated at approximately US$ 2 million per aircraft.

On 11 September 1994 a group of *Armée de l'Air* Mirage 2000s of EC1/2 Cicognes from Dijon-Longvic made a friendly visit to Minsk-Mazowiecki. For the occasion one of 1PLM's MiG-29s, 115, was adorned with a large EC1/2 squadron badge (a flying stork on a blue shield) on the fuselage upper surface.

The Polish MiG-29 fleet in 1996 is listed below.

Serial	Model	C/n	Remarks
15	MiG-29UB	N50903014615	
28	MiG-29UB	N50903014528*	Ex CzAF 4402
38	MiG-29	2960532038	Ex CzAF 3810
40	MiG-29	2960532040	Ex CzAF 4012
42	MiG-29UB	N50903014642	
54	MiG-29	2960532354	Ex CzAF 5414
56	MiG-29	2960532356	Ex CzAF 5616
59	MiG-29	2960532359	Ex CzAF 5918
64	MiG-29UB	N50903014664	
65	MiG-29	2960526365	
66	MiG-29	2960526366	
67	MiG-29	2960526367	
70	MiG-29	2960526370	
77	MiG-29	2960526377	Ex CzAF 7702
83	MiG-29	2960526383	Ex CzAF 8304
86*	MiG-29	2960526386*	Ex CzAF 8906
92	MiG-29	2960526392	Ex CzAF 9207
105	MiG-29	2960535105	
108	MiG-29	2960535108	
111	MiG-29	2960535111	
114	MiG-29	2960535114	
115	MiG-29	2960535115	

* Note: Polish sources quote the serial as 86 and the c/n as 2960526386. However, this does not agree with the aircraft's previous identity as CzAF 8906, as on Czech MiG-29s the first two digits of the serial match the last two digits of the c/n (which thus should have been 2960526389!). It is hard to say who made a mistake when applying the serial (the Poles or the Czechs) and what the c/n actually is. Likewise, the c/n of MiG-29UB 28 quoted in Polish sources (N50903014528) does not match the aircraft's previous CzAF serial 4402.

Romania

In 1989 a group of Romanian Air Force (*Fortele Aeriene Romãne*) pilots completed their conversion training at the Kiev Air Force Academy. In November-December they ferried their new mounts, ten single-seat MiG-29s (*izdeliye* 9.12A standard) and two MiG-29UBs, to Mihail Kogalniceanu airbase near Constanţa. Later deliveries brought the total up to about 30 aircraft. In 1997 the 'Fulcrums' were based at Giamata AB near Timişoara, home to the 57th fighter regiment. The last aircraft arived only a few days before the 1989 revolution which ended the rule of the Romanian dictator Nicolae Ceauşescu. Since the unit was not fully operational it did not participate in the fighting between regular army units which supported the revolution and the infamous secret service, Securitate, which remained loyal to Ceauşescu.

Two aircraft were lost in a mid-air collision in 1990 while practising for an aerobatics display at Baneasa AB near Bucharest, killing both pilots and a ground crewman. Another aircraft, a MiG-29UB, crashed after making a barrel roll at low altitude, killing the pilot. The cause was probably G-loc, as the Romanian pilot without wearing a G suit was trying to repeat a manoeuvre demonstrated by a MAPO-MiG test pilot.

Like most Communist nations, Romania was paranoid about security and details of the fleet remain scarce. Aircraft spotted hitherto are 'Fulcrum-As' coded 33 Red, 38 Red, 46 Red, 47 Red, 48 Red, 49 Red, 69 Red, 70 Red, 75 Red, 76 Red and 'Fulcrum-Bs' coded 15 Red, 23 Red and 29 Red; no c/ns are known. According to ANPK MiG, Romania purchased a single MiG-29 from neighbouring Moldova, quite possibly as an attrition replacement.

Slovakia

Unlike the Czech Republic, Slovakia still regarded Russia as a prime trade partner and military ally. Therefore the Slovakian air arm *(Slovenské Vojenské Létectvo)* retained the nine 'Fulcrum-As' and single 'Fulcrum-B' received after the division of Czechoslovakia. In the autumn of 1992 the fighters were flown to their new base at Šliač, home of the SVL's 1st Fighter Regiment (1SLP).

The original MiG-29UB 4401 crashed in March 1994. Unconfirmed reports state that the crash was caused by uncontained failure of an engine accessory gearbox and ensuing engine failure. However, in early 1994 Slovakia took delivery of five single-seat MiG-29s of an unspecified new version (0619, 0820, 0921, 2022 and 2123) and a single MiG-29UB, 1303. Eight more 'Fulcrum-As' were supplied later, bringing the total to 24 including the crashed trainer.

Slovakian MiG-29s became regular participants of various airshows at home and abroad. E.g., MiG-29 7501 performed at České Budějovice on Aviation Day (17 June 1994) wearing Slovakia's national colours (white, blue and red) on the nose, air intakes, fins and wings. Aircraft performing at RAF Mildenhall on 25-26 May 1996

included one MiG-29 and three SVL Mi-24V 'Hind-E' assault helicopters. One of the new Slovakian 'Fulcrum-As', 6829, was displayed at the Royal International Air Tattoo (RIAT) at RAF Fairford in June 1996. On 28-29 June 1997 a pair of SVL MiG-29s accompanied by an Antonov An-26 'Coke' twin-turboprop transport visited RAF Waddington.

Slovakian 'Fulcrums' are listed below.

Serial	Model	C/n
0619	MiG-29	
0820	MiG-29	
0921	MiG-29	2960535409
1303	MiG-29UB	N50903028113
2022	MiG-29	
2123	MiG-29	
3709	MiG-29	2960532037
3911	MiG-29	2960532039

A Slovak Air Force MiG-29. Slovakia is on good terms with Russia and pleased with Russian-built combat aircraft. (Thomas Müller)

4401	MiG-29UB	N50903013244
5113	MiG-29	2960532351
5515	MiG-29	2960532355
5817	MiG-29	2960532358
6829	MiG-29	
7501	MiG-29	2960526375
8003	MiG-29	2960526380
8605	MiG-29	2960526386
9308	MiG-29	2960526393
...24	MiG-29	
...25	MiG-29	
...26	MiG-29	
...27	MiG-29	
...28	MiG-29	
?		
?		

South Yemen (People's Democratic Republic of Yemen)

In mid-1993 Moldova sold four or five of its MiG-29s to the South Yemen Air Force via a third party. However, it turned out that the aircraft were delivered incomplete and two were in non-airworthy condition. The others were soon grounded as well.

Syria

The Syrian Arab Republic became the second export customer for the MiG-29. This Middle East country traditionally operated Soviet military hardware and needed new fighters to replace aircraft lost in wars with Israel. Besides, its MiG-21MF 'Fishbed-J' and MiG-23MS 'Flogger-E' fighters were getting long in the tooth.

Syrian Minister of Defence Mustaf Tlass officially ordered 150 'Fulcrums' in April 1987. Deliveries commenced quickly; the first aircraft, single-seat MiG-29s (*izdeliye* 9.12B standard) and two-seat MiG-29UBs, were handed over to the Syrian Air Force (*al Quwwat al-Jawwiya al Arabiya as-Suriya*) in July same year. The first MiG-29 squadron became operational in October 1988. A second batch was delivered by the end of the

SlovAF 'Fulcrums' sporting non-standard colour schemes include this MiG-29UB which took part in the Tiger Meet at the 1996 Fairford RIAT. (Air Power International)

ABOVE: *Bulgarian AF MiG-29s. (Yefim Gordon archive)*

year, bringing the total strength to one regiment (three squadrons).

There have been no confirmed reports of Syrian 'Fulcrums' in action against Israeli jets. Rumour has it that a Syrian pilot defected to Israel in a MiG-29 but again this has not been officially confirmed. What is known, however, is that the Syrian Air Force never got the 150 MiG-29s originally ordered. It has generally been believed that deliveries stopped at 80; however, the latest reports from ANPK MiG and other sources state that only 20 were delivered. There were unconfirmed reports originating from Israeli sources that a Syrian MiG-29 pilot defected to Israel in 1990 and that at least one more MiG-29 was lost in a shootout with IDF/AF fighters in early 1991.

Turkmenistan

Turkmenistan's small air arm includes 12 to 40 ex-VVS 'Fulcrum-Cs' (*izdeliye* 9.13 or 9.13S); it is not known if other versions are operated.

ABOVE: *Indian Air Force MiG-29 (izdeliye 9.12B). (World Air Power Journal)*

The Ukraine

After the breakup of the Soviet Union the newly-formed Ukrainian Air Force (UAF) took possession of all ex-VVS aircraft based in the republic, as well as some of the CISAF aircraft being withdrawn from reunified Germany. These included 216 MiG-29s, including 155 'Fulcrum-Cs' (*izdeliye* 9.13 and 9.13S). Thus, the Ukraine is the world's second-largest MiG-29 operator (Russia is the largest).

Ukrainian MiG-29s had their share of accidents, including fatal ones. On 30 July 1996 a single-seat 'Fulcrum' crashed during a training sortie, killing *Deputy Squadron Leader* Vadim Kiril'chuk. The aircraft was on a ferry flight from the Crimea and the pilot lost his way, eventually ejecting over the sea.

In the early '90s the UAF got its own display team, the *Ookrains'ki Sokoly* (Ukrainian Falcons). The team operates five single-seat 'Fulcrum-As' (101 White, 102 White, 103 White, 106 White and 108 White) and two MiG-29UB trainers, one of which is 104 White (the other is probably either 105 White or 107 White). The aircraft wear an attractive livery with the wings and tail unit painted in stripes of blue and yellow, the Ukraine's national colours. The fuselage is white with a red stripe running the full length of it, and the team's

name is carried in Ukrainian on the port side and in English on the starboard side. The tactical codes are applied to the fins rather than the usual position on the air intakes.

The Ukrainian Falcons had their début on 9 May 1997 during the VE-Day celebrations in the country's capital, Kiev.[10] On 19–20 July the same year the team performed at Fairford RIAT'97. However, on 26 March 1998 the group suffered a loss during a training session for a display in France when one of the single-seaters crashed on approach in poor weather to Kirovskoye AB (the UAF's training centre on the Crimea Peninsula). The pilot suffered critical injuries and died in hospital.

Once again, because of economic difficulties and the inability to keep large armed forces the Ukrainian Government has been trying to sell off part of its military aircraft, including some of the MiG-29s. Sales prospects, however, have been hampered by the inability to provide spares (as these have to be sourced in Russia) and adequate maintenance.

---

10 In the Soviet Union (and the CIS), Victory Day is celebrated on 9 May rather than 8 May as elsewhere.

A Ukrainian Air Force MiG-29 (izdeliye 9.13). (Yefim Gordon archive)

ABOVE: *Ukrainian MiG-29s retain the standard two-tone grey colour scheme. Subtle differences from Russian 'Fulcrums' include tactical codes which are invariably white (Russian MiG-29s usually have red or blue codes) and squadron markings on the nose – a practice seldom seen on Russian aircraft. (Sergey Popsuyevich)*

OPPOSITE: *Ukrainian AF insignia evolution. The trident was originally superimposed on a blue circle, later replaced by a shield. (Yefim Gordon archive)*

BELOW: *An unusual sharkmouthed Ukrainian MiG-29 (izdeliye 9.13) on landing. (Sergey Popsuyevich)*

Ukrainian AF MiG-29UB 80 White sporting a leaping tiger as a squadron badge and colourful air intakes. (Sergey Popsuyevich.)

United States of America

The United States Air Force got its first chance to evaluate the MiG-29 when one of the *Luftwaffe's* 'Fulcrum-As', 29+06, was loaned to the Air Force Systems Command (AFSC) in 1990. The objectives included development of anti-MiG-29 tactics and countermeasures for the impending Operation *Desert Storm*, during which USAF and USN fighters were expected to be opposed by the 'Fulcrum'. The aircraft remained in the US at least until August 1992.

In late 1997, as mentioned earlier, the USAF bought 21 ex-Moldovan MiG-29s – six 'Fulcrum-As', 14 'Fulcrum-Cs' and a single MiG-29UB. The deal was part of the Co-operative Threat Reduction Program initiated in 1993. The aircraft were bought in dismantled condition and delivered to Wright-Patterson AFB, Ohio, by Military Airlift Command McDonnell Douglas C-17A Globemaster IIIs.

Having thus placed the MiGs beyond the reach of Iran and other 'bad guys' the USAF will use them to study the type's performance and technical details. While the 'Fulcrum-A' is nothing new, the nuclear-capable 'fatback' is of special interest to the US. The MiGs may be used as 'aggressor aircraft' during Red Flag exercises after restoration to airworthy status; *AFM* believes that the Red Eagles, a secretive unit at Groom Lake and Tonopah in Nevada operating MiG-21s and -23/27s in the Cold War years, might even be reinstated. Having real MiG-29s is better than using the time-honoured aggressor F-5s and T-38 Talons – or even F-16Ns and F/A-18s masquerading as 'Fulcrums'!

Incidentally, to quote *AFM*, 'some say Uncle Sam has created a precedent that will allow any country trying to find a few extra dollars to suggest the possibility of selling hardware to countries like Syria, Iraq or Iran in order to secure a better deal. Just mention the fact that Damascus, Baghdad or Tehran is interested, and you will get a bundle of dollars, say the opponents. And this is a realistic scenario, bearing in mind how many of those countries that emerged from the former Soviet Union have an enormous pile of dual capable weaponry – be it aircraft, subs or artillery.'

Uzbekistan

After the collapse of the Soviet Union, Uzbekistan took over 36 'fatback' MiG-29s (*izdeliye* 9.13 or 9.13S); the exact quantity is unknown. It is not known if other versions are operated.

Yugoslavia/Serbia

Yugoslavia that is, the *big* confederacy of old, not the remnant that is left under the same name after the prolonged civil war became the first European export customer for the 'Fulcrum' in 1987. By early 1988 the Yugoslav Air Force (JRV – *Jugoslovensko Ratno Vazduhoplovstvo*) had taken delivery of 14 single-seaters (*izdeliye* 9.12A standard) and two MiG-29UB trainers. They were operated by the 127th LAE (*lovacka aviacijska eskadrila* – fighter squadron)/204th LAP (*lovacki aviacijski pulk* – fighter regiment) at Batajnica airbase. An immediate problem arose when the 'Fulcrums' arrived: they were too big to fit into the underground hardened aircraft shelters (HAS) built for the MiG-21s they supplemented, and new shelters had to be built.

Yugoslavia traditionally allocated indigenous designations to new types included into the JRV inventory; thus, the MiG-29 became L-18 (L = *lovac* – fighter in Serbian). Yugoslav 'Fulcrums' were displayed publicly for the first time during the open doors day at Batajnica on 15 May 1988. Another 16 aircraft were due for delivery that year but no additional MiG-29s were supplied before the Serbo-Croat civil war broke out and all weapons sales were embargoed. After the breakup of Yugoslavia into five separate states in the wake of the civil war the fighters were retained by the Serbian Air Force.

The original 14 aircraft are listed below.

Serial	Model	C/n
18101	MiG-29	2960525005
18102	MiG-29	
18103*	MiG-29	
18104	MiG-29	
18105	MiG-29	
18106	MiG-29	
18107*	MiG-29	
18108	MiG-29	
18109	MiG-29	
18110*	MiG-29	
18111	MiG-29	2960525136
18112	MiG-29	
18113	MiG-29	
18114	MiG-29	
18301	MiG-29UB	
18302	MiG-29UB	

Aircraft marked by * were either destroyed in accidents or shot down by Bosnian Moslems during the civil war.

Yugoslav (since Serbian) Air Force MiG-29s had small white serials on the fuselage. The MiG-29's centreline ferry tank is visible in the background. (Lotnictwo)

8
The MiG-29 vs. the Rest

A fighter's development history inevitably includes a comparison of the future aircraft's performance and operational characteristics, including serviceability and operating costs, with other aircraft in the same class. Initially this analysis is made by company engineers designing the aircraft proper and its systems; later, when the fighter enters production and becomes operational, the analysis is made by air force specialists. The MiG-29 was no exception. This chapter is a comparison of the 'Fulcrum' with Western fighters based on press reports and analyses made by Mikoyan and Western military experts.

Few Western fighters are readily comparable with the MiG-29. These are the General Dynamics (Lockheed Martin) F-16C Fighting Falcon, McDonnell Douglas F/A-18C Hornet and F-15C Eagle, Dassault Mirage 2000-5 and Eurofighter EF2000. Former project chief Mikhail R. Val'denberg, however, has been quoted as saying that 'the Hornet is no match for the MiG-29 in thrust-to-weight ratio or manoeuvrability or whatever, and the Mirage 2000-5 even more so. Of the fighters listed above only the F-16 is comparable to the MiG-29 in design philosophy, rôle and combat capabilities.'

The F-16 has become the world's most numerous fourth-generation fighter. In mid-1994 about 1,700 Fighting Falcons were in service with the air forces of 17 nations. A total of 3,989 had been ordered by operators around the world by the spring of 1994, including 2,208 for the USAF. The MiG-29 became the F-16's most serious competitor on the world fighter market. By mid-1994 more than 500 'Fulcrums' had been delivered to or ordered by 16 nations.

Differences between the F-16 and MiG-29 are due mainly to differing views on fighter tactics, which in turn are due to the different war experience the USA and the Soviet Union have had. In drawing up operational requirements for second-generation fighters the USAF relied mainly on WW II and Korean war experience; in both cases the USAF usually enjoyed air superiority way beyond the frontlines which meant American ground troops were well protected against enemy air strikes. Later, however, the USAF concentrated on nuclear strike capability, underestimating the importance of close-range aerial combat. As a result, the McDonnell F-4 Phantom II,

the main US air superiority fighter of the late '60s, could be easily outmanoeuvred by the obsolescent MiG-17 'Fresco' – and often fell victim to the latter's guns in Vietnam.

Thus, when the USAF launched the Advanced Light Fighter (ALF) programme in 1972, it had to readopt the high thrust-to-weight ratio/low wing loading policy, as this gave the fighter good acceleration and a short turn time. American fighter designers began developing lightweight and compact aircraft optimised for air-to-air combat within visual range at transonic speeds and medium altitudes; i.e., optimised for escorting strike groups. Maximum manoeuvrability would be attained at Mach 0.6–1.6; special attention was given to speeds around Mach 0.8–1.2.

The Soviet approach to the problem was somewhat different. As in Great Britain and France, the work of Soviet design bureaux after WW II was directed mainly at creating interceptors with the highest possible speed, ceiling and rate of climb to ward off nuclear strikes against specific targets of importance. The aircraft were required to have maximum engine power and low wing loading. The latter was necessary to give the interceptor a good service ceiling but gave a bonus in the form of good manoeuvrability and field performance.

During the Korean war MiG-15 'Fagot' fighters outperformed USAF fighters at high altitude. The new MiG-17 and MiG-19 'Farmer' that followed were high-performance jets in their day but dogfighting at low altitude was not exactly their strong point. The next fighter from the Mikoyan stable, the MiG-21 'Fishbed', was an outstanding aircraft in its class but its combat capabilities were somewhat hampered by poor rearward visibility making it vulnerable to attack from behind. The variable-geometry MiG-23 'Flogger' had heavier armament, a bigger combat radius and better field performance but poor handling at low speed.

The MiG-29 was a light fighter, continuing the MiG-15/17/21 philosophy. Like its predecessors, it was required to have high speed, rate of climb and service ceiling because high-flying spyplanes were among its main targets. Obtaining good field performance (without resorting to VG), low-speed handling and all-round visibility were priority design tasks.

ABOVE: *MiG-29.* *BELOW:* *F-16B*

Briefly, the F-16 and the MiG-29 compare as follows. The F-16 is an air superiority fighter designed to operate together with the heavier F-15. The exceptionally high performance, heavy armament and powerful fire control radar of the latter allowed the USAF to slacken the design requirements for the F-16 somewhat; still, the Fighting Falcon has a combat radius no less than the Eagle's. Conversely, the MiG-29 was to gain air superiority in the forward battle area without working in concert with the heavier Su-27 'Flanker', the F-15's Soviet counterpart: the latter is tasked primarily with air defence of priority targets and long-range escort. The MiG-29 is designed for higher speeds and has highly effective armament, including short- and medium-range air-to-air missiles. Thus, as regards armament and equipment the 'Fulcrum' fits into a niche between the F-16 and the F-15 but has shorter range than the American fighters. Both the F-16 and the MiG-29 are stressed for 9 Gs. Both aircraft have prominent LERXes and air intakes suited to high-alpha operation.

The fundamental differences between the two types, however, were laid down at an early design stage. Research done in the USA did not show twin-engined fighters to have any decisive advantages over single-engined aircraft. On the other hand, in the Soviet Union, unlike the USA, twin-engined fighters had a much lower accident rate than their single-engined counterparts. The choice of a twin-engined layout for the MiG-29 was also influenced by wind tunnel research at TsAGI which showed that twin-engined fighters had an advantage because of their higher thrust-to-weight ratio. The MiG-29 utilises an integral layout in which the wings and fuselage are blended into a single lifting body. The F-16 is designed along more conventional lines with a classic separate fuselage.

Since the Fighting Falcon was optimised for maximum manoeuvrability at transonic speeds, a fixed-area monoshock air intake was chosen. This enabled the engine to run steadily at up to Mach 2.0. Research in the USA showed that incorporating a variable air intake would add 180 kg (397 lb) of airframe weight without giving any appreciable improvement in performance at speeds below Mach 1.6. The MiG-29 was designed for higher speeds, so Mikoyan engineers opted for variable four-shock intakes enabling steady engine operation at up to Mach 2.3. In both cases the intakes were located ventrally to minimise airflow distortion at high alpha or during tight turns. For the same reason General Dynamics made the inlet duct as short as possible but this was

limited by the nose gear unit which stowed below the inlet duct. Mikoyan achieved the same result by placing the intakes under the LERXes which directed the airflow.

The different air intake design was also explained by the different approach to the FOD prevention problem. American specialists believed the F-16's air intake design made foreign object ingestion unlikely, since the intake was located forward of the nose gear unit and the distance from intake lower lip to ground was 1.2 times the intake's mean diameter; which, as statistics showed, was quite enough for safe operation.

In the Soviet Union, airfields were usually in much worse condition than in the USA or Western Europe. When several 1st TFW F-15s from Langley AFB, VA, were to make a friendly visit to the Lipetsk Combat Training Centre, a group of USAF experts arrived in advance to examine the airfield and stated that the F-15 could not operate from such poor-quality runways and taxiways. Fortunately, this was not true and the visit went as planned; still, the F-15 pilots exercised extra care during takeoff, landing and taxying. Besides, the VVS knew better than the USAF that fighters have to be capable of operating from semi-prepared tactical airstrips. From the MiG-23 onwards, Soviet (Russian) fighters are always fitted with mudguards on the nosewheels; on the 'Fulcrum' the engineers took the idea further, with the characteristic FOD protection doors and dorsal auxiliary intakes already described in detail. Incidentally, Russian pilots are completely satisfied with the runways and taxiways in Lipetsk.

Another important difference is the tail unit design. General Dynamics had considered both single and twin vertical tails for the F-16 at the PD stage. Wind tunnel tests showed that the vortices generated by the LERXes maintained their direction at high AOAs and twin tails gave slightly better directional stability. Eventually, however, a single fin and rudder was chosen because of the lesser technical risk. Mikoyan opted for twin tails because the MiG-29 was designed for higher speeds and more stringent requirements applied to directional stability; besides, the twin-tail layout had been tried and tested on the MiG-25 'Foxbat'. The tail unit worked with four vortices generated by the LERXes and vortex generators on the pitot boom.

The F-16 has trapezoidal wings (actually almost a cropped delta) with 40° leading-edge sweep, an aspect ratio of 3.2 and a 4% thickness-to-chord ratio at the roots. Wind tunnel tests revealed the necessity of automatic leading-edge flaps increasing lift and improving stability

In 1987 the former Yugoslavia was the first European country to operate the type. (World Air Power)

at high AOAs. At Mach 0.8 the LE flaps increase turning speed 18% as compared with wings with zero leading-edge camber and by 10% as compared with the best wings with a modified aerofoil incorporating leading-edge camber. The MiG-29's wings have similar LE sweep (42°) and a marginally higher aspect ratio (3.5); theoretically this should result in slightly higher drag.

The F-16 is the world's first production fighter to feature an FBW control system. In contrast, the MiG-29 has conventional mechanical controls. Test pilot John Farley who had a chance to fly the 'Fulcrum' says the characteristics of its control system are similar to the F-15's. As mentioned earlier, Mikoyan decided to play safe. The advanced MiG-29M incorporates FBW controls which enhanced its combat capabilities a good deal.

The F-16A's AOA limit is 25°, though some sources quote 27.5°. Early production MiG-29s had a 26° AOA limit; in the MiG-29S (*izdeliye* 9.13S) and MiG-29SD/SE/SM, however, it was increased to 28°, while the FBW-equipped MiG-29M has a 30° limit. If the limiter system is used the MiG-29 can safely exceed 30° alpha, providing no roll control input is given. The MiG-29's roll control circuit is similar to that of the MiG-23. At AOAs up to 8.7° the ailerons and differentially movable

stabilators work in concert; beyond 8.7° the ailerons are locked neutral, leaving only the stabilators for roll control. Despite the MiG-29's good high-alpha handling the pilots cannot use it to the full to shorten the landing run since the landing gear is fairly short. Touching down at 240 km/h (133 kts), the fighter has a 600-m (1,968-ft) landing run with brake parachute, increasing to 900 m (2,952 ft) on a wet runway. Similarly, with a normal landing weight the F-16A fighter has a 650-m (2,132-ft) landing run on a dry runway.

The F-16 features a miniature side-stick instead of a traditional control stick. This allows the pilot to fly the aircraft by moving his wrist only, increasing control precision; on the minus side, however, the pilot can use only his right hand to work the stick. Currently the F-16 is the world's only production fighter to have a side-stick. The MiG-29, both the production 'Fulcrum-A/B/C' and the MiG-29M, has a conventional stick; so do the F-15E Strike Eagle, F/A-18 and EF2000.

The F-16's ejection seat is inclined at a greater angle than the MiG-29's (30°). This allows the pilot to withstand higher G forces during vigorous manoeuvring but makes it harder to look back over his shoulder. The F-16's one-piece frameless canopy offers better forward visibility; yet it is heavy and has to be jettisoned before ejection, as the glass is too thick to eject through it (for birdstrike protection reasons) and presumably even a micro-detonating cord wouldn't do the job. Cockpit visibility in the MiG-29 is marginally worse (though the pilots are quite pleased with it) and likewise the canopy has to be jettisoned before ejection.

The Zvezda K-36 zero-zero ejection seat fitted to most of Russia's current combat jets, including the MiG-29, has demonstrated its considerable capabilities more than once. The most spectacular demonstration was at the 1989 Le Bourget airshow when the seat saved test pilot Anatoliy Kvochur's life in a minimum-altitude ejection. The seat can be used at up to 1,300 km/h (722 kts) IAS and 25,000 m (82,020 ft); if a pressure helmet is used, safe ejection is possible at 1,400 km/h (777 kts) IAS. On the minus side, the K-36 is much heavier than its Western counterparts (205 kg/452 lb). The F-16 is equipped with a McDonnell Douglas ACES II zero-zero ejection seat permitting ejection at up to 1112 km/h (617 kts) IAS and 15,240 m (50,000 ft).

Dimensionally the two fighters are similar. The 'Fulcrum' is slightly longer and has a bigger wing span and wing area but the F-16 is taller. The MiG-29's empty weight is higher but normal TOW with six short-range AAMs is only 24–27% higher than the F-16's because of the lower fuel volume relative to total internal volume; in fact, the F-16's MTOW is higher than the MiG-29's.

The F-16 has a much bigger combat radius but, in fact, this is due mainly to the use of larger drop tanks. With two 1,400-lit. (308 Imp. gal.) underwing tanks and a 1,136-lit. (250 Imp. gal.) centreline tank, the Fighting Falcon's ferry range is 3,900 km (2,166 nm) versus the MiG-29's 2,900 km (1,611 nm) with two 800-lit. (176 Imp. gal.) underwing tanks and a 1,520-lit. (334.4 Imp. gal.) centreline tank or 2,100 km (1,166 nm) with centreline tank only. On internal fuel only, however, the two fighters have almost identical range; 1,600 km (888 nm) for the F-16 and 1,500 km (833 nm) for the MiG-29.

Moreover, in a situation resembling a typical Vietnam war engagement when the adversaries began a dogfight with a full internal fuel load, no drop tanks and short-range AAMs only, the F-16 will undoubtedly have a higher specific wing loading and a lower thrust-to-weight ratio than the MiG-29. Combat specific wing loading is 3% higher for the F-16A and 16% higher for the F-16C; thrust-to-weight ratio is 14% and 5% worse respectively. This gives the 'Fulcrum' an advantage, even though the Russian fighter has G load limits at speeds above Mach 0.85.

In 1993 US analysts compared the F-16C and MiG-29 in typical combat configuration (i.e., with a 50% fuel load and two dogfight AAMs on the outer wing pylons). Their verdict was that the F-16 would have a minor advantage over the MiG during transonic manoeuvring at low and medium altitude. According to US experts, in these conditions the MiG-29 would be handicapped by a G limit of 7 versus the F-16's 9 Gs, meaning the F-16 can make tighter turns. It should be noted, however, that these estimates were based on educated guesswork as to the MiG-29's performance characteristics, some of which were unknown at the time. They are largely confirmed by a special combat efficiency evaluation programme held by *Luftwaffe*, the results of NATO exercises and mock combat between the MiG-29 and Western fighters. These showed the 'Fulcrum' to be vastly superior to Western types in a dogfight. Not so much because of its excellent manoeuvrability but first and foremost thanks to the weapons control system and the weapons proper.

When *Luftwaffe's* (JG 73) MiG-29s participated in mock combat with USAF F-16Cs in 1994 the German pilots usually got the 'enemy' in their sights first, which meant victory (first shoot, first kill). The MiGs were armed with R-73 dogfight AAMs and the pilots used Schchel'-3UM helmet-mounted sights. Col. Jochen Both (USAF) detached to the *Luftwaffe* for the duration of the exercise stated that the Fighting Falcons showed better manoeuvrability 60% of the time; but then, the F-16s flew in clean condition while the MiGs had six pylons and carried a centreline drop tank and two fixed R-73 acquisition rounds. Still, the HMS enabled the MiG pilots to fire first. Incidentally, this gave rise to a new term. The Russian for helmet is *shlem*, and when talking of target acquisition with an HMS it soon became customary to say the target had been *schlemmed*!

Mock combat was performed one-on-one or in pairs. In Both's opinion, the MiG-29's radar had the serious drawback of being able to track only one target at a time; this made it harder for the 'Fulcrum' pilots in a mêlée with F-16Cs whose radars could track several targets. In reality, however, the standard N-019 radar can track ten targets while the F-16C's AN/APG-68 tracks only eight. On the other hand, the Fighting Falcon can attack up to four separate targets at a time with a salvo of AIM-120A AMRAAM missiles while the Russian fighter can only fire R-27 AAMs at one target at a time. Before that, JG 73 'Fulcrums' had engaged in similar mock combat with US Marine Corps F/A-18Cs.

Col. Both says *Luftwaffe* MiG-29 pilots have no problems using the R-73 missiles or the Russian helmet-mounted sight. The latter fits the standard NATO flying helmet perfectly and weighs only 300 g (10.59 oz), which means the pilot will not suffer injuries in an ejection because of the added weight. The pilot simply turns his head towards the target and pushes the missile fire button; the time required for the missile's heat seeker to get a lock-on and the missile to blast off is one second: 'excellent performance', as the German pilots put it.

On the other hand, MiG-29 pilots have to pay more attention to the instruments than those flying the F-16C which has a higher degree of automation. Also, they have to keep certain flight envelope limits in mind during a dogfight; this forces them to check on the instruments every now and again, distracting their attention at a critical moment, which may cause them to lose target lock-on. The F-16C's control system automatically keeps the aircraft within the prescribed limits. German pilots say they began to practice using the R-73 AAMs and HMS in a dogfight only after Germany's reunification and their integration into the *Luftwaffe*. According to Col. Both in Cold War times the East German Air Force (LSK/LV) concentrated on GCI-assisted intercept. Thus German 'Fulcrum' pilots realized the full strength of their weapons only when Western combat tactics were adopted.

The combat efficiency of the German MiG-29s in a dogfight was indeed increased by implementing a special dogfight mode: the radar or IRST automatically locked on to the target when it entered a predetermined area and was displayed on the HUD. The HMS and the wide-angle seeker heads of the R-73 missiles contributed most to the advantage, enabling the pilot to attack targets at large sighting angles without wasting time to turn the aircraft

One of the 24 'Fulcrum's evaluated and subsequently retained by Luftwaffe – *single-seater 29+20. (Yefim Gordon archive)*

squarely towards them ('If you can see them, you can shoot them'). This, incidentally, was demonstrated once again when *Armée de l'Air* and Belgian AF delegations visited the Czech Republic in 1996. Czech AF MiG-29s invariably emerged as the winners in mock combat against French Mirage 2000s and Belgian F-16As. In the West, production F-22As, Rafales and EF2000s will feature an HMS as standard.

The Vympel R-73 (AA-11 Archer) is a fire and forget weapon which can destroy violently manoeuvring targets day and night over land and water, even if the pilot's aim is not very good. It is immune to ground clutter, active and passive ECM since it is equipped with an omnidirectional passive IR seeker head. The R-73 has a combined jet/aerodynamic control system giving it superb manoeuvrability in all flight modes, especially immediately after launch when the missile's speed is low and rudder efficiency is poor. The seeker head's field of view is 90°; the missile has a 30-km (16-nm) range, a minimum target altitude of 5 m (16 ft) and can be fired during manoeuvres with up to 12 Gs. The cylindrical warhead weighs 8 kg (17.63 lb).

In an interview, Vympel's General Designer Sokolovskiy revealed that a new version designated R-73M had been developed. The R-73M features a seeker head with a 180° field of view and twice higher sensitivity (and hence detection range). The seeker head has a multi-facet two-band IR sensor for better IRCM resistance. It is programmed to shift its aim from the engine efflux to the centre of the airframe when the missile gets close to the target so that the R-73M does not lose its lock-on so easily.

In two consecutive issues (16 October and 25 October 1995) *Aviation Week & Space Technology* published a report by a group of American aviation writers on the problems of creating a modern short-range air-to-air weapons system. The report contained specialist opinions on progress in this direction in the US, the UK, Germany and Russia. Research made by McDonnell Douglas Corporation showed that in combat the MiG-29 would have first shot, first kill capability much more often than the F-15. Israeli reports state that the combat potential of a fighter equipped with an HMS is three times that of an identical fighter lacking this system if both are armed with AIM-9 Sidewinder missiles; if the MiG-29 carries AAMs with wide-angle seeker heads the advantage is nine times. A former senior USAF official has been quoted as saying that 'the billions of dollars spent on the F-4 and F-15 are no use if the enemy is armed with missiles with wide-

angle seeker heads and a helmet-mounted sight'. Evaluation of the R-73 and the MiG-29 resulted in the beginning of top-priority research for similar weapons systems in the US and Germany and in stepped-up research in the same direction in the UK, Israel and the South African Republic.

The MiG-29's advantage in a dogfight is enhanced by its highly effective internal gun. The IRST measures the target's coordinates and the laser rangefinder determines target range. The asynchronous aiming method based on these data gives the 'Fulcrum' excellent gunfire accuracy during manoeuvring. This method is also used when there is no direct visibility of the target (i.e., in IMC conditions). When the target is plainly visible a gunsight reticle is projected on the HUD and must be placed over the target in order to fire. In IMC conditions the HUD displays targeting error values calculated by the computer; these increase or decrease as the aircraft manoeuvres. When the error values drop to zero the pilot knows that the reticle is over the unseen target and it's time to fire. The heavy calibre (30 mm) and the fairly high rate of fire (1,500–1,800 rpm) enable the MiG-29 to score a kill with the first burst of gunfire – some five or seven rounds.

A fly-off between the F-16C and MiG-29 showed that the Fighting Falcon has a much higher roll rate thanks to its FBW control system and wing planform. Theoretically this should give it a higher turn rate, reducing turn time. However, during the MiG-29's airshow début at Farnborough International '88 specialists noted that the 'Fulcrum' could perform 360° turns without losing altitude; a crucial asset for a fighter. At 800 km/h (444 kts), turning radius is 350 m (1,148 ft); in the same situation the F-16 had a turning radius around 400 m (1,312 ft). At speeds above 400 km/h (222 kts) the MiG-29 can turn with a 225-m (738-ft) radius, pulling 3.8 Gs. At 10,000 m (32,808 ft) and Mach 0.9 the MiG-29 can pull 4.6–5.0 Gs in a turn.

Turn rate and linear acceleration are two of the most important factors determining a fighter's manoeuvrability. At Mach 0.85 the MiG-29's linear acceleration is 11 m/sec^2 (36 ft/sec^2) at S/L, which means the fighter can go from 500 km/h (277 kts) to 1,000 km/h (555 kts) in just 13 seconds. At 6,000 m (19,685 ft) and Mach 0.85, linear acceleration is 6.5 m/sec^2 (21.32 ft/sec^2).

The two engines located in spaced nacelles increase combat survivability significantly, as there is little probability of both engines being damaged by a single missile or burst of gunfire. This feature also reduces accident attrition in peacetime as compared with single-

ABOVE: *The Ookrains'ki Sokoly during a practice session. (Ryszard Jaxa-Malachowski)*
BELOW: *Slovak Air 'Fulcrum-A' 7501 in a special display colour scheme. (Peter Davison)*

engined types such as the F-16, Mirage 2000-5, SAAB JAS39 etc. In its 16-24 August 1995 issue *Flight International* analysed military aircraft accident statistics for 1994; of the 22 accidents that year involving F-16s eight were caused by engine failure. By comparison, since its service entry in 1983 the MiG-29 had only four accidents caused by engine failure. The RD-33 turbofan can be easily restarted at low speed (right down to 300 km/h or 166 kts), whereas the Pratt&Whitney F100-PW-200 of the F-16C/D requires a speed of 390–460 km/h (216–255 kts) for a successful relight.

General Electric offered one of their engines for installation in the export MiG-29 subject to certain conditions (engine model and other details remained undisclosed in 1997). MAPO-MiG engineers said yes, providing GE modified the engine to make it at least as good as the RD-33 in certain respects. One particular parameter MAPO-MiG was dissatisfied with was surge resistance; in the GE engine it was six conventional units (as per US standards), while in the RD-33 it was 12.[1] The RD-33 has a fairly low SFC: 2.05 kg/kgp·hr (lb/lb st·hr) in full afterburner and 0.77 kg/kgp·hr at full military power. By comparison, the SNECMA M53-P2 powering the Mirage 2000-5 has an SFC of 2.08 and 0.89 kg/kgp·hr in these respective modes.

A critical factor reflecting an aircraft's operations is its accident rate. Over the first ten years in service the mean accident rate per 100,000 flight hours is 7.8 for the MiG-29 and 14 for the F-16. All in all, 34 MiG-29s were lost in accidents between 1983 and 1995, only six of these because of design and manufacturing defects. Within the same time frame (excluding 1991-93 for which no data are available) there were 110 serious accidents involving F-16s, 44 of which were caused by design and manufacturing defects.

The above comparative analysis applies mainly to early MiG-29s ('Fulcrum-A/B/C') and late production (Block 50) F-16Cs. Late versions of the 'Fulcrum' – the MiG-29SE, MiG-29SM and especially the MiG-29M – have much-improved performance over the initial *izdeliye* 9.12 and a wider weapons range including R-77 (RVV-AE) AMRAAMski missiles, various AGMs and (on the MiG-29M) heavy-calibre guided bombs. The latest versions of the MiG-29 have better performance, combat efficiency, reliability and serviceability than most Western fighters.

Comparative data are given in the tables below.

Table 1. Thrust-to-weight ratio

| | Thrust-to-weight ratio: | |
	combat*	takeoff
Mikoyan MiG-29SE/SM	**1.52**	**1.08**
Mikoyan MiG-29M	**1.43**	**1.05**
GD F-16C	1.05	1.09
McDD F/A-18C	1.00	0.93
Eurofighter EF2000	1.30	1.22
Dassault Mirage 2000-5	0.95	n/a

* at 1000 m (3,280 ft) and Mach 1.0 with a full internal fuel load

Coupled with the excellent aerodynamics, the higher thrust-to-weight ratio gives the MiG-29 an advantage in manoeuvrability over its opponents.

Table 2. Rate of climb at 1,000 m (3,280 ft) and Mach 0.9 with a full internal fuel load

	Rate of climb, m/sec (ft/sec)
Mikoyan MiG-29SE	**330 (1,082.67)**
Mikoyan MiG-29M	**320 (1,049.86)**
GD F-16C	265–275 (869.42–902.23)
McDD F/A-18C	256 (839.89)
Eurofighter EF2000	300 (984.25)
Dassault Mirage 2000-5	285 (935.0)

Table 3. Maximum turn rate at 3,000 m (9,842 ft) with 50% fuel

	Turn rate, deg/sec
Mikoyan MiG-29SE	**23.5**
Mikoyan MiG-29M	**22.8**
GD F-16C	21.5
McDD F/A-18C	20.0
Eurofighter EF2000	22.0
Dassault Mirage 2000-5	20.0

---

1 Incidentally, in one case the westernization trend has been reversed. The RD-33 has been selected to re-engine the Atlas Cheetah, a South African spinoff of the Dassault Mirage III.

Table 4. Specific wing loading at takeoff

	Wing loading, kg/m² (lb/sq.ft)
Mikoyan MiG-29SE	**403 (1,963)**
Mikoyan MiG-29M	**439 (2,139)**
GD F-16C	435 (2,119)
McDD F/A-18C	420 (2,046)
Eurofighter EF2000	300 (1,461)

Table 5. G limits of fourth-generation fighters

	Airframe G limit	Max G force in a turn
Mikoyan MiG-29SE	**9.0**	**7.0**
Mikoyan MiG-29M	**9.0**	**7.0**
GD F-16C	9.0	6.4
McDD F/A-18C	7.5	6.2
Eurofighter EF2000	9.0	7.0

Table 6. Acceleration from 600 to 1,000 km/h (333–555 kts) at 1,000 m (3,280 ft)

	Acceleration time, sec
Mikoyan MiG-29SE	**13.5**
Mikoyan MiG-29M	**13.5**
GD F-16C	14.0
McDD F/A-18C	18.0
Eurofighter EF2000	14.0
Dassault Mirage 2000-5	

The upgraded fire control radars of the latest MiG-29 versions have a large field of view. In the MiG-29M's Phazotron N-010 Zhuk radar and the Phazotron N-019M Topaz of the MiG-29S the beam is scanned in azimuth through 180° and 140° respectively. By comparison, the Hughes Electronics AN/APG-65 radar fitted to the F/A-18C and the F-16C's Westinghouse AN/APG-68 have 140° and 120° scanning in azimuth respectively.

Table 7. Fire control radar performance data

	N-019	AN/APG-66	AN/APG-65
Weight, kg (lb)	250 (551.14)	160 (352.73)	224 (493.82)
Volume, m³ (cu. ft)	n/a	0.11 (3.88)	0.12 (4.23)
Scanner diameter	n/a	0.6 m (1 ft 11.62 in.)	0.7 m (2 ft 3.55 in.)
Mean radiation power, W	n/a	150–250	400–450
Aerial target detection range, km (nm)*:			
in open airspace	75 (41)	40 (22)	65 (36)
in look-down/shoot-down mode, forward hemisphere	65 (36)	n/a	60 (33)
in look-down/shoot-down mode, rear hemisphere	35 (19)	n/a	40 (22)

* fighter-type targets with an RCS of 3 m² (32.25 sq. ft)

Western and Russian assessments of the fighters' armament, weapons control systems and combat potential differ somewhat, to say the least. US specialists claim that the F-16A's Westinghouse AN/APG-66 radar is superior to the N-019, having, e.g., 20% longer detection range. MAPO-MiG, however, maintain that the N-019 has longer range not only than the AN/APG-66 but the much more powerful AN/APG-65!

Table 8. Weapons control system data of fourth-generation fighters

	MiG-29SE	MiG-29M	F-16C	F/A-18C	EF2000
Fire control radar					
Model	**Phazotron N-019ME**	**Phazotron N-010**	Westinghouse AN/APG-68	Hughes AN/APG-65	GEC-Marconi ECR90
Aerial target detection range, km (nm)**:**					
in open airspace	**60–70 (33–38)**	**80 (44)**	50–60 (27–33)	60–65 (33–36)	70–80 (38–44)
in 'look-down/shoot-down' mode, forward hemisphere	**60 (33)**	**80 (44)**	50–60 (27–33)	60 (33)	70 (38)
in 'look-down/shoot-down' mode, rear hemisphere	**30–35 (16–19)**	**40–50 (22–27)**	30–35 (16–19)	35–40 (19–22)	40 (22)
Targets tracked	**10**	**10**	10	10	10
Targets attacked simultaneously	**2**	**4**	4	4	4
Scanning in azimuth	**140°**	**180°**	120°	120°	140°
Surface ship detection range, km (nm)**	**n/a**	**120–150 (66–83)**	120–150 (66–83)	120–150 (66–83)	120–150 (66–83)†
Optoelectronic targeting system					
Aerial target detection range, km (nm)**:**					
head-on mode	**n/a**	**10 (5.5)**	none	none	n/a
pursuit mode	**15 (2.7)**	**30 (16)**	none	none	n/a
Laser rangefinder	**yes**	**yes**	yes‡	yes‡	no
Use in strike mode	**no**	**yes**	yes‡	yes‡	yes†
Active ECM	**yes**	**yes**	yes	yes	yes

Notes:
** surface ship with an RCS of 3,000 m^2 (32,258 sq. ft)
† To be introduced around 2005
‡ Podded laser ranger/designator only

Table 9. Armament of fourth-generation fighters

	MiG-29SM	MiG-29M	F-16C	F/A-18C	EF2000
Internal gun	1×GSh-301 30 mm	1×GSh-301 30 mm	1×M-60A1 20 mm	1×M-60A1 20 mm	1×Mauser 27 mm
Air-to-air missiles ('kill' range, km/nm)*: semi-active radar homing	2×R-27ER (60/33) 2×R-27R1 (50/27)	2×R-27ER (60/33) 2×R-27R1 (50/27)	2×AIM-7 Sparrow (40/22)	2×AIM-7 Sparrow (40/22)	n/a
active radar homing	6×R-77 (50/27)	6×R-77 (50/27)	6×AIM-120 AMRAAM (50/27)	6×AIM-120A AMRAAM (50/27)	6×AIM-120A AMRAAM (50/27)
passive IR homing	2×R-27T/ET (50/27) 6×R-73 (20/11)	2×R-27T/ET (50/27) 8×R-73 (20/11)	6×AIM-9 Sidewinder (20/11)	4×AIM-9 Sidewinder (20/11)	6×AIM-9 Sidewinder (20/11)
Air-to-surface missiles: passive radar homing	2×Kh-31P	4×Kh-31P	2×AGM-88A HARM	2×AGM-88A HARM	n/a
active radar homing	2×Kh-31A	4×Kh-31A	4×AGM-84 Harpoon	4×AGM-84 Harpoon	n/a
TV-guided	2×Kh-29T	4×Kh-29T	6×AGM-65A Maverick	4×AGM-65A Maverick	n/a
laser-guided	none	4×Kh-25ML	6×AGM-65E Maverick	4×AGM-65E Maverick	n/a
passive IR homing	none	none	6×AGM-65F Maverick	4×AGM-65F Maverick	n/a
Guided bombs	2×KAB-500KR	2×KAB-500KR	2–4×GBU-15	2–4×GBU-15	n/a
Unguided rockets and free-fall bombs	yes	yes	yes	yes	yes

* against fighter-type targets with an RCS of 3 m^2 (32.25 sq. ft)

Table 10. Maximum air-to-air missile launch range of fourth-generation fighters

	Medium-range AAMS in head-on mode	Medium-range AAMs in pursuit mode	Short-range AAMs in pursuit mode
MiG-29M	60 km (33 nm)	27 km (15 nm)	20 km (11 nm)
MiG-29	50 km (27 nm)	20 km (11 nm)	20 km (11 nm)
F-16C	40–45 km (22–25 nm)	18–20 km (10–11 nm)	18–20 km (10–11 nm)
F/A-18C	40–45 km (22–25 nm)	18–20 km (10–11 nm)	18–20 km (10–11 nm)

Table 11 below illustrates the so-called combined combat efficiency quotient calculated by MAPO-MiG experts. This is a relative unit which includes the performance of the WCS and other mission avionics, the fighter's top speed in intercept mode and the characteristics of its weapons.

Table 11. Combined combat efficiency quotient of fourth-generation fighters in intercept mode

Mikoyan MiG-29SE	0.82
Mikoyan MiG-29SM	0.82
Mikoyan MiG-29M	1.00
GD F-16C	0.76
McDD F/A-18C	0.85
Dassault Mirage 2000-5	0.68
Eurofighter EF2000	0.9–1.0

In dogfight mode the MiG-29's combined combat efficiency quotient, which here includes the characteristics of the ESM suite and the aircraft's acceleration as well, will be even higher (see below).

Table 12. Combined combat efficiency quotient of fourth-generation fighters in dogfight mode

Mikoyan MiG-29SE	0.90
Mikoyan MiG-29SM	0.90
Mikoyan MiG-29M	1.00
GD F-16C	0.79
McDD F/A-18C	0.65
Dassault Mirage 2000-5	0.82
Eurofighter EF2000	0.9–1.0

In strike mode the F-16 is superior to the MiG-29 due to its higher MTOW. E.g., with 2,000 kg (4,409 lb) of bombs and two R-60M AAMs the MiG-29 can only carry a single drop tank; with a similar ordnance load the F-16 can carry three drop tanks giving it longer range. Besides, the Fighting Falcon has aerial refuelling capability which production versions of the 'Fulcrum' lack (it is to be introduced under a mid-life update programme only). According to US experts, with two 900-kg (1,984-lb) bombs and two AIM-9 Sidewinder short-range AAMs the

F-16C has a 1,200-km (666-nm) combat radius on a hi-lo-hi mission profile; in similar conditions (two 900-kg bombs, two R-60M dogfight AAMs, hi-lo-hi) the MiG-29's combat radius is 500 km (277 nm). With the same armament on a lo-lo-lo mission profile the two fighters' combat radius should be 740 km (411 nm) and 315 km (175 nm) respectively.

Table 13. Combined combat efficiency quotient of fourth-generation fighters in strike mode

Mikoyan MiG-29SE	0.34
Mikoyan MiG-29SM	0.75
Mikoyan MiG-29M	1.00
GD F-16C	1.00
McDD F/A-18C	1.00
Dassault Mirage 2000-5	0.70
Eurofighter EF2000	0.8–1.0

According to Russian analysts, combat radius in supersonic (Mach 1.5) intercept mode with four medium-range AAMs, two short-range AAMs and three drop tanks is 410 km (227 nm) for the MiG-29M, 389 km (216 nm) for the F-16C, 370 km (205 nm) for the F/A-18C and 345 km (191 nm) for the MiG-29S. In low-level penetration mode (200 m/656 ft) with drop tanks the fighters have a combat radius of 385 km (213 nm), 400 km (222 nm), 372 km (206 nm) and 340 km (188 nm) respectively. Thus, Russian and US fourth-generation light fighters are similar in range.

Table 14 below illustrates the summarized combat efficiency evaluation of fourth-generation fighters.

Table 14.

	Combined combat efficiency quotient	
	air-to-air mode	strike mode
Mikoyan MiG-29SE	0.86	0.34
Mikoyan MiG-29SM	0.86	0.75
Mikoyan MiG-29M	1.00	1.00
GD F-16C	0.78	1.00
McDD F/A-18C	0.79	1.00
Dassault Mirage 2000-5	0.75	0.70
Eurofighter EF2000	0.9–1.0	0.8–1.0

The previous data indicate that the F-16 is an air superiority fighter optimised for air-to-air combat at subsonic and transonic speeds at low and medium altitude. The F-16's high MTOW also gives it strike capability. While the MiG-29, too, was conceived as an air superiority fighter, its early versions had limited strike capability; however, it is effective in the air defence rôle against high-flying high-speed targets.

MAPO-MiG calculations show that the MiG-29SE and MiG-29SM are a much more cost-effective solution as compared to their Western counterparts, as illustrated by Table 15 below.

Russian defence industry analysts claim that the most advanced version of the 'Fulcrum', the MiG-29M, is two to three times more cost-effective than the Eurofighter EF2000. Speaking of the Anglo-Italo-German-Spanish EF2000, Anatoliy Belosvet, Deputy General Director of ANPK MiG, said the aircraft was outdated even before it left the drawing board. 'We have carefully analysed the Eurofighter's capabilities but could not find anything we didn't know already', said Belosvet. He is convinced that the EF2000 is a less capable aircraft than the MiG-29 and putting it into production would be 'primarily a political decision with no viable technical background'.

MAPO-MiG also believe that the latest versions of the MiG-29 have better reliability and serviceability than their US competitors. MTBF is 7.3 hrs for the MiG-29M and 13.6 hrs for the MiG-29S versus 3.7 hrs for the F/A-18C and 2.9 hrs for the F-16C. Specific maintenance labour intensity is 11 man-hours per flight hour for the MiG-29M/S, compared to 16 hrs for the F/A-18C and 18

hrs the F-16C during the initial service (IOC) period as illustrated by Table 16 below..

Experts from Germany's Federal Accounting Office (BRH – *Bundesrechnungshof*) state that in the configuration selected for the *Luftwaffe* – i.e., without IRST and built-in DASS ECM suite – the EF2000 will be inferior to the MiG-29. Belosvet claims that the production MiG-29S (*izdeliye* 9.13S) armed with R-77 AAMs is a more capable dogfighter than the F-15C, F-16C and F/A-18C with AIM-120A AMRAAM missiles or the Mirage 2000-5 with Matra Mica AAMs, and that the MiG-29M has similar combat potential to the high-tech Boeing/Lockheed Martin F-22A Raptor.

Western aviation experts have often criticised the MiG-29's cockpit as sixties-style. Mikhail R. Val'denberg's answer was something like 'If a state-of-the-art cockpit is all you need, then the MiG-29 is not your best buy. But if you need a good aircraft for the counter-air rôle, well, that's something else again.' However, now that a 'glass cockpit' has been developed for the 'Fulcrum', this should make the critics think differently. The MiG-29's EFIS has been displayed in mockup form at various international airshows and in 1997 was undergoing tests on a modified 'Fulcrum-C' (331 Blue).

Of course, any analysis should be taken with a grain of salt. Analysts are never completely objective on either side, and of course all companies try to advertise their aircraft. Still, the MiG-29's impressive displays at various airshows speak for themselves; also, appraisals by Western experts, and not least fighter pilots, show beyond doubt that the 'Fulcrum' is, and ought to be, treated with respect.

Table 15. Cost-effectiveness of fourth-generation fighters

	Mikoyan MiG-29SM	Mikoyan MiG-29SE	GD F-16C	McDD F/A-18C	Dassault Mirage 2000-5
air-to-air mode	**1.0**	**1.23**	0.87	0.75	0.76
strike mode	**1.0**	**0.74**	1.02	0.88	0.67

Table 16. Reliability and serviceability parameters of fourth-generation fighters

	Mikoyan MiG-29SE	Mikoyan MiG-29M	GD F-16C	McDD F/A-18C
Operational readiness quotient	**0.9**	**0.9**	0.8	0.85
Specific maintenance labour intensity, man-hours per flight hour	**11.3**	**11.0**	18	16–18
MTBF, hrs	**13.6**	**7.3**	2.9	3.7
Airframe life, hrs	**7,000**	**7,000**	8,000	8,000
Relative cost	**0.7**	**0.8**	0.7	1.0

Table 17. MiG-29 and F-16 compared

	MiG-29	MiG-29SE	MiG-29M	F-16A Block 1-15	F-16C Block 25	F-16C Block 32	F-16C Block 42	F-16C Block 50
First flight	1983	1986	1986	1979-82	1984	1986	1989	1992
Powerplant	2×Izotov RD-33	2×Izotov RD-33	2×Izotov RD-33K[1]	P&W F100-PW-200	P&W F100-PW-200	P&W F100-PW-220	P&W F100-PW-220	GE F110-GE-129
Rating in full afterburner, kgp (lb st)	2×8,340 (2×18,386)	2×8,340 (2×18,386)	2×8,800 (2×19,400)	11,340 (25,000)	11,340 (25,000)	12,300 (27,116)	12,300 (27,116)	13,421 (29,588)
Length	17.32 m (56′ 9.88″)	17.32 m (56′ 9.88″)	17.32 m (56′ 9.88″)	15.03 m (49′ 3.73″)	15.03 m (49′ 3.73″)	15.03 m (49′ 3.73″)	15.03 m (49′ 3.73″)	15.03 m (49′ 3.73″)
Wing span	11.36 m (37′ 3.24″)	11.36 m (37′ 3.24″)	11.36 m (37′ 3.24″)	9.54 m (31′ 3.59″)	9.54 m (31′ 3.59″)	9.54 m (31′ 3.59″)	9.54 m (31′ 3.59″)	9.54 m (31′ 3.59″)
Height on ground	4.73 m (15′ 6.22″)	4.73 m (15′ 6.22″)	4.73 m (15′ 6.22″)	5.09 m (16′ 8.39″)	5.09 m (16′ 8.39″)	5.09 m (16′ 8.39″)	5.09 m (16′ 8.39″)	5.09 m (16′ 8.39″)
Wing area, m[2] (sq. ft)	38.00 (408.6)	38.00 (408.6)	38.00 (408.6)	27.87 (299.67)	27.87 (299.67)	27.87 (299.67)	27.87 (299.67)	27.87 (299.67)
Normal TOW, kg (lb)	15,000 (33,068)	15,300 (33,730)	16.680 (36,772)	11,200 (24,691)	11,470 (25,286)	n/a	12,000 (26,455)	12,933 (28,511)
MTOW, kg (lb)	18,000 (39,682)	19,700 (43,430)	22,000 (48,500)	16,060 (35,405)	17,010 (37,500)	17,010 (37,500)	19,187 (42,300)	19,187 (42,300)
Internal fuel, kg (lb)	3,630 (8,002)	3,832 (8,448)	4,460 (9.832)	3,104 (6,846)	3,104 (6,846)	3,104 (6,846)	3,104 (6,846)	3,104 (6,846)
Thrust-to-weight ratio[2]	1.11	1.09	1.11	0.95	n/a	n/a	1.03	1.03
Top speed, km/h (kts): at S/L	1,480 (822)	1,480 (822)	1,500 (833)	1,450 (805)	1,450 (805)	1,450 (805)	1,450 (805)	1,450 (805)
at altitude	2,450 (1,361)	2,450 (1,361)	2,500 (1,388)	2,100 (1,166)	n/a	n/a	2,000 (1,111)	2,000 (1,111)
Landing speed, km/h (kts)	260 (144)	260 (144)	260 (144)	245 (136)	245 (136)	245 (136)	245 (136)	245 (136)
Service ceiling, m (ft)	17,500 (57,414)	17,000 (55,774)	17,000 (55,774)	15,200 (49,868)	15,240 (50,000)	15,240 (50,000)	15,240 (50,000)	18,000 (59,055)
Rate of climb,[3] m/sec (ft/sec)	330 (1,082)	330 (1,082)	300 (984)	245 (803)	n/a	265 (869)	265 (869)	265 (869)

Table 17. continued

	MiG-29	MiG-29SE	MiG-29M	F-16A Block 1-15	F-16C Block 25	F-16C Block 32	F-16C Block 42	F-16C Block 50
Range, km (nm):								
on internal fuel at S/L	**710 (394)**	**n/a**	**900 (500)**	700 (388)	700 (388)	700 (388)	700 (388)	700 (388)
on internal fuel at altitude	**1,500 (833)**	**n/a**	**2,000 (1,111)**	1,600 (888)	1,600 (888)	1,600 (888)	1,600 (888)	1,600 (888)
w. 1 drop tank	**2,100 (1,166)**	**n/a**	**n/a**	n/a	n/a	n/a	n/a	n/a
w. 3 drop tanks	**2,900 (1,611)**	**n/a**	**3,200 (1,777)**	3,900 (2,166)	3,900 (2,166)	3,900 (2,166)	3,900 (2,166)	3,900 (2,166)
Long-range AAMs	–	**R-27ER R-27ET**	**R-27ER R-27ET**	–	–	–	–	–
Medium-range AAMs	**R-27R1 R-27T1**	**R-27R1 R-27T1**	**R-27R1 R-27T1**	–	–	–	AIM-120	AIM-120
Short-range AAMs	**R-60M R-73**	**R-60M R-73E**	**R-60M R-73**	AIM-9	AIM-9	AIM-9	AIM-9	AIM-9
Air-to-surface missiles	–	–	**Kh-25ML Kh-25MP Kh-29T Kh-31A/P**	AGM-84† Popeye-2‡ Gabriel‡	AGM-65	AGM-65 AGM-45	AGM-65 AGM-88	AGM-65 AGM-88

Notes:

[1] Land-based version lacking the 9,400-kgp (20,723 lb st) takeoff contingency rating of the naval engine

[2] With normal TOW

[3] At 1,000 m (3,280 ft)

† Royal Norwegian Air Force only

‡ Israeli Defence Force/Air Force (IDF/AF) only

Table 18. Comparative performance data of MiG-29 and the best Western fighters

	MiG-29SE	MiG-29M	F-16C	F/A-18C	EF2000
Powerplant	**2×Izotov RD-33**	**2×Izotov RD-33K**	Pratt&Whitney F100-PW-220	2×General Electric F404-GE-400	2×Eurojet EJ2000
Rating in full afterburner, kgp (lb st)	**2×8,300 (2×18,386)**	**2×8,800 (2×19,400)**	12,300 (27,116)	2×7,300 (2×16,093)	2×9,175 (2×20,227)
Normal TOW, kg (lb)	**15,300 (33,730)**	**16,680 (36,772)**	12,100 (26,455)	15,700 (34,611)	15,000 (33,068)
MTOW, kg (lb)	**19,700 (43,430)**	**22,000 (48,500)**	19,187 (42,300)	23,500 (51,807)	21,000 (46,296)
Internal fuel, kg (lb)	**3,832 (8,448)**	**4,460 (9,832)**	3,104 (6,846)	4,900 (10,802)	4,000 (8,818)
External fuel, kg (lb)	**3,040 (6,702)**	**3,290 (7,253)**	3,066 (6,760)	3,100 (6,834)	3,600 (7,936)

Table 18. continued

	MiG-29SE	MiG-29M	F-16C	F/A-18C	EF2000
Ordnance load, kg (lb)	**4,000** **(8,818)**	**4,500** **(9,920)**	5,443 (12,000)	4,500 (9,920)	6,500 (14,330)
Top speed, km/h (kts): at S/L	**1,480** **(822)**	**1,500** **(833)**	1,450 (805)	1,300 (722)	n/a
at altitude	**2,450** **(1,361)**	**2,500** **1,388)**	2,000 (1,111)	1,900 (1,055)	2,200–2,300 (1,222–1,277)
Range, km (nm): on internal fuel only (at altitude)	**n/a**	2,000 (1,111)	1,600 (888)	2,200 (1,222)	1,800–2,200 (1,000–1,222)
with 3 drop tanks	**n/a**	3,200 (1,777)	3,900 (2,166)	3,200 (1,777)	3,000–4,000 (1,666–2,222)

Mikoyan MiG-29 Comparison Graphs

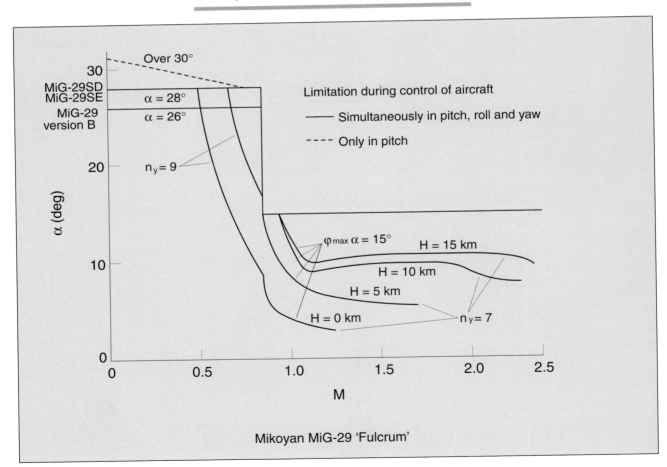

Mikoyan MiG-29 'Fulcrum'

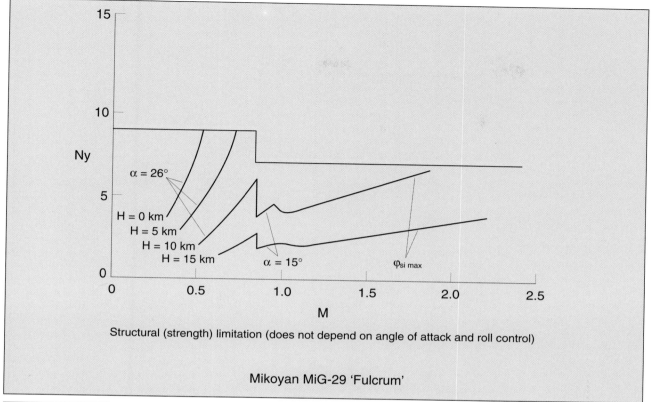

Structural (strength) limitation (does not depend on angle of attack and roll control)

Mikoyan MiG-29 'Fulcrum'

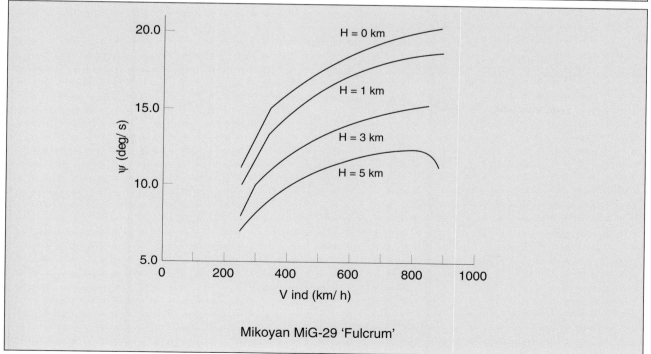

Mikoyan MiG-29 'Fulcrum'

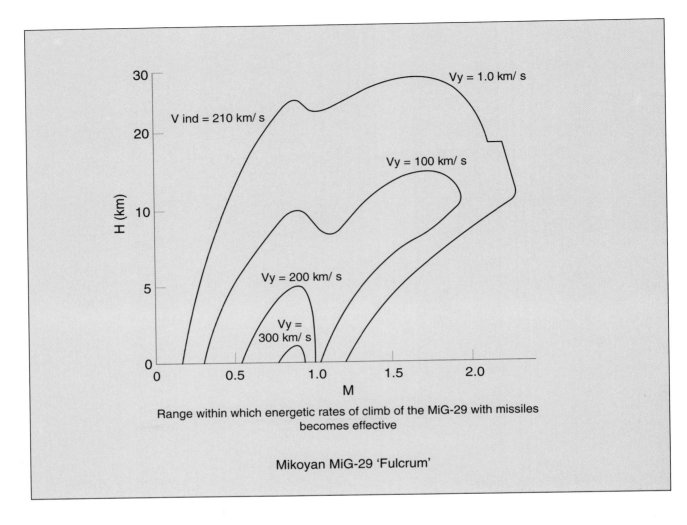

Range within which energetic rates of climb of the MiG-29 with missiles becomes effective

Mikoyan MiG-29 'Fulcrum'

The MiG-29 in Detail

T he MiG-29 is a twin-engined jet fighter of blended wing/body design. The fuselage (lifting body) and wings generate 40% and 60% of the total lift respectively; at AOAs above 17° the proportion of the lift generated by the fuselage and leading-edge root extensions is increased. The airframe utilises large extruded panels which reduces the number of stressed joints. Aluminium alloys (aluminium-lithium alloy on the MiG-29K and MiG-29M) and high-strength steel are the main structural materials. Some airframe components subjected to high stress and/or temperature (e.g., the wing spars and aft fuselage structure) are made of titanium. Composites account for approximately 7% of airframe weight. The airframe incorporates numerous access panels for ease of maintenance.

Fuselage (lifting body): semi-monocoque stressed-skin structure with 10 mainframes absorbing the main structural loads, interspersed with regular frames and bulkheads. Structurally the fuselage consists of three subassemblies: the forward fuselage (up to mainframe No. 4), centre fuselage (mainframes No. 4 through 7) and rear fuselage (mainframes No. 7 to 10) incorporating the engine bays (mainframes No. 7 and 8) and aft bay.

The forward fuselage includes the ogival glassfibre radome, the forward equipment bay, the pressurized cockpit and canopy, two avionics bays aft of the cockpit and the nosewheel well. The radome mounts the PVD-18 main pitot boom (*preeyomnik vozdooshnovo davleniya* – air pressure sensor) with horizontal vortex generators; besides the radar scanner it houses the marker beacon receiver antenna.

The forward equipment bay houses the radar set and IRST/laser ranger; the transparent sensor 'ball' of the latter is mounted dorsally, offset to starboard. The undersurface of the bay mounts IFF transponder, ATC,

The engine nozzles and open airbrakes of the 'Fulcrum-A'. (Andrey Yurgenson)

SHORAN and radio altimeter antennas and the air data system's yaw vane; AOA vanes are mounted on both sides. A PVD-7 backup pitot is mounted on the starboard side of the bay (the MiG-29K and MiG-29M have a third pitot head mounted ventrally beneath the cockpit). The IFF interrogator antenna is mounted ventrally or dorsally (ahead of the windscreen), depending on the version. On the MiG-29K the forward equipment bay also houses a retractable flight refuelling probe offset to port.

The pressurised cockpit is contained by frames No. 1 and 2 and has an aft-hinged canopy. The one-piece curved windscreen is made of electrically de-iced Triplex glass and has a magnesium alloy frame mounting three rear-view mirrors. The aft section is hinged to fuselage frame No. 3 and secured by four locks. The canopy is pneumatically actuated and has three positions, including partially open for taxying. Normally the canopy is operated by external and internal handles; a warning light and a voice information system warn the pilot if the canopy is not fully closed. In an emergency the canopy can be jettisoned manually; jettisoning prior to ejection is automatic. The pilot sits on a Zvezda K-36DM zero-zero ejection seat set at a 16° angle; the guide rails are attached to the aft cockpit bulkhead (frame No. 2). Seat height can be adjusted within ±85 mm (3.34 in.) to suit different pilots. Downward view over the nose is 14°.

A second equipment bay housing electrics is located between frames No. 2 and 3; it is accessible only when the canopy is fully open. An avionics bay further aft (between frames No. 3 and 3-D)[1] contains, among other things, the ARK-19 automatic direction finder. The ADF aerials are located dorsally (a blade aerial aft of the cockpit and a loop aerial beneath a dielectric panel between frames No. 5 and 6). The nosewheel well is contained by frames No. 2 and 4; the nose gear unit's hydraulic actuator is attached to the bottom of frame No. 2 and the unit itself to frame No. 3.

The leading-edge root extensions (LERXes) built integrally with the fuselage begin at frame No. 1. Their area is 4.71 m² (50.64 sq. ft); leading-edge sweep is 73° 30'. The port LERX houses the internal gun and its magazine box (frames No. 1 to 3) while the starboard LERX accommodates air conditioning equipment; these are accessed from below via removable and opening panels. The port LERX features a gun blast panel made of heat-resistant steel near the gun muzzle and numerous

cooling vents in the gun bay's upper skin between frames No. 2 and 3. Each LERX incorporates two dielectric panels over various aerials depending on the version (IFF, ATC, RHAWS and/or ECM).

The main engine air intakes are mounted ventrally on the LERXes between frames No. 3 and 4. On the 'Fulcrum-A/B/C' the LERXes have a rounded leading edge and incorporate auxiliary dorsal air intakes between frames No. 3-D and 4; the MiG-29K and MiG-29M have sharp-edged LERXes with no dorsal air intakes.

The MiG-29UB trainer differs markedly from the single-seaters in forward fuselage design. Mainframe No. 1 is moved forward by 900 mm (2 ft 11.43 in.), increasing the pressurised cockpit's length to some 3 m (9 ft 10 in.). The trainee and instructor sit in tandem on identical K-36DM ejection seats enclosed by a common aft-hinged canopy; the latter incorporates a retractable periscope for the instructor improving his forward view on takeoff and

The port LERX with the dorsal blow-in doors in open position. (Aleksey Mikheyev)

---
[1] This is a transliteration of the **Russian** designation. Since D is the fifth letter of the Cyrillic alphabet, the English equivalent should really be frame 3-E!

174

ABOVE: *The engine nozzles and open airbrakes seen from above. (Andrey Yurgenson)*
BELOW: *The aft fuselage of the MiG-29K, showing arrester hook. (Andrey Yurgenson)*

landing. All flight, engine and weapons controls, flight instruments and indicators are identical in the front and rear cockpits. The electric system's overload protection panel is moved forward from equipment bay No. 2 to a space between the front seat and rear instrument panel.

Since the MiG-29UB lacks radar, the nosecone is made almost entirely of metal, incorporating only a small dielectric fairing over the marker beacon receiver antenna. The forward equipment bay houses the IRST/LR, automatic control system components and avionics. Thus Mikoyan have managed to make the trainer completely identical with the 'Fulcrum-A' aft of mainframe No. 3 at the expense of only a 100-mm (3.93-in.) increase in overall length.

The centre fuselage of the MiG-29, MiG-29S/SD/SE/SM and MiG-29UB incorporates three main integral fuel tanks and the mainwheel wells. Tank No. 1 is limited by frames No. 4 and 5, tank No. 2 by frames No. 5 and 6 and tank No. 3 by frames No. 6 and 7. The latter tank is the main structural element of the fuselage, absorbing the vertical loads from the wings, engines and main gear units. Frame No. 6 incorporates the forward fitting of the centreline drop tank and frame No. 7 features the engines' forward fittings. The main gear units are attached to special boxy structures fitting in between frames No. 6 and 7. Frames No. 7 and 8 delimit the engine bays. Integral fuel tank No. 3-A split into two sections is located between frames No. 7 and 7-Zh.[2] A bay in the aft fuselage houses the auxiliary power unit and the engine accessory gearbox[3] with associated generators, fuel, oil and hydraulic pumps.

The aft fitting of the centreline drop tank is located at frame No. 8 incorporates. Further aft is the rear bay mounting the tail unit and afterburners. Frame No. 9 incorporates attachment points for the airbrakes and brake parachute canister, as well as the engines' rear fittings. The airbrakes are hydraulically actuated; the upper airbrake with an area of 0.75 m^2 (8.06 sq. ft) is deflected 56° and the lower airbrake with an area of 0.55 m^2 (5.91 sq. ft) is deflected 60°. The brake parachute is released electropneumatically and has an area of 17 m^2 (182.79 sq. ft). The MiG-29K and MiG-29M have a different aft fuselage structure with a single large airbrake between frames No. 8 and 9 and a non-integral fuel tank (No. 3-B) added between frames No. 7 and 8. The MiG-

29K is also equipped with an arrester hook attached to frame No. 8.

Wings: Cantilever all-metal mid-wing monoplane of trapezoidal planform. Leading-edge sweep 42°, anhedral 3°, taper 4.41, aspect ratio 3.5. The wings utilise TsAGI P-177 airfoil. Area of the wings proper (excluding LERXes) is 38.056 m^2 (409.2 sq. ft); chord is 5.6 m (18 ft 4.47 in.) at root and 1.27 m (4 ft 2.00 in.) at tip.

The wings have a three-spar structure with two false spars ahead of the wing torsion box and a third false spar aft of it, 16 ribs and upper and lower skins reinforced by stringers. The outer wings are attached to the fuselage by five fittings each at frames No. 6, 6-V and 7. The wing torsion box doubles as an integral fuel tank. The wings have three-section leading-edge flaps, one-piece trailing-edge flaps and ailerons. The LE flaps are deflected 20° by six hydraulic actuators each (one inboard, two on the central section and three outboard). The TE flaps are deflected 25° for takeoff and landing by single hydraulic actuators equipped with uplocks; the high-lift devices move in concert. LE and TE flap area is 2.35 m^2 (25.26 sq. ft) and 2.84 m^2 (30.53 sq. ft) respectively. The ailerons have an area of 1.45 m^2 (15.59 sq. ft) and are deflected through +15°−225° by RP-280A hydraulic actuators.

Each wing incorporates attachment points for three weapons pylons. The innermost pylons are attached to the spars in three places, the others in two. The wingtips mount navigation lights, RHAWS and (on some versions) ECM antennas.

The MiG-29M features two-section LE flaps. The MiG-29K has a radically different wing design; the wings are made of steel, not Al-Li alloy as on the M, and fold upwards for carrier stowage. Wing span is increased by 630 mm (2 ft 0.8 in.) to 11.99 m (39 ft 4.04 in.), slightly increasing wing area; with wings folded span is 7.8 m (25 ft 7.08 in.). Likewise, two-section LE flaps are fitted, and the conventional ailerons are replaced by flaperons of slightly reduced area. The capacity of the wing tanks is identical to that of the 'Fulcrum-A/B/C'. The MiG-29K and MiG-29M have two additional underwing hardpoints.

Tail unit: The slab stabilizers (stabilators) are mounted on the outer sides of the engine nacelles and move symmetrically for roll control and differentially for pitch control. Leading-edge sweep 50°, anhedral 3° 30'. The stabilators utilise TsAGI S-11S airfoil. Span is 7.78 m (25 ft 6.29 in.) and total area 7.05 m^2 (75.80 sq. ft); the MiG-

---

[2] The English equivalent is 7-G.

[3] The MiG-29 is probably unique among twin-engined fighters in having a common gearbox for both engines.

The wing folding hinge of the MiG-29K. (Andrey Yurgenson)

29K and MiG-29M have increased-area stabilators with extended chord resulting in a characteristic dogtooth.

Each stabilator is a single-spar structure with a false spar, 16 ribs, upper and lower skins and a honeycomb core composite trailing edge. The stabilators are controlled by RP-280A hydraulic actuators mounted on aft fuselage frame No. 10; the skewed axles are rigidly attached to the stabilators, turning in bearings mounted on frames No. 9 and 10. Stabilator deflection is +15°−225° on takeoff and landing and +5° 45′−217° 45′ in cruise flight. The twin fins with fillets and inset rudders are attached to the aft fuselage bay outboard of the engine nacelles. The fins are canted 6° outboard; leading-edge sweep is 47° 50′, total fin area 10.1 m² (108.6 sq. ft) and total rudder area 1.25 m² (13.44 sq. ft).

Each fin is a two-spar carbonfibre reinforced plastic (CFRP) structure with front and rear false spars, 9 ribs, skins and a honeycomb core trailing edge. Structurally the fins consist of rectangular root sections rigidly attached to the aft fuselage, detachable trapezoidal upper sections and root fillets with 75° leading-edge sweep. Each rudder

is mounted on three brackets and has a nose section and a honeycomb core trailing edge. All aircraft manufactured from 1984 onwards have rudders with 21% longer chord extending beyond the fin trailing edge. The rudders are deflected ±25° by RP-270 hydraulic actuators mounted in the root sections

The fins have glassfibre tips housing communications radio and ATC/SIF aerials (port fin) and IFF and GCI command link aerials (starboard fin). A SHORAN antenna and the tail navigation light are located on the port fin trailing edge and backup IFF and ATC/SIF aerials on the starboard fin trailing edge. RHAWS and ECM are mounted on the outer surfaces of the fins. The number and placement of the aerials may vary between versions.

'Fulcrum-As' built from 1984 onwards, 'Fulcrum-Cs' and the MiG-29S/SD/SE/SM have strake-like structures ahead of the fin fillets housing BVP-30-26 chaff/flare dispensers. These are absent on early-production 'Fulcrum-As', the MiG-29UB and MiG-29K and MiG-29M prototypes. Early-production 'Fulcrum-As' featured twin ventral fins outboard of the engine nacelles. These

ABOVE: *A Russian Air Force 'Fulcrum-A' (31 White, c/n 2960535121) undergoing maintenance shows the partially deflected LE flap and AKU-58M ejector rack for an air-to-ground missile. (Yefim Gordon)*

BELOW: *The 1,500-lit. centreline drop tank. It is not clear whether the number 2727 is the aircraft's fuselage number or pertains to the tank itself. (Yefim Gordon)*

were deleted on later aircraft, as directional stability was found to be adequate without them.

Landing gear: Hydraulically retractable tricycle type; wheel track 3.09 m (10 ft 1.65 in.), wheelbase 3.645 m (11 ft 11.5 in.). All three units are equipped with oleo-pneumatic shock absorbers.

The semi-levered suspension nose unit is equipped with twin KT-100 brake wheels[4] (tyre size 570×140 mm/22.4×5.5 in.) and retracts aft into the tunnel between the air intakes. The combined steering mechanism/shimmy damper allows the nosewheels to turn ±31° for taxying and ±8° for evasive action during an aborted takeoff or landing. The nosewheels are fitted with a scraper-type mud/snow/slush guard for foreign object damage (FOD) protection. On the first two 'Fulcrum-A' prototypes, Aircraft 901 and Aircraft 902, the wheelbase

----

[4] KT = *koleso tormoznoye* – wheel, brake-equipped

LEFT: *The nose gear unit. (Aleksey Mikheyev)*
BELOW: *The main gear units. (Andrey Yurgenson)*

was approximately 5.2 m (17 ft 0.72 in.). The much longer nose gear strut was attached to mainframe No. 2 and the nosewheels were semi-enclosed by a MiG-23-style mudguard. Each main unit is equipped with a single KT-150 brake wheel (tyre size 840×290 mm/33.0×11.4 in.); the MiG-29M has KT-209 wheels. The main units retract forward; the axes of the retraction hinges are tilted outboard and aft so that the mainwheels rotate through 90° during retraction to lie horizontally in the wing centre section. The MiG-29K has a reinforced landing gear with longer-stroke oleos which are shortened by special links during retraction. On production aircraft each wheel well is closed by three doors, one of which is attached to the retraction jack. On 'Fulcrum-A' prototypes and a few initial production aircraft the nosewheel well was closed by three doors (the fourth door segment was attached to the strut ahead of the nosewheels). All doors remain open when the gear is down. The struts are secured by mechanical locks and (in the down position) by shutoff valves trapping hydraulic fluid in the retraction jacks. The landing gear is normally operated by the main hydraulic system, with pneumatic emergency extension for the nose unit and free-fall emergency extension for the main units. The wheel brakes are pneumatically operated by two systems (normal and backup); the nosewheel brakes can be selected off. An electromechanical anti-skid system is provided, operating only in normal braking mode.

Powerplant: All versions except the MiG-29M and MiG-29K are powered by two Klimov NPP (Izotov) RD-33 afterburning turbofans rated at 5,040 kgp (11,111 lb st) at full military power, 5,600 kgp (12,345 lb st) at minimum afterburner and 8,300 kgp (18,298 lb st) in full afterburner.

The RD-33 is a two-shaft turbofan with a bypass ratio (BPR) of 0.475, a four-stage axial low-pressure (LP) compressor, an adjustable nine-stage high-pressure (HP) compressor, an annular combustion chamber, a single-stage air-cooled HP turbine, a single-stage air-cooled LP turbine, an afterburner and a convergent-divergent axisymmetric supersonic nozzle. Core and bypass flows are mixed aft of the turbine. For greater reliability the combustion chamber is equipped with an oxygen feed system. It increases the chances of a successful relight at high altitude where the air is thin and prevents flameouts caused by gas ingestion during gun firing and missile launches. The RD-33 has proved to be virtually immune to surge during violent manoeuvres – even at negative airspeed during a tailslide. On the ground the engine runs

steadily at ambient temperatures between 260°C and +60°C (276–+140°F); in the air it runs at inlet temperatures up to +200°C (392°F) which are reached in Mach 2.35 cruise.

Specific fuel consumption (SFC) is 2.05 kg/kgp·hr (lb/lb st·hr) in full afterburner and 0.77 kg/kgp·hr at full military power. The two compressors provide an overall engine pressure ratio (EPR) of 21.5 and a mass flow of 76.9 kg/sec (169.5 lb/sec). Turbine temperature is fairly high; 1,525°K at idling RPM and 1,650°K in flight. Idling thrust is a mere 200 kgp (440 lb st). The engine accelerates from idling RPM to full military power in three or four seconds and another two seconds is needed to engage full afterburner; in case of need, however, the RD-33 can go from idling RPM to full afterburner in just four seconds.

The engine is 4.26 m (13 ft 11.71 in.) long, with a maximum overall diameter of 1.0 m (3 ft 3.37 in.) and an inlet diameter of 0.75 m (2 ft 5.52 in.). Dry weight is 1,050 kg (2,314 lb), which amounts to a weight/thrust ratio of 0.126. Engine life is 1,400 hrs (RD-33 Srs 2) or 2,000 hrs (RD-33 Srs 3); time between overhauls (TBO) is 700 and 1,400 hrs respectively. The RD-33 has a hydroelectronic control system featuring a BPR-88 analog RPM limiter, NR-59A variable delivery fuel pump, RSF-59A nozzle and afterburner regulator, RT-59I main fuel distributor and RTF-59 afterburner fuel distributor. The engines are controlled by throttles located on the port cockpit console via mechanical linkages.

The MiG-29K is powered by RD-33K engines uprated to 5,500 kgp (12,125 lb st) at full military power and 8,800 kgp (19,400 lb st) in full afterburner with a 9,400-kgp (20,723 lb st) contingency rating for high gross weight carrier takeoffs. A modified version of the RD-33K without this contingency rating powers the MiG-29M. The RD-33K is equipped with a full authority digital engine control (FADEC) system featuring the NR-59A fuel pump, RSF-59A regulator and ESU-21 digital control unit.[5] Afterburner SFC is improved to 1.97 kg/kgp·hr and weight/thrust ratio to 0.119.

The engines are inclined 4° upwards and set at 1.5° toe-in in spaced nacelles. The adjustable supersonic air intakes are raked and have rectangular cross-section at the inlets changing to circular at the compressor faces. To prevent boundary layer ingestion the intakes are set at a distance from the wing undersurface so that the upper

---

[5] NR = *nasos-regoolyator*; RSF = *regoolyator sopla i forsahzha*; RT = *raspredeleetel' topliva*; ESU = *elektronnaya sistema oopravleniya*.

The Izotov (NPP Klimov) RD-33 turbofan.

intake lip acts as a boundary layer splitter plate. A vee-shaped fairing spilling the boundary layer connects the intake lip to the wing. The horizontal airflow control ramps create four shock waves, optimising the airflow for various flight modes (subsonic, transonic and supersonic). These consist of four segments; the first (i.e., the splitter plate) is fixed at a 6° angle, the others are hydraulically-actuated. The rearmost segment is perforated to spill the boundary layer via triple dorsal windows closed by metal mesh.

To prevent foreign object ingestion during taxying, takeoff and landing the forward movable segments of the intake ramps double as FOD protection doors which block the intakes completely. When these are closed the engines breathe via the dorsal air intakes mentioned earlier (five rows of spring-loaded blow-in doors). The FOD protection doors close automatically during engine starting when hydraulic pressure reaches nominal and open when the aircraft accelerates to 200 km/h (111 kts) IAS during takeoff, i.e., past rotation speed. They close again when the airspeed drops below 200 km/h, reopening after engine shutdown. The dorsal blow-in doors may open to

admit additional air in low-speed flight, even when the FOD protection doors are fully open.

Each intake has an individual ARV-29D ramp control system[6] with three preset programmes which adjusts the ramp depending on engine RPM and operates the FOD protection door. The ARV-29D includes two airspeed sensors (triggered when the aircraft reaches Mach 1.15 and Mach 1.5) and two pressure relays triggered by altitude in excess of 3,000 m (9,842 ft) and airspeed in excess of 200 km/h. If the system fails the pilot can adjust the intakes manually.

The MiG-29K, MiG-29M and MiG-29SMT have redesigned air intakes with movable lower lips and no dorsal blow-in doors. FOD protection is offered by hinged grids which retract after takeoff to lie flat against the bottom of the inlet ducts, trapping any foreign objects retained by them. The mainwheel well walls are perforated to admit additional air at low speed. Besides,

---

[6] ARV = *avtomateecheskiy regoolyator vozdookhozabornika* – automatic air intake adjuster; D = *dorabotannyy* – revised. Early-production aircraft had the earlier ARV-29 version.

The port RD-33 turbofan of 'Fulcrum-A' 31 White (c/n 2960535121) with the large one-piece cowling removed for servicing, showing details of engine. (Yefim Gordon)

the MiG-29K and MiG-29M have reprofiled inlet ducts to cater for the higher mass flow of the uprated RD-33K engines.

On the ground the engines can be started singly or simultaneously by means of the NPP Klimov (Izotov) GTDE-117 auxiliary power unit (jet fuel starter) located in a bay in the aft fuselage between the engine nacelles. The APU's air intake offset to port is located at frame No. 7; the exhaust is located on the fuselage underside near the starboard nacelle and closed by a door to reduce drag when the APU is off. In flight the engines are restarted by windmilling at speeds down to 300 km/h (166 kts). The GTDE-117 itself is fired up by an ST-115B starter-generator, using ground power or batteries. It weighs only 40 kg (88 lb) and delivers 90 eshp. The APU provides electric and hydraulic power when the engines are shut down, allowing the aircraft's systems to be checked without using ground power: an undoubted asset on tactical airstrips where support equipment may be unavailable.

The same bay houses the engine accessory gearbox[7] which enables the engines to drive the generators, fuel, oil and hydraulic pumps and the APU to spin up the engines

by direct drive via couplings. The basic 'Fulcrum-A', MiG-29SD and MiG-29UB have a KSA-2 gearbox;[8] this was replaced by the KSA-3 on 'fatback' versions (***izdeliye*** 9.13 and MiG-29SE/SM). The engines, accessory gearbox and APU use IPM-10 brand mineral oil. Separating the engine accessories from the engines minimises disconnecting operations during an engine change. The engines are extracted downwards and enclosed by one-piece cowlings with quick-release fasteners; this means that a team of four technicians can change an engine in just 2 hrs 15 min.

Fuel system: Apart from its obvious purpose, the fuel system maintains the aircraft's CG and cools engine oil, bleed air for the air conditioning system (on the MiG-29S/SE only) and the radar set (in the latter case by means of a fuel/glycol heat exchanger). Fuel system components and hydraulic tanks are located inside the fuel tanks for better survivability.

On the 'Fulcrum-A' (including the MiG-29SD) and MiG-29UB internal fuel is carried in four fuselage integral tanks and two wing tanks. The fuselage tanks hold 650 lit./143 Imp. gal. (No. 1), 870 lit./191.4 Imp. gal. (No. 2), 1,810 lit./398.2 Imp. gal. (No. 3) and 310 lit./68.2

[7] The MiG-29 is probably unique among twin-engined fighters in having a common gearbox for both engines.

[8] KSA = *korobka (privoda) samolyotnykh agregahtov* = accessory (drive gear)box.

Imp. gal. (No. 3-A); each of the wing tanks holds 330 lit. (72.6 Imp. gal.). Fuselage tank No. 2 feeds the engines via a fuel accumulator in tank No. 3. Total internal fuel capacity is 4,300 lit. (946 Imp. gal.), which amounts to 3,200 kg (7,054 lb) of usable fuel at a specific fuel gravity of 0.785 g/cm^3. On the 'Fulcrum-C' the capacity of fuselage tank No. 1 is increased by 240 lit. (52.8 Imp. gal.) to 890 lit. (195.8 Imp. gal.), resulting in a characteristically bulged fuselage spine. This brings the total internal fuel capacity to 4,540 lit. (998.8 Imp. gal.) or 3,400 kg (7,495 lb) of usable fuel.

A 1,500-lit. (330 Imp. gal.) drop tank can be carried on the fuselage centreline. It obstructs the APU exhaust and hence incorporates a unique vertical duct enabling the APU to exhaust straight through it. The 'Fulcrum-C' introduced 'wet' inner wing pylons allowing the carriage of two 1,150-lit. (253 Imp. gal.) drop tanks; this feature was added to many 'Fulcrum-As' as a mid-life upgrade. With three drop tanks the 'fatback' versions have a total fuel capacity of 8,340 lit. (1,834.8 Imp. gal.) or 6,250 kg (13,778 lb).[9]

Structural changes have increased internal fuel capacity to 5,810 lit. (1,278.2 Imp. gal.) on the MiG-29M and 5,670 lit. (1,247.4 Imp. gal.) on the MiG-29K. These versions feature a new 1,710-lit. (376.2 Imp. gal.) No. 1 fuselage fuel tank whose capacity has been almost doubled by using the space in the LERXes formerly occupied by the dorsal auxiliary intakes. The capacity of No. 3-A tank is enlarged by 70% to 530 lit. (116.6 Imp. gal.), and a new strap-on No. 3-A tank holding 130 lit. (28.6 Imp. gal.) is added. No. 2 and 3 tanks hold 840 lit. (184.8 Imp. gal.) and 1,800 lit. (396 Imp. gal.) respectively.

The MiG-29K and MiG-29M have an internal fuel capacity of 5,720 lit. (1,258.4 Imp. gal.) or 4,460 kg (9,832 lb) of usable fuel. This is distributed as follows: 1,700 lit./374 Imp. gal. (fuselage tank No. 1), 840 lit./184.8 Imp. gal. (tank No. 2), 1,800 lit./396 Imp. gal. (tank No. 3), 480 lit./105.6 Imp. gal. (tank No. 3-A), 100 lit./22 Imp. gal. (tank No. 3-B) and 400 lit. (88 Imp. gal.) in each wing tank. The MiG-29K and MiG-29M also have provisions for three drop tanks. The MiG-29K features a refuelling probe enabling it to receive fuel from hose-and-drogue tankers (Il-78, Su-24 with UPAZ-1A buddy refuelling pack etc.). The fully retractable L-shaped probe is located ahead of the windscreen, offset to port.

The MiG-29SMT has an internal fuel capacity of approximately 5,300 lit. (1,166 Imp. gal.) thanks to a new No. 1 fuselage fuel tank similar to that of the MiG-29K and MiG-29M. This version and other export 'Fulcrums' can be fitted with the optional semi-retractable refuelling probe on the port side of the forward fuselage. The faired probe is attached to frames No. 1 and 2 and can be removed if necessary; it has a delivery rate of 900 lit./min (198 Imp. gal./min). Enlarged new 1,800-lit. (396 Imp. gal.) underwing drop tanks are also offered. Fuselage tanks No. 1 and 3 each have one GTN-7 turbopump, with three more in tank No. 2. The wing tanks each have one fuel jet pump; so do fuselage tanks No. 3 and 3-A. The turbopumps and fuel jet pumps are powered by a DTsN-80 centrifugal pump connected to the engine accessory gearbox. The fuel tanks are pressurised by bottled nitrogen for explosion suppression or by engine bleed air.

The MiG-29 uses RT, T-1 or TS-1 brand jet fuel or Western equivalents (JP-1, Jet A-1, AVTUR etc.).[10] Normal procedure is single-point pressure refuelling through a standardised connector in the port mainwheel well; gravity refuelling is also possible through filler caps in No. 1 and 3 fuselage tanks. The drop tanks are filled independently through filler caps. Refuelling options include 50% internal fuel, 100% internal fuel and 100% internal fuel plus one, two or three drop tanks. The STR-6-2(A) or STR-6-5(A) fuel metering system automatically calculates fuel quantity and range on remaining fuel, indicates empty tanks and alerts the pilot when he is down to 'bingo fuel', i.e., reserves (550 lit./121 Imp. gal.).

To maintain CG position the tanks are emptied in a certain sequence. On the 'Fulcrum-A' fuel is used as follows: centreline drop tank; 250 kg (551 lb) from tank No. 2; 200 kg (440 lb) from tank No. 3; wing tanks, tank No. 3-A; 600 kg (1,322 lb) from tank No. 3; 280 kg (617 lb) from tank No. 1; tanks No. 3 and 1 completely, tank No. 2 completely and fuel accumulator. On the 'Fulcrum-C' the sequence is as follows: centreline drop tank, tank No. 1 (partially), tank No. 3 (partially), wing tanks (partially), underwing drop tanks, wing tanks (completely), tank No. 3 (some more), tank No. 3-A, tank No. 3 (some more), tank No. 1 (some more), tanks No. 3, 1 and 2 completely and fuel accumulator.

Armament: The MiG-29's weapons range allows it to fill the counter-air and strike rôles, comprising an internal

---

[9] Latest Mikoyan data states drop tank capacity as 1,440 lit. (316.8 Imp. gal.) and 1,200 lit. (264 Imp. gal.) for the centreline and underwing tanks respectively.

[10] RT = *re'aktivnoye toplivo* – jet fuel

gun, short- and medium-range air-to-air missiles, unguided rockets and free-fall bombs. The MiG-29K, MiG-29M and MiG-29SM/SMT can also carry guided air-to-surface missiles and guided bombs. Guided and unguided weapons are carried on four (MiG-29UB), six ('Fulcrum'-A/C) or eight (MiG-29K and MiG-29M) underwing hardpoints equipped with launch rails and/or ejector racks. The maximum ordnance load is 2,200 kg (4,850 lb) for the MiG-29 (*izdeliye* 9.12) and MiG-29UB, 3,200 kg (7,054 lb) for the MiG-29 (*izdeliye* 9.13), 4,000 kg (8,818 lb) for the MiG-29S/SD/SE/SM/SMT and 4,500 kg (9,920 lb) for the MiG-29K and MiG-29M.

The TKB-687 (9A4071K) internal gun installation is housed in the port LERX and consists of a Gryazev/Shipoonov GSh-301 single-barrel 30-mm (1.18-in calibre) automatic gun and associated ammunition box for 150 AO-18 rounds; on the MiG-29K and MiG-29M capacity is reduced to 100 rounds. Rate of fire is 1,500–1,800 rounds per minute, muzzle velocity 860 m/sec (2,821.5 ft/sec) and recoil force 6,000–7,500 kg (13,227–16,534 lb). The gun is belt-fed and fires high explosive / fragmentation / incendiary (HEFI), HE/fragmentation/incendiary/tracer (HEFI-T) and armour-piercing/explosive (APE) rounds; the latter can penetrate armour up to 40 mm (1.57 in.) thick. An HEFI round weighs 836 g (29.5 oz) and an APE round weighs 860 g (30.36 oz), including belt link.

Firing is electrically controlled by a trigger on the stick. The gun can fire continuously, expending the entire supply in a single six-second burst,[11] or in short bursts. Alternative firing modes are automatic fire (three-quarters of the ammo supply), automatic fire with cutoff (firing 25 rounds in a one-second burst each time the trigger is squeezed) and training mode (a 7-round burst each time the trigger is squeezed). Effective range is 800–200 m (2,624–656 ft) in air-to-air mode and 1,800–1,200 m (5,905–3,937 ft) in strafing mode. The GSh-301 is water-cooled, with additional air cooling through vents in the gun bay to extend its service life. The gun can tolerate 2,000 shots; it is 1,978 mm (6 ft 5.87 in.) long and weighs 45 kg (99.2 lb).

The MiG-29 (*izdeliye* 9.12 and 9.13) is armed with two Vympel R-27R medium-range AAMs and/or two, four or six Vympel R-73 or Molniya R-60M short-range AAMs. The R-27R (*izdeliye* 470) can destroy all manner of aerial targets, including RPVs and cruise missiles, in all weather conditions, day or night, over land and sea, even

though the target manoeuvres violently, returns fire, uses ECM and generally misbehaves. Target flight level is 20–27,000 m (65–88,582 ft) and maximum target speed is 3,500 km/h (1,944 kts). The missile can be launched when the aircraft is pulling up to 5 Gs and the target is up to 10,000 m (32,808 ft) higher or lower.

The missile utilises the tail-first configuration with large forward-swept cruciform canards and cruciform wings. It features an inertial navigation system with mid-course radio correction and a model 9B-1101K semi-active radar homing (SARH) seeker head with a 100° field of view. The R-27R is compatible with all versions of the 'Fulcrum' except the MiG-29UB which has no radar for target illumination; export aircraft (*izdeliye* 9.12A and 9.12B) are armed with export R-27R1 missiles. R-27Rs are carried on APU-27 (APU-470) missile rails[12] on the inboard pylons.

The R-73 (*izdeliye* 72) is designed to destroy high-manoeuvrability aircraft and RPVs during close-range air-to-air combat in all weather conditions, day or night and in an ECM environment. It is likewise a tail-first missile with cruciform canards and wings but has a mixed jet/aerodynamic control system. The jet control (thrust vectoring) feature makes the missile extremely manoeuvrable, enabling it to score a kill on a target pulling up to 12 Gs. The R-73 is equipped with a Mayak high-sensitivity passive infra-red seeker head with cooling system, which makes it one of the world's first omnidirectional dogfight AAMs capable of destroying targets in both head-on and pursuit mode.

Target flight level is 20–20,000 m (65–65,616 ft) and maximum target speed is 2,500 km/h (1,388 kts). The IR seeker has a 90° field of view and can track targets at a speed of up to 60 deg/sec. The pilot can aim the missile in point-and-shoot mode by using a helmet-mounted sight. The R-73 is compatible with all versions of the MiG-29; export aircraft are armed with export R-73E missiles. R-73s are carried on APU-73-1D (P-72-1D) missile rails which can be fitted to any pylon.

The R-60M (*izdeliye* 62M) with a IR seeker head is designed to destroy high-manoeuvrability aircraft and RPVs within visual range. This again is a tail-first missile with purely aerodynamic controls. The wings incorporate so-called 'rollerons' for roll stabilization. The R-60M is a uniquely light and compact weapon in its class. Its low launch weight and refined aerodynamics make the missile extremely agile, enabling it to score a kill on a target

---

[11] Applies to the 'Fulcrum-A/B/C' with 150 rounds.

[12] APU = *aviatseeonnaya pooskovaya oostanovka* – aircraft-mounted launcher.

Missile pylons and MERs on 'Fulcrum-C' 101 Red at TsNII-30. (Viktor Drooshlyakov)

pulling up to 12 Gs.

Target flight level is 30–20,000 m (98–65,616 ft) and maximum target speed is 2,500 km/h (1,388 kts). The Komar-M passive IR seeker has a 40° field of view and can track targets at a speed of up to 35 deg/sec. It has a cooling system, enabling attacks in head-on mode. The missile can be launched when the aircraft is pulling up to 7 Gs. Export aircraft are armed with export R-60MK missiles. R-60s are carried on APU-60-1DB-1 (P-62-1D) missile rails which can be fitted to any pylon. The air-to-air weapons range of the MiG-29S/SD/SE/SM/SMT includes two R-27R/T/RE/TE medium-range AAMs (R-27R1/T1/RE1/TE1 for export), two, four or six R-77 (RVV-AE) medium-range AAMs and a like number of R-73 (R-73E) short-range AAMs. The R-27T is a passive IR-homing version of the R-27R; its IR seeker head has a 110° field of view. The R-27RE and R-27TE are

extended-range versions with longer-burn rocket motors. A mix of R-27s with different guidance systems can be used to increase resistance to countermeasures and improve the chances of a kill.

The R-77 is designed to destroy enemy fighters, bombers, attack and transport aircraft and helicopters in all weather conditions, over land and sea, day or night and in an ECM environment. It is a wingless missile with aft-mounted cruciform lattice-type rudders. The R-77 is a fire-and-forget weapon featuring an inertial navigation system with mid-course radio correction and an active radar homing seeker head which allows the missile to go for another target if the original one manages to break target lock-on.

Target flight level is 20–25,000 m (65–82,020 ft) and maximum target speed is 3,600 km/h (2,000 kts). The missile can be launched at up to the aircraft's G limit and destroy targets flying up to 10,000 m (32,808 ft) higher or lower. R-77s are carried on AKU-170 missile rails[13] which can be fitted to any pylon. The MiG-29K and MiG-29M can carry two R-27RE/TE AAMs, two or four R-27R/T AAMs, two, four, six or eight R-77s and/or a like number of R-73s.

In the attack rôle all versions of the MiG-29 can carry a range of unguided rockets, including two or four B-8M1 rocket pods with twenty 80-mm (3.15-in.) S-8 folding-fin aircraft rockets (FFARs) each and two or four 240-mm (9.44-in.) S-24B heavy unguided rockets on APU-68-85 launchers. Early 'Fulcrum-As' also used four UB-32A-73 rocket pods with 32 57-mm (2.24-in.) S-5 FFARs each. On the MiG-29K and MiG-29M the S-24s were replaced by two 266-mm (10.47-in.) S-25 rockets on PU-O-25 disposable launchers and/or two or four B-13L missile pods with five 122-mm (4.8-in.) S-13 FFARs each.

The unguided rockets are mainly used against enemy personnel and small single armoured, hardened and soft-skinned targets but may also be used against aerial targets. They have several types of warheads. The 57-mm FFAR has HE (S-5M), HE/fragmentation (S-5MO), shaped-charge armour-piercing (S-5K) and SCAP/fragmentation (S-5KO/KP) versions. The 80-mm FFAR comes in AP/fragmentation (S-8A/M/KO/KOM/T), concrete-piercing (S-8B/BM), HEF (S-8-OF), fuel/air[14] (S-8D/DM) and anti-personnel dart-filled (S-8AS/ASM) versions. The 122-mm FFAR comes in concrete-piercing (S-13 and S-13T), HE (S-13D) and HEF (S-13-OF) versions. The S-24B has an HEF warhead, while the 266-mm rockets are equipped with outsize warheads: fragmentation (S-25-O) or HEF (S-25-OF/OFM) of 420 mm (16.53 in.) and 340 mm (13.38 mm) diameter.

The weapons range of all versions includes 250-kg (551-lb) and 500-kg (1,102-lb) free-fall bombs. Typically these are HE bombs (FAB-250M54, FAB-250M62, FAB-500M54, FAB-500M62, FAB-500ShN etc.) and HE/fragmentation bombs (OFAB-250-270 etc.). The MiG-29 (*izdeliye* 9.12) and MiG-29UB can carry two or four bombs on BD3-UMK or BD3-UMK-2/-2B bomb racks fitted to pylons No. 1 through 4 – i.e., the inner and centre wing pylons. On the MiG-29 (*izdeliye* 9.13),

MBD3-U2T-1 multiple ejector racks can be fitted to the inboard pylons, permitting the carriage of two bombs in tandem and increasing the total to six; the MiG-29S/SD/SE/SM/SMT/M/K can carry up to eight bombs on four MERs.

Other air-to-ground weapons include ZB-500ShM, ZB-500ASM and ZB-500GD napalm tanks for strikes against personnel and large-area targets such as railyards and warehouses; two or four of these can be carried on BD3-UMK racks. Another option is KMGU or KMGU-2 submunitions pods used for bomblets without attachment lugs and for anti-tank or anti-personnel mines. The submunitions are packed into BKF cassettes,[15] eight per pod. The KMGU pod has pneumatically-operated doors and can be programmed to release the cassettes at intervals of 0.05, 0.2, 1 or 1.5 seconds. For MiG-29 operations KMGU pods are usually loaded with twelve 2.5-kg (5.5-lb) AO-2.5RT fragmentation bomblets, twelve 1.6-kg (3.5-lb) PTM-1 anti-tank mines or 156 800-g (1.76-lb) anti-personnel mines. Two or four pods are carried on BD3-UMK racks, giving a total of 384 bomblets or anti-tank mines and no less than 4,992 anti-personnel mines. 100-kg (220-lb) OFAB-100-120 HE/fragmentation bombs and 50-kg (110-lb) P-50-75 practice bombs can also be loaded.

Avionics and equipment:

a) **Weapons control system.** The MiG-29's WCS comprises a fire control radar for medium-range targeting and a short-range optoelectronic targeting system. It enables the aircraft to complete its mission (long-range intercept, dogfight or strike) in all weather conditions, day or night and in an ECM environment, operating singly or in a group. The functions of the WCS are:

- to seek and detect aerial targets and identify them jointly with the IFF system;
- to target aerial targets and ground targets within visual range;
- to determine whether conditions are OK for missile launch, download target data and illuminate targets for SARH missiles;
- to display and record targeting, flight and navigation data and weapons control commands.

---

[13] AKU = *aviatseeonnaya katapool'tnaya oostanovka* – aircraft-mounted ejector rack.

[14] Similar to the fuel/air bomb – a bomb filled with liquid explosive which is sprayed like an aerosol and then detonated. The resulting fireball burns up all oxygen inside, creating a vacuum, and outside air rushing in flattens everything in the epicentre of the explosion, which is why the fuel/air bomb is sometimes called the poor man's atomic bomb.

[15] BKF = *blok konteynernyy dlya frontovoy aviatsii* – containerised (submunitions) pack for tactical aviation.

The MiG-29 (*izdeliye* 9.12 and 9.13) is equipped with the SUV-29 (Sh-104) combined WCS comprising the RLPK-29 radar targeting complex (based on the Phazotron N-019 Rubin radar) and the OEPrNK-29 (S-31) optoelectronic targeting/navigation complex. Export aircraft (*izdeliye* 9.12A and 9.12B) have a downgraded RLPK-29E radar targeting complex (based on the N-019EA or N-019EB radar respectively) and an OEPrNK-29E2 (S-31E) optoelectronic targeting/ navigation complex. The MiG-29UB lacks radar, featuring only the OEPrNK-29UB complex.

The MiG-29S has a SUV-29S WCS comprising the RLPK-29M radar targeting complex (based on the Phazotron N-019M Topaz radar) and the OEPrNK-29-1 optoelectronic targeting/navigation complex. Export versions, MiG-29SD/SE, have a downgraded RLPK-29ME radar targeting complex (based on the N-019ME radar) and an OEPrNK-29-1E optoelectronic targeting/navigation complex. These are compatible with R-27T1/RE1/TE1 and R-77 AAMs and MERs increasing the bomb load to 4,000 kg. Additionally, the RLPK-29ME and OEPrNK-29-1E are integrated with the aircraft's automatic control system and have an enhanced self-test capability and a training mode helping pilots to master the WCS.

The MiG-29M has a SUV-29M (Sh-103) WCS and the MiG-29K has a SUV-29K WCS. Both comprise the Phazotron N-010 radar designated Zhuk for export and the OEPrNK-29M (K-048) optoelectronic targeting/navigation complex. The SUV-29M/K features a dogfight mode. The radar or IRST automatically engages a target within 1.5 seconds after it enters a predetermined area marked on the HUD.

The RLPK-29 complex can track up to ten targets at a time, automatically selecting a priority threat; the pilot can also designate a priority target manually. The radar determines the exact coordinates of the priority target as it is tracked. On the MiG-29SD/SE the system can engage two priority threats at a time and has a training mode simulating the target's evasive manoeuvres and countermeasures. The system has an automatic self-test feature. The RLPK-29 comprises the N-019 Rubin radar and a Ts100 series digital processor; the 'third-world' MiG-29 (*izdeliye* 9.12B) has a Ts100.02.06 processor. The radar has look-down/ shoot-down capability and is virtually jam-proof. Detection range for a fighter-type target in open airspace is more than 100 km (55 nm) and target lock-on range is 70 km (38 nm). Target tracking angles

are +60°–238° in elevation and ±67° in azimuth.

The RLPK-29M/ME comprises the N-019M/ME Topaz radar and a Ts101M digital processor. It can guide missiles to two targets at a time, is compatible with R-77 AAMs and has increased ECM resistance. The RLPK-29UM comprises the N-010 Zhuk radar and a Ts100 series digital processor. The radar has a flat-plate slotted array; the beam is electronically scanned in elevation and mechanically in azimuth. The N-010 can guide missiles to four aerial targets at a time, determine the coordinates of ground targets and track moving ground targets, has three ground mapping modes with different resolution and supports automatic terrain following.

The optoelectronic targeting/navigation complex has the following functions:

- day and night passive (i.e., stealthy) detection and tracking of targets with a high IR signature at short range or aerial targets within visual range in a dogfight;
- determining whether conditions are OK for unguided rocket and IR-homing AAMs launch, designating targets for rockets and missiles, targeting during gun firing, and bomb-aiming;
- navigation;
- presentation of target, flight, navigation and tactical information and;
- supporting the helmet-mounted sight (HMS);
- photographic registration of the attack's results;
- pre-flight testing of the WCS.

On the MiG-29SD/SE the complex has a training mode simulating the target's evasive manoeuvres and countermeasures and displays WCS test results.

The OEPrNK-29 consists of an OEPS-29 optoelectronic targeting system, an SN-29 navigation system, and a Ts100 series digital processor, an SUO-29M weapons selection system, an SEI-31 joint indication system (JIS) featuring the ILS-31 HUD, an FKP-EU gun camera and multi-function control panels. The MiG-29 (*izdeliye* 9.12B) features a Ts100.02.02 processor and an SEI-31-E2 JIS; the MiG-29SD/SE has a Ts100.02.07 processor and an SEI-31-1E JIS.

The OEPS-29 targeting system includes the KOLS (*izdeliye* 13S) infra-red search&track/laser ranger designed by NPO Gheofizika and the Schchel'-3UM HMS (Schchel'-3UM-1 for export). The IRST/LR, which can acquire targets independently or with data input from the radar, can determine the target's coordinates and range with greater accuracy than the radar. Since the IRST/LR does not emit electromagnetic pulse, it enables the fighter to attack covertly without switching on the radar. Some performance figures are given below.

Detection range (fighter-type target)	15 km (8.3 nm)
Steady tracking range	12 km (6.6 nm)
Laser ranger operating range	200–6,500m (656–21,325 ft)
Large field of view	±30° in azimuth, ±15° in elevation
Small field of view	±15° in azimuth, ±15° in elevation
Scanning time:	large field of view 3.5 sec small field of view 2.0 sec

The high-precision channel of the IRST/LR is used for targeting when firing the gun. The so-called asynchronous aiming method is the main one When the target is plainly visible (i.e., in VMC conditions) a gunsight reticle is projected on the HUD and must be placed over the target. In IMC conditions the HUD displays targeting error values calculated by the computer; these increase or decrease as the aircraft manoeuvres. When the error values drop to zero the pilot knows that the reticle is over the unseen target and it's time to fire. If autotracking is impossible an enhanced optical mode, the so-called predictive mode, is used. If targeting data are unavailable it is possible to launch missiles with the IRST sighting line in neutral position and fire the gun, using a fixed grid in the HUD as a reference point.

The MiG-29M and MiG-29K are equipped with an OLS-M IRST/LR featuring a more sensitive IR sensor with cooling, a more powerful laser ranger and a TV channel for long-range target identification. The IRST's detection range is 35 km (19.4 nm) in pursuit mode and 10 km (5.5 nm) in head-on mode. The TV channel's detection range and identification range is 10 km and 6 km (3.3 nm) respectively; the LR's maximum range is 8 km (4.4 nm).

The Schchel'-3UM HMS with NVU-2M goggles (*nashlemnoye vizeernoye oostroystvo* – helmet-mounted viewing device) increases targeting efficiency in a dogfight, offering the point and shoot targeting mode. By turning his head towards the target the pilot supplies targeting data both to the IRST/LR and to the R-73 IR-

homing AAMs. If the latter get a lock-on the pilot can fire missiles without waiting for target data from other systems to become available.

The SN-29 navigation system has the following functions:

- providing input to flight instruments, the automatic control system and JIS;
- determining the aircraft's heading, airspeed, altitude, pitch and bank angles, azimuth and range to waypoints and feeding airspeed information to targeting systems;
- computing the aircraft's coordinates, independently or using ATC beacons.

The SN-29 navigation system includes the A-323 short-range radio navigation/instrumental landing system, the IK-VK-80 (Ts-050) complex, the SVS-II-72-3-2i air data system and the BK-55 connector unit. The A-323 SHORAN/ILS enables the aircraft to follow a predetermined route, return to a preprogrammed airfield equipped with landing aids and land in manual, automatic or flight director mode, executing a landing pattern down to 50 m (164 ft) and making a go-around if necessary. The SHORAN works in conjunction with various tactical navigation systems: RSBN-2N, RSBN-4N, RSBN-6N, Pole-N (Field; pronounced like the poly- prefix), Udar-M (Blow; pronounced oodahr) and PRMG. Navigation signals are received by the Peon-NM-02 antenna and feeder system located under the nose and on the starboard fin. Early-production MiG-29s were fitted with A-312 Radikal-NP SHORAN.

Navigation error margins are given in **Table D** on opposite page.

The MiG-29M has an upgraded navigation suite featuring an INS-84 inertial navigation system, an SVS-2Ts-U air data system, an A-331 SHORAN/ILS with a Potok (Stream) antenna and feeder system, an Uragan (Hurricane; pronounced ooragahn) long-range radio navigation (LORAN) system and a Ts080 digital processor. The MiG-29M has a slightly different SN-K Oozel (Knot) navigation suite featuring a Resistor-K-42 SHORAN/ILS optimised for carrier operations instead of the A-331.

The SUO-29M (*izdeliye* 20PN) weapons selection system (*sistema oopravleniya orouzhiyem*) performs the following tasks:

TABLE D

Parameter	Error margin	
	normal computation	express computation
Bank and pitch angle	0.5°	1°
Heading: true	±0.5°	±1°
magnetic	±1°	±1.5°
coordinates: in autonomous mode	±8 km (4.4 nm)	±4% of distance covered since last correction
in radio correction mode	±0.04 D±300 m (984 ft)	±0.04 D±300 m (984 ft)

Note: D = distance to beacon

- delivering and interrupting electrical power to all weapons as required;
- issuing commands to arm and fire the weapons as required by the mission;
- indicating available weapons, the currently active weapon and its condition;
- jettisoning external stores in an emergency (in USAF terms, the panic button function);
- self-test.

The system includes a BTsL-10P-20P central processing unit, BUR-20PR-I and BUR-20PR-II missile control units, a BAP-20 gun automatic control unit, four BNO unguided weapons automatic control units and (on 'Fulcrum-Cs' only) two BUT multiple bomb rack (MER) control units. The MiG-29 (*izdeliye 9.12B*) has an SUO-29M2 weapons selection system. The MiG-29S/SD/SE features an SUO-29M4 system enabling the fighter to carry R-27T/T1, R-27RE/RE1, R-27TE/TE1 and R-77 AAMs and four MERs. The weapons selection system of the MiG-29SM/SMT/M/K has provisions for Kh-29L, Kh-31A/P air-to-surface missiles and KAB-500Kr guided bombs.[16]

The SEI-31 joint indication system (*sistema yedinoy indikahtsii*; SEI-31-01 on the MiG-29S) presents targeting, flight and navigation data and comprises the ILS-31 HUD (*indikahtor na lobovom stekle*) and the IPV direct vision CRT display (*indikahtor pryamoy veedimosti*). On the MiG-29M and MiG-29K this is replaced by the SOI-29 data presentation system (*sistema otobrazheniya informahtsii*) featuring a more sophisticated collimator HUD and two monochrome multi-function CRT displays. The latter will be replaced by four multi-function colour liquid crystal displays (LCDs) on the MiG-29SMT.

The attack results are documented by the FKP-EU gun camera (*fotokontrol'nyy preebor*) which can photograph targets within 3,000 m (1.6 nm). The gun camera 'fires' through the HUD glass and uses 35-mm film up to 30 m (98 ft) long; maximum camera speed is 10 frames per second.

b) Radio navigation equipment. The MiG-29's radio navigation suite comprises the ARK-19 ADF (*avtomateecheskiy rahdiokompas*), the A-037 radio altimeter, the A-611 (RPM-76) marker beacon receiver and the SO-69 ATC transponder. The ADF consists of a receiver, a control panel and two aerials on the fuselage spine (an omnidirectional blade aerial and a directional loop aerial). It enables navigation by means of ground VHF omnidirectional range (VOR) beacons by determining the angle between the aircraft's longitudinal axis and the beacon's bearing. The ADF's range depends on the aircraft's flight level and the power of the VOR (e.g., a 500-Watt beacon can be detected at 200–300 km/111–166 nm). The error margin is 3–5°.

The A-037 Doppler altimeter doubles as a ground proximity warning system (GPWS) when the gear and flaps are up. It consists of a transceiver, two aerials under the fuselage nose and an electromechanical indicator. Measurement range is 0–1,000 m (3,280 ft). Early-production aircraft were equipped with the RV-15 (A-031) altimeter; the MiG-29M and MiG-29K have the RV-21 (A-035) Impul's altimeter. The A-611 receiver informs the pilot that he has passed the outer and inner marker beacons during his landing approach; a beep sounds in the pilot's headset when the aircraft passes the beacons. The receiver's aerial is located inside the radome.

---

[16] BTsL = *blok tsentrahl'nyy logheecheskiy*; BUR = *blok oopravleniya raketami*; BAP = *blok avtomahtiki pushki*; BNO = *blok [avtomahtiki] neoopravlyayemovo oorouzhiya*; BUT = *blok oopravleniya tandemnymi podveskami* (tandem stores control unit)

The SO-69 transponder transmits the aircraft's callsign, true airspeed and altitude. These are displayed beside the aircraft's blip on the ATC radar screen, allowing better air traffic control and flight safety, especially in an ECM environment in combat. ATC transponder aerials are located under the nose, in the port LERX and on both fins. The MiG-29M and MiG-29K are equipped with an improved SO-72 (A-511) ATC transponder.

c) Communications equipment. The suite comprises an R-862 Zhooravl'-30 (Crane) UHF radio, an SPU-9 intercom *(samolyotnoye peregovornoye oostroystvo)* and an R-855UM Komar-2M emergency radio. The R-862 radio is used for communication with other aircraft and ground control. It is frequency-stabilised and operates in the metre and decimetre wavebands, with working frequencies changing in 25-kHz increments. The R-862 has 2,000 preset channels in the metre waveband (100–149.975 MHz) and 7,200 preset channels in the frequency range of (220–399.975 MHz). Minimum operating range for communication ground control is 120 km (66 nm) at 1,000 m (3,280 ft), 250 km (138 nm) at 5,000 m (16,404 ft) and 350 km (194 nm) at 10,000 m (32,808 ft).

The SPU-9 intercom enables the pilot to use the radio, listen to VOR identification signals, warning and caution messages given by the Almaz-UP (Diamond) voice information module and informing and warning 'beeps' from various systems ('marker beacon passed', 'GCI data link on', 'target lock-on' from the IRST/LR, 'enemy radar detected' from the RHAWS etc.). On the ground it can be used for communication with ground crew who plug into a connector on the forward fuselage. Finally, on the MiG-29UB the intercom can be used for communication between trainee and instructor.

The R-855UM emergency UHF radio is part of the survival kit and is used to call a search and rescue team in the event of an ejection or forced landing. It uses the 121.5 MHz emergency frequency, enabling two-way voice communication within a 50-km (27-nm) radius with SAR aircraft flying at up to 3,000 m (9,842 ft) and acting as a beacon to assist in the location of the downed pilot within a 60–70-km (33–38-nm) radius. The radio's batteries permit 55 hrs of continuous operation in transceiver mode (with reception 75% of the time) or at least 24 hrs in beacon mode. On the MiG-29M and MiG-29K the comms equipment is integrated into the TKS-2-29 suite.

d) IFF equipment. The IFF system identifies aerial targets detected by the fire control radar as friendly,

identity unknown or hostile and responds to identify yourself queries from other aircraft. The MiG-29's IFF system comprises the SRZ-1P (*izdeliye* 6231) interrogator *(samolyotnyy rahdiolokatseeonnyy zaproschik)* and the SRO-1P (*izdeliye* 6201) transponder *(samolyotnyy rahdiolokatseeonnyy otvetchik)* which constitute the Parol'-2D (Password) system. Both parts of the system are programmed with the current identification code. The pilot makes a query by pushing a button on the stick; the interrogator sends a coded signal and gets a coded response from the other aircraft's transponder. A friendly tag then appears beside the target's blip on the joint indication system display if the other aircraft is a 'good guy'. In an emergency the transponder can transmit a Mayday signal.

The MiG-29 (*izdeliye* 9.12B) features the SRZ-15 interrogator and SRO-2 (NATO 'Odd Rods') and SO-69 (version K-42E) transponders. The MiG-29SD/SE is equipped with the *izdeliye* 6231R interrogator (with the interchangeable *izdeliye* 035MR as an option) and *izdeliye* 6201R and SO-69 (version K-11E) transponders which utilise modern electronics components making them more reliable. The interrogator aerial is located dorsally or ventrally ahead of the cockpit. Transponder aerials are located under the nose, in the LERXes, on the port fin and (SRO-2 only) on the wingtips.

e) Electronic support measures suite. The ESM suite warns the pilot that he is under attack, indicates possible directions from which he could be attacked and diverts enemy missiles from the aircraft. The core of the MiG-29's ESM suite is the SPO-15LM (L006LM) Beryoza radar homing and warning system (RHAWS).[17] With a warning beep the system informs the pilot that he is being painted by enemy radars and the joint indication system display shows the direction and type of the radar and the signal's intensity.

A slightly different RHAWS is fitted to export aircraft: L006LM/version 101 on the MiG-29 (*izdeliye* 9.12B) and L006LM/version 108 on the MiG-29SE. On the MiG-29M and MiG-29K the Beryoza is replaced by a more efficient Pastel RHAWS which can download target data to Kh-31P anti-radiation missiles. The RHAWS aerials are located in the LERXes, on the wingtips and the outer surfaces of the fins to give complete 360° coverage.

To disrupt the operation of land-based and shipboard air defence radars and sidetrack radar-homing AAMs and SAMs the 'Fulcrum-C', MiG-29M and MiG-29K are

---

[17] SPO = *sistema predooprezhdeniya ob obloochenii* – lit. irradiation warning system

equipped with a Gardeniya-1FU (L203B) active jammer; the export version, Gardeniya-1FUE (L203BE), is fitted to the MiG-29SE. On the 'Fulcrum-C' the jammer works in concert with the Beryoza RHAWS, using an L138 commutation module. Depending on the type of enemy radar illuminating the aircraft the jammer can emit high-frequency noise, low-frequency Doppler noise or flashing interference signals. This allows it to neutralise at least two radars operating in continuous, quasi-continuous or pulse-Doppler emission mode. The jammer covers a sector of the aircraft's rear hemisphere measuring ±60° in azimuth and ±30° in elevation.

The 'Fulcrum-A/C' is equipped with two BVP-30-26M chaff/flare dispensers located on the wing upper surface ahead of the fin fillets and canted towards the aircraft's centreline. These are loaded with sixty 26-mm (1.02-in.) PPI-26 IRCM flares for protection against IR-homing missiles or PPR-26 chaff bundles for passive radar jamming, though the latter are seldom used. The flares or chaff are fired by the SUVP-29 (*izdeliye* 20SP) control unit determining firing sequence and duration.[18] These depend on the aircraft's speed, altitude and direction of the attack; on the 'Fulcrum-C' fitted with the L138 commutation module the launch is programmed automatically as directed by the RHAWS. On the MiG-29M and MiG-29K the chaff/flare capacity is doubled, with two BVP-60-26 dispensers buried in the aft fuselage upper surface.

f) Command link equipment. The E502-20 Biryuza command link system receives guidance signals, target coordinates, tactical and interaction data from ground command (GCI) centres. The commands prepared by the CGI computer are transmitted as modulated HF signals and received by the Bekas-R (Snipe), then converted into standard digital or analog form and fed to the radar, automatic control system, JIS, intercom etc. The main parameters transmitted via the command link system are the target's altitude and speed, range to target, closing speed, and required heading and elevation.

By customer request all export versions of the 'Fulcrum' may be fitted with flight instruments marked in the Imperial system of measurement units, Western TACAN tactical radio navigation, IFF and VOR/ILS equipment, an SO-69M ATC transponder using internationally-accepted frequencies (or a Cossor IFF transponder), GPS and an extra Western communications radio.

g) Built-in test equipment/crew alerting system (BITE/CAS) and data recording equipment. The MiG-29 features an Ekran-03M (Screen) common test and crew alerting system (alternatively, Ekran-03ME on the MiG-29 (*izdeliye* 9.12B) and Ekran-13ME on the MiG-29SE). The Ekran BITE/CAS is built around a programmable data collection and processing module which diagnoses systems down to subsystem level, informs the pilot of critical systems failures and records these for ground personnel to deal with later. It enables automated pre-flight systems check and monitors the aircraft's systems in flight. Malfunctions are memorised in priority order and automatically recorded on tape 20 seconds after touchdown along with the time of failure (i.e., time elapsed from system startup). Sixty-four malfunction messages can be memorised and recorded and 256 alpha-numeric messages displayed in priority order.

The BITE/CAS and self-test modules of certain systems monitor more than 80% of the aircraft's systems and equipment, including the engine controls, intake ramp controls, landing gear, hydraulics, electrics, automatic flight control, fuel and fire suppression systems, WCS, IFF and other avionics. The VSS-1-4K light indication system (*vnootrikabinnaya svetovaya signaleezahtsiya*) informs the pilot of systems operating modes and malfunctions by means of green information lights, yellow caution lights and red warning lights.

The Almaz-UP (P-591B) voice information module plays back 47 pre-recorded caution and warning messages, informing the pilot of dangerous flight modes and malfunctions (engine fire, accessory gearbox fire, exhaust gas temperature critical etc.). The most critical warning messages are also transmitted to the ATC operator by radio. The messages are triggered by sensors in the engines, intake ramp control, hydraulic, electric, life support and air data systems and by the BITE/CAS.

The Tester-UZLK flight data recorder (FDR) tapes coded information about flight modes and systems operation to be used in normal mission evaluation or accident investigation. It is housed in a crashworthy capsule in the aft fuselage and is switched on manually or automatically at the moment of unstick. The FDR records the engines' operating mode, RPM and exhaust gas temperature, fuel flow, intake ramp and landing gear position, G loads and pitch/roll/yaw rates, heading and

---

[18] PPI = *peeropatron infrakrahsnyy* – IR cartridge; PPR = *peeropatron (protivo) rahdiolokatseeonnyy* – radar suppression cartridge; SUVP = *sistema oopravleniya vybrosom pomekh* = chaff/flare launch control system.

vertical speed, operation of the WCS, automatic flight control, hydraulic, fire suppression and crew escape systems, marker beacon receiver and comms radio.

Depending on the version, the MiG-29 can be fitted with various aerials as detailed in **Table E** on opposite page.

Electrics: Three subsystems: 28.5 V DC, 115 V/400 Hz AC (three-phase) and 36 V/400 Hz AC (single-phase). Main power sources are a 30-kW GSR-ST-12/40A DC generator (peak output 83.3 A, 208/120 V) and a 12-kW GT30NZhCh12 AC generator (400 A, 28.5 V); both are driven by the accessories gearbox. Reserve DC power is supplied by two 15STsS-45B silver-zinc batteries (28 V, 45 A·h) located in the starboard LERX which are also used for APU starting if ground power is unavailable. Reserve AC power is supplied by a PTO-1000/1500M converter (1.5 kW, single-phase/1 kW, three-phase; peak current 13 or 16 A respectively). The electric system includes an AZU-400A overload protection and control unit *(avtomaht zaschchity i oopravleniya)*. Two ground power connectors are located on the port side of the forward fuselage.

Exterior lighting: Two FP-8 ('Fulcrum-A/B') or FP-15 ('Fulcrum-C') landing lights on the main gear doors *(fahra posahdochnaya)*; one FPK-250 taxi light on the nose gear strut or, on early-production aircraft, FR-9 *(fahra roolyozhnaya)*; ANO-15 navigation light *(aeronavigatseeonnyy ogon')* at the wingtips and on the port fin.

Control system: All versions except the MiG-29M and MiG-29K have a conventional mechanical flight control system with rod linkages and irreversible hydraulic actuators. The control system features an artificial-feel mechanism and trimming in all three control channels. Pitch control is provided by stabilators with separate RP-260A actuators *(roolevoy preevod)*. Roll control is provided by ailerons with RP-280A actuators and differential stabilator deflection, and directional control is provided by inset rudders with RP-270 actuators. The actuators have twin chambers allowing them to be powered by two different hydraulic systems for greater reliability.

The aircraft can be controlled manually or automatically. In the latter case by the SAU-451 automatic control system *(sistema avtomateecheskovo oopravleniya)*. The system acts as a yaw, roll and pitch damper, enhancing stability and control, especially at high alpha. It also stabilises heading, AOA and bank angle, brings the aircraft into straight and level flight from any attitude at the push of a button on the stick (the so-called panic button), stabilises barometric altitude, enables automatic climbout from dangerously low altitude (when the gear is up) and automatic landing approach down to 50–60 m (164–196 ft).

The 'Fulcrum'-A and -C (*izdeliye* 9.12 and 9.13) are equipped with the SAU-451-03 and SAU-451-04 versions respectively. The MiG-29S/SE has the SAU-451-05 version featuring a critical AOA warning horn, a bank angle limiter and bigger rudder deflection at high alpha; the MiG-29SD's SAU-451-06 is similar except for the latter feature. The MiG-29UB has the SAU-451-02 version with changes associated with the trainer's dual controls. The system has twin ARM-150M servos in the pitch channel and ARM-150K servos in the yaw and roll channels (*avtonomnaya roolevaya masheenka* – self-contained servo).

To prevent stalling and inform the pilot that he is about to exceed prescribed AOA and G limits the MiG-29 is equipped with an SOS-3M alpha and G limiter (*sistema ogranicheetel'nykh signahlov* – limiting signals system) which also controls the LE flaps to expand the AOA envelope. As the aircraft approaches critical AOAs the system engages a stick-pusher with a force of up to 17 kg (37.5 lb). On the MiG-29 (*izdeliye* 9.12) and MiG-29UB the alpha limit is 26°; the MiG-29S/SD/SE/SM is equipped with an SOS-3M-3 system with a 28° limit.

The MiG-29M and MiG-29K have a KSU-915 combined control system (*kompleksnaya sistema oopravleniya* – complex control system for *izdeliye* 9.15). The system has a quadruplex analogue fly-by-wire pitch control channel with no mechanical backup and triplex FBW roll and yaw control channels with mechanical backup enabling 50% control surface deflection. It enhances manoeuvrability by making the aircraft statically unstable.

Hydraulics: Two independent hydraulic systems. The main system powers one chamber of each control surface actuator and the stick pusher actuator, the artificial feel unit, operates the landing gear, airbrakes, LE and TE flaps, air intake ramps, nosewheel steering mechanism and APU exhaust door. The backup or booster hydraulic system powers the other chamber of each control surface actuator and the stick pusher actuator. The two systems have separate hydraulic tanks pressurised to 2.8 kg/cm² (40 psi).

A company demonstrator owned by MAPO MiG. Some test and demonstrator aircraft carried the tactical codes on the fins rather than on the air intakes – and non-standard three-digit codes at that. (Yefim Gordon)

A MiG-29 (izdeliye 9.13) on test at NII VVS, operating from Akhtoobinsk, displaying to advantage the wing-mounted racks for 100-kg (220-lb) or 250-kg (551-lb) bombs. The dorsal air intake louvres sometimes open during low-speed flight. (Yefim Gordon)

This MiG-29 (izdeliye 9.13) with white war game recognition markings on the spine and fins is operated by the Tactical Aviation Combat Training Centre (TsBP FA) in Lipetsk. (Yefim Gordon)

A MiG-29 (izdeliye 9.13) of the Lipetsk Centre taking off. (Yefim Gordon)

Another routine display flight is about to begin. (Yefim Gordon)

ABOVE & OPPOSITE ABOVE: *Typically the MiG-29K's weapons load consists of Kh-31A anti-shipping missiles and R-73 short-range AAMs. (Yefim Gordon)*

INSET: *An overall view of the Topaz radar. (Viktor Drooshlyakov)*

LEFT: *312 Blue at MAKS-95 with two R-27R medium-range radar-homing AAMs, two R-77s, two R-73s and two R-60Ms. (Yefim Gordon)*

INSET: *A single-seat MiG-29 of the Strizhi aerobatic team hangared at Kubinka AB. (Yefim Gordon)*

TOP: *A Blue Angels pilot is pleased with his flight in a MiG-29UB. (Yefim Gordon)*

OPPOSITE: *The pilots of the Kubinka unit have often had to stage aerobatics displays even before the team was officially formed. (Aviatsiya i Kosmonavtika)*

BELOW: *Four different versions of the MiG-29, photographed a Zhukovskiy. (Yefim Gordon)*

MiG-29UB 33 White (note short radome and single pylons) making a solo display, March 1998. (Yefim Gordon)

The traditional fireworks as each aircraft unleashes a salvo of IRCM flares at the end of the display. (Yefim Gordon)

Three MiG-29s taking off for a show past two An-26s and an An-72 of the airlift regiment based at Kubinka. (Yefim Gordon)

A MiG-29/izdeliye 9.13 fires an S-24 heavy unguided rocket. (Yefim Gordon archive)

The MiG-29SMT upgrade will allow the 'Fulcrum' to stay in front-line service until 2010. The second prototype is seen here during trials. (Yefim Gordon)

ABOVE & OPPOSITE BELOW: *Unlike the basic MiG-29UB the MiG-29UBT has full combat potential. (Yefim Gordon)*

ABOVE: *The first 'production' MiG-29SMT (01 Blue, c/n 2960720165), completed in the last days of 1998, came as a precious gift to the Russian Air Force. (Yefim Gordon)*

A Luftwaffe MiG-29 (29+03, ex LSK/LV 615). How long will the 'Fulcrum' remain in NATO service? (Yefim Gordon)
A Hungarian Air Force (5th Fighter Regt 'Puma' Sqn) MiG-29UB visiting RIAT'97. (Yefim Gordon)

TABLE E

Antenna/aerial	MiG-29 (*izdeliye* 9.12B)	MiG-29SD	MiG-29SE
1 Fire control radar antenna	+	+	+
2 SRZ-15 IFF interrogator aerial	+	–	–
Izdeliye 035MR IFF interrogator aerial	–	+	+
3 Marker beacon receiver antenna	+	+	+
4 Forward navigation antenna	+	+	+
5 Radio altimeter transmitting antenna	+	+	+
6 SRO-2 IFF transponder waveband III aerial*	+	–	–
Izdeliye 6201R IFF transponder waveband II, III and VII aerials	–	+	+
7 Radio altimeter receiving antenna	+	+	+
8 IFF transponder waveband III aerial	+	+	+
9 ECM receiving antenna symmetrically to starboard	–	–	+
10 IFF transponder waveband I and II aerial	+	+	+
11 SRO-2 IFF transponder waveband I aerial symmetrically to starboard	+	–	–
Izdeliye 6201R IFF transponder waveband I aerial symmetrically to starboard	–	+	+
12 RHAWS azimuth antenna symmetrically to starboard	+	+	+
13 SRO-2 IFF transponder waveband II aerial	+	–	–
14 ECM antennas	–	–	+
15 RHAWS wide-angle azimuth and elevation antennas	+	+	–
16 ADF blade aerial	+	+	+
17 ADF loop aerial	+	+	+
18 SRO-2 IFF transponder waveband II aerial	+	–	–
19 ECM antennas	–	–	+
20 ECM receiving antennas	–	–	+
21 RHAWS wide-angle azimuth antennas	–	–	+
22 UHF communications blade aerial	+	+	+
23 Aft navigation antenna	+	+	+
24 Command link aerial	+	+	+
25 SRO-2 IFF transponder waveband I aerial	+	–	–
Izdeliye 6201R IFF transponder waveband I aerial	–	+	+

* Note: IFF operating frequencies are divided into several arbitrary wavebands which cannot be disclosed here – for obvious reasons.

Hydraulic power is provided by NP-103A variable-displacement pumps driven by the engine accessory gearbox. In an emergency the backup hydraulic system is powered by an NS-58 pump. The systems are filled with AMG-10 hydraulic fluid and have a nominal pressure of 210 kg/cm^2 (3,000 psi); safety valves prevent the pressure from exceeding 240 kg/cm^2 (3,428 psi). If hydraulic pressure falls to 130 kg/cm^2 (1,857 psi) all hydraulically-powered equipment except the control actuators, LE and TE flap actuators and stick pusher actuator are automatically disengaged; when the pressure falls to 100 kg/cm^2 (1,428 psi) the emergency pump is automatically engaged.

Pneumatic system: Three separate systems. The main pneumatic system powers the wheel brakes, canopy actuator, fuel shutoff cocks and operates brake parachute deployment and jettisoning. The emergency system operates the mainwheel brakes and enables emergency gear extension. The third system pressurises the hydraulic tanks and avionics bays. Air is supplied by bottles charged to 150 kg/cm^2 (2,143 psi); the pressure is reduced to 63 kg/cm^2 (900 psi) for operation.

Radar cooling system: The radar set has a liquid cooling system filled with OZh-65 glycol antifreeze; it features a pump, an expansion tank, an air separator and a fuel/glycol heat exchanger. The radar is switched off automatically if the temperature exceeds 70°C (158°F) or glycol pressure exceeds 8.8 kg/cm^2 (125 psi).

Oxygen system and crew gear: The oxygen system provides life support to the pilot(s) at high altitude, during high-G manoeuvring and in the event of an ejection; it also ensures reliable engine restarting in flight and APU startup on the ground. The pilot's main oxygen supply consists of three 4-lit. (0.88 Imp. gal.) oxygen bottles charged to 150 kg/cm^2 (2,143 psi); the pressure is reduced to 8–12 kg/cm^2 (114–171 psi) for operation. An air/oxygen mix is supplied to the pilot's face mask up to 8,000 m (26,246 ft); at higher altitude the system switches to pure oxygen.

The KSKK-2M emergency oxygen system located in the ejection seat consists of a 0.7-lit. (0.15 Imp. gal.) oxygen bottle and the supply lasts four minutes. MiG-29 pilots can use the KKO-15LP oxygen bottle (*komplekt kislorodnovo oboroodovaniya* – oxygen equipment set) enabling the pilot to eject at up to 20,000 m (65,616 ft) and stay underwater for up to five minutes if he is unlucky

enough to ditch. The engine and APU oxygen feed system has one 4-lit. bottle.

Pilot gear includes a VKK-15K pressure suit (*vysotno-kompenseeruyuschchiy kostyum*), a ZSh-7A flying helmet (*zaschchitnyy shlem* – protective helmet) and a KM-35 oxygen mask. If the mission does not involve climbing above 12,000 m (39,370 ft), the lighter PPK-3 G suit (*protivoperegroozochnyy kostyum*) may be used at the expense of a slight reduction in the pilot's G limits. For overwater sorties the VMSK-4-15 maritime pressure/rescue suit (*vysotnyy morskoy spasahtel'nyy kostyum*) with added heat insulation may be used in case of ditching.

Air conditioning system: The cockpit is air conditioned by engine bleed air cooled by air/air heat exchangers and a turbocooler. Cockpit temperature is automatically maintained at +15–25°C (59–77°F). The system also pressurises the pilot's pressure suit, demists the windscreen and cools the gun bay.

Fire suppression system: One 3-lit. (0.66 Imp. gal.) fire extinguisher filled with Khladon-114V$_2$ chlorofluorocarbon (CFC) in the fuselage spine for extinguishing fires in the engine bays and APU/accessory gearbox bay. The system is activated by flame sensors within three seconds after fire breaks out.

Crew escape system: Zvezda K-36DM Srs 2 zero-zero ejection seat and canopy jettisoning system activated by external and internal handles. The seat guarantees safe ejection in horizontal flight at 0–1,400 km/h (777 kts) IAS or Mach 2.5, during manoeuvres with 22–+4 Gs, at AOAs up to 30°, sideslip angles up to 20° and any bank angles right up to inverted position, roll rates up to 3 sec–1. On the ground safe ejection is guaranteed at speeds down to 75 km/h (41 kts). Minimum ejection altitude is 85 m (278 ft) in a 30° dive and 55 m (180 ft) in inverted flight.[19] Maximum G load during ejection is 18 Gs.

The seat is equipped with a KSMU-36 two-stage combined ejection gun, a parachute deployment mechanism, a PSU-36 parachute system with a 28-line parachute (canopy area is 60 m^2/645 sq. ft) and a stabilization system with two drogue chutes and automatic and semi-automatic deployment devices. It also houses the NAZ-8 survival kit (*noseemyy avareeynyy zapahs* – lit. portable emergency kit) comprising the R-855UM Komar-2M UHF radio, the PSN-1 one-man inflatable

---

[19] Airspeed is 400 km/h (222 kts) in both cases.

rescue raft *(plot spasahtel'nyy nadoovnoy)*, a food
supply, camping gear, signal flares and a first-aid kit. The
seat weighs 123 kg (271 lb) complete with oxygen system
and survival kit.

TABLE F

MiG-29 (*izdeliye 9.12*) specifications

Length overall		17.32 m (56 ft 9.88 in.)
Length less pitot boom		16.28 m (53 ft 4.94 in.)
Fuselage length		14.875 m (48 ft 9.62 in.)
Wing span		11.36 m (37 ft 3.24 in.)
Wing area		38.056 m^2 (409.2 sq. ft)
Height on ground		4.73 m (15 ft 6.22 in.)
Landing gear track		3.09 m (10 ft 1.65 in.)
Landing gear wheelbase		3.645 m (11 ft 11.5 in.)
Empty operating weight		10,900 kg (24,029 lb)
Takeoff weight:	normal	15,000–15,200 kg (33,068–33,509 lb)
	maximum	18,480 kg (40,740 lb)
Fuel load:	with 1 drop tank	4,640 kg (10,229 lb)
	with 3 drop tanks	6,480 kg (14,285 lb)
Usable fuel (depending on specific gravity):		
OKB data:	with 100% internal fuel	3,150–3,800 kg (6,944–8,377 lb)
	with 50% internal fuel	1,200–1,500 kg (2,645–3,306 lb)
	with 1 drop tank	4,350–5,000 kg (9,589–11,022 lb)
	with 2 drop tanks	5,000–5,600 kg (11,022–12,345 lb)
	with 3 drop tanks	6,150–6,800 kg (13,558–14,991 lb)
VVS data:	with 100% internal fuel	3,150–3,700 kg (6,944–8,157 lb)
	with 1 drop tank	4,250–4,950 kg (9,369–10,912 lb)
	with 2 drop tanks	4,950–5,500 kg (10,912–12,125 lb)
	with 3 drop tanks	6,050–6,750 kg (13,337–14,880 lb)
Fuel remaining after landing (with reserves)		550 kg (1,212 lb)
Maximum ordnance load:	'Fulcrum-A'	2,000 kg (4,409 lb)
	MiG-29SE	4,000 kg (8,818 lb)
Top speed:	at sea level	1,480 km/h (822.2 kts)
	at 11,000 m (36,089 ft)	2,450 km/h (1,361.1 kts)
Unstick speed		260–280 km/h (144.4–155.5 kts)
Landing speed		250–260 km/h (138.8–144.4 kts)
Maximum Mach number		2.3
Service ceiling with 800 kg (1,763 lb) of fuel		18,000 m (59,055 ft)

TABLE F continued

Service ceiling at subsonic speed (900 km/h or 500 kts)		14,500 m (47,572 ft)
Rate of climb		330–335 m/sec (1,082–1,099 ft/sec)
Takeoff thrust-to-weight ratio	1.1	
G limits:	up to Mach 0.85	+9–22.5
	above Mach 0.85	+7–21.5
Range/combat radius:	w. 2 R-27s, 4 R-73s, internal fuel:	
	at 200 m (ft)	455/134 km (252/74 nm)
	at 10–13 km	900/180 km (500/100 nm)
	w. 2 R-27s, 4 R-73s, 1 drop tank:	
	at 200 m (ft)	670 km (372 nm)
	at 10–13 km	1,380 km (766 nm)
	clean:	
	at 200 m (ft)	535 km (297 nm)
	at 10–13 km	1,250 km (694 nm)
Endurance:	w. 2 R-27s, 4 R-73s, internal fuel:	
	at 200 m (ft)	0 hr 50 min
	at 10–13 km	1 hr 10 min
	w. 2 R-27s, 4 R-73s, 1 drop tank:	
	at 200 m (ft)	1 hr 11 min
	at 10–13 km	1 hr 38 min
	clean:	
	at 200 m (ft)	0 hr 57 min
	at 10–13 km	1 hr 22 min
Takeoff run:	in full afterburner	250 m (820 ft)
	at full military power	600–700 m (1,968–2,296 ft)
Time to unstick (in full afterburner)		6–7 sec
Landing run with brake parachute		600–700 m (1,968–2,296 ft)

Note: Range, combat radius and endurance figures are stated as per VVS documents. ANPK MiG state that the MiG-29 (*izdeliye* 9.12) has a maximum range of 1,430–1,500 km (794–833 nm) on internal fuel, 2,100 km (1,166 nm) with one drop tank at S/L and 2,900 km (1,611 nm) with three drop tanks.

MiG-29 versions: comparative specifications

	MiG-29 (9.12)	MiG-29 (9.13)	MiG-29UB (9.51)	MiG-29S (9.13S)	MiG-29SD (9.12SD)
First flight	1977	1984	1981	1990	1990[3]
Powerplant	2×RD-33	2×RD-33	2×RD-33	2×RD-33	2×RD-33
Rating in full a/b, kgp (lb st)	2×8,340 (2×18,386)	2×8,340 (2×18,386)	2×8,340 (2×18,386)	2×8,340 (2×18,386)	2×8,340 (2×18,386)
Length with pitot	17.32 m (56' 9.88")	17.32 m (56' 9.88")	17.42 m (57' 1.82")	17.32 m (56' 9.88")	17.32 m (56' 9.88")

TABLE F continued

MiG-29 versions: comparative specifications					
	MiG-29 (9.12)	**MiG-29 (9.13)**	**MiG-29UB (9.51)**	**MiG-29S (9.13S)**	**MiG-29SD (9.12SD)**
Wing span	11,36 m (37′ 3.24″)	11,36 m (37′ 3.24″)	11,36 m (37′ 3.24″)	11,36 m (37′ 3.24″)	11,36 m (37′ 3.24″)
Height on ground	4.73 (15′ 6.22″)	4.73 (15′ 6.22″)	4.73 (15′ 6.22″)	4.73 (15′ 6.22″)	4.73 (15′ 6.22″)
Wing area, m^2 (ft^2)	38.056 (409.2)	38.056 (409.2)	38.056 (409.2)	38.056 (409.2)	38.056 (409.2)
Normal TOW, kg (lb)	15,000 (33,068)	15,300 (33,730)	14,600 (32,186)	15,300 (33,730)	15,000 (33,068)
MTOW, kg (lb)	18,480 (40,740)	n/a	n/a	19,700 (43,430)	18,480 (40,740)
Ordnance load, kg (lb)	3,200 (7,054)	3,200 (7,054)	n/a	3,200 (7,054)	3,200 (7,054)
Internal fuel, kg (lb)	3,630 (8,002)	3,850 (8,487)	n/a	3,850 (8,487)	3,630 (8,002)
Thrust-to-weight ratio[1]	1.11	n/a	n/a	1.09	1.11
Top speed, km/h (kts): at 11,000 m (36,089 ft)	2,450 (1,361)	2,450 (1,361)	2,230 (1,238)	2,450 (1,361)	2,450 (1,361)
at S/L	1,480 (822)	1,480 (822)	1,400 (777)	1,480 (822)	1,480 (822)
Landing speed, km/h (kts)	260 (144)	260 (144)	260 (144)	260 (144)	260 (144)
Service ceiling, m (ft)	17,500 (57,414)	17,000 (55,774)	17,500 (57,414)	17,000 (55,774)	17,500 (57,414)
Rate of climb, m/sec (ft/sec)[2]	330 (1,082)	300 (984)	330 (1,082)	300 (984)	330 (1,082)
Effective range, km (nm): on internal fuel at S/L	710 (394)	n/a	680 (377)	n/a	710 (394)
on internal fuel at altitude	1,500 (833)	n/a	1,410 (783)	1,500 (833)	n/a
with 1 drop tank	2,100 (1,166)	n/a	n/a	n/a	2,100 (1,166)
with 3 drop tanks	2,900 (1,611)[10]	3,600 (2,000)	n/a	3,600 (2,000)	2,900 (1,611)
Subsonic G limit	9.0	9.0	9.0	9.0	9.0
AAMs: long-range	—	—	—	R-27ET/ER	R-27ET/ER
medium-range	R-27R1/T1	R-27R1/T1	—	R-27R1/T1 R-77	R-27R/T1 R-77
short-range	R-60M R-73	R-60M R-73	R-60M R-73	R-60M R-73	R-60M R-73
AGMs	—	—	—	—	—

30

TABLE F continued

MiG-29 versions: comparative specifications					
	MiG-29SE (9.13SE)	MiG-29SM (9.12SM)	MiG-29SMT (9.17)	MiG-29M (9.15)	MiG-29K (9.31)
First flight	1990[3]	1990[3]	1997[3]	1986	1988
Powerplant	2×RD-33	2×RD-33	2×RD-33	2×RD-33K[4]	2×RD-33K
Rating in full a/b, kgp (lb st)	2×8,340 (2×18,386)	2×8,340 (2×18,386)	2×8,340 (2×18,386)	2×8,800 (2×19,400)	2×9,400 (2×20,723)
Length with pitot	17.32 m (56' 9.88")	17.32 m (56' 9.88")	17.32 m (56' 9.88")	17.32 m (56' 9.88")	17.27 m (56' 7.92")
Wing span	11,36 m (37' 3.24")	11,36 m (37' 3.24")	11,36 m (37' 3.24")	11,36 m (37' 3.24")	11.99/7.8[5] (39' 4.04"/ 25' 7.08")
Height on ground	4.73 (15' 6.22")	4.73 (15' 6.22")	4.73 (15' 6.22")	4.73 (15' 6.22")	4.73 (15' 6.22")
Wing area, m² (ft²)	38.056 (409.2)	38.056 (409.2)	38.056 (409.2)	38.056 (409.2)	43.0 (462.36)
Normal TOW, kg (lb)	15,300 (33,730)	n/a	16,850 (37,147)	15,800 (34,832)	15,570 (34,325)[6]
MTOW, kg (lb)	19,700 (43,430)	n/a	n/a	n/a	18,210 (40,145)[7]
Ordnance load, kg (lb)	3,200 (7,054)	n/a	4,000 (8,818)	4,500 (9,920)	4,500 (9,920)
Internal fuel, kg (lb)	3,850 (8,487)	3,630 (8,002)	4,835 (10,659)	4,460 (9,832)	4,460 (9,832)[8]
Thrust-to-weight ratio[1]	n/a	n/a	n/a	1.11	1.06
Top speed, km/h (kts): at 11,000 m (36,089 ft)	2,450 (1,361)	2,450 (1,361)	2,450 (1,361)	2,500 (1,388)	2,300 (1,277)
at S/L	1,480 (822)	1,480 (822)	1,480 (822)	1,480 (822)	1,400 (777)
Landing speed, km/h (kts)	260 (144)	260 (144)	260 (144)	260 (144)	230–240 (127–133)
Service ceiling, m (ft)	17,000 (55,774)	n/a	n/a	17,000 (55,774)	17,400 (57,086)
Rate of climb, m/sec (ft/sec)[2]	300 (984)	n/a	n/a	320 (1,049)	260 (853)
Effective range, km (nm): on internal fuel at S/L	n/a	n/a	n/a	900 (500)	n/a
on internal fuel at altitude	n/a	n/a	2,100 (1,166)	2,000–2,200 (1,111–1,222)	n/a
with 1 drop tank	n/a	n/a	2,700 (1,500)	3,200 (1,777)	2,600 (1,444)
with 3 drop tanks	n/a	n/a	3,300 (1,833)	n/a	3,000 (1,666)

TABLE F continued

MiG-29 versions: comparative specifications					
	MiG-29SE (9.13SE)	MiG-29SM (9.12SM)	MiG-29SMT (9.17)	MiG-29M (9.15)	MiG-29K (9.31)
Subsonic G limit	9.0	9.0	9.0	9.0	8.5/6.0⁹
AAMs: long-range medium-range short-range	R-27ET/ER R-27R1/T1 R-77 R-60M R-73	R-27ET/ER R-27R1/T1 R-77 R-60M R-73	R-27ET/ER R-27R1/T1 R-77 R-60M R-73	R-27ET/ER R-27R1/T1 R-77 R-60M R-73	R-27ET/ER R-27R1/T1 R-77 R-60M R-73
AGMs	—	Kh-29T/TD	Kh-29T/TD Kh-31A/P	Kh-29T/TD Kh-31A/P Kh-25ML/MP	Kh-29T/TD Kh-31A/P Kh-25ML/MP

Notes:

1 With normal TOW

2 At 1,000 m (3,280 ft)

3 Design date, as the aircraft has not flown yet

4 Without 9,400-kgp contingency rating

5 With wings in flight position and folded respectively

6 With four AAMs

7 With four AAMs and three drop tanks

8 Normally limited to 4,000 kg (8,818 lb) because of weight restrictions during carrier operations

9 Subsonic/supersonic

10 Modified aircraft only (with 'wet' wing pylons)

MiG-29 Tactics

The MiG-29's main combat modes in the counter-air rôle are:

- maximum-range intercept, GCI-controlled or independent (using the fire control radar);
- medium-range air-to-air combat using R-27R/RE, R-27T/TE and R-77 AAMs;
- close-range air-to-air combat (dogfight mode) using R-73 AAMs;
- close-range air-to-air combat using the internal gun.

In all kinds of air-to-air combat the fighter's WCS enables:

- automatic target detection by means of the radar or IRST/LR, possibly with guidance from GCI centres or AWACS aircraft via command link;
- covert target detection by means of the radar (in passive tracking mode) at 70–80 km (38–44 nm) range or by the IRST/LR at 15–30 km (8.3–16 nm) range; in search mode the radar can track up to 10 targets;
- target lock-on and autotracking by the radar at up to 40 km (22 nm) or by the IRST/LR at up to 12 km (6.6 nm) with radar or laser ranging; the N-019M and N-010 radars can guide missiles to two or four priority targets respectively.

The IRST/LR is the main targeting system used with the gun. Targeting is possible in visual reference mode (by placing the gunsight reticle on the HUD over the target in VMC conditions) or error computation mode (in IMC conditions). A fixed grid on the HUD can be used as a reference point for gun and missile firing if no targeting information is available.

In strike mode 'Fulcrum' versions having no provisions for guided air-to-surface weapons (*izdeliye* 9.12, 9.12A/B and 9.13, MiG-29S/SD/SE) can use the following tactics:

- diving attack (dive-bombing, firing FFARs and strafing);
- dropping bombs at the moment of recovery from a dive;
- dropping bombs and submunitions in horizontal flight.

Targeting mode is selected automatically, depending on the flight mode. The WCS continuously measures target range with the laser ranger or, if this is impossible, computes target range based on altitude and attitude; this is then used to calculate weapon impact point, commence and cease fire. Once again a fixed grid on the HUD can be used as a reference point for gun and rocket firing if no targeting information is available.

The Shape of Things to Come

The MiG-29 is currently in service with the air arms of more than 20 nations. After delivery of MiG-29s to Malaysia the fighter is becoming increasingly popular in Southeast Asia; among other nations, the Philippines have expressed an interest in the 'Fulcrum'. This country, which is enjoying economic growth and has become one of the Asian tigers, not only needs lots of new military hardware but is considered a good customer; that is, a customer paying in dollars, not 'goatskins'. In the late '80s the USA accounted for 90 per cent of the Philippines' weapons imports; however, since then relations between the two countries have cooled and the Philippines are looking for new suppliers.

According to press reports, the Philippine Air Force (PAF) and the Navy top the waiting list for re-equipment. One of the high-priority programmes in the Air Force is the replacement of ageing Northrop F-5A/Bs. A contract for new fighters to replace them could be worth up to US$ 600 million.

The PAF called a competition for an F-5 replacement. Initially contenders included the IAI Kfir C7, ex-*Armée de l'Air* Mirage F1s, upgraded ex-Belgian Air Force Mirage 5BA/Ds, the South African Atlas Cheetah, the F-16A/B, ex-Republic of Korea Air Force F-5A/Bs and the MiG-29. Most of them, however, were soon rejected because they were second-hand aircraft offered at bargain prices. Thus, as Western observers noted, the Russian offer looked more attractive than the others. Sure enough, the MiG-29 was more expensive than some of the aircraft on offer but it was new, with a service life that enabled it to remain operational for 20 to 25 years; more importantly, however, it was a state-of-the-art combat aircraft, not a 'warmed-up' previous-generation fighter.

Later the leading Western fighter makers changed their proposals, and now the PAF is choosing from the F-16, the F/A-18, the Mirage 2000, the Kfir 2000 and the MiG-29MF. Aviation experts believe the 'Fulcrum's' chances are fairly good. The Malaysian neighbours have had positive experience with the type and Russian aircraft manufacturers have shown their ability to suit customer requirements and fulfil their contract obligations. The MiG-29's demonstration at the LIMA'95 airshow at Langkawi AB in Manila in March 1995 also helped.

Another extremely important factor is that the Russian exporters were ready to supply technologies and engage in mutually profitable joint projects from the start. This led to the signing of a technology exchange agreement between VPK MAPO and the Philippine International Trade Corporation (PITC) which allowed both states to expand high-tech product sales on each other's markets. However, Western weapons exporters are also taking active and rather unusual steps to get a bite of the Philippine market. E.g., the USA started increasing its military aid again in the early '90s. Thus, defence analysts believe the PAF's new fighter acquisition contract may probably be split between several manufacturers; the F/A-18 and the MiG-29FM are stated as the most likely winners.

The MiG-29's future prospects concern not only new exports but first of all product improvement. E.g., improved lateral stability and roll control introduced on the MiG-29S by optimising aileron and rudder movement and modifying the automatic control system have increased the MiG-29SD/SE/SM's AOA limit to 28–30°, giving better agility. A further improvement in manoeuvrability could be obtained by introducing thrust-vectoring control (TVC). A thrust-vectoring derivative of the RD-33 designated RD-43 (erroneously referred to in aviation magazines as RD-133) has been developed by NPP Klimov in St. Petersburg. Unlike other thrust-vectoring engines – e.g., the Lyul'ka (Saturn) AL-31FP turbofan intended for the production Su-37 and the Pratt&Whitney F119-PW-100 powering the Boeing/Lockheed Martin F-22A Raptor – the RD-43 has a two-plane vectoring nozzle. According to former chief project engineer Mikhail R. Val'denberg, the use of two-plane vectoring nozzles enables the fighter to use TVC even if one engine fails. The use of TVC both in the pitch and yaw channels offers sizeable advantages over pitch-only TVC while incurring only a negligible weight penalty.

NPP Klimov have retained maximum commonality with the current RD-33, which means the RD-43 can be easily retrofitted to all versions of the 'Fulcrum'. Unlike the Su-37 and F-22, however, production MiG-29s do not have a fly-by-wire control system into which the vectoring nozzle actuators can be integrated, so a special processor governing the nozzles has to be fitted. Incorporating TVC will significantly expand the fighter's AOA envelope, improve pitch and roll control and be a step towards ultra-manoeuvrability. A MiG-29 converted into a TVC testbed is expected to enter flight test shortly.

A few years from now the 'Fulcrum' may be re-engined with new-generation afterburning turbofans which will improve thrust-to-weight ratio, placing the MiG-29 alongside fifth-generation advanced tactical fighters. NPP Klimov are currently working on such an engine already dubbed RD-333 (!) by the Western press (which is actually again the RD-43). This engine will have an afterburner rating increased to approximately 10,000 kgp (22,045 lb st) by increasing turbine temperature by 100–150°K (to 1,800°K). A critical design requirement is that the dimensions of the new engine are kept within those of the RD-33 so as to enable current 'Fulcrums' to be upgraded without major structural modifications. Current MiG-29 project chief V. V. Novikov believes the new engine may be available before the turn of the century.

The next major issue is the upgrading of the avionics suite, primarily the fire control radar. The Phazotron N-019M/ME Topaz fitted to the MiG-29S/SD/SE/SM has reached the limit of its growth potential. It will be replaced by a new-generation radar using new components and having much greater capabilities. Such a radar, the Phazotron N-010 Zhuk, has been tested successfully on the MiG-29M prototypes. Unlike the N-019, it has a slotted-array antenna; the beam is scanned electronically in elevation and mechanically in azimuth. In air-to-air mode the N-010 can guide missiles to four priority threats (versus one and two for the N-019 and N-019M respectively), discern targets flying in close formation and attack hovering or slow-moving targets such as helicopters. In air-to-surface mode its capabilities are even more impressive: it can designate targets for Kh-31A and Kh-35U active radar homing anti-shipping missiles, work in ground mapping mode with low, medium or high resolution, enable blind bombing through overcast etc.

MAPO-MiG is offering two avionics upgrade options. Option 1 involves replacement of the N-019 or N-019M radar with the N-010 while the rest of the avionics remains largely unchanged; this can be done in service by the unit's tech staff. Option 2 is more radical, involving a complete replacement of the mission avionics. The new suite is built around a digital computer with powerful Intel 486DX2 processors and a MIL-STD-1553B multiplex databus. Thus the open avionics architecture principle is implemented and the targeting, navigation, communications equipment and flight instrumentation are integrated into a single complex. The navigation suite is to include an INS based on ring laser gyros and a Glonass/Navstar global positioning system (GPS). Western avionics may be integrated and part of the avionics may be podded.

To reduce pilot workload the HOTAS principle is to be implemented. The traditional analog flight instruments will be replaced by an EFIS with multi-function colour LCDs and conventional switches by a multi-function control panel. The cockpit will also have an upgraded HUD. The finished result will be similar to the definitive MiG-29M prototype (156 Blue). Other possible improvements include the installation of an advanced ESM suite including an ELINT/SIGINT pack, an RHAWS, an infra-red missile warning system, a programmable active jammer and chaff/flare dispensers. Additionally, the airframe is to be coated with radar-absorbent materials to reduce radar signature.

Combat capability may be enhanced by installing a data link enabling the fighter to pass target information to other aircraft in a group or receive target information from GCI centres, AWACS aircraft or other fighters. This will enable the MiG-29 to operate jointly with other fighters (e.g., the Su-27 or MiG-31 'Foxhound') and even SAM sites. In this case, MiG-31 and Su-30 two-seat interceptors can act as mini-AWACS aircraft, designating targets and guiding MiG-29s to them when the 'Fulcrums' are beyond the reach of GCI centres.

The weapons control system of the MiG-29SD/SE/SM is compatible with most Russian medium-range AAMs and IR-homing dogfight AAMs currently in production. Future AAMs having tracker heads with better ECM/IRCM resistance and longer-burn motors may be integrated as they come along. These may feature enhanced manoeuvrability enabling the aircraft to fire over the shoulder at a pursuing enemy fighter.

Plans concerning air-to-surface weapons include the integration of Kh-31P anti-radiation missiles followed by Kh-31A and Kh-35U anti-shipping missiles. Later, when the avionics suite is upgraded, new stand-off anti-shipping missiles with a range of up to 200 km (111 nm) and high-accuracy AGMs may be added, enabling the aircraft to destroy ground targets or surface ships without coming within range of the enemy's air defences.

Changes are likely to be made to standard operational procedures in order to cut operating costs. This will mean a switch from pre-planned maintenance to operation based on actual condition with periodic reliability checks and servicing every 1,000 flight hours. On an average basis this will cut annual maintenance costs by 15–20 per cent per aircraft. Operating costs are also to be reduced by effective training of highly skilled maintenance personnel using the latest techniques and computerised teaching aids. For foreign operators a joint aircraft maintenance centre could be established; currently Malaysia, Germany and India are working on it. VPK MAPO is offering a range of specialised teaching aids, including a flight simulator with six degrees of freedom and interactive tuitional software using the latest computer graphics.

On 24 December 1997 test pilot Sergey Tresvyatskiy made the first takeoff on a MiG-29 from a specially developed mobile ski jump. Experts believe this trials programme could be of great importance to tactical aviation. It is known that only a timely decision by the Iraqi Air Force to move its aircraft to Iran during the Gulf War had saved them from destruction; Allied bombardments had knocked out Iraqi airstrips soon after, rendering takeoff impossible. Statistics show that the distance between bomb craters on a disabled runway does not exceed 300 m (984 ft). No combat jets except V/STOL types can operate from such short runways; by comparison, the normal takeoff run is 600–700 m (1,968–2,296 ft) for a MiG-29 or Su-27 and 800 m (2,624 ft) for a Su-25.

The only possible solution, according to LII specialists, is a mobile ski jump reducing takeoff run by approximately 2.5 times. Such a structure could be transported in dismantled condition and quickly erected at the end of the undamaged section of the runway, permitting aircraft to be flown out.

LII's MT-1 *(mobeel'nyy trampolin)* ski jump is 14 m (45 ft 11 in.) long and 0.75 m (2 ft 5.5 in.) high. It weighs some 22 tons (48,500 lb) and is made up of seven sections, the largest of which weighs some four tons (8,818 lb). These are transported by two trucks or a truck with a trailer and assembled by three men within 40 minutes. The MT-1 can handle aircraft grossing up to 16 tons (35,273 lb).

ANPK MiG was interested in the project and supplied one of its development MiG-29s (407 Blue) for trials on the ski jump. The aircraft got airborne after a takeoff run of 200 m (656 ft); Mikoyan engineers plan to reduce this to 130–150 m (426–492 ft). With a full fuel load and four missiles the MiG-29 can take off from the MT-1 with a takeoff run of 230–250 m (754–820 ft).

MAPO specialists believe that this combined approach to improving the MiG-29 and stage-by-stage completion of the long-term upgrade programme will ensure that the 'Fulcrum' remains in service well beyond the year 2000. Development costs of new-generation combat aircraft are inevitably soaring, and development is protracted; thus one may confidently say that these aircraft will take some time entering production and will not be produced on a large scale. The resulting gap between third-generation fighters which are due to be phased out and fifth-generation fighters which are just entering flight test will be bridged by today's fighters which will stay around for another 15 or 20 years. And the MiG-29 is one of the best among them.

Even now many nations, notably Germany (which is a 'Fulcrum' operator) and SE Asian nations, are showing an interest in the MiG-29SMT. Germany is ready to act as an intermediary for MiG-29 upgrade orders from European nations (e.g., Poland, Hungary and Romania), using the capabilities of the technical facility established several years ago with VPK MAPO's assistance.

Yet of course the MiG-29SMT was developed primarily with the Russian Air Force in mind. Importantly, this is an affordable option for the Russian defence budget which has not been feeling too well lately. Starting in 1998, the Russian MoD planned to begin upgrading MiG-29s currently in service. Hopefully the first ten or fifteen aircraft would be completed in 1998; 40 late-model fighters are to be upgraded by the year 2000 and some 150 conversions are planned in all. This will boost the Russian Air Force's combat potential perceptibly, ensuring proper combat readiness until 2015 or 2020 when a next-generation fighter based on the MiG-29 will be available.

Appendix 1 Acronyms and Glossary

AAM	Air-to-Air Missile		FOD	Foreign Object Damage
ADF	Automatic Direction Finder		FX	Fighter, Experimental
AGM	Air-to-Ground Missile		G	Unit of gravitational effect
AMLF	Advanced Mass-produced Light Fighter project		G-loc	Loss of Consciousness induced by high G
AOA	Angle of Attack (alpha)		GCI	Ground Control Interception
APU	Auxiliary power unit		GOR	General Operational Requirement
ASW	Anti Submarine Warfare		GPS	Global Positioning System
ATC	Air Traffic Control		GPWS	Ground Proximity Warning System
ATF	Advanced Tactical Fighter		GSVG	Soviet forces in East Germany
AV-MF	Naval aviation		HAD	Head Down Display
BITE	Built In Test Equipment		HEFI-T	High Explosive, Fragmentation & Incendiary with Tracer ordnance
BVR	Beyond visual range		HMS	Helmet-Mounted Sight
c/n	Code Number		HP	High Pressure
CAS	Close Air Support or Crew Alert System		HOTAS	Hands On Throttle & Stick
CFE	Conventional Forces in Europe treaty		HUD	Head Up Display
CFRP	Carbon Fibre Reinforced Plastic		IAS	Indicated Air Speed
CG	Centre of gravity		ICAO	International Civil Aviation Organisation
CIS	Confederation of Independent States (post Soviet)		IFF	Identification Friend or Foe
CRT	Cathode Ray Tube		IFR	Instrument Flight Rules
CTOL	Conventional Take Off & Landing		IK	IR search, target identification and memory system
ECM	Electronic Countermeasures		INS	Inertial Navigation System
EFIS	Electronic Flight Instrumentation System		IOC	Initial Operating Capability
ELINT	Electronic intelligence		IR	Infra-red
ESM	Electronic Support Measures		IRCM	IR Countermeasures
f/n	Fin Number		IRST	IR Search and Tracking
FADEC	Full Authority Digital Engine Control		KAB	Guided bomb
FBW	Fly-by-wire		kg	Kilogrammes
FDR	Flight Data Recorder		kgp	thrust in kg.
FFAR	Folding Fin Aircraft Rockets		km/h	kilometres per hour
FLIR	Forward Looking Infra-Red		kts	knots

LCD	Liquid Crystal Display		RCS	Radar Cross-section
L/D	Lift/Drag ratio		RDTC	Centre for testing systems
LE	Leading Edge		S/L	Sea Level
LERXes	Leading Edge Root eXtensions		SAR	Synthetic Aperture Radar
LLTV	Low Light TV		SARH	Semi-Active Radar Homing
LORAN	Long-range radio Navigation aid		SHORAN	Short-range radio navigation aid
LWF	Light Weight Fighter		SibNIA	Soviet aviation research centre at Novosibirsk
MAP	Ministry of Aircraft Production		SIF	Selective Identification Facility
McDD	McDonnell Douglas (Boeing)		SOR	Specific Operational Requirements
MTBF	Mean Time Between Failures		stabilator	stabiliser/elevator
MTOW	Maximum Take Off Weight		TE	Trailing Edge
NIIR	Radio research institute		TsAGI	Central Aerodynamics Institute
nm	nautical miles		TsIAM	Central R&D for engines
NPO	Phazotron electronics institute		TsNII	Central R&D centre No. 30
OKB	Soviet central design office		TOW	Take Off Weight
PD	Preliminary Design		VHF	Very High Frequency
PFI	Advanced tactical fighter		VFR	Visual Flight Rules
PVO	Air Defence Force		VIAM	Institute for aviation structural research
R&D	Research & Development		V/STOL	Vertical & Short Take Off & Landing
RAHWS	Radar Homing & Warning System		VVS	Soviet airforce
RAM	Radar Absorbent Material		WCS	Weapons Control System

Appendix 2 Detail Plans

9.12

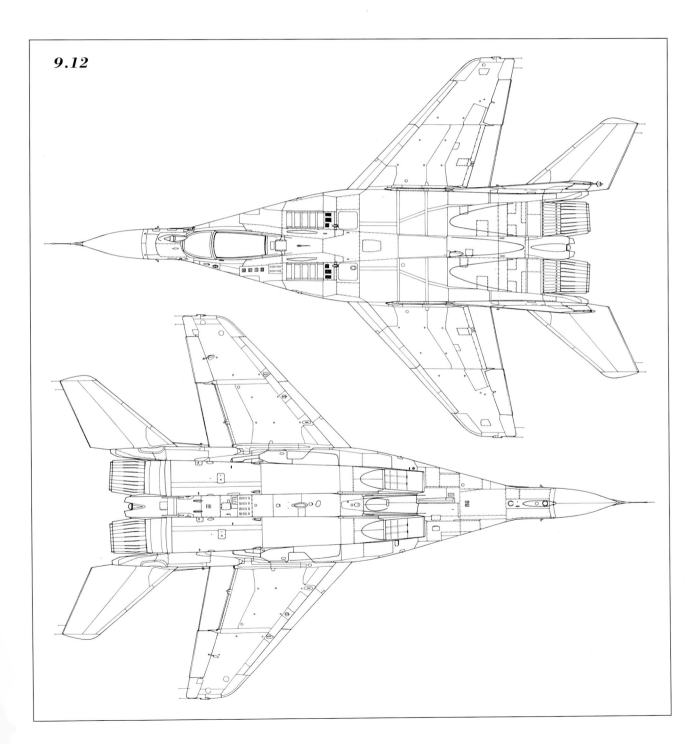

9.12 continued

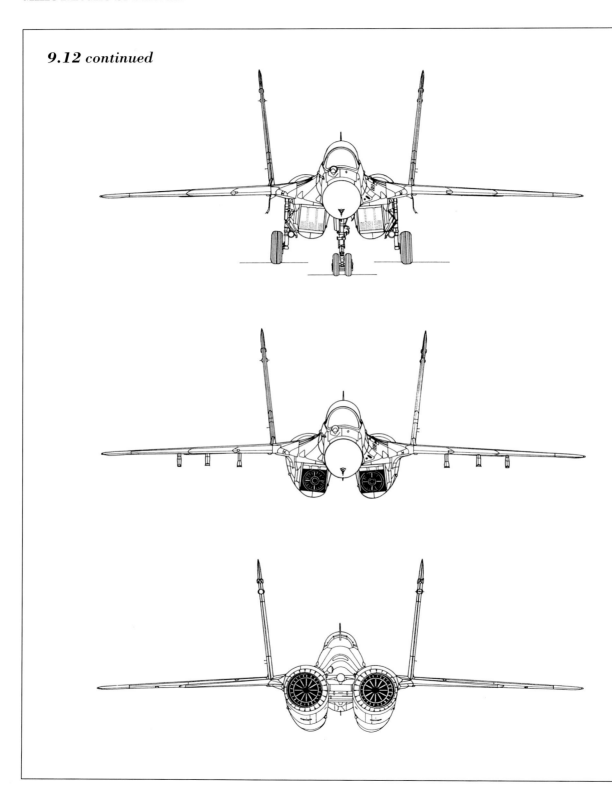

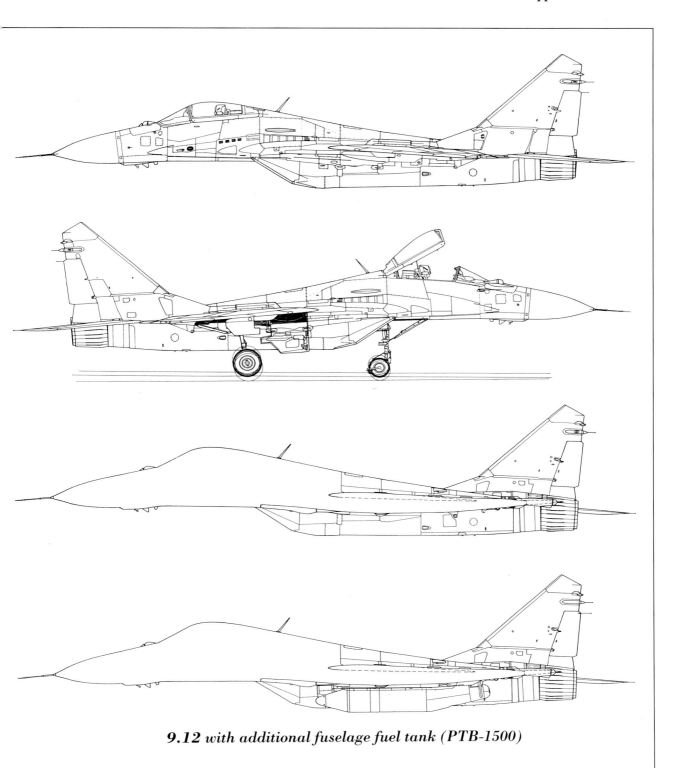

9.12 with additional fuselage fuel tank (PTB-1500)

9.12 *First production*

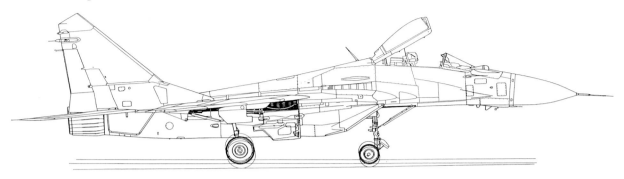

9.12 *First production with missiles and additional fuel tank*

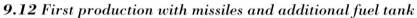
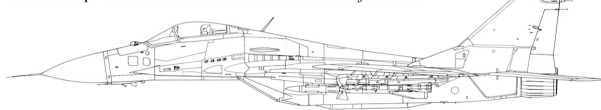

9.12 *First production 'Blue 29'*

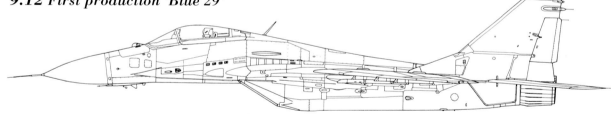

9.12 *First production 'Blue 21'*

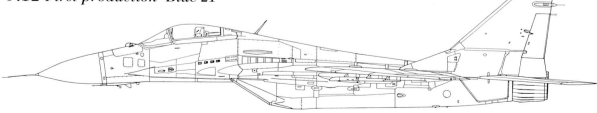

9.12 *Soviet Navy*

9.12 *Production (Red '33')*

9.12 *(Blue '33') LII test-bed*

9.12 *Production with S-24 rockets ('Blue 48')*

9.12 *'Aircraft 211' test-bed*

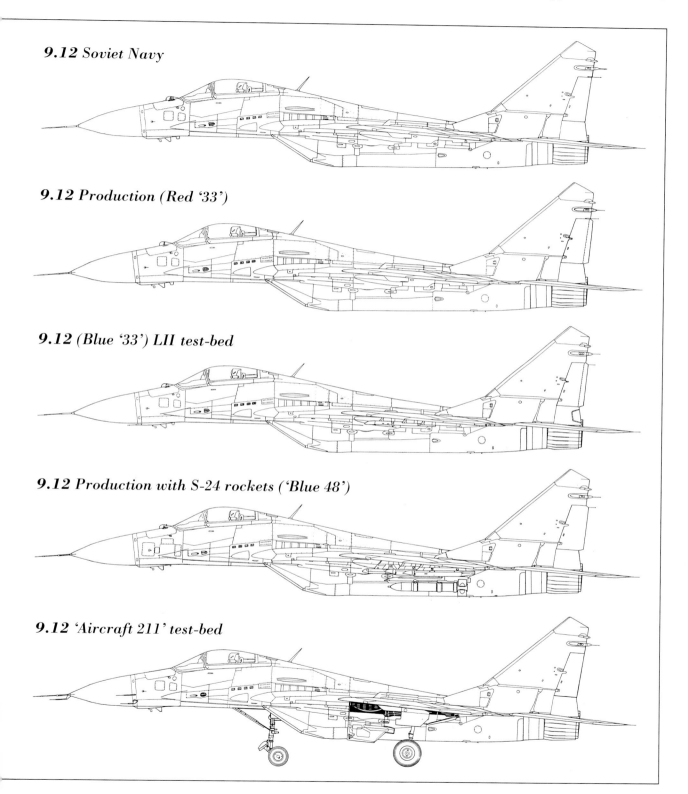

MiG-29UB Prototype ('Aircraft 95 1')

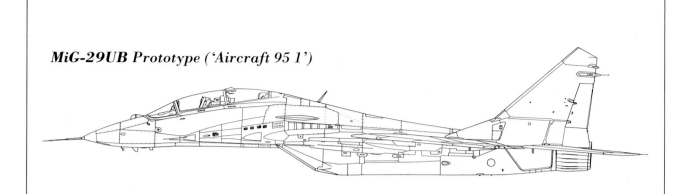

MiG-29UB Prototype ('Aircraft 95 1')

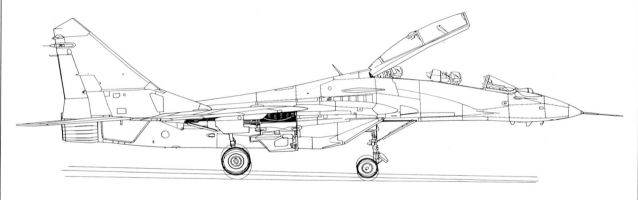

MiG-29UB Production

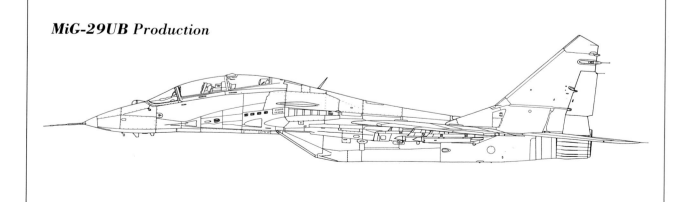

MiG-29UB Production

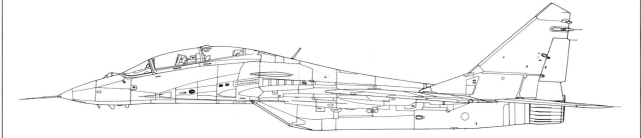

MiG-29UB Production with additional fuel tanks (PTB-1150)

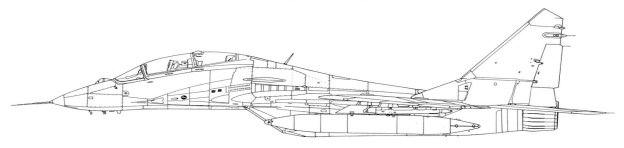

MiG-29UB Production (fuselage number '99')

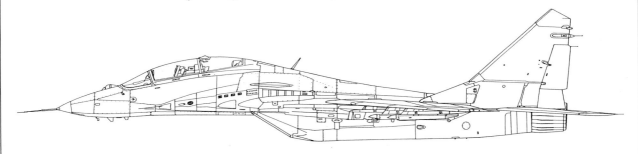

MiG-29UB

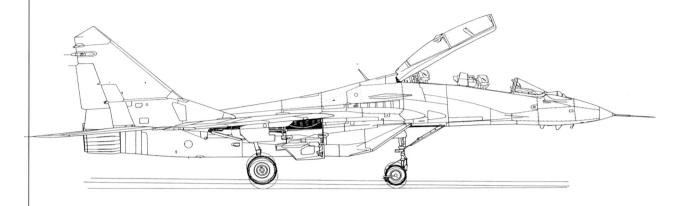

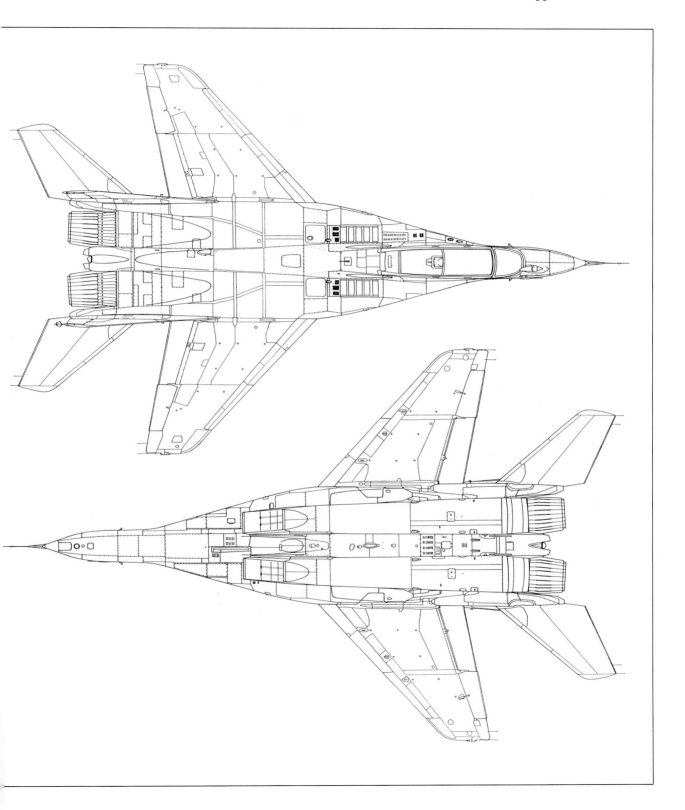

9.13S

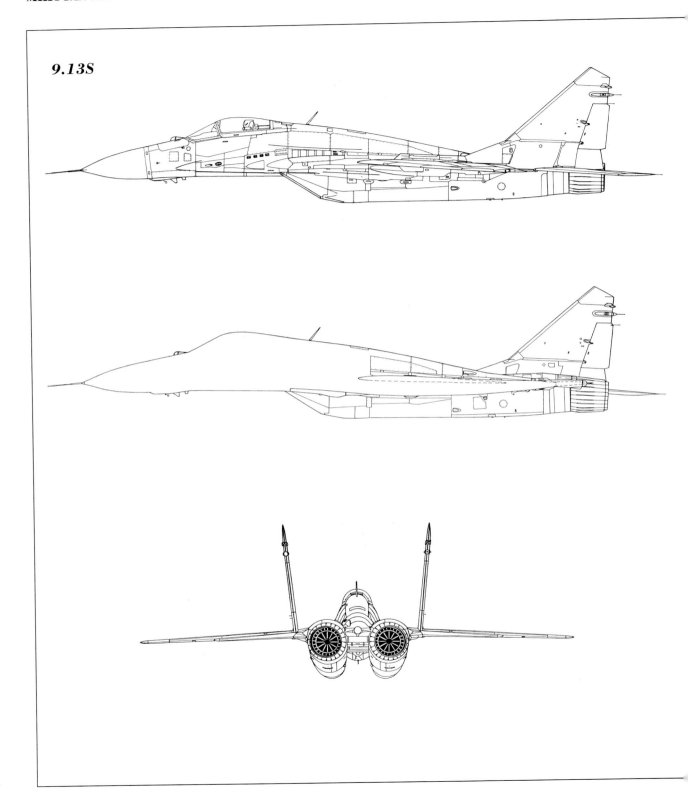

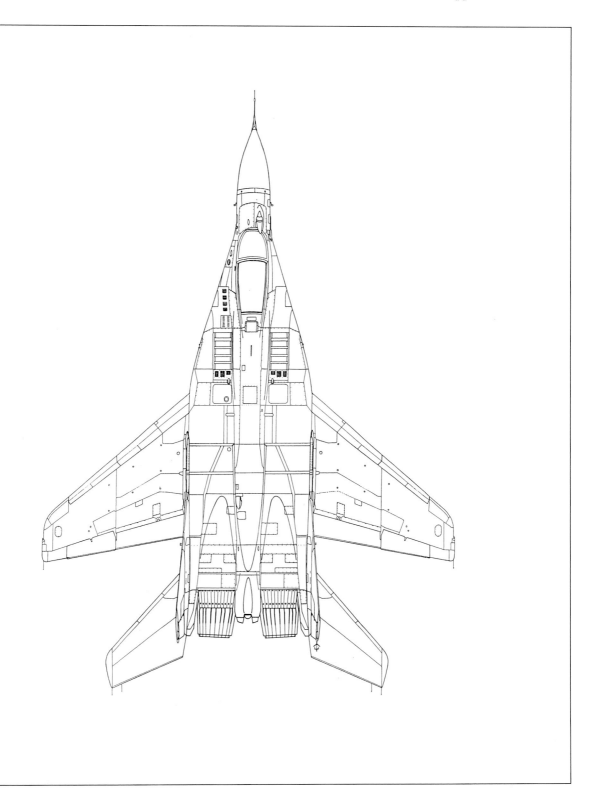

MiG-29 (Blue '407') with 6 R-77 missiles

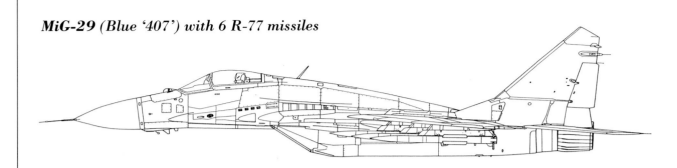

MiG-29SM with 2 R-73, 2 R-77 and 2 Kh-29T missiles

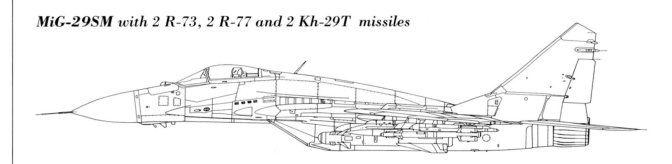

MiG-29 Test-bed (Blue '357')

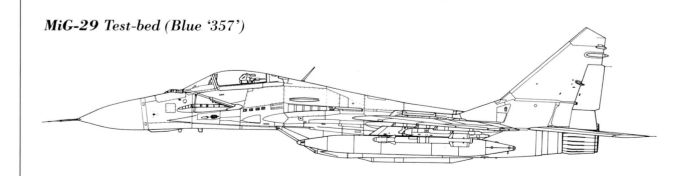

MiG-29 *Test-bed (Blue '357')*

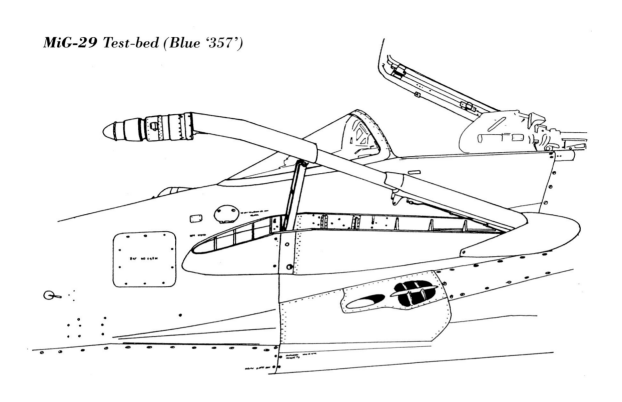

MiG-29SMT *with 2 R-73, 2R-77 and 2 Kh-31P missiles*

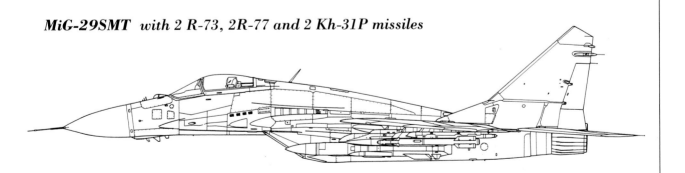

MiG-29M Prototype No.5 (Blue '155')

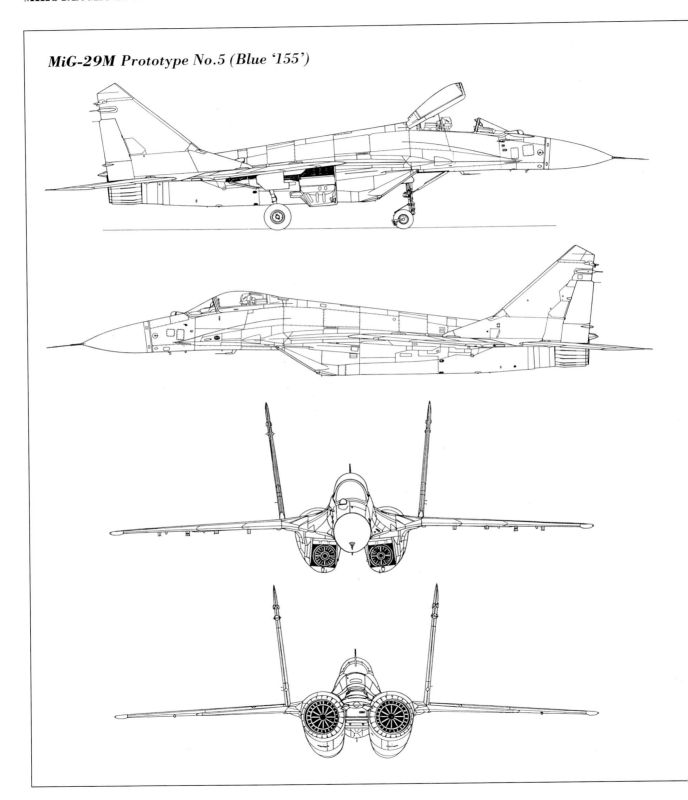

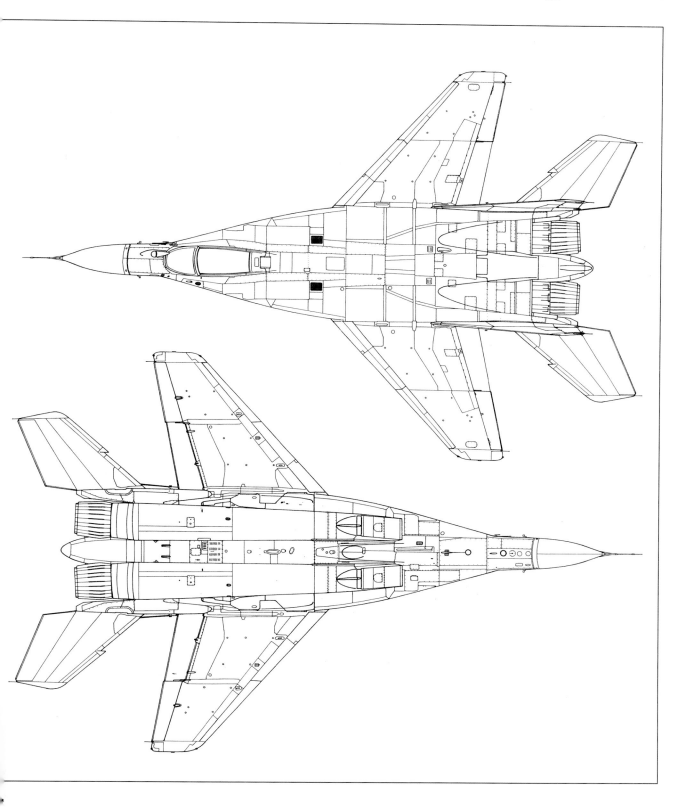

MiG-29M First Prototype (Blue '151')

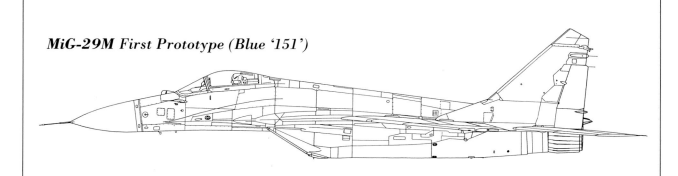

MiG-29M First Prototype No. 6 (Blue '156') with 2 R-73, 2 R-77 and 4 Kh-31A/P missiles

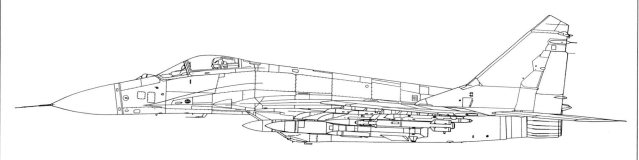

MiG-29M First Prototype (Blue '151')

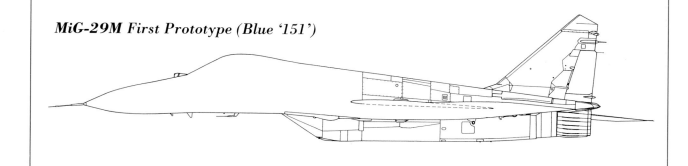

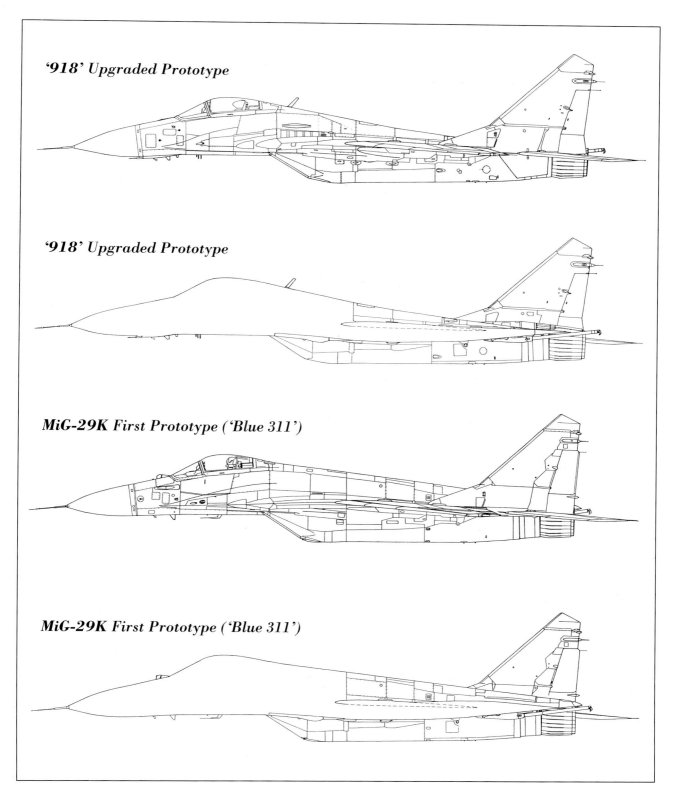

'918' *Upgraded Prototype*

'918' *Upgraded Prototype*

MiG-29K *First Prototype ('Blue 311')*

MiG-29K *First Prototype ('Blue 311')*

MiG-29K Second Prototype (Blue '312')

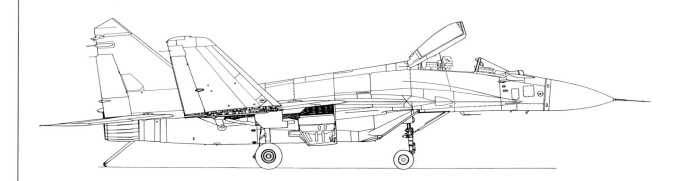

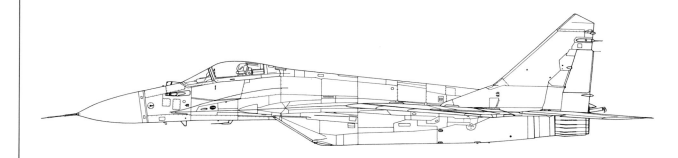

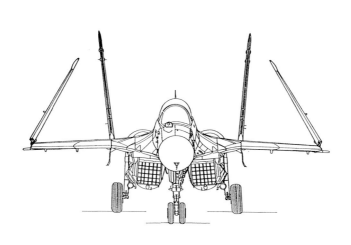

MiG-29K *Second Prototype (Blue '312') continued*

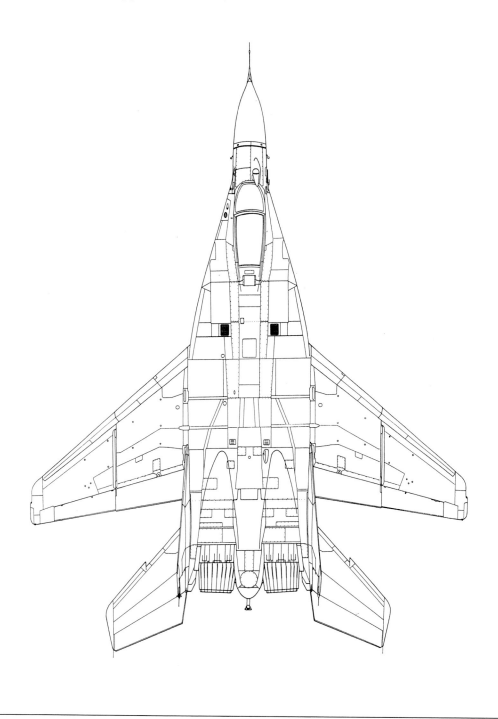

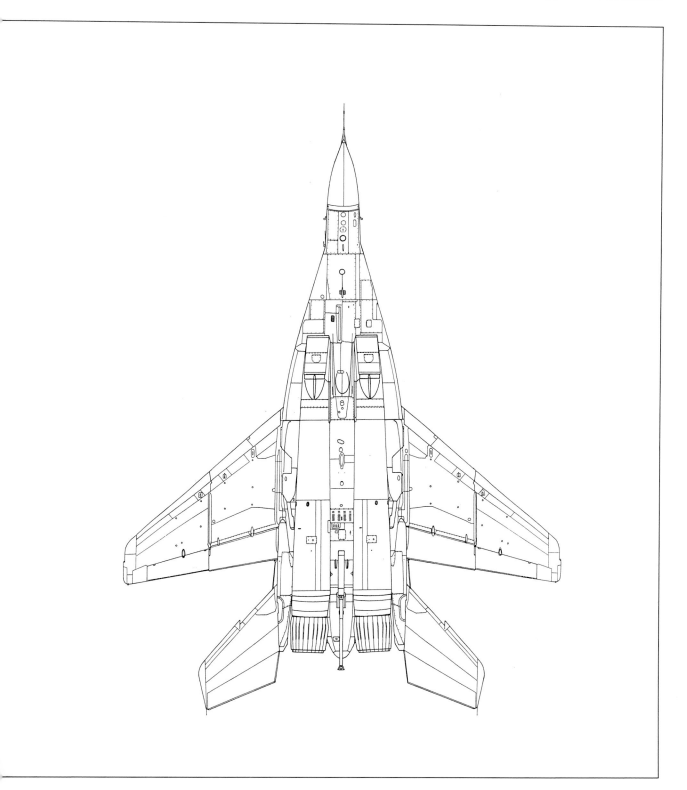

MiG-29K Second Prototype (Blue '312') continued

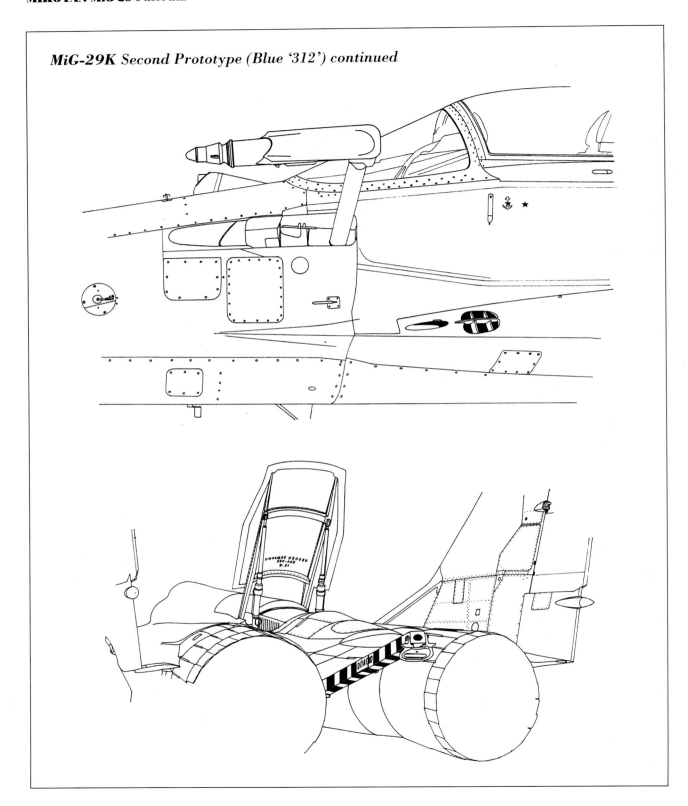

Index